UNITY
IN
THEOLOGY

Lonergan's Framework for Theology in Its New Context

Michael C. O'Callaghan

UNIVERSITY
PRESS OF
AMERICA

81-10396

/19   Co 1/8/82

To the Trapp Family
of Tübingen

iv

ACKNOWLEDGEMENTS

I wish to thank the following publishers for granting me permission to quote from their publications: Suhrkamp Verlag, Frankfurt; Benziger Verlag, Köln; University of Chicago Press, Chicago; Regis College Press, Toronto; Wilfrid Laurier University Press, Waterloo; Harper & Row, New York; and Darton Longman & Todd, London.

I wrote this book in partial fulfillment of requirements for the doctoral degree in theology at Tübingen, West Germany. Professor Dr. Walter Kasper guided my research, and I am grateful to him, not only for his constructive criticism, but also for his gentlemanly openness to the work of North American theologians. As well, I wish to thank Aline Uebelmesser for the care and proficiency she demonstrated in preparing the Tübingen typescript. Similarly, I thank Lynette Kent for her work on the present typescript.

Fr. Fred Crowe of Regis College in Toronto has provided an invaluable service there, in establishing the Lonergan Center; I am indebted to him for his cooperation throughout my years of study. Archbishop Anthony Jordan, O.M.I., and his successor Joseph MacNeil, have generously supported me in every way; to them, as well as to my faculty associates at Newman Theological College, Edmonton, I am profoundly grateful.

I am especially thankful to Bernard Lonergan, who has guided me through changing times with the breadth of his thought and the depth of his friendship.

CONTENTS

ABBREVIATIONS

DTC   Dictionnaire de théologie catholique
EK   Evangelische Kommentare
ITQ   Irish Theological Quarterly
KuD   Kerygma und Dogma
LThK²   Lexikon für Theologie und Kirche (2.Auflage)
MThZ   Münchener theologische Zeitschrift
NCE   New Catholic Encyclopedia
QD   Quaestiones disputatae
RGG³   Die Religion in Geschichte und Gegenwart (3.Auflage)
ScEc   Sciences ecclésiastiques
SM   Sacramentum Mundi
StZ   Stimmen der Zeit
ThPh   Theologie und Philosophie
ThQ   Theologische Quartalschrift
TS   Theological Studies
ZKTh   Zeitschrift für katholische Theologie
ZM   Zeitschrift für Missionswissenschaft (und Religionswissenschaft)
ZThK   Zeitschrift für Theologie und Kirche

A BIOGRAPHICAL NOTE

Bernard Joseph Francis Lonergan was born in
Buckingham, Québec, Canada, on December 17, 1904.
The eldest of three sons, he entered the Jesuit
novitiate at Guelph, Ontario, in 1922. He did
his philosophical studies at Heythrop College in
England from 1926 to 1929, and an extra year at
the same college enabled him to earn a degree in
the humanities from the University of London.
Following a period of teaching at Loyola College
in Montreal he went to the Gregorian University,
Rome, for theological studies. He was ordained
a Jesuit priest in 1936. After a year in France
he returned to the Gregorian for three years of
doctoral studies in dogmatic theology. The next
thirteen years were spent teaching theology in
Canada, at L'Immaculée-Conception in Montreal and
at what is now Regis College in Toronto. In 1953
Lonergan returned to the Gregorian in Rome, where
he was professor of dogmatic theology until 1965,
when he moved back to Regis College in Toronto.
In 1976 he accepted a position at Boston College,
where he is currently Visiting Distinguished Professor of Theology.

FOREWORD

The problem is familiar. Traditional theology knew many divisions and subdivisions. But the success of the German Historical School has added a new dimension to all of them, to emphasize their separateness, and to make unity less a problem for highly specialized professors than for disoriented students.

Such in brief is the new context of theology. But this book also offers a new context for Lonergan's framework. The old context was the cognitional theory presented in Insight. The new context comes out of the German theological milieu where contemporary theologians unify their work in different manners: Pannenberg stresses theology's scientific character; Rahner its churchly role; Metz the timeliness of its summons. Each of the three emphasizes a necessary quality. Each treats the same material object in a different manner. But together they offer not one theology but three overlapping theologies. The problem of unity remains.

In this fashion Dr. O'Callaghan keeps the issue not only purely theological but also contemporary and concrete. His work was done at Tübingen, and his numerous, extensive and apposite quotations from influential German theologians reveal an enviable mastery of the current situation. His anticipation of objections brings to light his searching exploration of opposed viewpoints. His treatment of them is both inconspicuous and persuasive. Finally, while his work is specialist, still it solidly if only implicitly recalls specialists from totalitarian ambitions.

Bernard Lonergan, S.J.

Boston College

INTRODUCTION

To situate Lonergan's work within the context
of contemporary Catholic theology, I will discuss
briefly (1) the renewed theology; (2) the need for
a new fundamental theology; (3) the work of Bernard
Lonergan; and (4) the scope of my own work here.

1. The Renewed Theology

Like all ecumenical councils so Vatican II was
both an end and a beginning. It was the culmina-
tion and consolidation of a theological renewal that
had been taking place in Catholic thought since the
last century; and it was the beginning of a theological revolution, the aim of which was to provide the
renewed theology with a secure foundation and an integrated structure. Throughout the Council's various constitutions and decrees homage is paid to the
work of historical scholars, to the reflections of
systematic theologians, to the energy of those im-
mersed in the pastoral communication of the gospel;
yet nowhere do we find a detailed account of the
unity of such work, of the common basis from which
the various specialists operate, of the cooperation
among them, of the unity of purpose that unites them
all in a common endeavor. Indeed, a careful reading
of the documents leaves the impression that, while
theological renewal is recognized, the foundation
and structure of that renewal is far from being settled: it is one thing to affirm the legitimacy of
critical-historical exegesis and the urgent need of
a truly pastoral theology, but it is another to reveal the complementarity of these concerns. This
latter task was not resolved at Vatican II. The
Council called indeed for an overhaul of the theological structure, but wisely recognized that this
was the burden, not of an ecumenical council, but
of the community of post-conciliar theologians themselves.

In the next section I will outline the response
thus far given by theologians to the need for a new

INT

foundation and structure of theology. For the moment, however, I wish to comment briefly on the
renewal that had been going forward in different
areas, and that stood in need of a new basis and
a new organization. For sake of brevity I will
describe this renewal in terms of a new theological memory, a new theological orientation, and a
new theological understanding.

The new theological memory resulted from the
gradual and often controversial reception by Catholic theology of the methods of historical-critical
exegesis and scholarship. Theologians had always
been conscious of their need to turn to scripture
and tradition in theological work, but since especially the sixteenth century that turn was mostly
a search for evidence of eternal truths to serve as
the premisses for theological conclusions. There
was lacking to theologians a sense of historical
development, so that scripture and later texts were
simply depositories of proof-texts used to demonstrate the truth of church doctrines or to bolster
the authority of theological opinions.

The renewal that occurred in this area was the
recognition that scripture and tradition provide,
not the premisses for theological arguments, but
data for theological investigation. No longer was
the appeal to history made to prove the rectitude
of present thought and praxis. Instead, theologians began to confront the immense complexity of
the Christian social and cultural tradition in its
origins and subsequent development or decline. In
consequence, a multitude of specialized exegetical
methods were applied to the documents and other
traces of the past, in order to piece together as
much as possible their original meaning and eventual
influence. The result has been a tremendous outpouring of scholarly studies in the past few decades
of Catholic theology, an outpouring that even yet
is being received with difficulty by dogmatic and
systematic theologians. Still, historical work has
greatly enriched the whole of theology by bringing
theology once again into contact with its life-giving

sources - something that moves theology beyond the
logical confines of the medieval summa and Melchior
Cano's de locis theologicis. Catholic historical
studies have ceased to be merely the "positive" handmaid of a dogmatic theology, and have become an autonomous specialization with its own experts, its own
methods, its own publications, its own goal.

Besides its new awareness of the Christian past,
theology has received a new orientation towards the
present and future. The old dogmatic theology was
largely an instrument or spokesman for the teaching
office of the Catholic Church; it would serve the
Church precisely by transmitting eternal and universally valid dogmatic truths to seminarians who after
ordination would pass these truths on to the faithful in Catholic parishes.

In its new orientation, theology would be eminently pastoral, where "pastoral" has quite a new
meaning. It would proclaim Christian truth, but it
realizes that truth has meaning only within a given
context, that social and cultural contexts change
over time and from place to place, that effective
communication of the Christian message may demand a
plurality of expression in order to make the message
intelligible and spur its hearers to ministry in the
world. So a contemporary theology would be truly
contemporary, sensitive to the signs of the times,
responding to the concrete questions, problems, concerns, hopes, and sufferings of men and women whoever and wherever they may be. It would speak precisely to these people, and not to those of the
first, fourth, sixteenth, or nineteenth century. It
would announce a living message, the gospel that the
Kingdom of God is near, indeed it is present already
among us and demanding a metanoia, a radical change
of direction in life and in thought. So it is, that
a renewed theology, in becoming more critically aware
of the Christian past in all its complexity, achievement, failure, quite rightly has come to recognize as
well the complexity of living in the present.

Clearly, such an orientation has had repercussions on the way that theology makes the transition from the Christian past into the world of today. It cannot simply repeat verbatim the findings of exegetes and historians, for times have changed. Nor can it ignore the findings of exegetes and historians, for then there would be no Christian message to proclaim. It cannot merge uncritically with the social and cultural movements of the present day, for this would leave the Christian message identified with the violence of error and decline as well as with the heroism of truth and progress. Nor can it ignore the social and cultural movements of the present day, for this would leave the Christian message an irrelevant relic of a distant past. So the renewed theology is struggling to develop the sort of speculative understanding and sound theory that is both historically-minded and pastorally oriented yet also is critical, normative, and authentically Christian.

Accordingly, the renewed theology has a renewed systematic or theoretical function. It is to be speculative, but not in the sense of some idealism that would ignore concrete history past and present. It is to be theoretical, but not in the sense of an ideology that removes itself to the ivory-tower of empty words and hollow promises. It would be instead a truly thinking theology, at home in the world of science and equally concerned with shaping and guiding historical process, aware that the only way to do this is to develop and implement ever better theories that systematize Christian truth and value.

We live then, as C. Geffré has said, in a new age of theology.[1] The former positive theology, that was never really more than a tool of dogmatism, has been transformed into an autonomous historical-critical scholarship. The former classicist dogmatics that presumed the Christian culture to be the only culture has given way to a pastorally-minded theology acutely aware of cultural pluralism and diversity. That same dogmatics, that was confined to the transmission or contemplation of eternal truths, has given way to a historically-minded theoretical search for understanding of what Christian truth might possibly mean in the complex world of today. Each of these developments was recognized at Vatican II. It is not surprising, then, that the theologians who were behind the scenes at the Council would experience the difficulty of reconciling the pluralism of the renewed theology with the unity of the Christian faith. Clearly, there was need for cooperation of the sort that could give coherence and integration to the work of the entire theological community. It was with such a concern in mind that the periodical, Concilium, was founded with an international and multi-disciplinary basis. It was a similar concern that prompted an extensive study of theological pluralism by the International Commission of Catholic Theologians. Finally, this same concern for coherence and integration seems to underlie recent efforts towards the renewal of fundamental theology and explicit concern for theology's foundation, methods, and goals in the world of today.

2. The Need for a New Fundamental Theology

If theology is not conceived as a wordless, mystical withdrawal into a cloud of unknowing, then theological reflection needs a conceptual apparatus, a Begrifflichkeit. For this reason, the Christian message and tradition has invariably had to borrow and adapt the language of this world in order to speak of other-worldly reality, of God and of all things in relation to God.

Such speech, such a conceptual apparatus, may or may not be systematically structured. In an earlier stage the language is pre-philosophical and pre-systematic; there is no uniform conceptual apparatus, no universally recognized manner of expressing what is meant, but rather a spontaneous, self-correcting process of teaching and learning that adapts what is meant to a huge variety of social structures and cultural channels. This accounts for the great diversity to be found in the New Testament writings, and gives rise to the need for a careful

and detailed historical exegesis to determine in each
particular case just what is meant.

At a later stage, however, a comprehensive and
coherent structure may be needed. Just why this is
so will be discussed later in this work. For now, I
would note only the fact that, in the medieval period,
theology became structured and systematized. To develop this structure, theologians turned mostly to
the genius of Aristotle, at once taking over the Aristotelian framework while adapting it to Christian purposes. Within that framework the memory, orientation,
and understanding of theology had a common basis and a
common conceptual structure: theology was a unified
system.

For reasons that must await a later explanation,
a series of developments occurred that made the Aristotelian structure inadequate to modern types of intellectual development. And in Catholic theology the
renewal that has been going forward since the last
century has only served to emphasize what thinkers in
other fields have often stressed since the seventeenth
century: the Aristotelian framework cannot possibly
systematize and integrate modern thought in all its
various specializations. Here we have in briefest
form an account of the dilemma facing Catholic theologians in these days of renewal, especially since Vatican II: if the former structure has been superseded,
is there any possibility of developing a new structure
on a new foundation?

The problem is very complex, yet in urgent need
of solution. Firstly, there is an autonomous historical-critical scholarship, uncovering for us the massive complexity of the Christian past, and speaking
to us about what this Christian past possibly or probably was. Secondly, there is a pastorally oriented
theology that has an eye on the concrete complexity
of Christian living and thinking in the pluralistic
world of today. Thirdly, there is a dogmatic or systematic theology that would reflect theoretically and
critically on the Christian past in light of present
situations and needs, in order to gain an understand-

ing of the meaning of the Christian tradition in the world today. Finally, and tending now to merge with the concerns of dogmatic and systematic theology, there is appearing a new fundamental theology, struggling to find the key which will open the door to a modern system in which memory, orientation, and reflection will again share a common foundation, integrated procedures, and a unified purpose.

This search for a new fundamental theology is perhaps most characterized by its scope. It would not confine itself to the renewal of this or that particular theological treatise, nor would it strive merely for better techniques in communicating the gospel. Rather, it would reflect critically on the entire theological scene and uncover its presuppositions, its diverse methods, its present social and cultural context, its aims and goals. It is the recognition that a renewed theology needs a new foundation and a new integration.[2]

Most commonly, this search for a new fundamental theology is being conducted by theologians working in dogmatic or systematic theology, for it is here especially that the need for a new foundation and structure is most acutely felt. Later in Chapter One, I will discuss in more detail the various issues involved in such work, and so will note here only the broad lines of development and the names most commonly associated with this whole question.

A critical examination of the foundation, methods, and scope of theology was initiated by the theologians of the Catholic Tübingen School at the beginning of the nineteenth century. Not only did they strive to bring about a new understanding of theology in the cultural context of their day; as well, they suggested lines of development that are significant for our own day but that only recently have begun to receive new attention. For the spirit of the Tübingen School was precisely its effort to deal with the dimensions needed by theology in the modern world and that I mentioned in the previous section. As Walter Kasper notes, the con-

cern of the Tübingen School was an integrated theology: a theology that balanced <u>Wissenschaftlichkeit</u>,
<u>Kirchlichkeit</u>, and <u>Zeitoffenheit</u>, described by
Kasper in the following way:

> Wissenschaftlichkeit ist hier jedoch nicht
> gleichbedeutend mit geisttötenden abstrak-
> ten Einzelanalysen, denen das geistige Band
> fehlt und di geistliche Frucht abgeht,
> Kirchlichkeit ist hier nicht Grenze, son-
> dern Lebensraum christlicher Freiheit, weil
> die christliche Freiheit durch den in der
> kirchlichen Gemeinschaft vorgegebenen Glau-
> ben an Jesus Christus begründet wird,
> schliesslich ist Zeitoffenheit etwas an-
> deres als Mode und marktgängige Meinung;
> wahre Zeitgemässheit kann vom Theologen
> auch einmal das gegenüber der öffentlichen
> Meinung und ihren Tabus kritisch-befreiende
> Wort verlangen.[3]

At once I would note that the balanced and integrated theology hoped for by the Tübingen School is
not yet a common achievement. But I would hasten to
add that the scope of the problem has remained the
same, inasmuch as the fundamental concern of theology
in our own day is precisely the need to reconcile the
<u>Wissenschaftlichkeit</u>, <u>Kirchlichkeit</u>, and <u>Zeitoffenheit</u>
of theological reflection. Indeed, since the middle
of the nineteenth century, Catholic theology has been
engaged in a constant struggle to integrate these various factors - a struggle largely unsuccessful because
invariably one dimension would be over-emphasized, to
the neglect of the others.

An initial phase of this development stressed the
<u>Kirchlichkeit</u> of theology and tended to ignore its ra-
tional and practical dimensions. The balance which
marked the Tübingen School was followed by a retreat
to a traditional dogmatic stance, immunizing church
and theology from an increasingly autonomous and secular society and culture. There was developed a defen-
sively-minded apologetics that was at best a prologue
to theology itself and was concerned with the <u>praeam-</u>

INT

bula fidei. Theology itself was grounded in dogmatic truths that were self-evident to orthodox believers and that stood above any critique based on
purely rational grounds.[4]

     In a second phase, the emphasis shifted to the
Zeitoffenheit of theology. It was the era of Lebens-
philosophie, of stress on the external objective
world, of a return to the categories of life, experience, feeling, personal dialogue. In the work of
theologians such as Guardini and Adam, Catholic theology assimilated this spirit and tried to move theological reflection away from logical speculation to
a more life-related and concrete reflection on Christian living in the world.[5]

     A third phase concentrated on the Wissenschaft-
lichkeit of theology, spurred by the need for a more
critical approach to the world than had been dominant
in the theologies of life. Such critical thought was
underpinned by the reception into Catholic theology
of critical-historical methods of investigation and
by the attempts of theologians to come to terms with
the various philosophies which, since Descartes, had
eroded the scholastic and neo-scholastic foundation
of theological reflection.[6]

     The current phase of development is the emer-
gence of a new fundamental theology, especially since
the Second Vatican Council. Its main novelty lies in
the fact that it would reflect on theology itself in
an explicit effort to discover just what is meant by
Wissenschaftlichkeit, Kirchlichkeit, and Zeitoffenheit; it would expose the very foundations of theology and the principles upon which a truly contemporary theology should build.

     For the reader wishing to gain some initial in-
sight into where Lonergan's work relates to contemporary theology, I would suggest that his work be
understood as a contribution to this search for a
new fundamental theology. Accordingly, he is concerned with those issues that are receiving the at-

xxiii

tention of such theologians as Pannenberg and Sauter, Rahner and Kasper, Metz and Peukert. As mentioned, the main issues are the ecclesial, rational and practical dimensions of theology: the relation of history and dogma, theory and praxis, theology and <u>Wissenschafts-</u> or <u>Handlungstheorie</u>. To indicate the broad lines of Lonergan's concern with these questions, I wish now to discuss the main characteristics of his work over the past fifty years.

3. The Work of Bernard Lonergan

A distinction sometimes is made between the specifically theological aspects of a particular topic and the scientific or philosophical approaches to this same topic. So, for example, Walter Kasper discusses various notions of dogmatic theology and then introduces his own suggestion in the following way:

> Sieht man zunächst einmal von den verschiedenen religionsphilosophischen und wissenschaftstheoretischen Neuansätzen ab und beschränkt man sich auf die innertheologische Diskussion, . . .[7]

Implicit in this statement is a well-known fact: any theological statement has its context of interpretation that includes any number of philosophical, scientific, or even commonsense presuppositions. Moreover, the complexity of present-day issues and the subsequent division of labor in modern thought makes it imperative that a specialist restrict himself or herself to the acquired specialization, leaving to others the task of working out the further aspects of any given problem. So it is, that theologians quite properly speak mostly of theological dimensions of a question, and confer with their philosophical or scientific colleagues to round out their thought.

As it happens, this fact serves as a good starting-point for my introduction of Bernard Lonergan. While theologians prefer to concentrate on the specifically theological component in the theological

structure, Lonergan has devoted the vast majority
of his efforts to the non-theological or anthropological component to that structure. To paraphrase the passage just quoted from Kasper's article, Lonergan would generally prescind from the
specifically theological discussion in order to
concentrate on the philosophical and cognitional
aspects of various issues. To put it another way:
while Kasper would generally attend to the objects
of theological reflection, though without ever losing sight of the underlying philosophical questions,
Lonergan would attend principally to the philosophical issues regarding the constitution and development of the theologian as human subject, without ever
losing sight of the specific objects with which theologians are concerned.[8]

My aim in the present section is to describe
this interest of Lonergan in the human or anthropological side of theology; an account of precisely
what Lonergan has to say about this matter is the
topic of the chapters which follow. Already I have
drawn attention to the current interest in developing a renewed fundamental theology, and located
Lonergan's work within this general framework. I
noted the ongoing difficulty of integrating the
Wissenschaftlichkeit, Kirchlichkeit, and Zeitoffenheit
of theology. Here, I would note further that this
difficulty was encountered as well by medieval theologians, and to reach an integration they turned to
Arabic and Greek philosophy, particularly to Aristotle,
in order to find a system in which all three dimensions
could be brought together. It was the rise of modern
science, modern philosophy, and modern scholarship
that signalled an end to the medieval foundation and
that challenged theologians to work out a new foundation for their various reflections. The results have
been at best ambiguous, and as I shall indicate in
Chapter One there is still no agreement on the anthropological component that is to serve as the
integrating foundation of a theology that would be
at once rational, ecclesial, and pastorally related
to its social and cultural contexts.

xxv

For Lonergan, the challenge of working out the
foundations of theology demands a threefold response. Firstly, there is the matter of historical
continuity; to transpose theology from one sort of
system to another demands that we first understand
the original system in its achievement and limitations. Secondly, there is need to take account of
the modern developments that made elements of the
original system inadequate for contemporary needs.
Finally, there is the task of transposing the original system to the modern context in such a way as
to assimilate the new context while also critically
adapting it in order to retain a specifically theological identity.

It is possible to understand Lonergan's work
as his response to each of these three interrelated
tasks. In an initial period, to 1949, he was chiefly
concerned with understanding the achievement of medieval theology. From 1949 to 1965, he concentrated on
studying the modern developments in science, philosophy, and scholarship that demanded a new systematic
structure for theology, a new approach to theology.
And since 1965 he has been working on the transposition of theology from its medieval to its modern context - a transposition that preserves the Wissenschaftlichkeit, Kirchlichkeit, and Zeitoffenheit of
theology in a dynamically integrated unity.

(1) Lonergan's Studies in Medieval Theology

I have already mentioned the renewal of Catholic theology that has been occurring since the last
century. One aspect of this renewal was the reception of critical-historical scholarship in studying
the Christian tradition. One of the earlier fruits
of this scholarship was the revival of interest in
medieval scholasticism. The medieval period had been
a turning point in theology, for it was then that theology became a comprehensive and systematic discipline,
unified by borrowing and adapting Arabic and Greek
philosophical thought. It is true that there had been
a similar revival of interest in medieval theology by

theologians in the sixteenth century; but their neo-scholasticism lacked the critical-historical spirit that could unveil the original achievement of medieval theology, and the neo-scholasticism deteriorated into a series of endless disputes. But with the modern critical studies of such scholars as Baeumker, Grabmann, and Landgraf, the dimensions of medieval thought came to light. In particular, attention focused on the work of Aquinas who emerged as the principal authority and guide in medieval and subsequent scholasticism, and whose relevance for contemporary theology was consistently emphasized by the teaching office of the Catholic Church between the First and Second Vatican Councils.[9]

It was the availability of these critical studies that allowed Lonergan access into the world of medieval theology. During the 1930's, when he was taking his theology studies at the Gregorian University in Rome, his interest in the medieval period was stimulated by two main sources. A fellow-student, who had studied under the Louvain philosopher Maréchal, informed Lonergan of the main dimensions of Maréchal's project of transposing Aquinas to the modern context; and one of Lonergan's professors, Bernard Leeming, offered a course on the Incarnate Word and drew heavily on Aquinas' theology. By the time Lonergan began doctoral studies in theology at the Gregorian, he considered himself a Thomist and, at the suggestion of his dissertation director, Charles Boyer, Lonergan set to work on a historical study of operative grace in the writings of Aquinas.[10] For present purposes I would note only that his study allowed Lonergan to identify the specifically religious or theological component in Aquinas' system; in more contemporary terms, Lonergan calls it a study of religious conversion set within the framework of scholastic and mostly Aristotelian thought.[11]

After doctoral studies Lonergan complemented his first major work with a further historical study of Aquinas, this time focusing attention on the anthropological or rational dimension of Aquinas' theological structure. It was a matter of tracing Aquinas' thought on the conditions of the possibility for human acceptance of operative grace, and this demanded a study of Aquinas' cognitional theory. This is developed in its fullest form in Aquinas' trinitarian theology, and the results of Lonergan's inquiry were published in a series of articles in the periodical, Theological Studies, between 1946 and 1949.[12]

In the course of the present work I shall have occasion to mention in more detail the actual content of Lonergan's studies on Aquinas. For the moment it is important to note that Lonergan found in Aquinas a theological system grounded solidly in phenomenology and psychology of the human subject - an existential rather than an essentialist theology.[13] Moreover, it is important to note that his studies of Aquinas allowed Lonergan to re-confirm what he already knew from earlier studies in Newman and Augustine: that the key component in the rational dimension of theological reflection is to be found, not in beginning from a metaphysics or from an epistemology, but rather in a cognitional theory that accounts for developing understanding. And for Lonergan the only sure way to work out a cognitional theory is to objectify the operations of our own mind - to discover what we are doing when we are knowing. Lonergan found this to be the procedure of Aquinas in the latter's trinitarian theology. Aquinas was not content with a deduction of the existence of intellectual operations from the fact that objects are in fact understood and known; as well, he identified these operations as themselves given in his own consciousness. In a word that currently is popular, Aquinas explicitly appealed to experience and, indeed, to experience in the profoundest meaning of that word: the inner experience of one's own conscious and intentional operations whereby we come to know ourselves, not as souls or substances, but as human subjects.[14]

I have been presenting Lonergan's studies of Aquinas as part of the broader movement within Catholic theology to recover the medieval, and particularly Thomist, heritage. The need was for a truly critical and historical assessment of medieval theology, for

only on the basis of such an assessment could theology begin the work of transposing the medieval
system to the modern context.[15] And in Aquinas,
Lonergan found a model for the construction of a
theological system that at once was methodical,
truly theological, and in dialogue with the world
of medieval thought.

(2) Lonergan's Studies in Modern Science, Philos-
    ophy, Scholarship

As soon as he had completed his studies on the
medieval theological system, Lonergan set to work
on writing an account of theological method in the
contemporary cultural context. This context differs
immensely from that of the medieval period, and to
do theology in this modern context demands that theologians have an accurate grasp of just what this
context is. To put the problem in terms that I have
already mentioned: the Zeitoffenheit of theology demanded that theologians investigate just what Wissenschaftlichkeit and Kirchlichkeit mean in the world of
today, a world in which science, philosophy, and history differ radically from their medieval counterparts.

Already at the beginning of the last century the
theologians of the Catholic Tübingen School attempted
a renewal of theology along precisely these lines, as
did subsequent generations of theologians. I cannot
here, of course, attempt even an outline of their suc-
cesses and failures in this regard, but one thing at
least is clear: the problem of working out the function of theology in the context of modern science,
modern historical scholarship, and modern philosophy
is far from being resolved. Among those trying to
come to terms with this question is Bernard Lonergan.

The guiding question for Lonergan could be formulated as follows: how is it possible to accomplish
in our own day what Aquinas did in his? The answer
to this question depends, of course, on one's assessment of the achievement of Aquinas. Lonergan placed
that achievement in the fact that Aquinas came to un-

derstand Aristotelian psychology by understanding
his own psychological operations; through a self-
appropriation of his own mind, in its conscious and
intentional operations, Aquinas was able to reach a
critical understanding of the mind and work of Aristotle.

Again, Lonergan himself had come to understand
Aquinas' psychology, particularly the psychological
analogy underpinning Aquinas' trinitarian theology,
by understanding his own psychological operations;
through a self-appropriation of his own mind, in its
conscious and intentional operations, Lonergan was
able to reach a critical understanding of the mind
and work of Aquinas.[16]

For Lonergan, the next step was clear. In order
to situate theology in a context wherein Aristotle
had been replaced by developments in modern science,
modern scholarship, and modern philosophy, there was
needed an understanding of these developments.[17] And
Lonergan knew that the best way to understand modern
science was by doing modern science, rather than listening to the opinions of scientists or philosophers
regarding the meaning of science. Moreover, in doing
modern science Lonergan attended, not just to the objects of scientific investigation, but to himself as
coming to understand scientifically.

In other words, just as Aquinas had assimilated
Aristotelian thought by attending to his own acts of
understanding, so Lonergan assimilated modern science
and modern historical scholarship by doing science
and history, attending all the while to what he himself was doing in his pursuit of scientific and
scholarly understanding. And what Lonergan uncovered
in this process was not just the methods specific to
various fields of human inquiry, but a basic pattern
of conscious and intentional operations that was the
core common to all specific methods. Moreover, this
core of operations is common as well to theology, for
theologians too are actively engaged in reaching an
understanding of things. Without doubt theology has

its specific method, its specific operational relationship to its object of inquiry; but this in no
way takes away from the fact that theology is a
search for understanding and that human understanding, if objectified through a heightening of consciousness by the theologian, is the key to method
in theology.

I have been giving a very concise account of
the project which Lonergan set for himself, and must
hasten to add that the full meaning of this project
will emerge only in the chapters to follow. An introduction can do no more than point to a general
direction, with the hope that the reader will ac-
quire a certain feeling for what Lonergan was up
to.[18] I hope, however, that enough has been said
to clarify the purpose which Lonergan had in writing
Insight: A Study of Human Understanding.[19] It is
intended as a study of methods operative in various
fields of human inquiry, in order to prepare the way
for a study of method in theology;[20] the various
fields of human inquiry together constitute the new
context in which theology operates, so that Insight
is the initial investigation of the Zeit to which
theology is to be offen. Yet, at the same time, Insight is more: it would attend, not just to the objects of human inquiry, but would invite the reader
to discover in himself or herself just what happens
when one comes to understand something in mathematics, in physics, in everyday commonsense knowing:
an invitation to understand one's own understanding
in its preconceptual dynamism:

> The first eight chapters of Insight are a
> series of five-finger exercises inviting
> the reader to discover in himself and for
> himself just what happens when he under-
> stands. My aim is to help people exper-
> ience themselves understanding, advert to
> the experience, distinguish it from other
> experiences, name and identify it, and
> recognize it when it recurs. My aim, I
> surmise, is parallel to Carl Rogers' aim
> of inducing his clients to advert to the

feelings that they experience but do not
advert to, distinguish, name, identify,
recognize.[21]

Throughout Insight Lonergan invites the reader
to compare the results of this personal experiment
with the views both of the Aristotelian system and
of modern philosophers, especially since the time of
Descartes. Insight itself is best understood as Lonergan's "response" to Kant, for it was Kant who had
pronounced the end of traditional metaphysics and who
turned attention to the critical problem of cognitional
theory. That this is Lonergan's intention is clear
from the Introduction to Insight.[22]

Again, I would reiterate that Lonergan's aim is
to identify and objectify the anthropological component of a method in theology. This component is the
human mind itself, in its conscious and intentional
operations; the process of self-appropriation, of
heightening one's consciousness and discovering this
for oneself, is what Lonergan calls transcendental
method or generalized empirical method;[23] and while
the precise meaning of this will become clear only
later in Chapter Three, I would like here to refer
to a passage from Method in Theology, that relates
this method to theology:

. . . the introduction of transcendental
method abrogates the old metaphor that
describes philosophy as the handmaid of
theology and replaces it by a very precise fact. Transcendental method is not
the intrusion into theology of alien matter from an alien source. Its function
is to advert to the fact that theologies
are produced by theologians, that theologians have minds and use them, that
their doing so should not be ignored or
passed over but explicitly acknowledged
in itself and in its implications. A-
gain, transcendental method is coinci-
dent with a notable part of what has been
considered philosophy, but it is not any

philosophy or all philosophy. Very precisely, it is a heightening of consciousness that brings to light our conscious
and intentional operations and thereby
leads to the answers to three basic questions. What am I doing when I am knowing?
Why is doing that knowing? What do I know
when I do it? The first answer is a cognitional theory. The second is an epistemology. The third is a metaphysics
where, however, the metaphysics is transcendental, an integration of heuristic
structures, and not some categorial speculation that reveals that all is water,
or matter, or spirit, or process, or what
have you.[24]

It might be helpful to the reader if I indicate
briefly some of the main developments in Lonergan's
thought prior to Insight; that the only way of appropriating the modern context of theology is the
way of "personal experiment" was evident to Lonergan
early in his career. His own personal experiment in
mathematics and modern science was initially stimulated by a book by H. B. W. Joseph, Introduction to Logic,
and with the guidance of the mathematics tutor at Heythrop College, in the late 1920's. An initial formulation of cognitional process was suggested by Lonergan's study of Newman's Grammar of Assent; here, Newman made a clear distinction between the ideas we happen to have on a given subject, and the assent whereby
we determine some ideas to be in fact true. For Newman, this latter assent was the illative sense, whereby
we can infer that something is truly so and thus reach
a concluding judgment, as distinct from having just a
number of bright but possibly mistaken ideas. This
distinction became crucial for Lonergan, who in later
years formulated it as the distinction between insight,
on the one hand, and the reflective act of understanding (judgment), on the other.[25]

In the early 1930's Lonergan studied both Plato
and Augustine. In their early development, both had

INT

stressed the dynamic process of coming to understand, a process that was built on asking and answering questions, searching for insights, striving to reach conclusions, reaching judgments and
truth, and then continuing the process, ever open
to refinement or revision of what one already understood or knew. Later, Lonergan commented that
these studies put an end to his previous nominalism, and convinced him of the centrality of understanding in cognitional process.[26]

     I have already mentioned Lonergan's interest
in Aquinas,[27] but it is worth noting a further influence that these studies of scholastic theology
had on Lonergan. He so entered the spirit of scholastic thought that he first expressed his own account of cognitional theory in scholastic categories. It is therefore not surprising to find Insight
expressed in terms of a faculty psychology; but as
Lonergan later remarked, despite the terminology he
was developing in Insight an intentionality analysis.[28]

     As it turned out, Insight had to be published
earlier than expected, because Lonergan had been
asked to take a professorship of theology at the
Gregorian University in Rome. Accordingly, Insight
was a study of the human subject as knower; still
to be integrated in his analysis was the higher
viewpoint of the existential subject, the subject
as doer, the subject as one who acts. And it was
in developing this viewpoint that Lonergan studied
the phenomenologists and existentialists, and it
was during this period that he replaced his faculty
psychology with the vocabulary appropriate to an
intentionality analysis. The greatest influence on
Lonergan's new formulation of his transcendental
method was the work of the educational psychologist,
Jean Piaget. To note this difference, one has only
to compare Insight (completed in 1953) with Lonergan's brief monograph on that work - an article entitled Cognitional Structure, written in 1964.[29]
To put this in another way: although Lonergan stud-

ied the existentialist philosophers and phenomenologists, and borrowed a goodly number of their conceptual categories, he did not take over whole-
heartedly the "system" of a Heidegger or a Jaspers
or a Husserl; Lonergan's study of human understanding and human existence in the world was an original
creation, in the sense that it was the product of
Lonergan's own self-appropriation and his own convictions. He invariably had to rely on conceptual
terms borrowed from elsewhere, but it is worth emphasizing that he turned most often to psychology,
rather than to modern philosophies, in formulating
his account of cognitional process.

In Insight Lonergan had concentrated on grounding mathematical, scientific, and commonsense knowing. Still to be worked out was that dimension of
the modern context which had most directly affected
theology, namely, the problem of the "Geisteswissenschaften." Not only were these hermeneutical sciences very much part of the modern context, but as
well they seemed to stand in direct opposition to
any theology resting on "dogmatic" assumptions.
Lonergan's initial entry into the meaning of critical history, as opposed to classicist history, probably came in the early 1930's with his study of
Christopher Dawson's The Age of the Gods. A few
years later, in conjunction with his historical
studies on Aquinas, Lonergan was greatly influenced
by the thought of Ernst Cassirer, particularly as
introduced to him by Klibansky's and Paton's Fest-
schrift for Cassirer, published in 1936.[30] Lonergan's own historical "experiment" was his two studies of Aquinas; the initial formulation of Lonergan's
cognitional hermeneutics appears in an unpublished
introduction to his doctoral thesis,[31] while a few
additional and more elaborate comments may be found
in chapter 6, 7, 18, and 20 of Insight. A further
experiment was done in relation to Lonergan's courses in Rome on the Trinity and the Incarnation.[32]
But to formulate this hermeneutics in contemporary
terms demanded that Lonergan turn attention to the
developments in hermeneutics associated mostly with
nineteenth-century Germany and the Dilthey-Troeltsch

problematic. It was for Lonergan a matter of developing a conceptual apparatus for an intentionality analysis approach to critical-historical scholarship. Here, the central category for Lonergan was "meaning," and he drew on the thought of Jaspers, Bruno Snell, and most especially of Piaget in developing this notion.[33]

By the early 1960's, then, Lonergan had completed two of the three tasks needed to transpose the medieval theological system to the contemporary context. He had investigated the original system that needed transposing; and he had uncovered the structural unity of the modern context to which the transposition had to be made. There remained only the final task, that had motivated Lonergan's work from the beginning; the actual transposition of theology itself from its medieval to the modern context. If the anthropological component had been identified, it remained to work out the specifically theological principle: for while theology shared this anthropological component with modern science and modern scholarship, it was clear that theology was more than just science or historical scholarship. So it was, that Lonergan set to work on objectifying his own thought precisely as theological; and this self-understanding of himself as theologian received expression in the phase of Lonergan's work that we may now consider.

(3) Lonergan's Transposition of Theology

While Lonergan was teaching at the Gregorian, he gradually began to apply the results of his investigations to Catholic theology. This happened especially in the early 1960's, as Vatican II was meeting and the inadequacy of the former structures of theology was becoming more and more apparent. Lonergan seems to have conducted a series of experiments in the reorganization of theology, particularly during various summer institutes in the early 1960's. His aim, of course, was not to start from nothing and invent something entirely new, but rather to start from existing structures and current theological work,

transposing this to a foundation in transcendental
method while preserving a specifically theological
dimension to that foundation.

There were three main parts to this transposition, that I may mention briefly. There was a need
to re-structure "dogmatic" or "speculative" theology.
There was a need to re-structure "positive" or "historical" theology. And finally there was a need for
a new sort of "fundamental" theology, that could account for the integration of speculative and positive
theology. A word may be said on each of these tasks.

The key distinction in speculative or dogmatic
theology (Lonergan soon dropped this terminology) was
between doctrines and systematics: theological understanding was not a matter of proving or demonstrating
the truths of the faith, but rather of trying to understand what one already knows to be true because of
one's faith. Nor is theology, however, simply iden-
tical with expressions of faith, or confined merely
to repeating what is the common faith of the church
(as in a Denzingertheologie). Rather, theology is
properly an effort to understand, in line with Vatican I's insistence on the possibility of reaching a
partial understanding of what is already believed.
This search for systematic understanding, however,
presupposes that into which some understanding is
sought. And the question asked by Lonergan was,
Who determines the doctrines into which the systematic theologian inquires? Remotely, of course, the
doctrines in question are the content of the church's
confession of faith; yet where are we to find this
confession? Clearly, we think of the official teaching of the church, yet with equal clarity we know
that this teaching is but one aspect of the church's
confession of faith. To put it all very briefly,
Lonergan postulated the need of a distinct task in
theology, namely, the task of stating the teachings
of the community - determining as accurately as possible the various doctrines into which some understanding would be sought. This was the basis for
Lonergan's distinction between two specializations

in theology, two quite distinct functions that
theologians are to perform. The doctrinal theologian has the task of setting forth the doctrines or teachings of the community; the systematic theologian has the task of searching for
some insight into the possible meaning of these
doctrines, drawing on analogy, the relation of
the doctrines to one another, and the orientation
of the doctrines to their eschatological end.
Lonergan does not doubt that one and the same
theologian may be called upon to do both tasks;
but he would insist that different methods are
involved in each task, and a great deal of confusion could be avoided by distinguishing the different jobs.[34]

    This led Lonergan to the second set of prob-
lems - the historical dimension of theology. For
clearly the doctrinal theologian will set forth
all the more clearly just what the current doctrines of the church are if he or she has a grasp
of their historical background and development,
of what the community has professed and believed
in its past tradition, of what is contained in
scripture, the church Fathers, the various councils and synods, in earlier theological speculation, in the ever-present sensu fidelium. This
took Lonergan into the sphere of "positive" theology (he soon dropped this terminology), and to
a distinction between doctrines (that are theological statements of what Christian doctrine is
at the present time) and that which underpins the
doctrines - their origins, development, controver-
sies in history. This was Lonergan's effort to
integrate within theology the critical work of exegetes, patristic scholars, medieval historians,
etc. The task was difficult, because these specialists did not attempt to "prove" anything, but
rather set forth hypotheses about what Christian
belief and practise possibly or probably was; yet
the doctrinal theologian could not ground his
work solely on hypotheses, but had somehow to mediate Christian truth. This hiatus or gap between
historical and doctrinal theology was, of course,

nothing new, yet Lonergan sharpened the precise nature of the difference between the two areas and this set the stage for Lonergan's attempt to work out a new fundamental theology that could bridge the gap between encountering the past (history) and mediating truth to the present.[35]

This latter problem of specifying the foundations of theology was for Lonergan the most difficult. He hit upon the solution rather dramatically in the Spring of 1965, at which time his notion of functional specialization in theology really began to take shape. But, as it happens, I may conclude this introduction of Lonergan's work at this point, for the study which follows is basically an account of the breakthrough that was Lonergan's insight into the foundations of a new theology. I will try to clarify this in the next section.

4. "Unity in Theology"

In order to state precisely my intention in writing the present work, I would begin by noting briefly the main studies already done on Lonergan's thought. To do this I find it convenient to refer to the three dimensions of Lonergan's own studies that I outlined in the previous section: his medieval studies, his investigations of the modern scientific, philosophic, and scholarly context, and his transposition of theology to this new context.

To the best of my knowledge there have appeared no major studies on Lonergan's interpretation of the medieval theological achievement, particularly that of Aquinas.[36] A discussion of specific aspects of Lonergan's interpretation of medieval scholasticism has been done in articles by such people as David Burrell, Frederick Crowe, and Matthew Lamb, as well as in various reviews of Lonergan's two historical works.[37] My own work here is _not_ intended as a study of Lonergan's interpretation of medieval scholasticism.

Secondly, a number of major studies have appeared

INT

that investigate Lonergan's cognitional theory and
method in relation to major thinkers in the modern
context such as Kant, Hegel, Dilthey, Husserl, and
Gadamer.[38] Again, specific questions have been
treated in article form by a large number of authors,
both in monographs and in reviews of Insight or minor
publications.[39] My own work here is not concerned
with a critique of Lonergan's thought in relation to
any of the major figures in the development of modern
science, modern scholarship, or modern philosophy.
Nor is it a study of Lonergan's transcendental method
itself.

Finally, there have been both major and minor
studies of the genetic development of Lonergan's
thought in relation to contemporary theology.[40] Further, there have been a few articles that have treated
Lonergan's transposition of theology to a contemporary
context, as well as a large number of reviews of work
published by Lonergan since 1965 - especially reviews
of Method in Theology.[41]

To date, however, there has been no major study
that has been systematic, that has tried to bring together in coherent fashion Lonergan's notion of theology: its foundations, its structure, its role in
the Christian community and in human history. My
work hopes to be such a study.

While my project is ambitious, I feel it is
needed. All too easily one loses sight of the entire
project that motivated a significant thinker in all
his work. And with this oversight, subsequent interpretations of that person's thought may tend to miss
the point of a particular element in the system. Accordingly, I felt that a systematic overview was
needed, not only to prevent as much as possible a
misunderstanding of Lonergan's thought, but especially
to provide the broader context where such thought may
be better understood and judged.

The study which follows, then, is not genetic but
systematic. It would ask, not about the development

in Lonergan's thinking in whole or in part over
the past fifty years, but rather about the way in
which the results of fifty years of thought might
be ordered in a systematic fashion. This implies
that I have selected a theme around which the
"fragments" may be gathered, and the theme chosen
is "the unity of theology in its new context."
This theme, I believe, has motivated Lonergan's
work throughout his career.

Secondly, I acknowledge that a systematic
study of the sort I am attempting relies on genetic and interpretative studies of Lonergan's thought.
I am indebted to the many people who have done such
studies, even if occasionally I choose to disagree
with their findings. For while utilizing the work
of others, my principal task was nonetheless to assess Lonergan's work on the basis of my own self-
appropriation in assimilating that work, judging it
by what I myself discovered in my investigation of
Lonergan and other contemporary theologians.

Thirdly, although an exercise in systematic
thinking, the present work would hope to be as well
an effort to present Lonergan's thought in such a
way as to highlight its relevance to contemporary
theology: it would, then, facilitate the communication of Lonergan's thought. Such communication
implies a more or less specific audience, for clearly
an author can structure his work differently for different groups of readers. In the main, then, I have
in mind German theologians, whether Catholic or Protestant. Most especially in Chapter One I wish to
present things in such a way as to raise issues that
currently are receiving extensive attention in German theology, namely, the issues grouped around the
development of a new fundamental theology. In particular, I shall discuss the suggestions for such a
fundamental theology by Wolfhart Pannenberg, Karl
Rahner, and Johann Metz, and then I will add a concluding section to Chapter One relating these suggestions to that of Lonergan. And while the remainder of my work will concentrate on Lonergan's thought,

xli

INT

I shall attempt to highlight the relation of this
thought to discussions currently taking place in
German theology.

It remains that a brief word be said on the
actual structure of the study. To present a notion
of theology in terms of method, rather than in the
more traditional categories of formal and material
objects, demands a rather extensive context. Following the **Fragestellung** in Chapter One I shall
present Lonergan's understanding of the sort of
systematic reflection that underpinned the unity
of medieval theology; that unity disintegrated as
new types of intellectual development emerged in
modern science, modern historical scholarship, and
modern philosophy, so that it was no longer clear
just what function was to be performed by reflection on religion, or how that reflection should be
done. Such is the problem inherited by the new
fundamental theology, and Chapter Three begins on
a note or urgency by discussing the absence of God
in modern culture - an absence due in large part
to the absence of an adequate theology. In the
task of renewing theology, Lonergan suggests we
build on a new foundation, in a manner of a "theological anthropology," proceeding to objectify
that horizon in a series of steps. Chapter Three
itself presents Lonergan's account of the manner
in which we can move from religious experience to
an interpretation of this experience that draws
upon the tradition of the religious community; from
there we move on to his account of a new manner of
reflecting systematically on this experience and
its interpretation, where the "reflecting systematically" occurs both in a generalized way and in the
specialized ways of historical scholarship, dialectic, and praxis. Chapter Four examines how generalized and specialized methods can be put in theology, as theologians strive for some partial understanding of the realities to which religious experience and tradition bear witness. A final chapter
turns to a brief consideration of Lonergan's understanding of the role that a methodical theology can
play in the broader contexts of church community and
human community.

I. THE PROBLEM OF PLURALISM IN THEOLOGY

> Besides the pluralism implicit in
> the transition from classicist to
> modern culture, besides the pluralism
> implicit in the coexistence of undif-
> ferentiated and variously differen-
> tiated consciousness, there is the
> more radical pluralism that arises
> when all are not authentically human
> and authentically Christian.[1]

In order to set the stage for a study of Lonergan's notion of unity in theology, it seems well
to begin by examining the need for such unity.
This need arises from the fact of pluralism in
theology, and it is possible to distinguish three
distinct sources of that pluralism. Firstly,
there are the cultural differences among those to
whom Christ's message is communicated. Secondly,
there are the various specializations within theology. Thirdly, opposed convictions of theological
specialists concerning truth, morality, and religion give rise to fundamentally opposed theologies and, subsequently, to opposed fundamental
theologies. I shall discuss each of these topics
in turn, and add a final section relating Lonergan's thought to this whole discussion.

1. Cultural Pluralism and the Mission of the Church

Each of us to a greater or lesser extent has
experienced the fact of cultural pluralism, of the

tremendous diversity among the peoples of the
earth. Spontaneously we adapt to our immediate
surroundings and grow comfortable with the local
language, the societal network of family, neigh-
borhood, church, the cultural heritage of specific
viewpoint, mentality, belief. Spontaneously we
feel out of place and uncomfortable if there is an
unfamiliar context: a new language or strange dia-
lect, the ceremonies and rituals of a different
church or sect, the attitudes and customs of a foreign country. What to me is plain common sense is,
for another, puzzling, strange, or even nonsense.
These differences in common sense that result from
differences in sex, age, language, societal and cultural heritage is the fact of cultural pluralism.[2]

The implications of such cultural pluralism are
many, but of special concern here is the matter of
human communication. To communicate effectively is
to set up a world of common meaning, yet this is extremely difficult because of the almost endless diversity among people. Viewpoints and mentalities
differ depending on whether we are female or male,
old or young, black or white, parent or child, Catholic or Protestant, Christian or Hindu, German or
Canadian. And to communicate with someone who differs
from us in viewpoint and mentality, who has quite a
different brand of common sense, who is of another
cultural background, is no automatic achievement but
demands a learning process that is ongoing and never
complete.

Christianity is by no means exempt from cultural

pluralism or from the need to take seriously this
pluralism in its communication of the gospel of
Christ. Both in word and praxis it has taken hold
in a huge variety of individuals, societies, and
cultures to yield different brands, not just of
Christianity, but of Catholicism or Protestantism.
There results an impressive variety of local, re-
gional, and national churches, each reflecting its
own particular way of understanding and practising
the Christian gospel. Moreover, there is an ever-
increasing awareness that ministry to those who have
already received the gospel as well as to those who
have not yet encountered it demands a sensitivity to
the linguistic, social, and cultural heritage of
each particular group hearing the gospel message.
Without this sensitivity it is all too easy to make
the mistake of imposing one's own brand of common
sense, of social structures, of political systems,
of economic policies, of ideology, of cultural
traits on those to whom the gospel is being preached.

Such mistakes were made frequently by otherwise
well-intentioned teachers, preachers, catechists,
and missionaries; indeed, the danger of such mistaken attitudes and practices has been with the
Christian community since its origins, especially as
the gospel came to be preached in gentile contexts.
With the explorers' discovery of the 'new world' in
the fifteenth century, this problem of communication
took on enormous complexity yet it was all too often
resolved with a commonsense simplicity that, in the
western world, resulted in the preaching of European

3

culture along with the Christian gospel. The error
of this approach has come to be recognized in the
practice of the present century that has witnessed
a steady sensitivity by pastors and missionaries to
the concrete circumstances and cultures in which the
gospel is preached. And such practice received formal recognition and approval in Catholic circles at
the Second Vatican Council.[3]

After the Council, both the culturally sensitive
practice and the formal approval of such practice by
church authorities have received considerable attention by theologians. There is emerging a new kind of
pastoral theology that is concerned to read the signs
of the time before attempting any communication. And
this in turn has had repercussions on the whole of
theology, that is far more conscious than before of
the complexity involved in assimilating the meaning
of the Christian message and tradition, and in transposing that meaning for all classes and cultures. In
other words, cultural pluralism is entering into the
very heart of theology and is leading to the development of different theologies for different cultural
groups.

Just what this recognition of cultural pluralism
eventually will mean for theology is not yet clear,
but at least the main lines of the challenge have
been drawn. One of the most precise statements of
this challenge appears in the ninth thesis of a document by the International Commission of (Catholic)
Theologians on the unity of the faith and theological
pluralism; and the commentary on this thesis, by Pet-

rus Nemeshegyi, is a clear and unambiguous work of
interpretation.[4] The thesis itself recalls that the
Christian gospel is directed to all people and is
essentially a missionary gospel. For this reason,
God's revelation in word and deed is ever to be newly
reflected upon, newly expressed, and newly translated
into praxis for each and every human culture. Only
then can this divine revelation be truly an answer to
the questions rooted in the heart of mankind, and
only then will this revelation become the soul of
prayer, worship, and daily life in the people of God.
In this way, the gospel of Christ promotes the fulfillment of cultural aspirations, yet also is a creative critic of those aspirations. To accomplish this
task of incarnating the gospel in each culture, the
local churches need always continuity and community
with the universal church both past and present.
Through such efforts, the local churches contribute
extensively both to the deepening of Christian living
as well as to the progress of theological reflection
in the universal church, thereby promoting the di-
vinely-willed unity of all mankind, despite cultural
multiplicity.

Such is the challenge set forth in the thesis of
the theological Commission, and Nemeshegyi's commentary leaves no room for misunderstanding just what is
intended. He recalls the example of Paul who knew
that to preach the gospel to all nations meant being
a Jew for the Jews and a Greek for the Greeks. With
the spreading of the gospel to the Hellenic world,
the radical newness of Christ's gospel found expres-

sion only in the cultural <u>Denkformen</u> of Hellenism.
Nemeshegyi refers to this process as the <u>Kulturüber-
brückung des Christentums</u>, and notes its continuance
into the patristic era that occasioned considerable
controversy. The eventual success of the process,
however, was not without its price for there occurred
a tendency to canonize patristic and conciliar expressions as permanent and lasting achievements, applicable for all cultures and peoples. Such classicist thinking is now largely admitted as inadequate
and in its place is the contemporary recognition of
cultural pluralism. For the Vatican Council (according to Nemeshegyi), this does not mean some weak
'adaptation' of the Christian gospel to local conditions; rather, it is a matter of a creative encounter between divine revelation and the languages,
thoughtworld, religious and philosophical experiences
and images, traditional morality, social structures,
etc. of each different people and culture. This
whole cultural heritage is a specific brand of common
sense as well as specific trends in science, philosophy, and religious living; it is that culture's 'vocabulary' or 'Vorverständnis' through which alone the
Christian gospel can be assimilated, understood, and
lived.[5]

Professor Nemeshegyi continues his commentary
with a wealth of observations on the need for such
cultural sensitivity and on the dangers implicit in
such a process. Here, I would note only a single
point that serves admirably to conclude the present
section and to introduce the next. If such encounter

is to be both creative and specifically Christian,
if it is neither to ignore the given cultural heritage nor merge uncritically with it, then there is need
of a massive effort on the part of the theological
community to determine as precisely as possible just
what the Christian message is in its origins, subsequent development, and present meaning. For only then
is it possible to give that meaning an expression
which can challenge a particular culture with the radical call of Christ to repent and believe. As it happens, the community of theologians is indeed conscious
of the urgency and magnitude of the challenge. This
magnitude, however, implies that no one theologian can
do everything and become an expert in all areas of interpreting and communicating the gospel. Contemporary
theology is highly specialized, and this fact of
specialization is the second source of pluralism in
theology to which we may now turn attention.[6]

2. Performative Pluralism Within Theology

In attending schools, colleges, and universities,
we are usually doing something more than merely refining our spontaneous commonsense abilities. Undoubtedly
a good measure of common sense is an indispensable as-
set to us and forms the basis on which we begin our
bloody entry into the heights of academia. Nonetheless, those heights are something quite different from
common sense and perhaps for that very reason are
often judged obscure, remote, and quite irrelevant to
the immediate and more practical concerns of everyday

living. It is only with the greatest difficulty that
most of us enter the worlds of mathematics, natural
science, history, the behavioral sciences, perhaps
even philosophy. Even the subject matter of religion
seems strangely remote and distant, though it, along
with the other academic spheres, still retains a certain aura of mystery and importance.

While it is difficult enough to gain even a
basic working knowledge in any of those disciplines,
it remains close to impossible to relate any one of
them to the others. The curriculum is divided and
sub-divided into a huge variety of subjects, and we
move from mathematics to history to psychology with
little if any idea of what they possibly might have
in common. And if eventually we choose to pursue an
academic career, we find it necessary to select, not
all of the available disciplines, but generally a few
or only one in which to specialize, leaving the others
behind to be cared for by other specialists.

This fact of specialized areas of learning is not
to be denied. Presupposed, of course, is commonsense,
everyday living, but such ordinary living, while the
substructure of our cultural living, is by no means
the whole story. For any number of reasons, we try to
reflect on this living in order to understand it as
thoroughly as possible, to evaluate it critically, to
maintain, modify or completely change it in line with
newer and better ideas and theories. We try in different manners to objectify our everyday living, to
state its meaning and value explicitly and deliber-

ately, thereby subjecting the different patterns of our everyday living to careful scrutiny and study.

The various specializations of human knowing arise out of such reflection on everyday living. It is good common sense to use one's head in figuring things out, but a group of specialists like psychiatrists can help us figure out why we don't always figure things out, while another group, the psychologists, can give us positive hints on how we in fact operate in solving problems and what we might do to solve problems more effectively. Again, it is common sense to work skilfully at a craft, with maximum efficiency, but a group of specialized natural scientists can replace us with computerized technology that matches us in our skill and minimizes human error. Further, all of us share the wisdom of common sense that has a saying or proverb for all occasions, but a specialized group of philosophers may arise to probe the meaning and value of human life as such. To a greater or lesser extent, each of us has religious inclinations and may even pray or worship, but a specialized group of theologians is needed to analyze our religious living and clarify for us its role and significance in the world of today.

Such and many more are the various groups of specialists. Each somehow begins from commonsense living, but each eventually deserts this beginning for what seems a world apart - a world with its own technical language, its own experts, its own learned books and periodicals, its own conventions and meetings, its own niche in the educational system. Further, all this is done with at least a remote intention to enrich everyday living; and if some specializations seem to lag behind in this enrichment, it remains that our own day is conspicuously marked in its very ordinariness by the achievements of natural science and its technology. Closely related to this is the sense of autonomy, of human control over the world and its destiny, over mankind and oneself. Things are in process, and it is up to us, especially with steady advance in scientific progress, to assure a world without illness or discomfort and one with economic stability and equality for all.

It remains, however, that the fact of specialization makes it difficult indeed to determine just which of the specialties is to have the greatest influence on shaping and directing human life. As noted, the specializations tend to be rather autonomous entities, closed groups. At best, they are isolated from one another, and at worst they compete with one another in offering to mankind an interpretation of humanity and its world. Such isolation and competition cannot but affect everyday living, and accounts for the disorientation experienced by ourselves in a world that has become strange and broken. We are in need of solutions, of an orientation in life, yet the answers are not forthcoming from the academic world, from those precisely who supposedly are coolly reflecting on things for our benefit. Such is the current existential crisis.[7]

For the moment, my concern is not with this existential crisis but rather with the fact of pluralism
that is related to it. The pluralism here, then, is
not the sort concerned with the almost infinite specializations of common sense - the cultural pluralism
mentioned in the previous section. Rather, I am
speaking here of what might be called performative
pluralism, the sort of specializations that begin from
common sense only to withdraw from it in objectifying
reflection of one kind or another. Later in this work
I will sketch the main specializations of the contemporary period that are relevant to theology. For now,
I wish to indicate merely that the fact of specialization is relevant to theology.

Clearly, then, theology as such may be considered
one of these specializations, along with natural
science, history, philosophy; theology has had the
character of a specialization in this formal sense
ever since the great medieval systems of theology were
constructed to provide an integrated and systematic
reflection on the meaning of Christianity.[8]

On the other hand, however, there is a real sense
in which autonomous specializations are found within
theology itself. This is a very complex topic, indeed
it is a main motivation behind the present work, but I
find it important to sketch it here in this introductory chapter. What I have in mind, then, are especially three dimensions of theological work that present us with at least the tendency to be three autonomous entities: historical scholarship, systematic

I.

reflection, and pastoral communication.

Firstly, then, there is the work of historical scholars. Included here are such people as archeologists, experts in ancient languages, exegetes or interpreters of ancient and modern texts, church historians and historians of doctrine. Common to this group is a fidelity to what has come to be known as historical-critical method. Just what this method involves is a matter of considerable debate and discussion, but it is enough for present purposes to note that the method is empirical rather than deductive. This means that historical scholars understand scripture and the Christian tradition, not as supplying us with universally valid and eternally true principles from which conclusions could be deduced, but rather as data for investigation and interpretation by a developing and never more than probable understanding.[9] The fact of such critical scholarship in Catholic theology is today beyond doubt and is evident to anyone familiar with the massive exegetical and historical literature that has appeared in recent decades.

Secondly, there is the work of dogmatic or systematic theologians, and such work is quite different in its methods and aims from that of historical scholars. Without at all denying the validity of historical scholarship and even insisting that such scholarship is integral to their work, the dogmatic and systematic theologians are nevertheless moving in a different world. As a group they are concerned with

12

reaching a current understanding of the Christian "faith" - the meaning of the Christian message and tradition in the world of today. Accordingly, they need the work of historical scholars to suggest how past witnesses to that message and tradition actualized it in their own day; but dogmatic and systematic theologians would insist that they themselves have the quite distinct task of actualizing the meaning of scripture and tradition for the present day. To perform this task demands a historically-oriented speculative approach to Christian truth,[10] and this in turn means philosophizing within a theological perspective.[11] Here again the fact of such dogmatic and systematic reflection in Catholic theology is beyond doubt and it has brought forth an ongoing multitude of studies examining the meaning of Christ, church, sacrament, God, revelation, etc. in the world of today.

Thirdly, there is the work of pastoral or practical theologians, and such work is today quite different in its methods and aims from both historical scholarship and dogmatic or systematic theology. Such practical theology would indeed maintain a close working relationship with historical and systematic theologies, but especially in recent years has come to insist on its own proper methods and aims. It does not any longer understand itself as merely the practical conclusions that flow from dogmatic and systematic reflection, yet it too would take a stand on Christian truth. Nor does it understand itself as merely the interpreter of current Christianity,

I.

though such historically-minded interpretation is
vital to its task. In a sense, practical theologians
see their distinctiveness neither in historical interpretation nor in speculative or systematic reflection but rather in a praxis that communicates effectively the Christian message in the almost infinite
variety of individual, social, and historical contexts
of today's world. As such, practical theology in
Catholic circles is in the process of becoming autonomous from (though related to) dogmatic or systematic
theology, and in this process is acquiring its own
specialized experts, methods, publications.[12]

I have been giving a very concise outline of
three distinct dimensions of contemporary Catholic
theology. To some extent, each is concerned with
the Christian message and tradition, but each is differently concerned with that message and tradition.
The problem, of course, is the interrelationship of
the various groups of specialists and the problem of
integrating the efforts of each group, and I will
discuss this problem in the next section. My aim for
now, though, is to do nothing more than draw attention
to the various directions or dimensions of current
work in theology. Each has its validity and each is
very operative in Catholic theological circles. Most
theologians would readily admit the need of all three
groups, even though most tend to specialize in one or
the other. Disagreement, however, first arises when
theologians begin to discuss the unity of the various
groups. In recent years, this discussion has occurred
mostly under the rubric of "fundamental theology," and

so we come to the final source of pluralism that lies
in the varieties of fundamental theologies.

3. The Pluralism of Fundamental Theologies

    I began this chapter by drawing attention to the
pluralism in the cultural contexts within which the
Christian church is to communicate the gospel of
Christ Jesus. I went on to note that the recognition
and reception of such pluralism by theology has resulted, indeed, in a renewed and contemporary theology, but that this renewed theology is anything but a
unified and integrated discipline. This fact has led
a number of theologians to reflect on the nature or
function of theology as a whole, in all its various
specializations, in an effort to work out the unity
within theology and the relation of theology to other
disciplines and sciences. Generally speaking, this
discussion is considered to be the main task of a new
fundamental theology.[13] As perhaps might be expected,
the answers being given by theologians to the question
of the foundation, organization, and function of theology are not always the same. Indeed their answers are
so different as to give rise to yet a third source of
pluralism that we may call foundational pluralism or,
more descriptively, the pluralism of fundamental
theologies. To borrow a phrase from the human sciences, theology is undergoing an "identity crisis" as it
struggles to understand itself in its internal structure and in its external relations to other disciplines
and to Christian and human living.

I.

The fact of theology's identity crisis is due
in large part to the end of an era wherein the legitimacy of theological work was taken for granted and
stood in no need of justification. As I shall indicate later in this dissertation, that era ended with
the rise of modern science, modern scholarship, and
modern philosophy. These new disciplines, each in
its own way, gradually liberated themselves from dependence on metaphysical principles and from a worldview that presupposed both divinity and theological
reflection on that divinity. The foundations of
these new disciplines were squarely within this world
and human history, and this invariably posed identity
problems for a theology that claimed to speak of what
lay beyond this world.

At first, theology met the new challenge by re-
affirming its traditional role and by clearly isolating itself from the changes that were taking place;
such was the dogmatic age of theology. But as I
pointed out in the previous sections of this chapter,
Catholic theology has recently begun to follow the
example of Protestant theology in breaking through
this isolation and re-defining itself in the modern
world. To date, the results have been impressive,
yet it seems that a stage has been reached when further development is possible only if theology pauses
to take stock of itself and reflect on where it has
come from, what it has become, and where it is going.
And, as mentioned, such reflections have become the
task of the new fundamental theology.

16

Previously, then, it was enough to define theology as the science that dealt with revealed truths. Now, however, such a description seems grossly inadequate. There is a new notion of "science," and one wonders to what extent theology may be called a science in this new sense. There is a new notion of truth, as historically conditioned, and one wonders to what extent eternal truths can be historically conditioned. There is, finally, an age of agnosticism, atheism, and rationalism which refuses to acknowledge the existence of other-worldly reality and of possible revelations of this reality. The very foundations upon which theology rested so comfortably have been cast aside, and theologians face the choice of clinging to the past in increasing irrelevance, or of building on new foundations that place theology in the world of today. The task is far from easy. On the one hand, there is to be identity with the world of the present; on the other hand, there is to be a non-identity that preserves the unique role both of the Christian gospel and of the theology that reflects this gospel. But if the task is not easy, it nonetheless is urgent and, in response to this urgency, a number of theologians have suggested various ways in which theology can meet its identity crisis.

Among these theologians is Bernard Lonergan and I shall outline his approach to the problem in the next section. First, though, I wish to present three quite different views regarding the identity of theology in the world of today. The main representatives of these views are Wolfhart Pannenberg, Karl Rahner,

and Johann Metz. Pannenberg stresses the historical
and philosophical dimensions of religion and Christianity; he proposes a notion of theology built around
the Wissenschaftlichkeit of theological reflection,
thereby highlighting the parity of theology with other
academic disciplines. Karl Rahner tends to be concerned with preserving the specifically religious,
sacred, Christian dimensions of religion and Christianity; he proposes a notion of theology built around
the Kirchlichkeit of theological reflection, thereby
highlighting theology's specific function of witnessing in community to our experience of divine mystery.
Metz emphasizes the practical and political functions
of religion and Christianity as a critical force in
history and society; he proposes a notion of theology
built around the Zeitoffenheit of theological reflection, thereby highlighting theology's practical responsiveness to the signs of the times.

For the moment I wish to present these three
kinds of fundamental theology as more or less complementary: each of them highlights a dimension of theology that is important and that cannot be overlooked by
contemporary theologians. Each of them tries to take
account of the pluralism facing the church's mission.
Each of them tries to relate the various theological
disciplines to one another. Later in my work I will
try to show the legitimacy of each notion of theology,
and I shall draw on the work of Lonergan to relate all
three in a systematic and critical fashion. As well,
I shall indicate that problems and confusion can enter

in whenever we ask any one of the three theologies
to do too much - when we demand of any one of them
the accomplishment of all theological tasks.   But
for now I simply want to describe the main characteristic of each of the three fundamental theologies.

In general terms, then, the authors to be discussed here all are concerned with history, revelation, and praxis. Pannenberg would employ a foundation in history to explain both revelation and praxis.
Karl Rahner would employ a foundation in revelation
to explain both history and praxis. Metz would employ
a foundation in praxis to explain both history and
revelation. Lonergan would employ the foundation
common to history, revelation, and praxis to understand all three and to relate each to the others. I
wish to discuss each of these positions, and I shall
do so by concentrating on what I believe to be the
fundamental component of each notion of theology.
Clearly, I am not attempting to present these notions
of theology in an exhaustive manner, but rather would
offer just a few ideas that will help the reader to
relate the thought of Pannenberg, Rahner, Metz, and
Lonergan.

(1)   Wolfhart Pannenberg: The Priority of Wissen-
      schaftlichkeit

A moment ago I mentioned the identity crisis for
theology that occurred with the rise of a new notion
of science, historical scholarship, and philosophy.

I.

Each of these disciplines was part of the Age of
Reason, that tended to replace the earlier age when
faith was presumed and theology rested on principles
of faith that were revealed truths. I further noted
that the challenge to faith and theology was met by
a theology that insisted on faith over against reason, on authority over against autonomy, on dogma
over against history and science. This reaction on
the part of theology was perhaps inevitable in light
of the anti-religious spirit of much that occurred
in the Age of Reason and Enlightenment. Still, the
anthropological turn of modernity, that placed mankind and this world at the center of attention, was
and is too deeply rooted to be eradicated by appeals
to an earlier era of faith and authority. Another
approach to Enlightenment was needed, and one of the
most comprehensive and penetrating studies of theology in its modern context has come from Wolfhart
Pannenberg.

Pannenberg is convinced that the best way to
meet the Enlightenment's criticism of revealed religion and theology is by discovering the legitimate
insight of Enlightenment thought, rather than by de-
fensively condemning it or ignoring it by an insistence on fidelity to past authorities. Once the legitimate insight has been acknowledged, it can be
employed to up-date and purify religion and theology
in this post-Enlightenment era. But as well, similar
work must be done to discover the error in Enlightenment thinking that caused it to reject religion and
theology as detrimental to human living; and once the

error has been uncovered, it can be corrected to restore to religion and theology a vital role in the
modern world.   Such is Pannenberg's intention:

> Die rationale Kritik der Aufklärung und
> ihrer Erben an der christlichen Über-
> lieferung muss von der Theologie positiv
> aufgenommen werden, um überwunden werden
> zu können. Bei dieser Aufgabe handelt
> es sich keinesfalls um eine belanglose
> Apologetik. Sondern hier besteht doch
> wohl bis heute eine Notlage, der die
> Theologie nicht aus Bequemlichkeit aus-
> weichen darf, die sie vielmehr redlich
> bestehen muss als einen von der Sache
> her erforderten Klärungsprozess.[14]

For Pannenberg the legitimate insight of Enlightenment thought lies principally in its insistence on a
critical approach to history and on human autonomy and
responsibility.[15] Within that framework the Enlightenment was quite justified in rejecting as inadequate
authoritarian notions that grounded religion and theology exclusively on other-worldly, eternal truths imposed upon mankind from without, oblivious of human
freedom and response. But Pannenberg insists that the
oversight of Enlightenment thought was its claim to
ground human freedom in the ontic reality of the human
individual subject, simply as given in history. For
Pannenberg, the ultimate ground of freedom and human
personality cannot be the private, isolated, individual
subject; rather, the ground of autonomy lies outside
the historically conditioned individual in the "other,"
to whom the individual responds in love. In making
this response, the individual breaks loose from the
past, from what is already given and determined, and

becomes truly a person, reaching beyond himself and his ready-made world. Such freedom-as-response, moreover, must be carried out, and is possible, only in reference to (anticipation of) a personal reality that lies beyond this world - a person who is the totality of reality and meaning, and this is God. It is here that Pannenberg transposes the Enlightenment thesis of autonomy and atheism to demand precisely a link between autonomy and theism. For to think that the realm of society, of interpersonal response, can bestow upon mankind its true autonomy is an illusion; this society is itself the very sphere of bondage and unfreedom. Only response to a personal and other-worldly God can guarantee human autonomy and lead to both personal and societal progress; pure rationalism and atheism can lead only to further slavery or decline.

If, however, we are not simply to fall back into the errors of postulating an exclusively supernatural divinity removed from human history and imposed authoritatively on human freedom, then theology has the task of beginning precisely from human history and valid human freedom in speaking responsibly of God and the meaning of divine revelation. Somehow, the reality of God and revelation must be approached from within history, for modern historical consciousness finds any other approach both very unreal and intellectually unacceptable. Pannenberg here does not at all intend to diminish the subjective reality of individual religious experience; but he would urge that a scientific theology, if it is to be admitted to the modern academic community, has to work within the framework of reference guiding that community - what empirically and historically is intelligible. Accordingly, Pannenberg proposes a notion of theology that as a science takes its point of departure from the reality of this world of human history and human freedom and human response.[16]

Such is Pannenberg's basic project, and it has occupied his attention for some two decades. Throughout this period he has attempted to re-think the major doctrines of Christianity on the basis of critical history and a philosophy of religion. I wish to draw attention here, however, not to Pannenberg's reinterpretation of specific Christian doctrines, but rather to his explanation of just how such reinterpretation is to be done. In particular, I wish to present Pannenberg's thought on the relation of historical reason and faith, for it is against this background of the interaction of Wissen and Glauben that Pannenberg develops his new notion of theology. Further, it is this question of reason and faith that is the point where I would like to compare Pannenberg, Rahner, Metz, and Lonergan.[17]

In a paper given in 1960 and published the following year, Pannenberg set forth a number of theses regarding the doctrine of revelation.[18] His third thesis proposes that God's self-revelation through history (Geschichtsoffenbarung) can be grasped by anyone who has eyes to see it, and thus it has a universal character. In explaining this thesis, Pannenberg first notes that we usually understand revelation

as a process that lies beyond the apprehension of our
natural vision, that can be communicated to us only
in some secret and hidden manner. But Pannenberg insists that God's self-revelation in activity (<u>Handeln</u>),
as recorded in the Bible, is not some secret and mys-
terious happening; to think that it is would be to
confuse historical revelation with some gnostic secret
knowledge. Both the Old and the New Testaments show
clearly that God's activity through history is something that can be grasped by all peoples and in no way
is restricted to some special nation or group. Moreover, it is not some "supernatural" truth that is revealed, and that demands a special sort of knowledge
perfecting or completing our ordinary knowledge;
rather, revelation is fully on the level of what can
be seen by ordinary human knowing. In particular, the
Holy Spirit is not the condition whereby we know God's
self-revelation in Christ; Pannenberg agrees with
Bultmann that Paul describes faith, not as a gift of
the Spirit, but as the presupposition for receiving
the gift of the Spirit. That there are those who refuse to see this truth of God's self-revelation through
history in no way exempts theology and preaching from
the task of stating clearly and pointing to the quite
unpretentious revelation of God in the destiny of Jesus
Christ.

In clarifying what he means by this, Pannenberg
observes that knowledge of God's self-revelation is
more than just a confirmation of what we can already
know by our reasoning (<u>Vernunft</u>). Indeed, no one can

have knowledge (Erkenntnis) of God simply from one's own reasoning and ability (Kraft). This is so, moreover, not just in regard to our knowledge of God but as well in regard to many things that we experience (Erfahrungen). The fact of the matter is, that the events revealing God, and the message announcing these events, lead people to a knowledge that they cannot have by virtue of their own personal abilities and reasoning. But if people come into contact with these events and with the message reporting them, if they apprehend them in the reality of their historical relatedness, then the events speak their own factual language and lead people into knowledge of the God revealed in this language of historical facts. Such apprehension in no way demands the introduction of some external principles that cause us to see something "special" in the historical facts: for what we apprehend is nothing more than that which already is contained in the facts themselves. That so many fail to see God's self-revelation is all the more reason to appeal to people's true reasonableness, rather than to insist on the need of some higher knowledge or gnosis.

The position of Pannenberg, then, is clear. In order to find the revelation of God in this history of Israel and Jesus Christ, it is not necessary first to have faith; on the contrary, it is impartial apprehension of these events that first awakens authentic faith. Nor is such faith merely superfluous, for faith is tied intimately to the future (Zukunft) inasmuch as the essence of faith is trust and trust is

25

essentially oriented to what is future: it is the
future that will justify or crush such trusting.
Trust, however, is not to be some blind act but rather
is to build on what is given and can be grasped because it is manifest already in history. If there
were constantly doubts about what is actually given in
history, then the theologian and Christian would lack
a solid foundation on which to base their trust and in
which to find their salvation. Hence, the knowledge
of God's revelation in the history manifesting this
revelation must be the foundation of faith.

> Das Wissen von Gottes Offenbarung in der
> seine Gottheit erweisenden Geschichte
> muss also Grund des Glaubens sein.[19]

Doubtless, notes Pannenberg, the historical knowledge
(Wissen) of God's self-revelation is subject to
change and development; but this changing interpretation in no way will destroy the conviction of faith
as long as the interpretation bears witness to the
basic event of God's self-revelation itself. Thus,
faith as an act of trust transcends its own picture
(Bild) of the historical event (Geschehen). In the
trusting gift of one's very existence in faith, the
believer goes beyond even his or her theological formulations of faith and becomes open to others and
open as well to an ever better knowledge of the history by virtue of which he or she lives. It is such
faith that binds together people of very different
theological formulations as well as those who have no
idea of theology. So it is that knowledge is the
foundation of faith, although it is only by the trust

that follows such knowledge that one shares in the
salvation of God.

Pannenberg's account of the relation of knowledge and faith (Erkennen and Glauben) was questioned
by various critics. Pannenberg responded to this
criticism in a postscript to the second edition of
Offenbarung als Geschichte that appeared a few years
later.[20] Here, Pannenberg further clarified what he
meant by the priority of knowledge over faith (Erkennen vor dem Glauben). What he has in mind is a
logical priority; this does not necessarily mean a
psychological priority, as if someone was first allowed to believe only after reaching full and con-
clusive knowledge. Indeed, psychologically speaking,
the believer exists only in virtue of an anticipatory
knowledge, in anticipation of a truth to be conclu-
sively known only in the Eschaton though already now
manifesting itself to the believer.[21]

In this same postscript Pannenberg mentions the
need for a "Theologie der Vernunft," as noted also by
R. Röhricht, in order to clarify just what is meant
by Wissen and Erkennen. Pannenberg himself does not
attempt to develop this point at any length, but he
does make a couple of pertinent observations that are
very important to my present dissertation. He notes,
then, that Wissen does not mean some measurable "exact" Wissen, but must include the element of Einsicht.
Accordingly, a theology of reasoning (Vernunft) would
examine, not the a priori capacity of reasoning, but
rather what reasoning is in its historical structure

I.

of proposal and reflection, and in its openness to
truth that reasoning always presupposes and never
fully realizes. Such, Pannenberg contends, is in
line with the Thomist tradition of the unity of truth
and of the rationality or intelligibility of the
Christian message.

Against this background we can now understand
better what Pannenberg conceives to be the function
of theology.[22] Whoever believes in Jesus, thereby
setting his or her trust in Jesus, is the recipient
of salvation, regardless of one's historical and theological knowledge of Jesus. This presupposes that
communion with Jesus in fact guarantees and mediates
salvation. And it is precisely the task of theology
to reflect on the truth of this presupposition of
faith. Accordingly, theological knowledge is not a
condition for salvation, but it does tend to provide
a solid grounding for faith as well as an apologetic
that refuses to reduce faith to some merely subjective self-deception.

> Hier hat das theologische Wissen, um das
> die Arbeit theologischer Forschung sich
> bemüht, seine Funktion für den Glauben:
> Es sorgt dafür, dass der Glaube reiner
> Glaube, der vorgegebenen Wahrheit seines
> ihn tragenden Grundes vertrauen kann und
> nicht als grundlose "Entscheidung" zum
> Werk einer - illusionären - Selbsterlösung
> verdirbt. . . . Es bedarf also der Gründe
> für die Entscheidung des Glaubens. Dabei
> braucht der Glaube, um Glaube im Vollsinn
> zu sein, sich dieser Gründe nicht in jedem
> Fall und vor allem nicht in ihrer letzt-
> gültigen Klarheit und Gestalt bewusst zu

28

sein. Es genügt, dass die Entscheidung
des Glaubens <u>faktisch</u> auf stichhaltigen
Gründen beruht. Die Frage, ob und wie
das der Fall ist, bildet das Thema theologischer Reflexion, an der der einzelne Glaubende in dem Masse teilnehmen
wird und soll, wie es zur Auseinander-
setzung mit den ihn selbst bewegenden
Zweifeln nötig ist.

Die Theologie hat es also, in freilich
stets vorläufiger Weise, mit der Vor-
aussetzung des Glaubens zu tun, mit der
im Glaubensakt schon vorausgesetzten
Wahrheit und Verlasslichkeit des "Gegen-
standes," an dem der Glaube hängt.[23]

It is worth noting that Pannenberg thereby
clearly recognizes the limits of theological reflection. More accurately stated, theological reflection
as operative is always to be conscious of its own
limitations: as anticipatory knowledge of truth that
remains only indirectly revealed, even in the event
of Jesus Christ, theology ultimately confronts the
mystery of that with which it deals; thus theology
eventually must pass over into faith, it is to be a
<u>reductio in mysterium</u>.[24]

This eventual encounter of theological reflection with the mystery of God, in which theology passes
over into faith, provides an excellent opportunity to
consider the work of Karl Rahner. Whereas the <u>reductio</u>
<u>in mysterium</u> is for Pannenberg the terminal point of
theological reflection, such a <u>reductio</u> provides Karl
Rahner with the starting point of theological reflection, as I shall now attempt to indicate.

29

I.

(2) Karl Rahner: The Priority of Kirchlichkeit

I have mentioned that for Wolfhart Pannenberg
the reality of God as mystery is accessible to theological reflection only to the extent that this mystery indirectly reveals itself in the history of mankind - especially in the religions of mankind and
above all in Christianity. Theological reflection,
then, is basically the indirect sort of inquiry that
finds its verification in the historicity of religious experience in the various religions of mankind.
As such, theology is both historical and philosophical
investigation of the reality of mystery in history.
Theology is an evaluative sort of historical scholarship, in no way demanding the commitment of the theologian to God in faith. Instead, what counts is the
fidelity of the theologian to the critical methods of
historical and philosophic reflection, in order to
investigate, compare, and criticize the ability of
especially religious traditions to embody and reflect
the self-communication of divine reality.

Karl Rahner, on the other hand, is concerned to
emphasize precisely the foundational significance of
religious experience and faith in the theologian. At
first sight this seems to be directly contradictory
to Pannenberg's notion of theology, but I shall indicate later that the two positions are more complementary than contradictory. For the moment I wish to
draw attention to a single but fundamental aspect of
Rahner's notion of theology, namely, his attention to

the theologian as human subject; to the sort of human subject who is needed to do theology, and to the manner in which this human subject comes to function as theologian.

Perhaps the first thing to note is that Rahner, like Pannenberg, is very much concerned to acknowledge the fact of the Enlightenment: to accept its anthropologische Wende, and to overcome its rejection of revealed religion and theology precisely by proposing a notion of theology rooted in the anthropological turn of modern thought. Theology simply cannot operate as if the Enlightenment never existed, or as if it could be dealt with by a global condemnation.[25]

For Rahner, accepting the challenge posed by the Enlightenment means first and foremost coming to terms with modern philosophy.[26] Negatively, this means that theologians have to admit the inadequacy of scholastic and neo-scholastic philosophy as a tool for constructing their theological systems. Positively, it means that theologians have to turn to transcendental method if they wish to provide theology with a foundation adequate to the modern context, especially to the context provided by modern philosophy. It is clear to Rahner that modern philosophy, as exemplified in the work of Descartes, Kant, the German idealists, and in Existentialism, represents a complex of quite contradictory systems; accordingly, when Rahner says that modern philosophy may be studied as a series of efforts to develop a

I.

transcendental philosophy, he is quite aware of using
the word "transcendental" in an inexact, descriptive
manner. Having noted this, Rahner describes the
Fragestellung of modern philosophy (and hence of a
modern theology) as follows:

> Wir sagen darum ganz einfach und fast
> vorphilosophisch: Eine transzendentale
> Fragestellung, gleichgültig, in welchem
> Gegenstandsbereich sie auftritt, ist dann
> gegeben, wenn und insoweit nach den Bed-
> ingungen der Möglichkeit der Erkenntnis
> eines bestimmten Gegenstandes im erkenn-
> enden Subjekt selbst gefragt wird. Dass
> eine solche Fragestellung grundsätzlich
> in sich möglich, legitim und unter Um-
> ständen auch notwendig ist, braucht wohl
> im allgemeinen nicht lange erörtert zu
> werden. Erkenntnis bringt nun einmal
> nicht nur das Erkannte, sondern auch den
> Erkennenden ins Spiel, ist nicht nur von
> den Eigentümlichkeiten des Gegenstandes,
> sondern auch von der Wesensstruktur des
> erkennenden Subjektes abhängig. Das
> gegenseitige Beziehungsverhältnis und
> das gegenseitige Bedingungsverhältnis
> zwischen erkennendem Subjekt und erkann-
> tem Gegenstand als Erkanntem und Erkenn-
> barem sind der Gegenstand einer trans-
> zendentalen Fragestellung.[27]

The question about "the conditions of the possibility of knowledge" is of course very complex and it
may be answered in a variety of ways. The question
may be raised in the context of idealism, and the result is a series of philosophies that take their
stand on the priority of speculative reason. The
question may be raised in the context of existentialism, and the result is a series of philosophies that

take their stand on the priority of practical reason. Amidst such philosophical pluralism it is extremely difficult for the theologian to appeal to
transcendental method and to pinpoint the conditions
of the possibility of theological knowing: the disagreements are so pronounced that trying to build
theology on this or that modern philosophy seems
doomed to failure even before the project is undertaken. Nevertheless, the lack of agreement among
modern philosophers in no way detracts from the fact
of their unanimity in insisting that the central
question concerns human knowing - what knowledge is
and what we are to do with the knowledge that we
have.

Karl Rahner is very much aware of the pluralism
of modern philosophies. Moreover, he is extremely
conscious of the complexity within modern theology
itself, caused especially by the introduction of
critical-historical methods studying the Christian
message and tradition. At the same time, however,
he is convinced that there is a way of reflecting on
the Christian fact that at once does justice to the
spirit of modern philosophy and also provides the
various theological specializations with the categories they need to perform their highly technical
and scientific work. It is my conviction that Rahner
himself practised this "middle course," this new way
of doing theology, in almost all of his work as a
theologian over the past forty years. But it is also
my conviction that Rahner first adequately thematized

33

I.

just what he was up to in his "Grundkurs des
Glaubens" published in 1976.[28]   In due course I
shall have occasion to mention the remarkable
similarity between Rahner's thematization of his
transcendental method and Lonergan's thematization
of this same method. For the moment, however, I
wish to restrict attention, not to the thematization or objectification of transcendental method,
but rather to the reality which is thematized and
objectified.

   There is no doubt whatsoever that for Rahner
the fundamental reality is the human subject as
experiencing divine mystery.[29]   It is crucial to
note here that it is not the human subject alone,
nor divine mystery alone, but the human subject as
related to divine mystery that is the foundational
reality. This is quite in accord with the transcendental Fragestellung described by Rahner earlier
in this section. Moreover, it is important to note
that the human subject's experience of divine mystery, in its radical simplicity, is just given: it
is conscious without being known, meaning that it
is not the human subject knowing he or she is experiencing divine mystery or knowing that it is
divine mystery that is experienced. Rahner explains this in connection with his commentary on
the meaning of Ignatius of Loyola's consolación
sin causa precedente (consolation or trust that has
no cause):

           Von da aus lässt sich nun begreifen,

was mit dem Trost "ohne vorhergehende
Ursache" gemeint ist. Das Entscheidende
ist nicht irgendeine Plötzlichkeit des
Erlebnisses, sondern, wenn wir es einmal
deutlich sagen sollen, seine Gegen-
standslosigkeit. Was damit gemeint ist,
wird noch zu erklären sein. Es ist kein
"alcun obiecto" gegeben, und zwar auch
nicht im Trosterlebnis selbst. Wenn man
nun rasch mit dem Einwand dazwischen-
führe: da wird ja ein gegenstandsloses,
also unbewusstes Erlebnis behauptet, was
eine contradictio in adjecto ist, dann
hätte man die ganze Lehre des heiligen
Ignatius gründlich verkannt. Die ge-
meinte Objektlosigkeit ist die reine Of-
fenheit für Gott, die namenlose, gegen-
standslose Erfahrung der Liebe von dem
über alles Einzelne, Angebbare und Un-
terscheidbare erhabenen Gott, von Gott
als Gott. Es ist nicht mehr "irgendein
Objekt" gegeben, sondern das Gezogensein
der ganzen Person mit dem Grund ihres
Daseins in der Liebe über jedes bes-
timmte, abgrenzbare Objekt hinaus in die
Unendlichkeit Gottes als Gottes selbst
. . .[30]

This radical experience by the human subject of
divine mystery is, for Rahner, the horizon or the
very condition of the possibility of cognitional operations which intend some kategorial-gegenständliches
Objekt; it is the Vorgriff as opposed to the Begriff;
it is the subject in existentiell encounter with divine mystery, as the prior and illuminated reality of
the subject prior to this subject's objectification,
prior to the subject as existential.[30a]

While a great deal could be said at this point
regarding Rahner's notion of religious experience,[31]

I.

I wish only to draw attention to the relation of
this experience to theologizing. As far as I am
concerned, it is this relationship that distinguishes
Rahner's notion of theology from that of Pannenberg
and Metz, and thus I wish to study it quite carefully. What characterizes Rahner's notion of theology, then, is his insistence that theology is the
work of human subjects objectifying their encounter
with divine mystery. Whereas for Pannenberg theology
is a reflection on the indirect manifestation of mystery in history, Rahner would say that theology is
the indirect or transcendental reflection by the theologian on his or her religious tradition in light of
the theologian's own experience of divine mystery.[32]
It is this insistence on the theologian's own experience as being the "specifically theological principle" that I now wish to clarify.

As a first approximation Rahner notes that the
context of theology is the believing church in the
world:

> Die zukünftige katholische Theologie wird
> eine Theologie des bleibenden Bekenntnisses
> dieser Kirche sein. Wir wissen nicht, wie
> gross an Zahl und wie gesellschaftlich ein-
> flussreich diese Kirche in der Zukunft sein
> wird. Aber sie wird auf jeden Fall bleiben,
> und sie wird immer konstituiert sein durch
> das Bekenntnis zum lebendigen Gott, der sich
> in seiner gnadenhaften Selbstmitteilung der
> Welt als die letzte Kraft ihrer geschicht-
> lichen Bewegung und als ihre absolute Zu-
> kunft eingestiftet hat, durch das Bekenntnis
> zu Jesus Christus, in dem diese absolute
> Nähe Gottes zur Welt ihren geschichtlichen
> Höhepunkt und die Erscheinung ihres eschat-
> ologischen Sieges gefunden hat, durch das

> Bekenntnis zur bedingungslosen Liebe
> des Nächsten und zur Hoffnung des
> ewigen Lebens. . . . Und auf diese
> bleibende und immer neue Bekenntnis
> der Kirche bleibt auch die Theologie
> der Zukunft in der katholischen
> Kirche bezogen. Bleiben wird das
> Bedenken dieses Bekenntnisses mit
> aller Energie des Geistes und aller
> Kraft des Herzens aus der jeweils ge-
> benen neuen Situation des glaubenden
> und denkenden Menschen heraus.[33]

This link of theology to the believing church is the initial reason why I entitled this section on Rahner "Kirchlichkeit." It is a dimension of theology that has been emphasized by both Catholic and Protestant theologians, and generally it is what one is refer- ring to when one speaks of the ecclesial nature of theology.

It would, however, be a serious oversight if we restricted Rahner's meaning to some sort of external link between theology and the living church. What is meant by Rahner is something deeper, and to get at this requires our attention to a second approxi- mation.[34] This concerns the relation between ortho- praxis and orthodoxy, as set forth by Rahner on sev- eral occasions.[35] There is, then, such a thing as a practical "knowledge" ("Wissen") that Rahner identi- fies with experience of the divine mystery, that is pre-reflective, that is praxis in its deepest sense, that has meaning which can never be exhausted by re- flection:

> . . . Wir "wissen" alle im Geist Gottes
> mehr, Einfacheres, Wahreres und Wirk-

licheres, als wir in der Dimension un-
serer theologischen Begriffe wissen und
sagen können.[36]

This is true, not only for the individual in his or
her own religious experience, but as well for the religious community living in history:

Der heutige Mensch, der die geschicht-
liche Bedingtheit seiner Erkenntnis und
die Unmöglichkeit einer adäquaten Reflexion auf die Voraussetzungen seiner
eigenen Erkenntnisse reflex erfasst,
kann in einer frühen so gar nicht mög-
lichen Weise sich selbst gegenüber
kritisch sein. Er kann deutlicher re-
alisieren, dass seine Ansichten im sel-
ben Augenblick zu subjektiven Beliebig-
keiten zu werden drohen, wo sie nicht
in einer offenen Weise und in einem
grundsätzlich und praktisch aufrechter-
haltenen Dialog mit den Überzeugungen
der Gesellschaft konfrontiert bleiben.
Er kann heute besser verstehen,
dass die Wahrheit sogar mit Institution
etwas zu tun hat, dass man auch in der
Erkenntnis nicht das isolierte Einzel-
subjekt sein kann, dass die Wahrheit
weithin an ihrer gesellschaftlichen Ef-
fizienz gemessen werden kann, mehr als
man bisher meinte, dass die praktische
Vernunft und Entscheidung nicht nur
Derivate der theoretischen Vernunft sind,
sondern auch für die Erkenntnis als
solche selbst Eigenständigkeit und Ur-
sprünglichkeit haben, selbst aber nur
innerhalb eines gesellschaftlichen Kon-
textes denkbar sind.[37]

Such for Rahner is the priority of practical reason and, immediately following the passage just quoted,
he sets forth just what this means for theology in the
world of today. Theology should be reflection on the

faith of a church - a church living and acting (handeln) by virtue of this very faith. Rahner clarifies
this in the following important statement:

> Damit wird nicht ein kollektiver Subjekt-
> ivismus (im Unterschied zu einem individ-
> uellen) und ein Pragmatismus kanonisiert,
> sondern nur auf das Wesen der Theologie
> die Einsicht angewendet, dass das radikal
> Subjektive, das notwendig das interkom-
> munikativ Subjektive ist, auch das Ob-
> jektivste sei und dass die höchste Wahr-
> heit nur in der Tat der allumfassenden
> freien Liebe erreichbar bleibt. Von da
> aus gesehen gehört es zur selbstverständ-
> lichen theologischen Methode, von dem
> durchschnittlichen Glaubensbewusstsein
> der konkreten Kirche auszugehen.[38]

It is this link of theology to the faith of the living church that prevents theology from being merely
the private Weltanschauung of each individual theologian or even the communal Weltanschauung of a fully
autonomous and independent theological community.
Once again, this conviction of Rahner would, I suspect, cause little disagreement among contemporary
theologians. But then Rahner pursues this point to
its radical conclusion, and this brings us to a third
and final approximation that sets Rahner quite apart
from the mainstream of contemporary theologians.

I think the best way to approach this deepest
meaning of Rahner's ecclesial theology is to begin
with a passage from a letter written by Rahner to
Klaus Fischer:

> . . . kein Mensch kann das Ganze seines
> Lebens, seiner Grundentscheidung voll zu[39]

I.

einer expliziten, ausdrücklichen Aussage
bringen. Er lebt immer aus mehr, als er
sich selbst und anderen reflex sagen
kann. Er kann sein Tun trotz aller not-
wendigen Reflexion und reflexen Rechen-
schaft, die er sich und anderen über
sein Handeln gibt und geben muss, nie
adäquat reflektieren. Darum ist alle
Orthopraxis (aber so auch alles konkrete,
gelebte Glauben) nie die blosse Exekution
der (reflex ausgesagten, satzhaft ver-
gegenständlichten) Orthodoxie. Das gilt
für alle Lebensbereiche. Das gilt darum
auch für das christliche Leben und Glauben. Die reflektierte und reflektie-
rende Theologie holt nie den im Leben
vollzogenen Glauben ein. Theologie als
argumentierende Reflexion muss sein,
darf sein, darf entwickelt und auch mit
eigentlich wissenschaftlicher Methodik
durchdacht und dargestellt werden. Aber
das Christsein und sein Glaube ist immer
mehr, als was bei solcher Theologie zum
Vorschein kommt. Doch auf eben diese
Tatsache der Differenz zwischen Theorie
und Praxis, zwischen Glaube (als Tat der
Freiheit des Lebens) und Theologie kann
und muss nochmals reflektiert werden.
Die nie adäquate Reflektierbarkeit des
Lebens und des Christseins ist selbst
noch einmal ein Gegenstand der Reflexion
und so der Theologie. Nicht als ob sie
dadurch diese Diastase aufheben würde.
Aber die Theologie kann aus dieser re-
flektierten Diastase Konsequenzen ziehen.
Und eine davon ist eben die Möglichkeit
und das Recht einer Theologie der ersten
Reflexionsstufe.[39]

In this passage the key phrase is the one referring
to the "nie adäquate Reflektierbarkeit des Lebens und
des Christseins" as itself being the object of theological reflection. From what has already been said

40

in this section, it is clear that Rahner is not asking for a theology that reflects "objectively" - as if from outside - on the dichotomy between theory and praxis, between faith and theology. On the contrary, the "first level of reflection" is a matter of the theologian objectifying the meaning of his or her own "praxis" (encounter with divine mystery), and employing this objectification as the criterion for critically evaluating the community's Glaubens-bewusstsein.

This fact is stressed again by Rahner later in this same letter to Fischer. Rahner does not at all deny that the objectification of religious experience is legitimately expressed in the Christian history of salvation and revelation. Such is the context of interpretation, the horizon, in which the individual lives and upon which he or she draws in interpreting experience of divine mystery. But the contrary is also true: because the individual in fact is conscious of religious experience, it can happen that the objectification by the individual of this experience can be a principle for critically evaluating the religious tradition or context. In other words, Rahner maintains that theologizing is a matter of reflecting on one's religious tradition by attending, not only to the historically given tradition, but as well to one's own objectified experience of divine mystery as the critical principle by which that tradition is critically evaluated.[40]

It is in this sense that Rahner conceives of

41

I.

theology as "reductio in mysterium": not as some
neutral and impersonal contemplation of some far-
away divine mystery, but rather as a manner of reflection that begins from religious experience, that
objectifies this experience to evaluate a religious
tradition, and that thereby relates this tradition
in ever new ways to that which mankind experiences
in its deepest existential reality.

Wenn sich aber die Theologie versteht
als die "Wissenschaft" vom Geheimnis
als solchem (freilich getragen von der
Nähe dieses Geheimnisses zum Menschen,
die mit dem bezeichnet wird, was die
Christen Gnade usw. nennen), wenn die
Theologie eine Überlebenschance für
morgen nur hat, wenn sie sich mit letz-
ter Entschlossenheit zu diesem ihrem
Wesen bekennt und es nicht verschüch-
tert vor dem heutigen Menschen ver-
steckt, dann darf sie dieses ihr Wesen
auch in ihrem inneren Alltagsbetrieb
nicht vergessen. Sie darf sich nicht
verstehen als jene Wissenschaft, die
sich immer mehr in eine in alle Details
hinein differenzierte Systematik aus-
breitet, sondern als jene Tat des
Menschen, in der er auch auf der Ebene
der Reflexion die Vielfalt siner Wirk-
lichkeiten, seiner Erfahrungen und
Begriffe zurücktreibt in das unsag-
bare, finstere Geheimnis, das wir Gott
nennen. . . . Und liesse sich nicht
auch die bisherige Dogmen - und Theol-
ogiegeschichte verstehen als immer
neue, immer radikalere reductio in mysterium aller theologischen Aussagen,
so dass gerade der glaubende, Theologie
treibende Mensch besser als jeder an-
dere weiss, dass jede theologische Aussage nur in dem Moment sie selber ist,
in dem der Mensch sie willig entgleiten

lässt in das schweigende Geheimnis
Gottes hinein?[41]

I have been drawing attention to what I believe
to be a unique contribution by Rahner to the development of a contemporary notion of theology. He has
placed theology squarely within the framework of modern thought. He has developed an ecclesiology that
situates both the Christian church and Christian theology in living reference to its source in the experienced mystery of God. Most especially, he has drawn
attention to the vital relationship between the subjectivity of the theologian and the theologian's task
of objectifying this subjectivity in reference to the
given truth of the Christian tradition.

In his letter to Klaus Fischer, Rahner makes a
passing comment that, for me, is highly significant.
Rahner acknowledges the "transcendental" nature of
his theology – its foundation in the objectification
by the theologian of his or her own subjectivity in
reference to the context of the religious tradition.
But he adds that this transcendental method, with its
first level of reflection, is perhaps the meeting
place between his own thought and that proposed by
Johann Baptist Metz in the latter's "narrative theology." As it happens, Metz is the third theologian
whom I wish to consider in this initial chapter. He
has proposed a notion of theology that clearly is different from that suggested by both Pannenberg and
Rahner; yet the mention by Rahner of a link between
his own theology and that of Metz leads us to believe

43

that the various notions are more complementary than
contradictory. To discover if this in fact is so,
however, demands attention to just what Metz conceives
the task of theology to be, and to this topic we may
now turn.

(3) Johann Metz: The Priority of Zeitoffenheit

No less than Pannenberg and Rahner is Johann Metz
concerned to come to terms with the challenge of the
Enlightenment. With Pannenberg he would uncover the
inadequacy of the Enlightenment critique of religion
and the blind spot in many of the Enlightenment's sub-
conscious presuppositions.[42] With Rahner he would
meet the Enlightenment on its own grounds of a turn to
the human subject, and would ground theology squarely
on the reality of this subject in history and in society.[43] But unlike Pannenberg and Rahner he would understand the Enlightenment primarily as a shift in the
cultural context within which religion and theology
function. He acknowledges, of course, that the Enlightenment signalled an end to the taken-for-granted
identity between Christian faith and religious consciousness - the latter tending to be a more general
and critical understanding of religion. But Metz
notes as well that the Enlightenment brought an end
to the identity of Christian living with societal
living, so that Christianity was now viewed as merely
an instance within a broader and more comprehensive
view of man and the world.[44] Indeed, within this new

44

I.

perspective, Christianity came to be treated as a
false or erroneous mentality, counter-productive to
the "true" autonomy of the automatic progress of
evolutionary logic.[45] So it is, that Metz conceives
the project of a new fundamental theology: "'Aufklärung' als epochales Ereignis ernst zu nehmen und
kritisch zu verarbeiten."[46]

For Metz, coming to terms with the Enlightenment
is something of a novelty for (Catholic) theology.[47]
Despite its achievements, neo-scholasticism tended to
isolate Catholicism from the socio-political movements
of the time, and it isolated apologetics from the
heart of Christian faith and theology. Nor was Traditionalism any answer for, although it acknowledged
the fact of the church's need to accept the signs of
the time, nevertheless did so for the explicit purpose
of restoring outmoded (monarchical) societal forms,
ultimately grounded in religious authority. But although Traditionalism itself was denounced by the
teaching church, its ulterior motive was implicitly
and explicitly recognized as valid, so that the (Catholic) church came to a self-understanding as the highest socio-cultural authority.

Metz notes that a creative and less defensive encounter with the Zeitgeist began to characterize theology following the Second World War. In an initial
phase theologians made serious efforts to deal with
the questions posed by Kant, by German idealism, by
the Romantic Movement and the various philosophies of
phenomenology, existentialism and personalism; through

45

I.

the work of such theologians as Söhngen, Welte, Fries, and Rahner, there was developed a fundamental theology that was closely tied to dogmatic theology, allowing extensive dialogue between theology and modern thought. In a second phase, however, Metz notes the beginnings of a new movement within theology that tried to get behind these modern philosophies to the deeper problematic posed by the Enlightenment itself: the positivistic and (later) Marxist critique of religion and theology itself. There followed a series of "secularization theologies" that viewed the Enlightenment as simply the coming of age of Christianity and religion. And while Metz himself saw some truth in these theologies, he was nevertheless concerned that the identification of theology with the Zeitgeist would empty theology of its uniqueness, making it a victim of historicity instead of a critical and liberating force over against historicity. If theology was not simply to become the ideological voice for the forces of historical decline, then a new sort of fundamental theology would have to be developed that treated the Enlightenment itself as a problem and refused to accept it in all its presuppositions.[48]

Accordingly, Metz sets out to develop just such a new fundamental theology -- one that gets behind the concepts and systems that propagate Enlightenment progress in order to reach the new human self-understanding of Enlightenment subjects themselves, prior to the concepts and philosophies that serve as propaganda for unquestioned assumptions. So it is that Metz formulates

46

his basic thesis:

> Die These . . . betont: dass es der
> Aufgang eines neuen Menschen, des Bür-
> gers ist, der sich in der Aufklärung
> vollzieht und der sich in den Prozessen
> der Neuzeit behauptet und verabsolutiert;
> dass sich folglich das bürgerliche Sub-
> jekt auf dem Weg über jene liberale Umar-
> mung der Aufklärung durch die moderne
> Theologie in dieser etabliert; dass
> schliesslich und vor allem ein bestimm-
> ter bürgerlicher Begriff von Praxis den
> genuin christlichen Begriff einer gesell-
> schaftskritischen Praxis und Freiheit
> verdrängt hat, d.h. reduziert hat auf
> das in der Gesellschaft problemlos ex-
> istierende private Subjekt und seine
> moralische Rechtschaffenheit.[49]

For Metz, a genuinely Christian praxis is the
foundation of theology.[50] Indeed, it would be more
correct to say that theology is genuine Christian
praxis. What Metz here has in mind is fundamentally
social (gesellschaftliche) praxis as embodied in
those who are following Christ in Nachfolge, Umkehr,
Exodus, Metanoia, etc. In insisting on this social
dimension of Christian discipleship, Metz would draw
attention to the fact that the individual subject is
the product of society or community, that Christianity - if it is to have any meaningful role in the
building of human subjects (Subjektwerden) - has to
be able to speak effectively to the social and cultural contexts in which subjects find themselves for
better or, most often, for worse. An over-concen-
tration by religion on the privatized, individual
subject tends to leave untouched the various influ-

ences on this subject by social and cultural factors. This stress on the socio-political dimension
of human living by no means is a reduction of all
morality to social norms nor is it a relativizing
of the individual moral subject; on the contrary,
Christian praxis as societal remains ethically determined.

At the heart of this praxis is memory in the
sense of anamnesis, Erinnerung, that is the historical component in Metz' fundamental theology. Such
anamnesis is not derived from existing societal and
cultural structures, but rather from the gospel of
Jesus Christ as ongoing critique of all structures.
Coupled with anamnesis is another key notion of Metz
- that of narrative, Erzählung. Narrative is the
tool whereby the anamnesis is brought to bear on existing structures, whether in the social sphere or
in its cultural superstructure. Finally, anamnesis-
narrative centers in the sort of praxis that is not
some progressive subjugation by mankind of nature
(Handeln) but much more is geared to the overcoming
of apathy by a genuine Christian pathos (Leiden),
related especially to solidarity with both the living
and the dead. Metz summarizes this in the phrase,
"Zukunft aus dem Gedächtnis des Leidens,"[51] that
places humanity squarely within the realm of nature,
and not above it.[52]

In contrast to current notions of theology, Metz
is trying to develop a notion that not only mediates
the Christian past into the present, but as well me-

diates the Christian present into the future. Accordingly, he asserts that the main concern of theology is not the relation of history to dogma, but
rather the relation of theory and praxis.[53] By this
he means that the deepest problem facing Christianity
is the task of relating the concreteness of living
faith experience and praxis to the concrete historical forms of society and culture that themselves are
constituted by (non-religious) praxis. To encounter
and correct social praxis, thereby promoting the a-
bility of mankind to become truly human, cannot be
done by developing some a priori theory and then deducing consequences for practical living; on the contrary, the only effective manner to heal society is
by developing and promoting true Christian Nachfolge,
whose meaning ("theory") is already contained in such
a praxis. Nor is a theoretical theology thereby ren-
dered obsolete, for to bring the meaning of Christian
praxis to social and cultural processes demands the
perennial task of giving a true and responsible accounting of the faith (praxis) that one performs (1
Peter 3,15).[54] In other words, specifically theological methods are demanded - methods that truly are
within history yet also point to what lies beyond
history (eschatological Naherwartung).[55]

This attention to guiding historical and social
praxis is the fundamental reason why political theology would be in active dialogue with the everyday
world of common sense, as well as with the reflec-

I.

tive world of science, scholarship, and philosophy.[56]
It would recognize the pluralism of concerns and
methods operative in modern culture, and would complement these methods by a theology that would provide a critique and finality, without however usurp-
ing what is specific to the various methods in question. It is in this manner that theology really begins to come to terms critically with the Enlightenment.[57]

In the title to the present section on the notion of theology proposed by Metz, I spoke of it as
Zeitoffenheit. In employing this word I by no means
wish to suggest that Metz ignores historical and
scientific knowledge as relevant to theology; it is
true that Metz has offered no extensive account of
the relation of his fundamental theology to critical
history, and much less has he offered us a reflective
and systematic ("theoretical") account of many of his
key notions. But I do not think that there is any
doubt that Metz' notion of fundamental theology is
quite open to such further reflections; particularly
his use of Erinnerung seems compatible with critical
scholarship, while his Erzählung needs reflective
and academic expression, as well as the more common
expression in commonsense story.

But if Metz could find a certain complementarity
in the sort of thing being proposed by Pannenberg in
the area of history and philosophy, it is also true
that his concern for praxis is deeply open to Rahner's

concern for religious experience and for theologians who speak of tradition from within the horizon of their own authentic appropriation of religion. Metz would insist that praxis be authentic and religious and Christian, and the ground of such authentic praxis is the personal authenticity of the individual.[58]

Nevertheless, Metz has chosen to emphasize a dimension of theology that he feels is missing from the work of Pannenberg and Rahner. Metz wants a theology that is deeply responsive and keenly sensitive to the concreteness of any given social, cultural, and historical context. He wants a theology that is to be relentless in bringing the power of the Christian faith to the concrete needs of the moment. In a word, Metz has stressed the practical dimension of theology in the fullest sense of that word - geared not merely to private morality but most especially to social and cultural morality. It is to be a theology that operates with the memory of Christ but with the non-identity with society that this memory often demands - not to destroy society, but to heal it and evoke the truly human potential that remains captive of ideologies. It is a dimension of theology that is vital, and Metz has done a service in indicating that a concern for praxis is integral to a fundamental theology. I do not believe that Metz himself has given an adequate account of just how "praxis" is to be both Christian and critical, but he continues to work on his basic project and these further clarifications may eventually be given.

I.

There remains, however, a further question. I
have presented three distinct notions of fundamental
theology. Pannenberg would insist that <u>Wissenschaft-
lichkeit</u> is the key to theology's identity in the
modern world. Karl Rahner insists that theology is
to be truly theological, in the deepest sense of objectifying, bringing to light, the reality of human
religious experience by drawing on the Christian religious tradition. Metz is neither anti-intellectual
nor anti-religious, but he would still urge that the
proper function of theology is a praxis that brings
both reflection and spirituality in focus by not just
knowing history but by making history. I believe
that each of these theologians has stressed a legit--
imate and vital dimension of theology in the world of
today. In this sense I cannot but commend the work
of each, even though I have reservations about the
claims made by each for the proposal entertained. At
this point, indeed, the reservations are quite secondary, and I would urge instead a recognition of the
achievement of each of these theologians, at least in
the single element that I have identified in each
system. I do not believe that the work of any of
these theologians is adequate to account for <u>all</u> dimensions of a fundamental theology, on the basis of
the categories that each has developed. It is here
that the work of Lonergan becomes relevant. He
would suggest a way of integrating the concerns for
history, religious experience, and praxis that re-

late theology to this post-Enlightenment era, yet in
a way that preserves the uniqueness of theology in
this era. To an outline of his thought we may now
turn.

4. Lonergan and the Unity of Theology

In the previous section I outlined three distinct notions of theology, three types of fundamental theology. In order to highlight what is most
characteristic of each, I suggested that these theologies be identified as grounded in Wissenschaftlichkeit, Kirchlichkeit, and Zeitoffenheit, according to
the fundamental concern of each theologian. I noted
that Pannenberg is very much concerned with the similarity between theology and other sciences or disciplines that take their stand on rigorous and critical methods of investigating natural and human reality. Rahner, on the other hand, wants to emphasize
the non-identity or uniqueness of theology amidst the
various sciences or disciplines, and thus stresses
the origins of theologizing in the unique experience
of other-worldly mystery. Finally, Metz has highlighted the function of theology as praxis in history;
it is neither totally identified with inner-world processes and praxis, nor is it totally other-worldly and
removed from concrete historical praxis.

It is to be noted that all three authors are concerned with relating critical religious history, revelation, and religious praxis. But each differs from

I.

the others inasmuch as each selects one of these
categories to explain the other two. Pannenberg employs the foundation of critical religious history
to work out the meaning of revelation and praxis.
Rahner begins from revelation as experience and employs this as the interpretative principle of history
and praxis. Metz takes a stand on religious praxis
and from that basis asks about the meaning of history
and revelation.

A rather interesting fact emerges if we examine
the critique of our three authors by present-day theologians. Generally, it is admitted that Pannenberg
is quite accurate on the need for evaluative and critical religious history, but that his views on revelation and praxis are not too satisfactory.[59] Rahner
is praised for his experiential notion of revelation,
but serious reservations are voiced about his views
on history and praxis.[60] Metz' concern to relate theology and praxis has found a positive response among
theologians, who nevertheless find his approach to
history and revelation either incomplete or superfi-
cial.[61]

The fact that none of the theologies in question
seems to provide an adequate account of the function
of theology in all its dimensions gives rise to the
need for a further reflection on these theologies
themselves. The present dissertation is an effort
to indicate the relevance of Lonergan's work to such
a reflection; for Lonergan would preserve the valid

54

insights in each of the various theologies, while
overcoming the limitations that keep them at odds
with each other. But before I begin a study of Lonergan's thought on this matter, it seems well to
point out the main directions that a reflection on
theologies might take. Bearing in mind, then, the
work of Pannenberg, Rahner, and Metz, the question
arises as to how the concerns of each are to be
brought together under a single roof.

A first solution is juxtaposition, whereby there
is affirmed the need of critical religious history, a
normative revelation, and a critical religious praxis,
but no real effort is made to indicate how each of
these needs is to be reconciled with the other two.
Most commonly, such a solution is proposed by those
who have some initial awareness of living in an era
when critical history, empirical philosophies, and
empirical sciences are having a profound impact on
human living. This awareness leads them to a certain
respect for theologians who are trying to relate theology to this modern context. But because this awareness is only rudimentary, because such people are not
really professional theologians but have some other
role in the community, then it is impossible for them
to grasp the fundamental issues and to suggest ways
of integrating the various concerns. In their presentation of the issues, they will not hesitate to
employ various technical terms operative in the different theologies; but nevertheless the entire context of presentation is shaped by a common sense that

I.

is content to tolerate the fact of opposition and the
absence of systematic integration. Such, for example,
would seem to be the level of thought operative in the
documents of ecumenical councils or other statements
from the teaching office of a church.[62]

A variation on this practice of juxtaposition is
compromise. It is best illustrated, perhaps, by the
debates among theologians themselves who are called
upon to help church authorities compose documents expressing the current teaching of the church community.
Whereas the final document is most often a straightforward juxtaposition of unreconciled trends, the work
that lies behind such documents is most often a matter
of compromise. Here, professional theologians are at
work; but because they operate from different horizons,
because they may differ not only in their presuppositions but also in their theological specializations,
they find it difficult or impossible to understand each
other. In the absence of a common viewpoint or lacking
a common Begrifflichkeit, there is no choice except
compromise if anything at all is to be said. And
while this is by no means the ideal solution, it should
be noted that both compromise and juxtaposition may
serve to sharpen the differences, may highlight the
need for further work and reconciliation, and may thereby
stimulate dialogue on the deeper level that goes beyond
mere juxtaposition to treat the fundamental issues of
unity and truth.[63]

A second solution is derivation. It is illustrated, for example, in the work of Pannenberg, Rahner, and Metz. Here, there is affirmed the need for the integration of quite different trends within theology. The solution is a matter of stressing one of these trends, and making it the principle of interpretation for the other elements. So, for example, Pannenberg takes a stand on critical religious history and a philosophy of religion and makes this the basis for understanding both revelation and ecclesial praxis. The limits of such an approach are generally well-known, and will be mentioned again later in this work. At the same time, however, it should be noted that such derivation seems to be a needed preliminary before further study can be undertaken. Far more than compromise or juxtaposition, it clearly delineates the various elements that stand in need of reconciliation, and also serves to bring home the limits of derivation - something that possibly will promote solutions that lie in other directions.[64]

A third solution is elimination or reductionism. One of the trends or elements thought essential to a theology is simply dropped as in fact unessential or at least as lying outside the theological framework. Here, I would draw attention especially to three varieties of reductionism: secularism, sacralism, and humanism.

Secularism would eliminate from theology any element which claimed a foundation in other-worldly reality and which sought to interpret the meaning of that reality. It would understand theology to be the empirical research of Christianity or philosophical speculation about Christianity or some combination of empirical research and philosophical speculation, but nothing more. It is permissible, of course, to speak of religious experience and revelation, but only as far as these elements are considered meaningful to mankind - not as existing in themselves or as having some other-worldly origin. Theology is to be the application of modern science or modern scholarship or modern philosophy to the observable world of Christianity; it is not immediately concerned with promoting religious values or identifying with political forces and praxis, for this is the function of the church. Theology, to be scientific, has to separate itself from ecclesial policy and devote itself to the academic study of mankind as the source of religious symbols.[65] And while perhaps most secularist notions of theology would prescind from the question as to whether religious symbols pointed to objective reality, there are more extreme versions that positively deny objective reality to religious symbols and that conceive the role of theology precisely as the scientific study of mankind's religious illusions.[66]

"Sacralism"[67] would be the reverse of secularism. It would eliminate from theology any meaningful role for human reason and understanding, and would insist that theology is absolutely grounded on other-worldly reality, on religious experience, on revelation, on the Word of God, but nothing more. Accordingly, sacralism tends to be rather atemporal, outside of human history, whether past or present. This means that the truth of religion or of religious faith is not mediated by historical studies or by philosophic reflections. With Kierkegaard, it would insist on the infinite qualitative distance between God and mankind and on the unbridgeable dichotomy between grace and nature. It would stress asceticism, mysticism, and flight from the world as the only legitimate Christian praxis, and would emphasize personal rather than communal, societal, or cultural salvation.[68] Against the secularist, the sacralist would insist that religious symbols are real only to the extent they are personally meaningful to the believing subject and are expressions by this subject of involvement with what is symbolized, of commitment to divine reality, of personal religious and existential conversion to what is symbolized. Theology, then, would be an initiation into the higher realm of religious symbolism (gnosis) and the working out of the inner meaning of the realities behind the God-given symbols - a task entrusted only to those already initiated into the mysteries and familiar with the revealed writings.[69]

Humanism, at least in its present-day variety,[70] would reduce theology to a commonsense reflection on Christianity as a principle of humanitarian action in a world that has become too complex and too academic. Modern science, modern scholarship, modern philosophy have to be pulled down from the lofty heights of speculation and placed in the hands of the everyday

I.

commoner. For it is in this domain of ordinary and
everyday thinking and acting that the vast majority
of people feel themselves to be really alive. To
speak to these people demands putting things in the
language they understand, and so it is that teachers
and popularizers arise to translate the genius of
Enlightenment to the educated, but less creative,
masses. Theology moves from the university to the
street, and in imitation of former times becomes the
possession of all men and women of good will. To
accomplish this demands the elimination or at least
neglect of scientific history of theological speculation. In its extreme form, intended for those truly
come of age, such humanism would minimize the objective significance of religious experience and revealed
religion, to concentrate instead on the native ability
of mankind to assert its moral autonomy in the service
of an ever more humane society. It would totally sec-
ularize religious symbols, or would accept totally secularized religious symbols, revealing them as nothing
more than useful maxims for good conduct in any given
situation. It would work towards a truly religionless
Christianity and would promote a theology identified
with the work of figuring out the most effective ways
of overcoming the social ills of mankind.[71]

I have been drawing attention to a number of possible approaches to resolving the problem of the pluralism of theologies. The initial solution was simply
to admit the fact of pluralism and to affirm the general validity of all the key elements in theology by

60

juxtaposition or compromise. A second solution was derivation, whereby one theological category became the principle for interpreting the others. A third approach was concerned to reduce theology to some one essential component by eliminating concern with superfluous or non-essential questions; and the one essential component was variously identified as secular scientific studies, or personal religious experience, or humanitarian social praxis.

There is a fourth approach and it is one suggested by Lonergan. Basically, it is a matter of transposing the problem to a new level, a new context, a new key. The transposition in question is away from theological categories and to the human subject, the theologian, who is correlative to the past and present world of religion. This is not an easy notion to grasp, and it will occupy us for the next several chapters. But perhaps here I may offer a few general observations that might help the reader to relate Lonergan to what has already been said in this chapter.

I would note, first of all, that Lonergan has not made an in-depth study of the work of Pannenberg, Rahner, and Metz, and then worked out the method by which the three might be brought together. Yet at the same time he has been concerned with precisely those problems that have occupied the attention of those three authors, and he has approached these problems in a manner that seems to provide a coherent and unified foundation to all of them. The issues, then, are principally three. There is the fact of critical history and the problem of working out a hermeneutic rooted in the past Christian message and tradition. There is the fact of religious experience and revealed religion, giving rise to the problem of working out a confessional hermeneutic that objectifies validly and critically such experience. Finally, there is the fact of Christian praxis and Christian community, and the problem of working out a practical hermeneutic that directs this practice effectively within any given context, practical or theoretical, of the present or of the future. It goes without saying that an adequate fundamental theology has to be able to take account of all three factors - grounding each and relating one to the others.

Here, the question arises as to the basis or foundation of such a fundamental theology. And a moment ago, I indicated a number of candidates for this position. Lonergan is of the opinion that the solution to the integration of the various methods and the various theologies can be discovered only by finding the method that underpins specific methods - not because it is different from these specific methods, but because it is the core of each and every specific method.

Lonergan, then, is aware of the fact of critical history in uncovering the Christian tradition;

he is aware that theology has to go beyond such
critical history and concern itself with what is
other-worldly, perhaps even revealed; he is convinced of the priority of praxis and of the need
for ongoing, adaptive communication of the Christian message in any given historical context, relating praxis to theory if necessary. And what
he has tried to do is to develop a notion of theology as method - a notion that grounds and inte-
grates the various factors in a dynamic unity. In
no way is his work opposed to that of Pannenberg,
Rahner, and Metz; indeed, it would be more correct
to say that the work of those three theologians is
the objectification of Lonergan's method in theology: if Lonergan is concerned with the operations
of the theologian as subject, then Pannenberg,
Rahner, and Metz are more concerned with that
which is objectified.

I hope that this will become clear in the
course of the present work, but perhaps here I
could offer a spatial metaphor. I would suggest,
then, that Pannenberg develops a notion of theology "from below," Rahner works "from above," Metz
operates "from without," and Lonergan operates
"from within."

Again, it is possible to compare notions of
theology in terms of symbol. Pannenberg would develop a theology that investigates, evaluates, and
compares the religious symbols of mankind in its

I.

history. Rahner would suggest that the task of
theology is to interpret the reality behind the
religious symbols of mankind - that which gives
rise to religious symbols in the first place.
Metz would stress the power of symbols to inform
and shape human life in all its dimensions, and
would urge a theology that creatively adapted religious symbols to the current historical context,
whether theoretical or practical. Lonergan would
suggest a notion of theology that moved methodically from the investigation of past religious
symbols to the effective communication of their
deepest meaning and value to all peoples of all
classes and all cultures. Nor is this just a juxtaposition of Pannenberg, Rahner, and Metz. More
correctly, it is a transposition of their work from
the realm of category to its underlying basis in a
generalized empirical method that underpins and
permeates each specific method. Just how Lonergan
effects this transposition and invites us to work
out for ourselves this "theology in a new key" is
the subject of the present work.

II. BACKGROUND: FROM MEDIEVAL THEOLOGY TO THE NEW STUDY OF RELIGION

> . . . the modern science or discipline
> of religious studies has undercut the
> assumptions and antiquated the methods
> of a theology structured by Melchior
> Cano's De locis theologicis. Such a
> theology was classicist in its assump-
> tions. Truth is eternal. Principles
> are immutable. Change is accidental.
> But religious studies deal meticulously
> with endless matters of detail. They
> find that the expressions of truth and
> the enunciations of principles are
> neither eternal nor immutable. They
> concentrate on the historical process
> in which these changes occur. They
> bring to light whole ranges of inter-
> esting facts and quite new types of
> problems. In brief, religious studies
> have stripped the old theology of its
> very sources in Scripture, in patristic
> writings, in medieval and subsequent
> religious writers. They have done so
> by subjecting the sources to a fuller
> and more penetrating scrutiny than had
> been attempted by earlier methods.1

In the previous chapter I discussed three distinct notions of theology as represented in the work
of Pannenberg, Rahner, and Metz. Each of these authors stresses what he feels to be the main characteristic of a contemporary theology, and this characteristic is different in each of the authors named.
This fact gives rise to a further reflection on the
possibility of relating these distinct notions of
theology, in an effort to find out if the concerns

II.

of each author might somehow be reconciled in an integrated manner. I noted several different approaches
to this question, and concluded by suggesting that
Lonergan's work might be helpful in arriving at a
solution.

I think that a good place to begin this discussion of Lonergan's potential contribution to a reconciliation of distinct notions of theology is to examine his thought on the historical background that
lies behind this whole search for a new notion of
theology. By studying Lonergan's understanding of
this historical development, we might be in a position to appreciate better the origins of the various
notions of theology currently being suggested. Each
of those notions rests to a greater or lesser extent
on each author's interpretation of the historical
background. So, for example, Pannenberg, Rahner,
and Metz all are concerned to work out a notion of
theology that comes to terms with the challenge associated with the Enlightenment; and part of the
reason why these authors suggest different notions
of theology perhaps might lie in their different interpretations of the Enlightenment challenge. By
presenting Lonergan's understanding of the historical background, especially his interpretation of the
Enlightenment, I think it will be possible to shed
considerable light on this problem. It will become
clear that each of the three notions of theology is
a legitimate, but partial, response to the historical challenge. This fact is significant for the

present study of unity in theology, for it will indicate at least a certain complementarity in the
various notions of theology, even though their integration has yet to be achieved.

My aim in this chapter, then, is to present
Lonergan's understanding of the historical background
that seems to call for a new notion of theology in
our own day. After an introductory note on Lonergan's notion of specialization, I shall add several
sections explaining how he employs that notion to
interpret the major turning points in the history
of theological reflection. For Lonergan, theology
emerged as a specialized and fully systematic manner of thinking within the Christian community in
the medieval period. It was a theology influenced
by the medieval cultural context and a theology that
in turn influenced that context. But Lonergan notes
that as the medieval context gradually gave way to
the modern, historically-minded, "enlightened" world,
theology failed to adapt adequately to its new surroundings and became instead a theology rooted in
the classicist assumptions of Renaissance thought.
Such theology eventually found itself in opposition
to the new spirit in science, philosophy, and historical scholarship. Lonergan observes that these
disciplines too were concerned with religion and
Christianity, but their concern, far from supporting
theology, seemed often to destroy the very foundation on which the classicist theology rested. I
conclude this chapter by pointing to the fact of

II.

Lonergan's agreement with the authors discussed in Chapter One, that these new approaches to religion and Christianity have their legitimate function in the contemporary context, but pose an identity problem for classicist theology. As those authors, so too Lonergan would urge a critique of these modern or "enlightened" disciplines as a preliminary step in developing a contemporary theology, and this critique will be our concern in subsequent chapters.

1. Specialization

The aim of the present chapter is to give Lonergan's understanding of the historical background that has resulted in our present need for a new foundation and structure in theology. A notion that Lonergan suggests as useful in understanding this historical background is that of "specialization." Just what he means by this will be explained in a moment, but first I might note that this approach to the historical background is rather a unique way of understanding the various developments that have occurred in medieval and modern culture, and that have so profoundly influenced theology.[2] Nevertheless, I suspect that most readers would admit at least the possibility of such a notion and, once they have studied it, might find it to be a useful way of tying together a number of developments that are familiar but rather fragmented. Thus, most readers are well aware of the ordinary meaning of "specialization," and what Lonergan has

68

done is simply to give that word a technical meaning. Again, most readers would readily grant that
modern science, modern historical scholarship, and
modern philosophy all have had a profound influence
on theology, and what Lonergan proposes is simply a
way of understanding this influence more precisely
by thinking of these disciplines as emerging in a
process of increasing specialization.

For present purposes it will be sufficient if
I offer Lonergan's notion of specialization as he
summarizes it in a 1974 lecture entitled, "Aquinas
Today: Tradition and Innovation."[3] Lonergan's intention is to set forth the dynamic interplay in
human history of tradition and innovation. In describing the innovations, he refers to the fact of
increasing specialization:

> The innovations I envisage are the suc-
> cessive large-scale developments in med-
> ieval and modern culture. They are spe-
> cializations: in theology, in philosophy,
> in science, in scholarship. They have oc-
> curred at different times. Each was pre-
> ceded by earlier stages in which their
> later separate tasks were undifferentiated
> parts in previous larger wholes. In each
> case their emergence generated identity
> crises in their former hosts and demanded
> the discovery and the development of new
> methods and procedures.[4]

Specialization, he notes, is commonly thought to be
a concentration on one field to the neglect of others. But Lonergan would draw our attention to the
meaning of this concentration in the human develop-

ment of the specialist. What occurs is a differentiation of outlook, mentality, horizon that has
people living in different worlds that tend to exclude mutual communication. If I might offer an
example, there is the world of the natural scientist, and that world is quite different from that
of historical scholars, just as both those worlds
are different from the world of the philosopher. In
each case there is a distinct manner of intellectual
development, a distinct mentality or horizon with
its distinct methods of investigation and its own
technical language.

To explain this meaning of specialization, Lonergan notes that "horizon" is the boundary or limit
to a person's interests and knowledge. This boundary varies, for some individuals or groups know more
than others, or know something different than others,
or have different interests than others. Further,
interest can grow or diminish in any given individual
or group, or can shift to include a greater or lesser
number of objects. So Lonergan urges that we conceive horizon as a dynamic notion - indeed, he realizes that most of us readily acknowledge this; so we
are aware, for example, that historical accounts of
a given event come to be modified or rewritten as
different historians with different horizons select
different aspects of the event, or even as the same
historian develops in his or her understanding of
what happened. Horizons, then, are subject to development, and so we come to a key passage in Lonergan's

lecture, where he links the notion of horizon with
that of differentiation or specialization:

> In any individual his actual horizon is
> the fruit of his past development, and
> his past development in the main is his
> participation in the earlier developments
> of others and only on rare occasions the
> product of his own originality and cre-
> ativity. Moreover, such development ad-
> mits categorization to yield a differen-
> tiation of horizons. It may pertain to
> the prelinguistic development to which
> the infant is confined; to the common-
> sense development of intelligence that
> specializes in the concrete and immedi-
> ate; to the religious development that
> orients man to God and in the universe;
> to the scientific development that uni-
> fies and relates, constructs and extra-
> polates, serializes and generalizes, to
> discover and reveal the cosmos; to the
> scholarly development that enters into
> the common sense of another place and
> time to understand its language, inter-
> pret its meanings, and narrate its deeds
> and achievements; to the philosophic de-
> velopment that, in what now may seem its
> final phase, reflects on all of these,
> assigns each its proper competence, and
> relates each to the others.[5]

Lonergan notes that initially development is
spontaneous, a matter of using already learned operations in slightly new ways on different objects.
But as we advance in mastery of what is new, as we
develop skills proportionate to the learning of a
different field, there gradually emerges a distinct
horizon, no longer just a variation on previous
achievement but something quite new and different.

II.

Such is our development as an individual, but it presupposes a level of achievement in the context or symbolic traditions that are available to us and from which we draw. In a word, Lonergan is suggesting that there is a development in the horizon of the society or culture, as the group succeeds in developing now this, now that specialized manner of operating. So Lonergan writes:

> I am urging, then, a source of radical cultural differences not to be identified simply with the diversity of traditions, the varieties of religious experience, the proliferation of languages, and the conflicts of philosophies. It is a differentiation that is concealed in its early stages by its symbiosis with preceding achievement, and this concealment is permanent in the minds of those who advance no further. But the same differentiation for those who reach its later stages is all the more striking and strange, for the new enterprise detaches itself from its original host and proceeds, in the main, to expand and to function on its own.[6]

Lonergan goes on to illustrate in further detail each of the possible differentiations of consciousness or specializations that he has referred to, and then adds three further sections relating this framework to Christian theology. I shall discuss this more fully in the course of the present chapter, and here will simply offer an overview or sketch of the main lines of the development to be considered.

Lonergan considers the notion of specialization

relevant to Christianity and Christian theology because Christianity is not simply an affair of the
heart.[7] At its root and core it is indeed a prelinguistic and preconceptual experience of the heart,
an experience identified by Lonergan in Christian
terms as God's gift of his love to us. But, as he
once mentioned, this gift of love, offered to all, is
a gift crying out in us for interpretation, and for
Christians that interpretation receives its focus in
the Word, Jesus Christ. That Word, and the tradition
grounded in that Word, are historical. What is historical is subject to development. Just as the Word
Incarnate developed in wisdom and understanding before God and man, so too the tradition witnessing to
that Word also may undergo successive developments
as the wisdom and understanding of the ages become
ever more specialized and refined.

The faithful development of the tradition is a
task imposed upon the entire Christian community.
At an earlier stage, the community itself may spontaneously exercise this function and, through a process of trial and error and supervised by overseers,
adapt the tradition from one brand of common sense
to another. As the community endures, however, the
more it is forced to reflect on its own proper tradition, to distinguish that tradition from other
traditions, and to guard against erroneous interpretations of the tradition.[8] Particularly when the
culture within which the Christian tradition is planted includes specialized horizons (science, scholar-

ship, philosophy, etc.), this task of reflecting on
the Christian tradition in a similarly specialized
manner becomes imperative, if the tradition is to
be preserved in its integrity yet also communicated
to all levels of a given culture.

With this emergence of specialized reflection
on the Christian tradition, the task of developing
or translating the tradition becomes the concern,
not just of the community and its official representatives, but of a group of specialists as well. Such
a process of reflective understanding applied to the
whole of the Christian tradition was for Lonergan the
achievement of medieval theology. Yet within that
achievement he notes that there were planted the seeds
of even further development and specialization. The
medieval specialization was colored by theological
considerations, but it was a theology that defined
itself only by distinguishing its proper sphere in
the supernatural as opposed to the natural order.
This distinction paved the way for an independent
study of the natural order, a study that relied less
and less on a theological worldview. This latter attention to the world and to mankind in the world initially was a mixture of science and philosophy, but
in time natural science worked out its own frame of
reference independent, not just of theology, but as
well of philosophy. The study of mankind became the
study of mankind in its historicity and endless variety, and a critical historical scholarship set itself

the monumental job of reconstructing the constructions of the human spirit. Philosophy turned first
to natural science, then to scholarship, in an effort to define its proper sphere until our own day
when, as Lonergan observes, philosophy is becoming
content with the function of reflecting on the poly-
morphic consciousness of man manifested in any and
all of its various differentiations.[9]

According to Lonergan, all of these specializations asserted their independence from, if not opposition to, their original theologically colored
host. Each of these fields became a specialized
world unto itself, with its own presuppositions,
methods, goals, technical language. With each successive development something of an identity crisis
was created for the group out of which the new specialists arose. In particular, Lonergan observes
that theologians found their Renaissance or classicist thought-forms to be challenged by a science
that would be empirical and not deductive, by a
scholarship that mercilessly studied the complexi-
ties and contradictions in what was assumed to be
a permanently valid tradition, by a philosophy that
became the ready spokesman for anything except theology. In a word, the task of developing the tradition of Christianity, of effecting the aggiornamento and Heutigwerden that may be needed in any
age, became engulfed in a multitude of problems as
each new group of specialists occupied the stage.
Theologians found themselves isolated, and in their

II.

isolation either clung to their classicist presuppositions or acknowledged now this or that innovation, without however emerging with a clear and
distinct identity.

Lonergan, then, suggests an approach to the
historical background of current problems that studies the interaction of theology with its cultural
context,[10] in order to trace the developments that
have undermined previous theological achievement.
He suggests that we begin by trying to recover the
secret of success that characterized medieval theology. From there, he would invite us to pinpoint the
developments that made medieval theology increasingly
inadequate. Finally, he would work out a notion of
theology that stands in continuity with the medieval
tradition, yet transposes medieval achievement in
light of the innovations that have been taking place
for several centuries. Such are the topics to be
considered in the remainder of my work.

2. Theology as a Specialization in the Medieval
   Period

According to Lonergan, theology first became a
specialization in the achievements of Byzantine scholasticism and medieval scholasticism.[11] In saying
this, he does not deny the fact of serious reflection
on the message of Christ prior to that period. Indeed, without those earlier efforts of Christian
thinkers and writers, the medieval achievement could

76

not have occurred. Still, it was only in the medieval period when "first there arose a collaborative,
ongoing, cumulative process of reflection and formulation that topically ordered and explanatorily developed the Christian tradition as a whole."[12] It
is this process that resulted clearly in a specialized consciousness within Christianity - an academic
specialization with its own experts, technical terms,
and distinctive method. It is this development from
gospel to Summa that I wish to examine, both in its
preparation and in its achievement.[13]

(1) Preparation

In the initial period of Christianity, there was
no group of theological specialists clearly distinguished from the rest of the community in outlook,
language, methods of studying the Christian message.
There were, of course, teachers and scholars, whose
task it was to explain and defend the message of
Christ. In time, this task grew in complexity as errors and problems multiplied, so that reflection on
the meaning of Christianity gradually grew, not merely
in extent or intensity, but also in distinct methods
of investigation. Lonergan describes this gradual
process of development as follows:

> So initially the Christian religion and
> Christian theology were not distinguished.
> Tradition was assimilated. Efforts were
> made to penetrate its meaning and recast
> it for apostolic or apologetic ends. Not
> all were happy. Innovators formed schools

that splintered off in various directions and by their very separation and
diversity emphasized a main, unchanging
tradition. The main tradition itself
was confronted with ever deeper issues.
Painfully, it learnt from Nicea the necessity of going beyond scriptural language to formulate what was considered
scriptural truth. Painfully it learnt
from Chalcedon the necessity of employing terms in senses unknown both to
scripture and to the earlier patristic
tradition. But it is in reflection on
such developments, as in Byzantine Scholasticism, and in the extension of such
reflective consideration to the whole of
Christian thought, as in medieval Scholasticism, that theology became an academic subject, at once intimately con-
nected with the Christian religion and
manifestly distinct from it.[14]

Perhaps the key phrase in the passage just
quoted is, " . . . the necessity of going beyond
scriptural language to formulate what was considered
scriptural truth." This does not mean that scriptural language is untrue. Rather, Lonergan is pointing out that the scriptures are written in a language
that springs from a commonsense view of the world.[15]
Such ordinary language may speak indeed of what is
true, what really is so, but its speech is elusive.
It is not the type of thought or speech that coolly
analyzes reality, sets forth definitions and explanations, builds up theories and hypotheses. Rather,
common sense is concerned with particular and concrete situations; it may offer general instruction,
not as a universally valid theory, but simply as wise

advice to keep in mind. Hence, what Lonergan says
of commonsense thinking generally can be applied to
the mode of thought that informs scripture:

> It follows that common sense has no use
> for a technical language and no tendency
> towards a formal mode of speech. It a-
> grees that one must say what one means
> and mean what one says. But its corres-
> pondence between saying and meaning is
> at once subtle and fluid. As the proverb
> has it, a wink is as good as a nod. For
> common sense not merely says what it
> means; it says it to someone; it begins
> by exploring the other fellow's intelli-
> gence; it advances by determining what
> further insights have to be communicated
> to him; it undertakes the communication,
> not as an exercise in formal logic, but
> as a work of art . . .[16]

A few observations are here in order. Firstly,
Lonergan's contention that scripture springs from a
commonsense mentality seems relevant to current discussions on the role of narrative or story, not merely
in interpreting scripture, but as a paradigm for communicating the gospel to the almost endless varieties
of contemporary common sense.[17]

Secondly, as mentioned in Chapter One, there are
many brands of common sense. This point is central to
the present topic, for it highlights Lonergan's conviction that there is a need to move outside one's own
brand of common sense and reconstruct the common sense
of another, if there arises the need to communicate
one and the same message to several diverse commonsense mentalities. Such differences of common sense

II.

are evident in scripture and the various traditions that led to the formation of scripture. Successive biblical writers did not hesitate to adapt the gospel to different audiences.[18]

Thirdly, while adaptation was carried out for different groups within Judaism, Lonergan notes that the more challenging problem arose in dealing with pagans. These did not accept the scriptures of Judaism nor those of Christianity; lacking any common basis for dialogue, inasmuch as they operated with a different horizon, they misinterpreted Christianity and persecuted Christians. A quite new mode of adaptation was called for, and the apologists sought to meet this need by probing the assumptions and beliefs of the non-Palestinian world. Simply to have preached the sermon on the mount to these people would have been useless, and the persecutions would have continued unabated; as Lonergan remarks, the gospel can be preached only if Christians are allowed to exist.[19]

Fourthly, Lonergan observes that such adaptations involved a gradual reinterpretation of scripture. Clement of Alexandria set forth principles of interpretation, in order to indicate the errors of the Gnostics' exegesis of scripture; he noted as well the fact that the Bible contained anthropomorphism, and urged Christians to adopt an allegorical interpretation of such matters. To move away from a literal interpretation of scripture, however, meant that Christians had to turn to some non-scriptural source in order to clarify their notion of God. From a straightforward use of scriptural language there emerged a reflection on the meaning of that language - a "second-level" reflection on propositions - in order to arrive at scriptural truth. With such reflection, however, Christian thinkers became involved in the problems of realism as they sought to clarify why the God of the scriptures had to be real. To distinguish the different meanings of "reality" is not a simple matter, however, and the story of these efforts is the gradual clarification of Christological thought from the third to the fifth centuries.[20]

Commonly, the process to which Lonergan here refers is understood to be the Hellenization of Christian doctrine.[21] This is a matter of not a little dispute, and I think it is important to outline Lonergan's notion of what precisely Hellenization involved.[22] Perhaps the best way to do this is to compare Lonergan's understanding with that of another theologian, and so I shall begin with the views of Professor Walter Kasper, who summarizes his thought on Hellenization in his book, Jesus der Christus.[23]

Kasper notes that the historians of dogma who are associated with liberal theology, especially Harnack, over-simplified the fact of Hellenization; they claimed that Christological doctrine was rooted in Greek philosophy, and urged a dehellenization that would eliminate that philosophy and return to a simple doctrine of Jesus' faith in his Father. This, for Kasper, is too global a judgment, and he stresses the need to develop a more nuanced evaluation of the Hellenization process. This process involved a legitimate and needed encounter between Christianity and the Greek philosophical world, for both claimed to offer comprehensive interpretation of the meaning of humanity and its world. From the Christian viewpoint, an encounter with Greek thought was a matter of re-affirming itself within a new cultural context - of accomplishing an aggiornamento that placed the Christian message squarely within the Fragestellung of the day. Kasper concurs with R. Seeberg's observations, that it is not a Hellenizing, Romanizing, or Germanizing that corrupts Christianity, for these simply witness to the need for Christianity to adapt to various cultural conditions; rather, the danger lies in the possibility that this process leads to an emptying-out or weakening of the material content of Christianity by reducing that content to some other religious level: acculturation is needed, but it has to be done critically.

With this in mind, Kasper goes on to describe the doctrines of Nicea and Constantinople as masterpieces of aggiornamento, inasmuch as they distinguished clearly between legitimate and illegitimate Hellenization by introducing specifically Christian perspectives into Hellenistic thought. Still, these

were responses to specific problems and not a systematic and comprehensive introduction of classicist
thought into Christianity; for this reason, the use
of homoousios at Nicea could be misunderstood and
theology could seize the opportunity to substitute
metaphysical thought for the eschatological, salvation-history perspective of scripture. This was a
loss to Christian theology:

> So konnte es kommen, dass im Gefolge des
> homoousios von Nikaia das metaphysische
> Wesensdenken in die Theologie seinen
> Einzug hielt und das eschatologisch-
> heilsgeschichtliche Denken der Schrift
> schliesslich doch weithin verdrängte.
> Das Christentum verlor dadurch vieles
> von seiner geschichtlichen Dynamik und
> Zukunftsperspektive. Hier liegt das
> ziemlich grosse Korn Wahrheit an der
> These von der Enteschatologisierung des
> Christentums als Voraussetzung und Folge
> seiner Hellenisierung. Die unmittelbare
> Folge war, dass das Gottesbild der Tra-
> dition im Grunde gegen die Intention von
> Nikaia und Konstantinopel geprägt blieb
> durch die griechische Vorstellung von
> der Unveränderlichkeit, der Leidens -
> und Leidenschaftslosigkeit (apatheia)
> Gottes. Die Menschwerdung Gottes und
> erst recht das Leiden und Sterben Gottes
> wurden so zum grossen Problem.[24]

Professor Kasper then goes on to discuss various
attempts to overcome a metaphysically grounded Christology by restoring a salvation-history perspective
rooted in human subjectivity and autonomy. For present purposes, however, I believe enough has been said
to outline Kasper's understanding of Hellenization,

II.

and the time has come to locate Lonergan's thought
within that context.

Lonergan would agree that a Hellenization of
doctrine occurred, that non-scriptural language was
employed, that it was not a wholesale but rather a
critical acceptance of Hellenistic thought, and that
it provided a needed aggiornamento in communicating
specifically Christian truth in a non-Judaic cultural
context. But what seems to me to be unique in Lonergan's position is that he asks a further question,
What precisely is the novelty in the Hellenization
process? It is in answering this question that he
goes beyond the reflections of Professor Kasper and,
I believe, hits upon a key point in the interpretation
of Hellenization. Kasper and other thinkers seem to
presuppose that the novelty of the homoousios and subsequent terms lies in the fact that these terms were
borrowed from Greek thought. As well, Kasper notes
that these terms were not employed in a philosophical
or technical sense, but rather in a non-technical,
soteriological manner.[25] It would seem, therefore,
that Professor Kasper understands the novelty of this
development to lie exclusively in the fact that Christian truth was now expressed in non-scriptural terms,
employed in a non-technical sense and drawn from the
resources of Hellenistic culture.

Now, Lonergan would not argue with these conclusions, and would agree that Hellenization involved a
transposition of scriptural truth from one cultural

context to another. Still, he would draw our attention to the process by which this transposition was
made, to the manner in which it was carried out. On
the one hand, it was not a matter of simply repeating scriptural language in a new cultural context,
for homoousios is not a scriptural term. On the
other hand, it was not a matter of identifying scriptural truth with a specific and already understood
word borrowed from ordinary or technical language in
the new culture, for what Nicea intended by homoousios
had specifically Christian overtones, unknown to Greek
philosophy. But if homoousios is not scriptural language nor Hellenistic truth, just what is it? We may
answer that it is scriptural truth; but quite obviously
it is a truth that is apprehended and expressed in a
non-scriptural fashion. In other words, homoousios
is not scriptural truth in the sense that it is found
in scripture, but in the sense that it is a statement
about what is found in scripture: it is a proposition
about (scriptural) propositions, a second-level or
second-degree reflection. It expresses what is Christian truth, not because it was pronounced at an ecumenical council, not because it can be reduced to
scriptural imagery and language, but because what homoousios means corresponds to what in fact is so and
to what is expressed in a symbolic, commonsense way in
scripture. The achievement of Nicea was to understand
that scriptural truth is not identified with scriptural
language but with what is intended or meant by that
language. The views of Tertullian, Origen, and Arius

85

were rejected because those views did not correspond to the truth intention of scripture; the views of Athanasius were accepted because they corresponded to that truth intention, without claiming to be a complete and universally permanent expression of just what scripture meant. Indeed, the homoousios was just a beginning, but it was a crucial and decisive step that brought Christian doctrine from a commonsense to an incipiently systematic level of thinking.

In other words, where Professor Kasper and other writers understand Hellenization in terms of a re-formulation of doctrine, Lonergan goes a step further and discusses the developing mentality - the specialization of consciousness - that was implicit in the new formulations. He would draw attention to the manner in which the level of thinking of an Athanasius differed from that found in scripture. Allow me to quote a rather long passage from Lonergan's The Way to Nicea in illustration of this point:

> Now if, when it emerged, the Nicene dogma
> was inevitable, it was nonetheless new.
> For it marks a transition from multiplic-
> ity to unity: from a multiplicity of
> symbols, titles and predicates to the ul-
> timate ground of all of these, namely,
> the Son's consubstantiality with the Fa-
> ther. Equally, it marks a transition
> from things as related to us to things as
> they are in themselves, from the rela-
> tional concepts of God as supreme agent,

Creator, Omnipotent Lord of all, to an
ontological conception of the divine substance itself. It marks, no less, a
transition from the word of God as accom-
modated to particular people, at particular times, under particular circumstances,
to the word of God as it is to be proclaimed to all people, of all times, under
whatever circumstances - the transition
from the prophetic oracle of Yahweh, the
gospel as announced in Galilee, the apos-
tolic preaching and the simple tradition
of the Church, from all of these to Catholic dogma. It also marks a transition
from the mystery of God as hidden in symbols, hinted at by a multiplicity of ti-
tles, apprehended only in a vague and confused manner in the dramatico-practical
pattern of experience, to the mystery of
God as circumscribed and manifested in
clear, distinct and apparently contradictory affirmations. Finally, it marks a
transition from a whole range of problems
to a basic solution of those problems.
For a definitive step was taken from
naive realism, beyond Platonism, to dogmatic realism and in the direction of
critical realism. To the hermeneutical
question, what is it that symbols symbol-
ize, it was answered that what they sym-
bolize is that which is, that which is
truly affirmed. To the theological question, how God was to be conceived, an answer was given that set aside the sublime
Platonic Ideas, reaffirmed the omnipotent
Creator and went beyond the notion of God
as agent to think of him in terms of the
substance that causes all substances, the
being that is for all beings the source
of their being. To the trinitarian question, finally, an answer was given that
laid the foundation on which, of its own
accord, as it were, the whole systematisa-
tion of Catholic theology would arise.

II.

> Given that later systematisation, how-
> ever, it is only with the greatest dif-
> ficulty that we who have inherited it
> can come to understand how the ante-
> Nicene authors could in fact have said
> what in fact they did say.[26]

Again, Lonergan admits that a price was paid for
this transposition from symbolic understanding (scripture) to partially systematic understanding (Nicene and
post-Nicene authors). But the price paid is not the
fact that Christian teaching became involved in systematic thinking, for such involvement was demanded
precisely in order to protect Christian truth; to have
remained within scriptural modes of apprehension and
expression would have been to leave unresolved the
dilemma surrounding the identity and meaning of Jesus
Christ. Nor did the problem lie in the fact that the
Hellenistic technique of reflecting on propositions
resulted in a God of the philosophers being opposed
to the God of salvation history and scripture; on the
contrary, the technique as such does not predetermine
the attributes of God, and leaves the Christian free
to understand God in scriptural, patristic, medieval,
or modern terms.[27] Rather, for Lonergan, the price
paid in using the Hellenistic technique of reflection
on propositions lies in the fact that such reflection
is both difficult and precarious. All too easily one
can slip back into a symbolic mentality that empties
second-level propositions of all meaning because they
are seen to be immobile, unrelated to religious experience or anything in the real world, mere academic

88

inventions that separate us from the true meaning
of Jesus Christ. In a word, to introduce the
Christian message within a cultural superstructure
is a move that easily will be misunderstood and
deprecated by those who have not managed to get
beyond commonsense thinking.[28]

The point Lonergan emphasizes, then, the true
novelty involved in Hellenization, has little to
do with the common assertion that "Greek philosophy supplied all the principal elements in which
we have for centuries conceptualized the basic
Christian beliefs of the Trinity and the Incarnation."[29] Rather, the novelty lies in the gradual
emergence within the Christian community of a manner of thinking that went beyond common sense. In
the developments at Nicea and in subsequent centuries, we have a process of differentiation from a
global, compact, symbolic, commonsense consciousness to a level of understanding that operates on
quite distinct criteria with distinct methods for
a distinct goal. It was a long process, and its
full achievement would emerge only in a medieval
scholasticism. But it was not an optional process,
the idle pastime of a few academic souls who had
nothing better to do than reflect on propositions.
The New Testament left unresolved the central and
fundamental question, Who is Jesus Christ? Many
answers were given to that question. Some coin-
cided with the community's sense of scriptural
truth. Other answers were suspect, and left to a

II.

gradual clarification before their authenticity
could be determined. Other answers were clearly
incompatible with the person and message of Jesus
Christ, and emptied salvation and redemption through
that Christ of all meaning and value. And when
these adversaries used the very scriptures of the
community to justify their errors, then a further
way to the truth, a further method, had to be uncovered. So it was that Athanasius adopted a Hellenistic technique to provide a more precise and
technical explanation, that left the Son clearly
in the realm of the Father's divinity, rather than
on the side of creatures. So it was that subsequent
writers and subsequent Councils gradually moved that
technique from a context of logic to a context of
metaphysics, and such was the medieval achievement.

(2) Achievement

     Various patristic writers continued to make oc-
casional use of systematic thinking in their explanations of the meaning of the Christian message.
For the most part, however, such systematic thinking
was, for Lonergan, within a logical context. Whether
Lonergan considers Athanasius' explanation of substance or Augustine's explanation of person, he does
not find these terms to possess a precise technical
meaning. Instead, Lonergan identifies what mostly
is a reflection on propositions, concerned with the
minimal task of identifying reality with whatever is
known by a true judgment, a true affirmation. For

example, the Son is God because we affirm the same
things about the Son as we do about the Father, ex-
cepting the name 'Father':   the divinity of the Son
is a reality because we make the same judgments about
the Son as we do about the Father. Lonergan is aware
that in a sense, of course, this technique of logic
seems a mere tautology, more a description than an
explanation. To claim that the Son is God because
we predicate the same attributes to the Son as to the
Father is a claim that leaves many questions unanswered. Yet although it is but a beginning and gives
rise to further and deeper questions involving metaphysics, Lonergan insists that this logical technique is not without its significance. In the main,
that significance lies in the fact that Christian
doctrine is raised to the order of verifiable truth;
and the verification is a matter, not of sense criteria alone nor of insights and ideas alone, but of
a reflective judgment that states what in fact is so.[30]

Such statements of logical truth may or may not
be accompanied by a further reflection that works out
the many presuppositions and implications of what is
affirmed as true. By and large, the patristic writings leave these further questions unanswered, or answered in only a partial manner to satisfy the particular issue at hand. The need was for clarity and
precision in confronting misinterpretations of the
gospel, and the rules of logic abound in both these
qualities. Still, as Lonergan frequently points out,

II.

logic has its limitations, and I would summarize
these in the following way. While confining itself
to one problem, it tends to neglect the full picture;
for example, the concern to preserve the integrity of
the Son's divinity was coupled with a forgetfulness
of human anthropology and a Pelagian controversy.[31]
Further, logic tends to state truth in terms which
only the local experts can interpret, so that Hilary,
for example, encountered endless difficulties in explaining the Council of Nicea to the Western bish-
ops.[32] Finally, logic tends to be removed from concrete historical circumstances and from particular
brands of commonsense living; while intelligible to
the educated classes, logic is quite beyond the grasp
of ordinary thinking, so that the conciliar decrees
of the early church did not easily lend themselves to
preaching and catechetical instruction.[33]

It is crucial to an understanding of Lonergan's
thought to note that these limitations of logic did
not go unnoticed by patristic thinkers. While there
seems to have been an ongoing attention to homiletic
and catechetical needs, in a language that spoke
movingly to the heart, Lonergan would draw attention
more to an effort to overcome logical limitations in
another manner - raising and answering questions
that arose from the logical statements. This tended
to move thinking to a speculative level of systematic
reflection that sought some insight into the meaning
of the realities affirmed in logical statements,
placing these statements within a broader context of

metaphysics. It is one thing, for example, to make
a logical distinction between person and nature,
and quite another to ask about the reality of that
distinction. To ask about the reality of logical
distinctions and technique is to raise metaphysical
questions, and for Lonergan it was this that led to
the emergence of systematic thinking as a fully distinct specialization within the Christian community.
Whereas the early church councils remained on a logical level, intelligible to the common sense of an
educated class, the introduction of metaphysical
thinking resulted in a new group of specialists.
These specialists raised questions that arose in
part from church doctrines, but that could not be
answered within the logical framework of those doctrines. For Lonergan, it was this development of
metaphysical thinking that set up a theological context quite distinct from the context of church doctrines, and that led to the development of an autonomous theological superstructure, with its own specialists and its own methods of inquiry.[34]

Lonergan is only repeating what commonly is
known when he states that the works of Aristotle
provided the basic framework within which theologians sought to present Christian truth.[35] In particular, Aristotelian metaphysics proved invaluable
in overcoming the limits of purely logical thought
by meeting needs that logic was unable to fulfill.
These needs that faced medieval theologians are
described by Lonergan in the following way:

II.

> First, there was the need for a coherent
> theological Begrifflichkeit: just as
> diverse statements in the Christian tra-
> dition needed to be reconciled, so too
> the many reconciliations devised by the-
> ologians needed the overall reconcilia-
> tion that was to be obtained only by un-
> derpinning theological invention by a
> comprehensive system of thought. Second,
> there was the need for a unified appre-
> hension of things: the search of faith
> for understanding could not be a merely
> partial understanding. It had to be
> coupled with an understanding of nature,
> else divine grace would be perfecting an
> unknown nature and divine faith would be
> illuminating an unknown reason. Third,
> there was the problem of the University
> of Paris. There had been translated the
> brilliant studies of Aristotle by Arabic
> thinkers; the Parisian Averroists had
> emerged; and there had to be performed
> an apologetic task if an alien faith was
> not to obtain by its books a hegemony
> that it had failed to obtain by its
> arms.[36]

This quotation serves as a good basis for discussing Lonergan's understanding of the medieval
achievement as the development of theology as a full-
fledged specialization. The threefold need sketched
in the quotation is sort of the medieval equivalent
of a search for a theology wherein Wissenschaftlichkeit, Kirchlichkeit, and Zeitoffenheit are held in
balance. The search for a Begrifflichkeit was the
effort to develop a truly academic theology located
in the medieval scientific world. The search for a
unified apprehension of things was the effort to develop a truly "theological" theology that related

94

divine mystery to what lay within this world. The
effort to come to terms with the situation at the
University of Paris was the search for a theology
that not only was colored by happenings in the culture but that also could influence that culture with
the strength of the Christian message. I wish, then,
to discuss Lonergan's assessment of medieval theology
under these three headings.

   (a) Medieval Wissenschaftlichkeit - An initial
need in medieval theology was for what Lonergan refers to as a coherent theological Begrifflichkeit, a
comprehensive conceptual system. If we wish to understand why Lonergan says that such a system was
needed in the medieval period, then I would suggest
we study the development of Christian thought up to
the thirteenth century. Yves Congar made such a
study, and he concluded that up to the end of the
twelfth century, theology would be basically biblical; in fact, reflection on the gospel was known, not
as "theology," but simply as the "sacred page" or
"sacred scripture."[37] Congar notes the example especially of Augustine and Gregory in their interpretation of Scripture, and adds that later writers too
continued to employ methods of interpreting scripture
that rested as much on allegory as on a literal interpretation, and more on latin grammatical analysis
than on a study of the original scriptural languages
or historical context. Lonergan, in his own studies
of the development of Thomistic, trinitarian, and
christological thought, confirmed the findings of

II.

Congar. Lonergan recognized the value in such approaches to scripture, but also noted their limitations. The main limitation was the fact that there emerged a tremendous multiplicity of interpretations and commentaries on one and the same text. Further, such commentaries were written by people in a variety of historical, social, and cultural contexts, often reflecting elements or questions peculiar to specific groups.[38]

A first need, then, was to collect the various interpretations and commentaries relevant to the entire Christian tradition, giving that tradition some semblance of order. But Lonergan adds that such thematic collections of authoritative writings only further highlighted the multiplicity of interpretations, so that the medieval writers faced the further task of reducing the differences and resolving various conflicts.[39] Thus, just as the Fathers attempted to reconcile the Old Testament with the New, so, when the patristic writers themselves became authorities, efforts were made to reconcile differences among them, in order to indicate the coherence and continuity of the entire Christian tradition. And here the problem was how to find a basis of reconciliation, a unifying structure. Medieval thinkers lacked a sense of critical history, so that differences which we today would reconcile by pointing to historical change and development had to be reconciled on some other level.

For Lonergan, an early step in this process was
the use of dialectic in a methodical manner. It appears in Abaelard's <u>Sic et Non</u> that is pivotal in
the whole development from commentary on scripture
to systematic <u>Summa</u>. Lonergan summarizes the process in the following way:

> As already explained, there was a slight
> tincture of (theoretically differentiated
> consciousness) in the Greek councils at
> Nicea, Ephesus, Chalcedon, Constantinople
> III. But in the medieval period there
> was developed in the universities a vast,
> systematic, and collaborative task of reconciling all that had been handed down
> in the church from the past. The bold
> speculative efforts of an Anselm had
> aimed at comprehension before a sufficiently broad basis of information had
> been obtained. A more precise approach
> was illustrated by Abaelard's <u>Sic et Non</u>,
> in which one hundred and fifty-eight
> propositions were both proved and disproved by arguments drawn from scripture,
> the Fathers, the councils, and reason.
> From this dialectical display there was
> developed the technique of the <u>quaestio</u>:
> Abaelard's <u>Non</u> became <u>Videtur quod non</u>;
> his <u>Sic</u> became <u>Sed contra est</u>: to these
> were added a general response that outlined principles of solution and specific
> responses that applied the principles to
> each of the alleged pieces of evidence.
> Parallel to this development was the erudite activity of composing books of sentences that collected and classified relevant passages from scripture and tradition. When the technique of the <u>quaestio</u>
> was applied to the materials set forth in
> books of sentences, there resulted the
> commentaries and with them a new problem.
> There would be no point in reconciling

>   the diverging materials in the books of
>   sentences if the solutions to the multi-
>   tudinous questions were themselves inco-
>   herent.   There was needed, then, some
>   conceptual system that would enable the-
>   ologians to give coherent answers to all
>   the questions they raised; and this need
>   was met partly by adopting and partly by
>   adapting the Aristotelian corpus.[40]

Lonergan finds an outstanding example of coherence
and methodical composition in the work of Aquinas,
particularly his Summa. It was in this and similar
achievements that theology reached a new level of
systematic technical expression and comprehensive-
ness.[41] And in this development of system Lonergan
locates the medieval anticipations of modern science,
inasmuch as there emerged a level of reflex thought
that reorganized, correlated and explained what previously had been fragmented and diverging.[42] To employ a phrase used earlier, the Wissenschaftlichkeit
of medieval theology is to be found in its metaphysically based systematization.

   (b) Medieval Kirchlichkeit - In his article on
the history of theology Congar notes that Augustine
thought of human understanding as the fruit of a
living faith, the contemplation of a believing and
loving spirit; that which pertains to the created
order is to be understood, not in itself, but in its
reference to divine mystery.[43] Lonergan observes
something of the same trend present in the work of
Anselm in the medieval period; like Augustine, Anselm
presupposed a context of faith from within which he

would construct a rational presentation giving coherence to such problems as the reconciliation of
divine grace and human freedom.[44] In a word, medieval thinkers were generally aware, not only of
divinely revealed mystery, but of naturally known
truths. Yet they were unable to grasp both in a
unified manner that preserved the distinctiveness
of each but that also clarified their interaction.
In such a situation, Lonergan notes that theologians
commonly proceeded in one of two ways. Following
Anselm, they could raise all problems to the order
of mystery and faith. Or, following the lead of
Peter Abaelard and Gilbert de la Porrée, they could
reduce all problems to the level of logic and natural
truth.[45] Clearly there was need of a middle course.
For Lonergan, it was prepared remotely by the work of
Peter Lombard who, though he was squarely in the tradition of Anselm, nevertheless revealed the incoher-
ence of Anselm's position by drawing attention to the
need to think of human liberty in terms of nature as
well as in terms of grace.[46] But Lonergan adds that
the real breakthrough, the "Copernican revolution"
in the realm of theory,[47] came with the achievement
of Philip the Chancellor who, around 1230, worked
out a clear distinction between two orders - the supernatural and the natural. This led the way for
other thinkers to study grace apart from liberty and
liberty apart from grace, thereby reducing confusion
in the discussion of their mutual interaction.[48]

II.

Such a distinction, notes Lonergan, presented
a new challenge to theologians. To acknowledge an
autonomous sphere of nature, reason, and natural
love of God led to the need of understanding just
what one meant by nature, reason, and the natural
love of God. If theology, then, was to be the
search of faith for understanding, that understanding no longer could be confined to the supernatural
order - to the mysteries of grace, faith, charity,
merit; as well, theology had to include an understanding of nature and reason, of the natural order
that was perfected by the supernatural order. Only
in performing this task could theology avoid con-
fusing things by imposing the categories of revelation and divine mystery upon a quite autonomous
sphere of human reason and natural knowledge. Lonergan sketches the whole problem as follows:

> Again, the middle ages inherited from
> Augustine his affirmation of both di-
> vine grace and human liberty. For a
> long time it was difficult to say that
> there existed any finite thing that was
> not God's free gift. Though it was ob-
> vious that grace named not everything
> but something special, still lists of
> graces properly so called not only dif-
> fered from one another but also betrayed
> not a little arbitrariness. At the same
> time it was very difficult for a theol-
> ogian to say what he meant by liberty.
> Philosophers could define it as immunity
> from necessity. But theologians could
> not conceive liberty as free from the
> necessity of grace, or good without
> grace, or even evil with it. But what
> tortured the twelfth century found its

100

solution in the thirteenth. About the
year 1230 Philip the Chancellor completed a discovery that in the next
forty years released a whole series of
developments. The discovery was a
distinction between two entitatively
disproportionate orders: grace was
above nature; faith was above reason;
charity was above human good will;
merit before God was above the good
opinion of one's neighbors. This
distinction and organization made it
possible (1) to discuss the nature of
grace without discussing liberty, (2)
to discuss the nature of liberty without discussing grace, and (3) to work
out the relations between grace and
liberty.[49]

The need for a unified apprehension of things,
then, was the need for a reconciliation, an integration of faith and reason, while acknowledging the
autonomy of each. Efforts to realize this unity
were made in the _Summae_, and Lonergan sees these
efforts culminating in the work of Aquinas. Aquinas
insisted on the need to distinguish clearly between
two orders of knowledge - one pertaining to faith
and the other to reason. To distinguish, however,
was not to separate and Aquinas proceeded to work
out the relationship between faith and reason by
assimilating and then adapting the Aristotelian synthesis of philosophy and science, assigning to theology a role within this synthesis.[50]

Lonergan describes this achievement of Aquinas
as follows. Aquinas observed that a theologian has
the initial task of organizing the truths of faith

101

II.

in a coherent manner and then moving to conclusions
from them which have not been revealed: such is
the ordo inventionis, and it relies on the techniques developed since Abaelard of listing seemingly
irreconcilable positions, dismissing unacceptable
alternatives, and from the obvious agreements setting down in coherent fashion the most obvious conclusions that could be predicated of the tradition,
along with arguments suggesting an analogy with the
truths known by reason alone. In a word, Lonergan
seems here to be ascribing to Aquinas the theologian's task of reconciling diversity through a Begrifflichkeit, a systematic and scientific organization of the data.[51]

But there is as well a second task for the theologian, and it is precisely in fulfilling this task
that a unified apprehension of things is achieved -
an apprehension by reason illuminated by faith. The
conclusions of the ordo inventionis become the elements in the ordo disciplinae seu doctrinae: understanding, illumined by faith, combines those conclusions into principles, and science (scientia
subalternata) expands them by a process of deduction. In this manner there is achieved a systematic presentation of revealed truth that aims, not
at determining what that revealed truth is (this is
the task of the ordo inventionis), but at reaching
an understanding of that truth by the human mind's
native procedures of forming and developing concepts.[52]

In this manner, notes Lonergan, Aquinas promoted a theological reflection yielding a unified
grasp of revealed truth and naturally known truth.
Both faith and human reason were autonomous principles of knowledge, and grace and nature were two
orders of truth. Yet, though distinct, they were
integrated within a systematic grasp that both consolidated past achievement, yet moved this past a-
chievement forward by means of a reflection solidly
grounded in the living faith of the present. If I
could be permitted an observation, Lonergan is here
describing the faith dimension or religious dimension or Kirchlichkeit of medieval theological reflection - that which is specific to theology as
distinct from other fields of human inquiry.

(c) Medieval Zeitoffenheit - In the article
referred to earlier, Congar points out that from
patristic times, and especially since Augustine,
reflection on the gospel had drawn upon the resources of whatever human studies were available.
Already in apologetic literature there is evidence
of an acculturation process, and in Clement there
is a conscious effort to assimilate the heritage
of Greek philosophy as a means of explaining elements of the Christian faith.[53] The letter of
Jerome to Magnus is another instance of the need
to employ secular studies in understanding the
Christian tradition.[54] Augustine, both by exhor-
tation and example, insisted on the use of every
resource that could shed light on the meaning of

the gospel, whether a knowledge of sacred languages, of nature, of dialectic, of eloquence, of numbers, of history, of law.[55]

Lonergan is by no means unfamiliar with these facts, but he would add that it was first in the medieval period when a systematic use of human sciences became possible, through the introduction of the Aristotelian framework that offered a metaphysics, a classicist physics, a biology and a psychology.[56] Nor does he view the choice of this framework as a merely optional affair, for both Christians and non-Christians were part of an era that had rediscovered classical philosophy and were employing it extensively as an instrument of education. So Arabic thinkers and the disciples of Averroes at Paris urged a study of Aristotle, not merely to master a magnificent example of the power of human reason, but as well to disprove the claims of Christians. And this explains why Lonergan holds it to the lasting merit of medieval Christian thinkers that they responded by studying Aristotle themselves, adapting his thought to explain the meaning of the Christian faith.[57] Lonergan, of course, is not alone in pointing out this fact, and so I may conclude this brief section simply by noting that the medieval willingness to provide theology with a non-theological structure is a concrete example of what Zeitoffenheit in theology means.

I have been discussing Lonergan's understanding

of the process whereby theology emerged from a stage
of undifferentiated reflection in a commonsense manner to a stage wherein it became a full-fledged specialization - a distinct manner of reflecting on the
gospel and on Christian life and tradition. This
movement to theory within the Christian community, a
movement that consolidated past achievement and placed
theology solidly within the cultural academic world,
was for Lonergan the medieval achievement. But Lonergan notes that all achievement of this kind is limited, being both an end and a beginning. While medieval theology met the needs of its day, it also prepared the way for a series of developments in the culture that challeged theology as well to develop and
change. And to Lonergan's analysis of this subsequent
development we may now turn.

3. The New Context

In speaking of the achievement of Aquinas, Lonergan notes that "he carried through a distinction
between natural and supernatural, and by it he prepared the way for the independent study of nature:
for a philosophy that was not just a tool for theology; for a science that against Aristotle vindi-
cated its own autonomy; for a scholarship that took
the history of religion out of the competence of theologians and into the hands of scholars."[58] Following, then, Aquinas' working out of the distinction
between natural and supernatural, reason and faith,

II.

the path lay open for a series of developments that
for Lonergan could, and eventually did, transform
Western culture. He summarizes the situation as
follows:

> Still, a distinction between reason and
> faith is a distinction within theology.
> It pertains to the theologian's delimi-
> tation of his own field and to the elab-
> oration of his own methodology. But it
> possesses implications outside the the-
> ological domain. Its meaning is not con-
> fined to the erection of distinct and
> subordinate departments of philosophy
> and science within theological schools
> and for the furtherance of theological
> purposes. For once reason is acknow-
> ledged to be distinct from faith, there
> is issued an invitation to reason to
> grow in consciousness of its native pow-
> er, to claim its proper field of in-
> quiry, to work out its departments of
> investigation, to determine its own
> methods, to operate on the basis of its
> own principles and precepts. Such was
> the underlying significance of the dis-
> covery of Aristotle by the medieval age
> of faith. Such too was the open signif-
> icance of Renaissance humanism, Renais-
> sance philosophy, and Renaissance sci-
> ence.[59]

Such is a description of what Lonergan later referred to as the successive specializations of philosophy, science, and scholarship - the emergence of each
of these fields as distinct and autonomous horizons,
each with its proper procedures, inner organization,
function, and goal. Lonergan does not mean by this
that prior to the modern period there was no such

thing as philosophy or science or scholarship; rather, he is suggesting that in the pre-modern period, these fields were simply constituent parts of a unified system. That system, he observes, was grounded on a general science of being (metaphysics), and the particular sciences were just further determinations of the metaphysical terms and relations.[60] Lonergan maintains, however, that in the modern period, philosophy, science, and scholarship have emerged as autonomous fields, each appealing in its own way, not to metaphysics, but to empirical observation and experiment.

Lonergan, of course, is quite aware that medieval theology was very much involved in the metaphysical system, and that theology secured a role that reduced philosophy to a mere handmaid and other sciences to merely auxiliary disciplines. Theology, then, could not help but be affected by changes in the system as first one then another part broke loose and claimed independence. It seems important, therefore, to offer an overview of the changes that occurred. In line with the aim of the present work, I will offer, not a history of these cultural developments, but rather Lonergan's understanding of that history: how he interprets it, and what significance he gives it both in itself and, in the next section, in its relation to modern theology.

(1) The Autonomy of Philosophy: Part One

It is a rather well-known fact, repeated by Lon-

ergan, that ancient and medieval philosophers were
concerned principally with objects; the most comprehensive and general object was, of course, being itself and so it was that the philosophical study of
being provided the basis of integration among the
various sciences, that were divided according to
their material and formal objects.[61] Medieval theologians capitalized on this unified system and in-
corporated it within a religious perspective: so
Lonergan remarks,

> The medieval decision to use the Aris-
> totelian corpus as a substructure in-
> volved an integration of theology with
> a philosophy and with a detailed account
> of the material universe. Such an in-
> tegration offered the advantage of a
> unified worldview, but neither classi-
> cist culture nor Aristotelian thought
> inculcated the principle that unified
> world-views are subject to notable
> changes.[62]

This merely confirms what I have already said about
Lonergan's conviction that the distinction between
natural and supernatural, reason and faith, philosophy and theology, implied that philosophical and
scientific questions could be treated quite apart
from theology; while theologians considered philosophy (and the sciences then included within philosophy) as the handmaid of theology, philosophers would
more and more assert their independence and autonomy
from theology.

What is claimed here by Lonergan is supported by

the historian of philosophy, Frederick Copleston;
he notes that as medieval thinkers became acquainted
with the entire scope of Aristotelian writings, they
realized that Aristotle's system was a masterful
product of human reason alone, unaided by revelation
or by the acceptance of supernaturally grounded
faith. Theoretically at least philosophy could
exist independently of theology. Theologians like
Aquinas realized this, but Copleston remarks that
because they were theologians they could integrate
philosophy within a theological context. However,
he adds that not only theologians studied Aristotle,
and it was only to be expected that the impressive
example of Aristotle's work would lead medieval philosophers to a "declaration of independence" of philosophy from theology.[63]

I am sure that Lonergan would agree with Copleston's conclusion that it was not the intention of
Aquinas to set up philosophy as a field of inquiry,
a specialization, totally independent of theology.
Aquinas wished to make use of Aristotle in building
a theological-philosophical synthesis, in which theology would play a leading role. Yet, as Copleston
remarks, "children, when they grow up, do not always
behave exactly as their parents expected or wished.
Bonaventure, Albert, Thomas utilised and incorpor-
ated an increasing amount of the new philosophical
materials, and all the while they were rearing a
child who would soon go his own way . . ."[64]

II.

Lonergan himself sees this move to independence beginning already at the end of the thirteenth century, as the Thomist synthesis of reason and faith began to break up under a cult of certitude that reversed the Thomist quest for developing understanding:

> . . . the via doctrinae of the Summa is a masterpiece of theology as science and the apex of trinitarian speculation. But I would not be misunderstood. Coherently enough on their position, conceptualists conceive science simply in terms of certitude. For them the scientific ideal is the certitude one has of the particular and contingent fact of one's own existence. For them the substance of theology is what they are certain about, while the separable accidents are what they consider probable. They cannot be expected to think much of the Thomist trinitarian theory which, on its own showing, is no more than an hypothesis which does not attempt to exclude the possibility of alternatives. Still, without in any way deprecating certitude or even solidity, one may point out that the cult of certitude, the search for rigorous demonstration unaccompanied by a still greater effort to understand, has been tried and has been found wanting. It is the secret of fourteenth-century scepticism.[65]

Here, Lonergan is referring to the Augustinian-Aristotelian controversy of the thirteenth and fourteenth centuries, that surrounded the very idea of systematic thinking in theology. He is talking about the perversion within systematic thinking, that engaged in a quest for necessary truths and abstract universal principles, leading to a neglect of the dynamic quest

110

for insight and understanding. In a more recent
commentary on this period, Lonergan writes:

> When one turns from (Aquinas') cool im-
> plementation of faith's search for un-
> derstanding, an understanding that may
> be certain or merely probable, to the
> writings of John Duns Scotus or William
> of Ockham, one finds oneself in a quite
> different world. They were by-products
> of the Augustinian-Aristotelian conflict.
> They accepted Aristotle's logical works.
> His other writings they disregarded as
> merely pagan. In consequence they took
> the Posterior Analytics at face value.
> Their basic concern was whether or not
> this or that issue could be settled
> demonstratively. When that approach
> combined with questions on what could
> be by God's absolute power, the one way
> to certitude was through the principle
> of non-contradiction. For absolutely
> God could do anything that did not in-
> volve a contradiction. There is no con-
> tradiction between the occurrence of a
> hallucination and the absence of the
> hallucinated object.[66]

Lonergan here is adverting to a fundamental
plank in the platform commonly associated with the
Nominalist movement of especially the fourteenth
century. The Thomist synthesis of faith and reason
began to fall apart as theologians attended more
and more only to their rational and deductive powers as determined by the rules of logic; as Lonergan notes in the passage just quoted, the Augustin-
ian reaction against Aristotelianism was an effort
to purify theology from its association with the
pagan Aristotle's views on science and philosophy.

II.

But the subsequent reliance on logic alone, to the neglect of the quest for developing understanding, resulted in an age that Lonergan sees characterized by scepticism, as it became impossible to demonstrate by logic the various attributes of God.[67]

This Nominalist movement is, for Lonergan, the initial phase in the separation of philosophy from theology. Philosophy becomes concerned with rational certitude, self-evident truths, necessary propositions; theology rests exclusively on faith for its premisses and conclusions. But while he sees the separation of philosophy and theology actually operative in the Nominalist movement, Lonergan observes that it was first with Descartes (1596-1650) that a fully deliberate separation was urged: Descartes wanted his philosophy based on certitudes quite distinct from the certitudes of faith.[68] I shall return to Descartes in a later section, but at once it would be useful to note an aspect of his thought. His concern for a philosophy of the human subject seems to have been very much a reaction against philosophies such as Nominalism, that Lonergan says ignored or truncated the human subject.[69] So Lonergan notes that a concern with self-evident truths and necessary conclusions leads to an understanding of philosophy that neglects the concretely existing human subject; regardless of who the subject is, regardless of the subject's interest or attention, truth is there for everyone to grasp as logically self-evident, immediately clear, leading to conclusions that are both

necessary and obvious. Moreover, Lonergan adds, this
concern for certitude leads to conceptualism - to attention to those things about which we can be certain
because of common linguistic usage or because we can
infer these things from general scientific premisses.
For Lonergan, this undue attention to concepts leads
to a philosophy that conceives itself as a permanent
achievement, closed to development; for once concepts
are determined, they become valid for all time, regardless of historical circumstances. Such, for Lonergan, are abstract philosophies whose metaphysics
treat "being," not as something concrete and particular, but rather as an abstract concept consequent to
our knowledge of particular being that we somehow in-
tuit.

   While philosophy was drifting away from theology,
Lonergan would draw attention to a quite distinct development that was occurring around the same time.
This was the rise of modern science that sought to
separate itself from Aristotelian philosophy and eventually claimed autonomy from all philosophy, and we
may now turn to Lonergan's understanding of this development of science as a specialization.

(2) The Autonomy of Science

   I have already mentioned Lonergan's conviction
that ancient and medieval philosophy was linked to
the various sciences of nature, so that questions
about the material universe were raised and answered

II.

within the framework of a metaphysics, a philosophy
of being. It was a framework that provided the different sciences with a common Begrifflichkeit, relating various disciplines to one another as parts
of a unified system.[70]

In the present section I wish to trace Lonergan's
thought on how this continuity of philosophy and science was threatened as the latter turned more and more
to empirical observation and to the explanation of
particular data. Basically, Lonergan holds that science became less concerned with searching for essences
or for the principles from which it could deduce explanations of reality; instead, a new understanding of
science was emerging that took its autonomous stand on
empirical verification, thereby asserting its independence from metaphysical philosophy. It was a gradual
process, whose roots can be traced to the scientific
discoveries of the medieval period and to the scepticism surrounding metaphysics that was introduced
through nominalist philosophy. But Lonergan agrees
with Butterfield's contention that it was only with
the Copernican revolution, and the scientific insights
of the seventeenth century, that a scientific context
emerged that was capable of replacing the Aristotelian
system with an entirely new notion of scientific knowledge:

> When Professor Butterfield placed the or-
> igins of modern science at the end of the
> seventeenth century, he by no means meant
> to deny that from the year 1300 on numer-
> ous discoveries were made that since have

114

been included within modern science and
integrated with it. But he did make the
point that, at the time of their first
appearance, these discoveries could not
be expressed adequately. For, the dominant cultural context was Aristotelian,
and the discoveries themselves had Aristotelian backgrounds. Thus there existed
a conflict between the new ideas and the
old doctrines, and this conflict existed
not merely between an old guard of Aristotelians and a new breed of scientists.
For new ideas are far less than a whole
mentality, a whole climate of thought and
opinion, a whole mode of approach, and
procedure, and judgment. Before these
new ideas could be formulated accurately,
coherently, cogently, they had to multiply,
cumulate, coalesce to bring forth a new
system of concepts and a new body of doctrine that was somehow comparable in extent to the Aristotelian and so was capable
of replacing it.[71]

As was the case with the initial emergence of an
autonomous philosophy from theology, so too Lonergan
is aware that the emergence of an autonomous science
from philosophy did not occur overnight. If the a-
chievements of the seventeenth century could be considered the initial stage in the scientific context,
then Lonergan associates two principal figures with
these beginnings. In the work of Newton (1642-1727),
particularly his "Mathematical Principles of Natural
Philosophy," there is in fact a real distinction and
separation of natural science from philosophy; but as
the title itself indicates the science was still
linked, even if loosely, to the former philosophical
context. With Laplace (1749-1827), there is a fully

II.

conscious separation of science from philosophy; in
this regard Lonergan notes the famous comment of Laplace when questioned about the place of the philosophical First Mover in his planetary system, "Nous
n'avons plus besoin de cette hypothèse."[72]

Further stages in the development of modern science deepened the autonomous spirit, but Lonergan holds
that it was only in the present century that a complete
break with the Aristotelian system occurred. Put very
briefly, modern science, since the time of Newton and
Laplace, had continued to assume that science was true
and certain knowledge of causal necessity - a hangover
from the Aristotelian notion of science. But with
Einstein's special relativity and Heisenberg's relations of indeterminacy or uncertainty, the aim of science shifted from necessary laws to verifiable possibility.[73] To clarify this, I will outline the three
main areas in which Lonergan places a difference between modern and Aristotelian science. This is not
irrelevant to theology, traditionally conceived as
the "science of faith," for just as theology sought
to explain how it was science in the Aristotelian
context, so theology today is busy trying to define
itself in terms of modern science, or at least in
comparison with modern science, and it would be wise
to ask just what this science is all about.[74]

Firstly, Lonergan says there is a difference in
the ideals of scientific work. Aristotle set forth
an ideal of science that was so rigorous it could be

realized only in mathematics and geometry, and merely approximated in other sciences. For he wanted scientific knowledge to be knowledge of the universal causes of things, and to this end insisted on the need to know the end, agent, matter, and form of the object under study. Not surprisingly, medieval theology as science also defined itself in terms of the material and formal objects with which it was concerned. Further, Aristotle wanted science to be knowledge of what necessarily is so, what cannot be otherwise; whatever fell short of this necessity was simply contingent, about which we have, not scientific knowledge, but opinion. So medieval theology came to understand itself, particularly in the fourteenth century, as concerned with absolute necessity. Finally, Aristotle wanted scientific knowledge to be immutable and true; for it was knowledge of effects that could not be otherwise, and what cannot be otherwise always will be just that way: for Aristotle science was to be a permanent achievement, just as late medieval and Renaissance theology considered itself a permanent achievement, resting on the perennial philosophy. It follows that science, for Aristotle, is speculative, contemplative knowledge; it is "theory" as opposed to contingence, knowledge of necessary things as opposed to opinion about fleeting reality.

In contrast, Lonergan observes that the ideals of modern science, while as ambitious as those of Aristotle, are nevertheless much more capable of in fact

being achieved. When it searches for causes, modern
science does not turn to philosophic considerations
of end, agent, matter, and form, but rather to the
correlation or concomitance that in fact is present
among observable data. Further, modern science in
the present century no longer searches for what necessarily is so, no longer insists on the need to work
out absolutely necessary laws and systems. Necessity
is at best a marginal notion, and attention has
shifted to what is contingent: to a determination
of what is possible and, by verification, in fact
happens to be the case.[75] Finally, modern science
does not see itself as a permanent achievement or
as an immutable, infallible system of eternal truth;
rather, its self-image is of a cumulative, ongoing,
and emerging system, open to constant revision and,
perhaps, occasional revolutions. Hence, modern science is "theoretical," but now, not as opposed to
practice, but rather as a stage in dealing with the
same realities that are the concern of "practical"
knowledge. Modern science grounds a vast array of
practical applications, precisely because it is a
specialization that has withdrawn from everyday concerns; hence, modern empirical science is continuous
with and influential in a practical concern for shaping the world.[76]

Secondly, besides a shift in the ideals of scientific endeavors, Lonergan says there is a further
shift from essence to system. Aristotle conceived

scientific knowledge in terms of scientific syllogisms. Syllogisms are logical arguments, whose conclusions are supported by two premisses. It is a
linguistic or verbal argument, for it is built around
the relation of the subject and predicate of premisses
and conclusions. For Aristotle, scientific syllogisms
were syllogisms in which the link of the predicate to
the subject was universal (holding in every case),
necessary (it could not be otherwise), and eternal (it
always will be true). Such syllogisms, of course,
were needed to meet the ideals envisioned by Aristotle.
But along with the shift in ideals, there has occurred
a shift from the logic of syllogisms to the insight of
method.

Accordingly, Lonergan notes that modern science
is concerned with the concrete explanation of all phenomena, all occurrence, all process. It is not concerned with the grammatical relations of words, that
really don't take us beyond what we already know, but
rather with empirical data. It is aware of logic,
and employs logic in clarifying terms, in promoting
coherence, in supplying rigor. But such awareness
is now within the broader context of method, that
relies on non-logical operations like observation,
description, problem formulation, discovery, experimentation, verification, revision, as well as on logical operations.[77] Modern science is not concerned
with the immutable essence of things, but with the
relations among data that fit together in empirical
laws and that can be expressed in open systems.

II.

These systems take us beyond what is empirically observable, but this "beyond" is not some sphere of
detached essences; rather, it is a "beyond" that for-
mally states no more than is implied in the empirical
data itself. Hence, the terms and relations of modern
scientific systems are rooted in laws that are established by empirical procedures.[78]

Thirdly, Lonergan says that there was a shift in
the manner of dividing-up the sciences. For Aristotle,
division of the sciences was a matter of conceiving the
material and formal objects of the different sciences.
As mentioned, this conception turned to the most general of sciences, metaphysics, for its basic principles and terms, so that the other particular sciences
were further determinations of metaphysics, governed
by philosophical procedures and aims. The material
objects were those things that persisted unchanged
through a process of change. The formal objects were
the essences or forms or patterns constituting what
something is as unchanging. The material objects
could be ordered as to their generality, so that metaphysics governed the less general sciences and determined their scope and procedures.

Modern science, on the other hand, proceeds, not
from "above downwards," but from observable data and
experiment. Thus, Lonergan observes that the distinctions among modern sciences are the result of distinguishing different fields of observable data and, especially, different methods of dealing with this data.

Because of this strictly empirical basis, coupled
with equally empirical methodology, the autonomy of
modern science from classical philosophy is beyond
question. To what extent, however, modern science
is completely free from philosophy is, for Lonergan,
quite another matter.[79]

The empirical basis and methodology of modern
science has another implication for the division of
the sciences. Where classical science and philosophy
could easily be taught and mastered by an individual -
for it was a compact and unchanging system - Lonergan
stresses that modern science is the possession only
of an enormous community of scientists - a possession
at best probable, ever subject to further development, and heavily reliant on belief. Further, while
Aristotle's conception of science was an ideal-type,
to which all sciences conformed to a greater or lesser
degree, modern sciences each have their own methods
and none has to appeal to a similarity with some ideal
science in order to prove itself scientific. Modern
sciences stand on their own two feet - a lesson that
modern theology could well learn. Clearly, the natural sciences enjoy such independence, some doubts
may arise when talk turns to the human sciences, and
even further suspicion surrounds theology. But Lonergan suggests that we stop thinking in Aristotelian
terms that would embody all sciences and disciplines
in a logical system of common terms and relations.
Instead, he urges that each specialization is marked
by its own fundamental terms and relations, worked

II.

out by the experience of practitioners in the specialization; nor does this mean that Lonergan de-
spairs of the unity of human knowing, as if there
were only an irreducible plurality of scientific
disciplines, for he understands each specialization
to be a variation on a basic pattern of operations -
something that I'll explain more fully in Chapter
Three.

For Lonergan, then, the development of modern
science as an autonomous specialization, separate
from philosophy and theology, was not without its
repercussions on these other fields. Until fairly
recently, both theology and philosophy were considered "scientific," in the sense of that word usually
associated with Aristotelian science. But with current developments, this is no longer the case. I
suspect that Lonergan would fully concur with the
following observation of Professor Copleston:

> In the Middle Ages theology and philosophy
> were universally regarded as "sciences";
> the great figures in university life were
> the theologians and the philosophers; and
> it was they who in general estimation were
> the possessors of knowledge. In the course
> of time, however, scientific knowledge in
> the modern sense has come to be popularly
> regarded as the norm and standard of know-
> ledge; and in many countries neither the-
> ologians nor philosophers would be com-
> monly regarded as possessing "knowledge"
> in the sense in which scientists are
> thought to possess it.[80]

The story of the identity-crisis that the rise of

modern science has created for theology will be told
in due course. Firstly, however, I wish to turn to
Lonergan's account of the identity-crisis that the
autonomy of science from philosophy created for philosophy itself, as the Aristotelian system began crum-
bling under the weight of empirical method.

(3) The Autonomy of Philosophy: Part Two

Hopefully it is clear to the reader that I am
not following a strictly chronological order in this
chapter. My intention rather is to ask with Lonergan
just what happened to the unified system of theology
that was worked out in the medieval period, and the
answer has been to the effect that various disciplines,
once integrated within a single system, have since
broken loose and gone their own ways, thereby creating
an identity-crisis for theology. The most significant
and influential of these developments were the rise of
modern science and modern historical scholarship. But
if these two developments were the most significant,
it remains that Lonergan points to the absence of due
development by philosophy and theology as contributing
most to the disunity prevailing in our own day. Philosophers and theologians were by no means idle in the
past seven centuries, but their responses, according
to Lonergan, were more reactionary and problematic
than calculated and explicitly methodical; and for
this reason I have had to break up Lonergan's discussion of the emergence of an autonomous philosophy

123

II.

into three sections, and relegate theology to a separate part of the present chapter. At present, I would like to discuss Lonergan's understanding of the impact on philosophy of the initial stage in the growth of modern science, in order to find out just what this meant for philosophy's self-understanding.

We may begin by recalling the previous section, wherein I outlined Lonergan's conviction that modern science presented an apprehension of reality that was quite different than anything previously known. It was not grounded in Aristotelian metaphysics, for it took its stand on empirical observation and remained anchored to that basis by its insistence on empirical verification. But neither was modern science just a sophisticated variety of the ordinary, commonsense apprehension of empirical reality, for science went beyond that which could be observed to that which explained things in their relation to one another. And usually its explanations were in a language that only the scientific specialist could understand, a language that signalled the entry of quite a new type of theoretical knowledge.

According to Lonergan, then, the rise of modern science gave a new form to the opposition between the world of theory and the world of common sense.[81] To clarify this, Lonergan would draw our attention to the earlier form of this opposition that emerged

124

with the discovery of mind in ancient Greece.

> The discovery of mind marks the transition
> from the first stage of meaning to the
> second. In the first stage the world me-
> diated by meaning is just the world of
> common sense. In the second stage the
> world mediated by meaning splits into the
> realm of common sense and the realm of
> theory. Corresponding to this division
> and grounding it, there is a differen-
> tiation of consciousness. In the first
> stage the subject, in his pursuit of the
> concrete good, also attends, understands,
> judges. But he does not make a specialty
> of these activities. He does not formu-
> late a theoretical ideal in terms of
> knowledge, truth, reality, causality.
> He does not formulate linguistically a
> set of norms for the pursuit of that
> ideal goal. He does not initiate a
> distinct economic and social and cul-
> tural context within which the pursuit
> of the ideal goal could be carried out
> by human animals. But in the second
> stage of meaning the subject continues
> to operate in the common-sense manner
> in all his dealings with the particular
> and concrete, but along with this mode
> of operation he also has another, the
> theoretical. In the theoretical mode
> the good that is pursued is the truth
> and, while this pursuit is willed, still
> the pursuit itself consists only in op-
> erations on the first three levels of
> intentional consciousness: it is the
> specialization of attending, understand-
> ing, and judging.[82]

Although the passage just quoted contains notions from

Lonergan's thought that will be clarified only in Chap-

ter Three, I include it here in order to point out

Lonergan's characterization of the common sense -

theory opposition prior to the modern era. This is important, for Lonergan's understanding of "modernity," especially of the function of modern philosophy, is in terms of the various specializations that sharpened this opposition and thereby set the critical problem with which modern philosophers have been struggling since the time of Descartes.

In the earlier (second) stage, then, Lonergan observes that theory was a specialty for the attainment of truth, for stating the truth about this or that kind of reality. He recalls that Aristotle conceived theory as concerned with what was prior in itself but posterior to us; and for Aristotle such theory was a philosophy that derived its basic concepts from metaphysics and that viewed the various sciences as prolongations of that philosophy and as further determinations of the basic concepts provided by that philosophy.[83]

This makes more precise what I referred to in the previous section, wherein I outlined the main differences noted by Lonergan between Aristotelian and modern science. So Lonergan notes that the sciences have become ongoing processes, whose aim is not to state the truth about this or that reality, but rather to reach an ever better approximation towards the truth by an ever fuller and exacter understanding of all relevant data. While in the previous stage theory was a specialty for the attainment of truth, now scientific theory has become a specialty for the advance

of understanding. Further, the modern sciences are
autonomous, having worked out their respective methods and repudiated any higher discipline such as
philosophy or metaphysics that could determine those
methods for them. Finally, Lonergan adds that because the sciences are ongoing processes, their unification too has to be an ongoing process: it cannot
be some single well-ordered formulation resting on a
logic, but rather has to be a succession of different
formulations resting on method.[84]

To draw closer now to the topic of the present
section, Lonergan observes that the emergence of the
autonomous sciences has repercussions on philosophy.
For if previously there had been a continuity of philosophy and science within a single system, the emergence of autonomous sciences could not but have repercussions on the function of philosophy. And for
Lonergan, the struggle by philosophy to work out its
proper method and function characterizes the history
of philosophy at least since the time of Descartes,
as philosophers tried to figure out if their work was
a theory in the manner of science or a technical form
of common sense or a matter of human wisdom. Lonergan himself conceives philosophy in none of these
ways,[85] but he does understand the history of modern
philosophy as an ongoing effort to overcome this new
form of the opposition between common sense and scientific theory, between everyday knowing and scientific knowing. And so, after speaking of the continuity of philosophy and science in the Aristotelian

127

system, Lonergan offers a sketch of subsequent developments:

>   This continuity of philosophy and sci-
>   ence has often been the object of nos-
>   talgic admiration. But if it had the
>   merit of meeting the systematic exigence
>   and habituating the human mind to the-
>   oretical pursuits, it could be no more
>   than a transitional phase. Modern sci-
>   ence had to develop its own proper basic
>   concepts and thereby achieve its auton-
>   omy. In doing so it gave a new form to
>   the opposition between the world of the-
>   ory and the world of common sense. This
>   new form, in turn, evoked a series of
>   new philosophies: Galileo's primary
>   qualities, which admitted geometriza-
>   tion and so were real, and his refrac-
>   tory secondary qualities, which were
>   pronounced merely apparent; Descartes'
>   mind in a machine; Spinoza's two known
>   attributes; Kant's a priori forms and a
>   posteriori filling of the sensibility.
>   But Kant's Copernican revolution marks
>   a dividing line. Hegel turned from sub-
>   stance to the subject. Historians and
>   philologists worked out their autonomous
>   methods for human studies. Will and de-
>   cision, actions and results, came up for
>   emphasis, Kierkegaard, Schopenhauer,
>   Nietzsche, Blondel, the pragmatists.
>   Brentano inspired Husserl, and inten-
>   tionality analysis routed faculty psy-
>   chology. The second stage of meaning
>   is vanishing, and a third is about to
>   take its place.[86]

In the present section I wish to make a few observations on Lonergan's understanding of this development up to and including Hegel; in the next
section I shall discuss the autonomy of scholarship,

and then will add a final section on the most recent phase in philosophy's self-understanding.

I have already mentioned Lonergan's assertion that with Descartes there occurs an explicit effort to provide philosophy with its own proper foundations, independently of theology. But Lonergan adds that Descartes in no way attempted to separate philosophy and science, but, on the contrary, attempted to prove the conservation of momentum by appealing to the immutability of God. Such a procedure, according to Lonergan, could not last under the rising autonomy of science: Newton's work in mechanics and the Royal Society's insistence on the scientific criterion of verifiable hypotheses effected the separation of science from the current philosophies.[87] Still, although scientists repudiated their philosophical heritage, Lonergan observes that philosophers were quite fascinated by the achievements of scientists and became the spokesmen for the new age of Enlightenment:

> Coincident with the origins of modern science was the beginning of the Enlightenment, of the movement Peter Gay recently named the rise of modern paganism. Moreover, while this movement is commonly located in the eighteenth century, the French academician Paul Hazard has exhibited already in full swing between the years 1680 and 1715 a far-flung attack on Christianity from almost every quarter and in almost every style. It was a movement revolted by the spectacle of religious persecution and religious war. It was to replace the God of the Christians by the God of the philosophes and, even-

tually, the God of the philosophes by
agnosticism and atheism. It gloried in
the achievements of Newton, criticized
social structures, promoted political
change, and moved towards a materialist,
mechanist, determinist interpretation no
less of man than of nature.[88]

Assessments of the "Enlightenment" are, of course,
many indeed; for some it is fundamentally a political
problem to be resolved by political means, for others
it is fundamentally a theological problem to be resolved by theological means, for still others it is a
moral problem to be resolved by a philosophy of praxis,
while others are convinced it is a cognitional problem
to be resolved by cognitional theory, epistemology, and
metaphysics. For Lonergan, the Enlightenment poses
tremendous problems: on political, theological, and
moral levels; but he insists that an eventual resolution of those problems will depend on resolving the
fundamental issue of cognitional theory. Accordingly,
Lonergan is most interested in examining modern philosophies from the specific viewpoint of their various
cognitional theories, for although these various philosophies each contains error as well as truth, the
manner of working out a suitable cognitional theory
will be a matter of developing a method to promote
the truth and reverse the errors of the various Enlightenment proposals. Lonergan devotes the initial
thirteen chapters of Insight to developing in the
reader such a method, thereby clarifying the fundamental antitheses involved in human knowing; and in the

II.

fourteenth chapter, he acknowledges his debt to modern
thought's struggle with those fundamental issues:

> If a clear and sharp formulation of the
> antitheses occurs only at the end of a
> long and difficult inquiry (the initial
> chapters of Insight - M. O'C.), still
> that inquiry today is prepared and sup-
> ported in a manner unattainable in ear-
> lier centuries. The development of
> mathematics, the maturity of some bran-
> ches of empirical science, the investi-
> gations of depth psychology, the in-
> terest in historical theory, the epis-
> temological problems raised by Descartes,
> by Hume, and by Kant, the concentration
> of modern philosophy upon cognitional an-
> alysis, all serve to facilitate and to
> illumine an investigation of the mind of
> man. But if it is possible for later
> ages to reap the harvest of earlier sow-
> ing, still before that sowing and during
> it there was no harvest to be reaped.[89]

In this same chapter of Insight Lonergan offers
a heuristic scheme for guiding the historical investigation of particular philosophies. He discusses a
series of alternative suggestions for the method of
philosophy, and in each case he tries to isolate the
valid insight as well as to identify the error or
oversight. He does not offer this scheme as a history
of philosophy, whether ancient or modern, but emphasizes that the scheme is valuable in interpreting both
ancient and modern philosophies. Further, he examines
the various suggestions from the viewpoint of method -
attempting in each case to note the function of philosophy itself, thereby prescinding from other ques-

131

II.

tions that deal with such matters as the social or
ethical or theological implications or dimensions of
the different philosophies. I find this scheme to
be a useful instrument in discussing Lonergan's understanding of the development of philosophy during
the age of "Enlightenment"; for while the scheme is
intended to be merely a guide to actual historical
investigation of the various philosophies themselves,
Lonergan nonetheless includes enough references to
these philosophies as to provide the main lines of
his critique of them. I should perhaps note that my
aim is not to prove the validity of Lonergan's contention that the fundamental problem of the Enlightenment is one of cognitional theory, epistemology,
and metaphysics; rather, it is merely to examine how
this contention leads Lonergan to interpret the Enlightenment in the manner that I shall now explain.

In order to set Lonergan's scheme in perspective,
I would recall his account of the problem that the
various philosophies sought to resolve. The rise of
modern science was the emergence of a new type of theory that brought home forcefully the fact that human
knowledge is of two different kinds – a knowledge of
what is not given in our immediate experience (conspicuous in scientific knowledge), and a knowledge of
what is given in immediate experience (conspicuous in
sensations and emotions). And, for Lonergan, the philosophical problem has been fundamentally a matter of
working out precisely what these two forms of knowledge are and what the relations are between them:

132

> I ask, accordingly, about the nature
> rather than about the existence of know-
> ledge because in each of us there exist
> two different kinds of knowledge. They
> are juxtaposed in Cartesian dualism with
> its rational 'Cogito, ergo sum' and with
> its unquestioning extroversion to sub-
> stantial extension. They are separated
> and alienated in the subsequent ration-
> alist and empiricist philosophies. They
> are brought together again to cancel each
> other in Kantian criticism. If these
> statements approximate the facts, then
> the question of human knowledge is not
> whether it exists but what precisely are
> its two diverse forms and what are the
> relations between them.[90]

A more complete account of attempts to deal with
this question is provided by Lonergan in the dialectic
of methods in metaphysics that he provides in Chapter
Fourteen of Insight, to which I adverted a moment ago.
There, he enumerates the possible arbitrary positions
of philosophy under the headings of (1) deductive
methods, (2) universal doubt, (3) empiricism, (4)
common-sense eclecticism, (5) Hegelian dialectic, and
(6) scientific method and philosophy. Here I wish to
offer a very concise account of these positions, for
I sense that such an account will help the reader to
assess Lonergan's understanding of the "Enlightenment"
in what he believes to be its fundamental inadequacy,
namely, the inability to resolve adequately the nature
of human knowledge in both its forms. It goes without
saying that Lonergan associates that inadequacy with
the current controversy surrounding a fundamental theology, but to this topic I shall return later in this

II.

work. For the moment, it seems important to discover what Lonergan finds to be inadequate in the
philosophies of the period under study - an inadequacy that he finds generally unresolved even in the
philosophies of our own day and that, as many others
too have suggested, force upon us a "return to the
Enlightenment" in order to get to the roots of the
difficulty. I shall present Lonergan's views generally without the use of footnotes, and the reader
desiring the full account is thus referred in advance
to the presentation in Insight.

Of the six possibilities discussed by Lonergan,
the first tends to ignore the human subject, the next
three would guide the subject, the fifth would include
the previous four in a dialectic, and the last would
reduce philosophy to scientific method. Common to all
positions is the effort to give an adequate account of
what human knowing is all about.

(a) Deductive methods - Deductive methods pre-
vail in those philosophies that are concerned with determining the primitive or ultimate propositions from
which all other propositions of human knowledge can
be logically derived or deduced. Such deductive methods are of two kinds, depending on whether the primitive propositions selected are universal and necessary truths, or some concretely existent reality.
The first kind of deduction is suggested by such
thinkers as Duns Scotus and Ockham. Because the
primitive propositions are universal, they are ab-

stract and cannot ground the affirmation of existing
and present reality as existing and present; hence
such thinkers usually complement their abstract systems by introducing some sort of intuition that grasps
concretely existing reality. Further, because the
system rests on necessary truths, it is unconcerned
with contingent truth and thus is unconcerned with
integrating the empirical sciences and common sense,
both of which are concerned with contingent truth.
Hence, such an abstract metaphysics of all possible
worlds is empty, and I discussed Lonergan's fuller
account of this emptiness in the first part of the
autonomy of philosophy.

A second kind of deduction claims that the primitive propositions refer in fact to some concrete existent, from which all concretely existing reality is
derived. Lonergan notes that such systems are many:
a monist deduction of attributes, an emanationist deduction of processions, an optimism that asserts God
must create the best of possible worlds, a mechanist
determinism that concludes that given an initial situation, all else can be deduced from it. He observes
that such systems are quite consistent inasmuch as if
their premisses are granted, then the conclusions
drawn must follow. Obviously, though, the prior question is: are the premisses to be granted? Such is the
question of the very possibility of concrete deduction
in the first place - whether, for example, the concrete
deduction occurring in Newton's mechanics is to be the

135

II.

possibility of metaphysics, is to be the primitive
proposition from which knowledge of reality may be
deduced. The needed premisses would have to be synthetic, a priori principles: synthetic, inasmuch as
they must account for knowledge of the actual world,
and not be just a matter of definitions and grammatical syntax; and a priori inasmuch as they are not to
be had simply by sense experience, by taking a good
look at the external world, but rather originate in
the factory of mind that works the materials of outer
and inner sense into appropriate syntheses.

According to Lonergan, the problem with the various efforts to determine such synthetic, a priori
principles (including the efforts of Kant) lies in the
fact that they each chose some one set of such principles (e.g. Newtonian deduction) and made it the one
fixed source of deduction. This is inadequate, for it
fails to account for other types of deduction (e.g.
Newtonian deduction leaves unexplained the sort of deduction proposed by Einstein). There is, then, a need
to give an account of a whole series of deductions,
none of which is absolutely necessary but rather offers some de facto intelligibility that is subject to
adjustment, improvement, or even rejection when a whole
new paradigm emerges. In other words, concludes Lonergan, there is not some fixed set of a priori syntheses
for such fixity cannot account for the dynamic and open
thrust of human understanding reaching successive insights and ever higher viewpoints.[91]

136

If the abstract deduction of a Scotus is inadequate, Lonergan notes that Aristotle and Aquinas
acknowledged the fact of a priori insight; but inasmuch as their presentations are formulated in metaphysical terms, both writers do not offer an explicit
account of that which generates the principles on
which the metaphysics is to rest. Lonergan himself,
in Verbum, concluded that there is enough material in
Aquinas' writings to show that Aquinas conceived of
"wisdom" in precisely cognitional terms, grounding
his metaphysics; but Lonergan acknowledges that the
variety of Thomist interpretations tend to leave a
cloud of suspicion over deductive methods generally,
so that some other method is needed:

> Our consideration of deductive methods in
> metaphysics found abstract deduction to
> be empty and concrete deduction to stand
> in need of a prior inquiry. This prior
> inquiry was not conducted with sufficient
> generality by Kant, nor with sufficient
> discrimination by Scotus. Finally, its
> possibility was implied by Aquinas, but
> the varieties of Thomist interpretation
> are as much in need of a prior inquiry
> as anything else. It would seem, then,
> that at least one positive conclusion
> can be drawn, namely, that deductive
> method alone is not enough. The fas-
> cination exerted by this method lies in
> its apparent promise of automatic results
> that are independent of the whims and
> fancies of the subject. The deducing
> proceeds in accord with a rigorous tech-
> nique; the primitive premises are guar-
> anteed by a self-evidence that claims
> to exercise an objective compulsion to
> which the subject must submit if he is

137

not to be guilty of a lapse in intellectual probity. In fact, however, it
is not so easy to leave the subject outside one's calculations, and so we now
must turn to directive methods that aim
to guide the metaphysical enterprise by
guiding the subject that undertakes it.[92]

Continuing, then, our investigation of Lonergan's understanding of the philosophical problem of cognitional theory, epistemology, and metaphysics, we may
now turn to the philosophical position that he describes as "universal doubt."

(b) Universal Doubt - A second philosophical
method that Lonergan finds operative in modern philosophy is the method that advises the subject to doubt
everything that can be doubted. And Lonergan would
simply draw our attention to the consequences that
follow from a rigorous application of that principle.

Firstly, then, concrete judgments of fact are to
be excluded from the system of universal doubt, for
such judgments yield certainty but not indubitability.
Again, both science and common sense are to be excluded
from the system, for both aim at ascertaining the facts
and neither reaches what is absolutely beyond doubt.
Thirdly, it follows that judgments may indeed be made
within the system, but their meaning remains obscure
and unsettled; for to determine the clear and precise
meaning of judgments demands a clarification of cognitional structure - a clarification that would be at
best certain, but never indubitable. Fourthly, the
exclusion of concrete judgments of fact leaves only

analytic propositions as indubitable, so that knowledge is basically a matter of merely supposing that
something is so and never reaching the judgment that
something is indeed so.

Fifthly, Lonergan notes the survival in the system of the existential subject - the subject who exists prior to the question, Am I?; hence one might
argue that before I doubt I must exist, but the system, if it follows rigorously its own principle, can
offer no clarification on the meaning of "I," of "existing," of "affirming," so that the existential subject would remain basically frustrated. Sixthly, and
to point to the usual argument against the system,
not even the criterion of indubitability is indubitable, for the criterion presupposes a concrete judgment of fact that states doubting to be a rational,
meaningful activity; and such judgments of fact are
excluded. It follows, seventhly, that philosophy itself has no meaningful function except perhaps to bear
witness to the supposition that perhaps philosophy has
no meaningful function. For, eighthly, the implications of following the criterion of universal doubt
are themselves subject to doubt, thereby making acceptance of such a method a leap in the dark. Finally,
the results of following the method will be both arbitrary and illusory: arbitrary, for the exact implications of following the method cannot be known;
and illusory, for one thinks that one's opinions have
somehow passed a test that others have failed to pass
- something that ignores the existence of basic and

II.

initial convictions. Hence, Lonergan formulates his
assessment of universal doubt in the following summary:

> However, if I believe that universal doubt
> was practised more successfully by Hume
> than by Descartes and, perhaps, more suc-
> cessfully by the existentialists and some
> of the logical positivists than by Hume,
> I must also recall that my topic has been,
> not the concrete proposal entertained by
> Descartes, but the consequences of inter-
> preting literally and applying rigorously
> the precept, Doubt everything that can be
> doubted. Clearly enough, the implications
> of that precept fail to reveal the profound
> originality and enduring significance of
> Descartes, for whom universal doubt was not
> a school of scepticism but a philosophic
> programme that aimed to embrace the uni-
> verse, to assign a clear and precise reason
> for everything, to exclude the influence of
> unacknowledged presuppositions. For that
> programme we have only praise, but we also
> believe that it should be dissociated from
> the method of universal doubt whether that
> method is interpreted rigorously or miti-
> gated in a fashion that cannot avoid being
> arbitrary.[93]

At this point, Lonergan would direct our attention
to one of the most influential philosophic methods that
sought to do justice to the programme of Descartes but
that would guide the subject, not by advocating universal doubt, but by urging that the human subject simply observe the significant facts, if he or she would
gain knowledge of concrete reality. Such is empiricism,
and although Lonergan understands it to be a constantly
recurring theme in the history of philosophy, he also

is convinced that it has reached its most sophisticated form and systematic expression in modern philosophy, as a consequence of the rise of empirical science as autonomous specialization.

(c) Empiricism - I believe that Lonergan's critique of empiricism has particular importance for his
understanding of philosophic methods generally, and
so I would begin by quoting a passage from Insight
that I find to be central to his thought:

> A second method that offers to guide the
> subject issues the precept, Observe the
> significant facts. Unfortunately, what
> can be observed is merely a datum; signif-
> icance accrues to data only through the
> occurrence of insights; correct insights
> can be reached only at the term of a pro-
> longed investigation that ultimately reaches
> the point where no further relevant ques-
> tions arise; and without the combination
> of data and correct insights that together
> form a virtually unconditioned, there are
> no facts. Such, I believe, is the truth
> of the matter, but it is an extremely par-
> adoxical truth, and the labour of all the
> pages that precede can be regarded as a
> sustained effort both to clarify the na-
> ture of insight and judgment and to ac-
> count for the confusion, so natural to
> man, between extroversion and objectivity.
> For man observes, understands, and judges,
> but he fancies that what he knows in judg-
> ment is not known in judgment and does not
> suppose an exercise of understanding but
> simply is attained by taking a good look
> at the 'real' that is 'already out there
> now.' Empiricism, then, is a bundle of
> blunders, and its history is their suc-
> cessive clarification.[94]

II.

From this passage it is possible to identify the
basic premise upon which Lonergan understands empiricism to rest. For the empiricist, human knowing must
be a matter of experiencing, looking, or intuiting; if
these operations are not present, then there is no
knowing. Accordingly, the empiricist notion of objectivity is experiential: objective reality is whatever
is experienced, looked at, intuited. And the empiricist thesis finds continual reinforcement in the perennial confusion of animal and human knowing that pre-
sumes human knowing must somehow be reduced ultimately
to external sense experience, especially to human vision and seeing.

In this regard, Lonergan mentions Augustine's
comment that for years he was convinced that the real
had to be a body. Later, with Neo-Platonist aid, Augustine got beyond that view and became convinced that
reality was _veritas_: and for Augustine, truth was
known, not by looking out, nor by looking within, but
rather by looking above in a contemplation of eternal
reasons. Lonergan notes that it is disputed by Au-
gustinian interpreters just how literally Augustine
intended this inspection of the eternal to be understood. One interpreter of Augustine was Aquinas, and
Lonergan says that Aquinas insisted that Augustine's
Uncreated Light grounds the truth of our judgments,
not because we _see_ that Light, but because our intellects are created participations of this Light. Still,
Lonergan observes that the ambiguity of Augustine's

142

meaning of "looking at the Uncreated Light" led a group of nineteenth-century Catholics (the ontologists) to appeal to Augustine for their insistence (against Kant) that the notion of being was an obscure intuition of God.

Just as empiricism can corrupt a notion of judgment, so Lonergan adds that it can corrupt a notion of human understanding. Here, he refers to Scotus again, whose notion of abstraction included a second step in which the intellect took a look at the conceptual content produced in the intellect by the automatic and unconscious co-operation of the intellective and imaginative powers of the soul. Lonergan attributes such intellectual empiricism as well to Platonist thought (the spiritual eye of the soul looking at or recalling universals), and adds that Aristotelian thought too probably is empiricist (physics as a study of 'bodies'). Even Aquinas is not above suspicion, for though Lonergan and other commentators of Aquinas are convinced that Aquinas was no empiricist, it remains that most commentators presume that Thomist psychology is much the same as that of Scotus.

The new problem, of course, arose with modern science. If one holds that human knowing must somehow be experiencing, looking, or intuiting, then science can reach knowledge of reality only if that which is given to sense is merely apparent and unreal. That is, if scientific knowledge is the ex-

143

emplar of human knowledge, then ordinary, commonsense knowledge must be of what is only apparent but
not really real. And so Lonergan summarizes the
modern philosophical conflict with science:

> The conflict between objectivity as
> extroversion and intelligence as know-
> ledge has provided a fundamental theme
> in the unfolding of modern philosophy.
> Cartesian dualism was the juxtaposition
> of the rational affirmation, Cogito,
> ergo sum, and of the 'already out there
> now real' stripped of its secondary qual-
> ities and of any substantiality distinct
> from spatial extension. While Spinoza
> and Malebranche attempted to swallow the
> dualism on the rationalist side, Hobbes
> reduced thinking to an unprivileged in-
> stance of matter in motion. The Cam-
> bridge Platonists endeavoured to accept
> Hobbes' conception of the real as 'out
> there now' and yet to affirm God as su-
> premely real because his omnipresence
> was the reality of space and his eter-
> nity was the reality of time. Berkeley
> sought the same end by a different route;
> he granted secondary qualities to be mere
> appearance, and concluded that primary
> qualities with still greater certainty
> were mere appearance; being then was be-
> ing perceived, and so reality shifted
> from apparent 'bodies' to the cognitional
> order. Finally, Hume brought analysis to
> bear effectively on the issue; our know-
> ing involves not only elements but also
> unities and relations; the elements con-
> sist in a manifold of unrelated sense im-
> pressions; the unities and relations have
> no better foundation than our mental hab-
> its and beliefs; whatever may be the prac-
> tical utility of our knowledge, at least
> it cannot pretend to philosophic validity.[95]

There is, perhaps, no need to remind the reader
that Lonergan is not advocating a wholesale rejection
of the philosophies mentioned in the passage just
quoted; rather, he is offering a critique centered in
the single yet (for him) foundational issue of cognitional theory, whereby these various philosophies
explicitly or implicitly propose a self-understanding
of the method and function of philosophy as a distinct
and specialized area of knowledge. Indeed, each of
the philosophies mentioned is for Lonergan a step in
the ongoing dialectic whereby philosophy sought to
clarify its identity in a world increasingly in awe
of scientific achievement; each is a mixture of valid
insight and erroneous oversight, and what Lonergan is
trying to do, in this fourteenth chapter of Insight,
is to sketch the underlying dilemma and confusion that
arises when human knowing itself is not understood in
both its forms.

An important step in this process was taken by
Kant, who sought to avoid the extremes of rationalism
and naive realism by reaffirming and bringing together
again the two forms of human knowing. Now Lonergan's
critique of Kant is a recurrent theme woven subtly
into the entire structure of Insight, and it is quite
beyond the scope of my present work to repeat that
critique in its entirety. But at least I can draw
attention to Kant's involvement in the problem of empiricism, as outlined by Lonergan in the historical
scheme I am presently considering. The immediate

background to this specific critique of Kant is the
Kantian effort to uncover the fixed set of a priori
and synthetic premises that could serve as the basis
for a concrete deduction of all human knowing; I discussed this earlier under the heading of "deductive
methods." Lonergan now adds a further approximation
that pinpoints more exactly the restrictive character
of Kantian thought that, for all its speculative power
and significance, nevertheless is entangled in empiricist presuppositions that demand the existence of an
unknown "thing-in-itself" - a problem that was seen,
not only by Lonergan writing today, but as well by
German idealists in the Kantian and post-Kantian era.
Firstly, then, the statement of Lonergan, then a few
additional comments:

> If it is merely confusion of thought that
> interprets objectivity in terms of extro-
> version, Kant's Copernican revolution was
> a half-hearted affair. He pronounced both
> primary and secondary qualities to be
> phenomena. He made absolute space and
> absolute time a priori forms of outer and
> inner sense. He regarded the things them-
> selves of Newtonian thought to be unknow-
> able. But he was unable to break cleanly
> from the basic conviction of animal extro-
> version that the 'real' is the 'already
> out there now.' Though unknowable, New-
> ton's things themselves were somehow known
> to produce impressions on our senses and
> to appear. The category of reality was to
> be employed by understanding when there
> occurred some filling in the empty form of
> time. The category of substance was iden-
> tified with the permanence of reality in
> time. However convinced Kant was that

'taking a look' could not be valid human
knowing, he devoted his energies to showing how it could seem to be knowing and
in what sense it could be regarded as
valid. Nor is the anomaly of his position surprising. If the schematism of
the categories comes within striking distance of the virtually unconditioned,
still Kant failed to see that the unconditioned is a constituent component in
the genesis of judgment and so he relegated it to the role of a regulative i-
deal of systematizing rationality. But
once extroversion is questioned, it is
only through man's reflective grasp of
the unconditioned that the objectivity
and validity of human knowing can be established. Kant rightly saw that animal
knowing is not human knowing; but he
failed to see what human knowing is. The
combination of that truth and that failure is the essence of the principle of
immanence that was to dominate subsequent
thought.[96]

A commentary on this passage seems possible only
by writing a separate book or by an over-simplification
of the issues. But perhaps I could note that for Lonergan, the inadequacy of Kantian philosophy lies neither in Kant's formulation of the philosophical problem nor in Kant's conviction regarding the a priori
of human understanding. Rather, Lonergan understands
the key inadequacy to lie in Kant's doctrine that the
a priori forms of sensibility and data constitute mere
appearances - a fundamentally empiricist viewpoint.
Hence, without an anchoring in concretely known reality,
the Kantian notion of judgment is incapable of being a
notion that insists on a grasp of an unconditioned as

II.

constitutive of judgment. As Lonergan elsewhere
noted, the Kantian judgment is only a mediate knowledge of objects, a representation of a representation, as Kant himself stated; so it is, that reason
is never related to objects themselves, but only to
understanding and, through understanding, to the
empirical use of reason itself; and Lonergan concludes:

> Since our only cognitional activity im-
> mediately related to objects is intui-
> tion, it follows that the value of our
> judgments and our reasoning can be no
> more than the value of our intuitions.
> But our only intuitions are sensitive;
> sensitive intuitions reveal not being
> but phenomena; and so our judgments and
> reasoning are confined to a merely phe-
> nomenal world.[97]

In other words, Lonergan criticizes Kant for an
inadequate notion of objectivity, one that rests on
empiricist principles. And, as Lonergan mentioned
in the earlier passage from Insight, this inadequacy
results in various doctrines of immanentism, according to which the human subject, as knower, is locked
up within himself or herself, quite unable to know
reality as real. So Lonergan mentions that Kant's
attempt to fuse disparate forms of knowing into a
single whole ended in the destruction of each form
of knowing by the other, thereby destroying the realism of both forms. And while this had the advan-
tage of overcoming an older materialism and sensism,
Lonergan finds that it opened the door to positivism

148

and pragmatism that are merely more cultured forms of
materialism and sensism. And in this context, Lonergan points to the inadequacy of Husserl's phenomenology as just a purified empiricism.[98]

Just as one can join the empiricists in insisting that only science gives knowledge of the real,
while sense offers only appearance, so Lonergan next
studies the contrary view that only commonsense can
reach knowledge of the real, while science is valid
only to the extent it can be reduced to a confirmation
of commonsense views. Such is what Lonergan refers to
as commonsense eclecticism, the third of the methods
that would guide the human subject towards the goal of
knowledge.

(d) Commonsense Eclecticism - Lonergan begins
his discussion of commonsense eclecticism by describing its relevance to the history of philosophy:

> The third of the methods that would guide
> the philosopher to his goal is common-
> sense eclecticism. If it rarely is adop-
> ted by original thinkers, it remains the
> inertial centre of the philosophic pro-
> cess. From every excess and aberration
> men swing back to common sense, and per-
> haps no more than a minority of students
> and professors, of critics and historians,
> ever wander very far from a set of assump-
> tions that are neither formulated nor
> scrutinized.[99]

He goes on to describe the programme of commonsense
eclecticism as giving due recognition to the world
of theoretical understanding and granting that world

a remote possibility of success. Still, common sense
would urge the existence of countless problems that
theory has failed to resolve in the past, present,
and foreseeable future; and common sense would direct
attention to this problematic past and complex present
and insecure future, insisting that the proper course
of action is simply sound judgment that rejoices in a
common touch, a healthy sense of reality, and a proportioned balance. Such sound judgment becomes the
guiding principle of a philosophic viewpoint and thoroughly enlightened stance. So Lonergan describes its
programme:

> . . . opinions are legion; theories rise,
> glow, fascinate, and vanish; but sound
> judgment remains. And what is sound judg-
> ment? It is to bow to the necessary, to
> accept the certain, merely to entertain
> the probable, to distrust the doubtful,
> to disregard the merely possible, to laugh
> at the improbable, to denounce the impos-
> sible, and to believe what Science says.
> Nor are these precepts empty words, for
> there are truths that one cannot reject in
> practical living, there are others which
> it would be silly to doubt, there are
> claims to truth that merit attention and
> consideration, and each of these has its
> opposites. List the lot, draw out their
> implications, and you will find that you
> already possess a sound philosophy that
> can be set down in a series of proposi-
> tions confirmed by proofs and fortified
> by answers to objections.[100]

From this comprehensive programme Lonergan chooses
to single out only what one's philosophy will be, if
one chooses commonsense eclecticism as a method. To

this end, he refers back to the initial part of Insight and his discussion there of the validity and limitations of common sense. Its limitations lie in its inability to know its own nature, to know it is restricted to the concrete and particular in familiar situations, to know its aberrations that so easily arise from dramatic, individual, group, and general bias. Doubtless it is a valid, necessary and quite irreplaceable type of human knowing, yet it is in need of a prior critique from outside itself if it is to function authentically within its own sphere. And commonsense eclecticism, as a philosophical viewpoint, rejects such criticism and purification, placing commonsense practicality as the aim of philosophy.

Accordingly, notes Lonergan, such eclecticism brushes aside the genuine aim of philosophy that lies in the unfolding of the pure desire to know and in the ordering comprehensively of all departments of human knowing. In its place there is substituted the spontaneous subject, for whom genuine theory is simply beyond that subject's horizon. It follows that commonsense eclecticism denies the vital growth of philosophy, and holds that all philosophy (except its own) is far too profound and very silly, if not actually dangerous to read. Finally, the principle of sound judgment is posited without a concomitant effort to understand what one judges, and the absence of due understanding leads one to ask irrelevant questions and to treat them indefinitely, and leads others to take up the slack left by unanswered issues by imposing authoritarian systems and bandwagon cultures. However, this blindness of common sense to its own limitations and the recurrent aberrations in human knowing may itself be raised to the level of speculation and made the dialectical pole in the unfolding of the human desire to know. And so we come to Lonergan's discussion of Hegelian dialectic.

(e) Hegelian Dialectic - Lonergan's discussion of Hegelian Dialectic in Chapter Fourteen of Insight is devoted largely to a comparison between Hegel's notion of dialectic and Lonergan's own notion of dialectic. Elements of Lonergan's critique of Hegel receive due mention, but throughout the discussion one has the impression that Lonergan is merely summarizing what he elsewhere said. This impression is accurate, and so I would here direct attention to Chapter Twelve of Insight, entitled The Notion of Being. As well, I readily confess the inadequacy of my procedure that attempts to treat sections of Insight quite out of context, and so beg the understanding of my readers.

Still, there is perhaps some justification for my method, inasmuch as Lonergan himself opens his Chapter Twelve discussion of Hegel with a reference to the discussion he will lead in Chapter Fourteen. Lonergan is discussing various notions of being in the history of philosophy, most of which were concerned with the perennial problem of the unity of

being and the multiplicity of beings. After mentioning the thought of Scotus, Lonergan turns to
Hegel:

> Five hundred years separate Hegel from
> Scotus. As will appear from our discus-
> sion of the method of metaphysics, that
> notable interval of time was largely de-
> voted to working out in a variety of man-
> ners the possibilities of the assumption
> that knowing consists in taking a look.
> The ultimate conclusion was that it did
> not and could not. If the reader does
> not himself accept that conclusion as
> definitive, certainly Hegel did and so
> Hegel could not take advantage of the
> Scotist escape from the identification
> of the notion of being with the notion
> of nothing. But Hegel was boxed on the
> other side as well. He effectively ack-
> nowledged a pure desire with an unre-
> stricted objective. But he could not
> identify that objective with a universe
> of being, with a realm of factual exist-
> ents and occurrences. For being as fact
> can be reached only in so far as the vir-
> tually unconditioned is reached; and as
> Kant had ignored that constitutive com-
> ponent of judgment, so Hegel neither re-
> discovered nor re-established it. The
> only objective Hegel can offer the pure
> desire is a universe of all-inclusive
> concreteness that is devoid of the ex-
> istential, the factual, the virtually
> unconditioned. There is no reason why
> such an objective should be named being.
> It is, as Hegel named it, an Absolute
> Idea. It is the all-inclusive summit of
> the pure desire's immanent dialectical
> process from position through opposition
> to sublation that yields a new position
> to recommence the triadic process until
> the Absolute Idea is reached.[101]

II.

Lonergan's critique of Hegel, then, is included mainly within the context of a discussion of the notion of being. Both Hegel and Lonergan acknowledge the fact of the unrestricted desire to know an unrestricted objective. Their difference lies in the fact that Lonergan identifies that objective with a universe of being, while Hegel identifies it with an Absolute Idea that is devoid of the factual, the existential, the virtually unconditioned. And Lonergan traces this inadequacy in the Hegelian system to the Kantian legacy that made the thing-in-itself existent but unknowable; it was but a small step to pronounce the unknowable as non-existent, and this step was taken by Hegel.

This mistaken view of human judgment, inherited from Kant, is the core of the Hegelian inadequacy, at least in the interpretation by Lonergan:

> (Hegel's) viewpoint is essentially the
> viewpoint of a thinker who does not and
> cannot regard the factual as uncondi-
> tioned, who cannot acknowledge any fac-
> tually fixed points of reference, who
> cannot advance by distinguishing the de-
> finitively certain, the more or less
> probable, and the unknown. Hegel's
> range of vision is enormous; indeed, it
> is unrestricted in extent. But it is
> always restricted in content, for it
> views everything as it would be if there
> were no facts. It is a restricted view-
> point that can topple outwards into the
> factualness of Marx or inwards into the
> factualness of Kierkegaard. It is a
> viewpoint that is transcended automati-
> cally by anyone that, in any instance,

grasps the virtually unconditioned and
affirms it.[102]

Clearly, Lonergan's critique of Hegel (as of Kant)
presupposes Lonergan's notion of judgment as a grasp
of the virtually unconditioned tied intimately to the
factual, to reality. I acknowledge this, and presuppose it in my presentation of Lonergan's philosophical
dialectic of methods in philosophy. Still, there is
at least little difficulty in offering a critique of
philosophies that have been judged generally inadequate, though I believe Lonergan has pinpointed the
inadequacy in a way that is both accurate and precise.
Nevertheless, despite the general rejection of empiricism and idealism by many thinkers, there is as well a
profound respect for the systems engendered by such
views. And it may be asked if, perhaps, Lonergan shares
in that respect or has just casually dismissed past
philosophies as totally irrelevant.

I have already mentioned that Lonergan is concerned with isolating the fundamental inadequacy in
the explicit or implicit cognitional theory of the
various philosophies, and thereby chooses to prescind
from other dimensions of those philosophies. But here,
in this discussion of Hegel, it seems well to draw attention to the fact that Lonergan acknowledges a profound debt to the past and present philosophers. Generally, that debt recognizes the philosophic heritage
which posed questions and gave answers that underpin
present-day philosophic discussion; Lonergan is not

II.

operating in some twentieth-century vacuum, aloof
from any and all philosophic tradition, but understands himself as inheriting that tradition and
seeking to come to terms with it. Specifically,
one could point to Lonergan's use of terms borrowed
from (and adapted from) empiricist, idealist, and
existentialist philosophies, all the while mindful
of the critique Lonergan makes of each of these philosophies. But here, the best proof of interdependence
is Lonergan's footnote to his discussion of Hegel:

> It is not to be inferred that my attitude
> towards Hegel is merely negative. In
> fact, characteristic features in the very
> movement of his thought have their paral-
> lels in the present work (Insight). As
> his Aufhebung both rejects and retains,
> so also in their own fashion do our higher
> viewpoints. As he repeatedly proceeds
> from an sich, through für sich, to an und
> für sich, so our whole argument is a move-
> ment from the objects of mathematical,
> scientific and common-sense understanding,
> through the acts of understanding them-
> selves, to an understanding of understand-
> ing.[103]

There is no doubt in my mind that Lonergan's thought
has been positively influenced by the great philosophical systems of the past and the present. Nor is
there any doubt that his fundamental proposal could
be enriched considerably by drawing upon these same
systems for a more detailed conceptualization. Indeed,
such enrichment is demanded by Lonergan's fundamental
concern and by his conviction that philosophies invariably are engaged in an ongoing dialectic of developing

insight and refinement. To paraphrase Hegel, Enlightenment is a permanent task, rather than a permanent
achievement.

To return now to our Chapter Fourteen of Insight,
it is worth noting that Lonergan devotes more space to
a discussion of the sixth proposal for philosophic
method than to any one of the previous five. That
proposal is the one put forth by scientists themselves
in their conclusions as to what philosophy should be
doing, and to it we may now turn.

(f) Scientific Method and Philosophy - I have
already mentioned Lonergan's account of the philosophic problem as the struggle to understand and to integrate two quite different kinds of knowledge. Further, I have been giving Lonergan's heuristic scheme
of philosophic methods proposed to resolve that problem, particularly in the modern era when the difference between common sense and theory has been brought
home so forcefully by theoretical empirical science.
In this final section Lonergan invites us to consider
the tendency of scientists themselves to pronounce on
this question of the integration of human knowledge.
Quite unexpectedly, such pronouncements occur within
the scientific horizon, so that the hoped-for integration is to be an achievement of scientific method
itself, consistently revealing the ignorance and use-
lessness of common sense, and with equal consistency
urging the identification of philosophy with scientific
method.

II.

Lonergan distinguishes two phases in this tendency by scientists to resolve the philosophic problem by scientific method and achievement. The earlier phase is described by Lonergan as scientific monism, that regarded the various philosophies as misguided efforts to attain the knowledge that science alone can bestow. In that phase, the integration of human knowledge was to be a matter of the unification of the various sciences, a unification to be achieved by empiricist procedures. Such was mechanist determinism that saw the universe as consisting of imaginable elements linked together in space and time by natural laws; for inasmuch as one could imagine the elements, the universe was mechanist; and inasmuch as the laws were necessary, the mechanism was determinist. Accordingly, notes Lonergan, the fundamental science was mechanics, while all other sciences were conceived as just macroscopic viewpoints of a reality that basically and actually was microscopic; and scientists operated with unquestioning belief that their mechanist views of objectivity, knowledge, and belief were uniquely valid.

That earlier phase, according to Lonergan, has been steadily disappearing under the weight of recent scientific achievements. Here, Lonergan mentions the work of Darwin, Freud, and Einstein, as well as the field of quantum mechanics, all of which reveal a universe that is neither mechanist nor determinist. In this second phase, scientists are increasingly aware of the complexity of human knowledge, of the error involved in thinking of knowledge in terms of looking,

158

of the need to think rather in terms of experiencing, understanding, and judging so that the 'real' is not what can be imagined, but rather what can be verified. Further, such verification is a matter, not of some particular scientific affirmation that approximates the facts, but of general affirmations wherein groups of groups of particular affirmations converge with hopefully increasing accuracy.

But Lonergan would draw our attention to the tendency of scientists to carry over into this new phase many of the totalitarian ambitions that characterized the old:

> Scientific monism not only identified science with philosophy but also concluded that the method of science must be the method of philosophy. While this implication cannot be challenged as long as the premise stands, the break-down of the premise cannot be expected to transform the long-established habits of mind that were generated and nourished by the conclusion. Only through a positive accumulation of new insights can scientists be expected to grasp the differences between the methods of empirical science and the method that must be followed if the detached and disinterested desire to know is to attain an integrated view of the universe.[104]

With this in mind Lonergan devotes the remainder of this section to a discussion of three main differences between scientific method and philosophic method, showing thereby the futility in trying to reduce one to the other. Because of the importance of this entire ques-

II.

tion in current discussions of Wissenschaftstheorie,
I wish to present a rather full account of Lonergan's
thought on this matter.

The basic difference, according to Lonergan, lies
in the quite different correlations of method and results. The scientist employs properly scientific method
in scientific investigations, but the use of that method
does not predetermine the results that the scientist
will achieve; rather, the same basic set of procedures
will lead to a variety of different goals, a variety
of different objects, each particular and determinate.
But in philosophy, the method that one chooses predetermines what one's philosophy will be; for philosophy is
concerned with an integrated view of the universe, and
there is only one integrated view of one universe and
only one set of directives that lead to it. And philosophy obtains this integrated view of a single universe, not by employing the categorically determinate
methods of science, but by relating the categorically
determined results of all scientific and commonsense
methods in a higher unification that, for Lonergan, is
the integral heuristic structure:

> Metaphysics does not undertake either to dis-
> cover or to teach science; it does not under-
> take either to develop or to impart common
> sense; it does not pretend to know the uni-
> verse of proportionate being independently
> of science and common sense; but it can and
> does take over the results of such distinct
> efforts, it works them into coherence by re-
> versing their counter-positions, and it knits
> them into a unity by discerning in them the
> concrete prolongations of the integral heur-

160

istic structure which it itself is.[105]

Besides this difference in the functions of scientific and philosophic methods, there is, secondly, a difference in linguistic technique. Scientists commonly reach a single, precise, universally accepted, technical language. Philosophers, on the other hand, employ language that is equivocal and literary. Here, Lonergan would point to the difficulties in developing a technical language for philosophy, a language that communicates accurately the meaning of knowledge, reality, and objectivity - the fundamental problems of philosophy. The difficulty lies in the very ambiguity of these terms and the failure of philosophers to agree among themselves on these fundamental issues. Hence, the task of working out a technical language for philosophy demands long and painstaking efforts that explore the meaning of fundamental terms in different systems, that evaluate tneir possible combinations, and that are open to continual refinement. Even then, however, philosophy invariably will have to have recourse to ordinary and non-tecnnical language, at least as a pedagogical tool in reaching the changing mentalities of different generations.

A third difference noted by Lonergan lies in the group mentalities of the scientist and philosopher. Scientists presuppose and build on the achievement of a four-centuries-old scientific community, and no scientist feels obliged to repeat all the work of his or her predecessors and contemporaries. But philosophers cannot be so presumptuous about their belief in the

II.

correctness of past philosophic achievement. Philosophies have been many, and the many have more often
than not been in dialectical opposition with one another; so Lonergan writes:

> Instead of a single tradition with dis-
> tinct departments as in science, philos-
> ophy has been a cumulative multiplication
> of distinct and opposed traditions. Nor
> is there anything surprising about this
> contrast. For in science a single method
> operates towards a variety of different
> goals, but in philosophy a single all-
> inclusive goal is sought by as many dif-
> ferent methods as arise from different
> orientations of the historically develop-
> ing but polymorphic consciousness of man.
> Hence, while a scientist is reasonable in
> entering into the scientific tradition
> and carrying on its work, a philosopher
> cannot be reasonable on the same terms;
> he has to become familiar with different
> traditions; he has to find grounds for
> deciding between them; and it is the rea-
> sonableness of that decision on which
> will rest the reasonableness of his col-
> laboration within any single tradition.[106]

Accordingly, Lonergan indicates the centrality of personal commitment and personal knowledge in doing philosophy, for philosophic issues cannot be settled by
consulting handbooks, referring to the successful experiments of others, or by urging acceptance of the
work of some philosophic genius. Instead, philosophic
evidence is within the philosopher himself or herself,
and it is only by the method of personal experiment
that one uncovers the meaning of attentiveness and in-
attentiveness, intelligence and stupidity, reasonable-

162

II.

ness and rashness, responsibility and indecision. And so Lonergan describes his notion of the philosophical vocation:

> Philosophic evidence is within the philosopher himself. It is his own inability to avoid experience, to renounce intelligence in inquiry, to desert reasonableness in reflection. It is his own detached, disinterested desire to know. It is his own advertence to the polymorphism of his own consciousness. It is his own insight into the manner in which insights accumulate in mathematics, in the empirical sciences, in the myriad instances of common sense. It is his own grasp of the dialectical unfolding of his own desire to know in its conflict with other desires that provides the key to his own philosophic development and reveals his own potentialities to adopt the stand of any of the traditional or of the new philosophic schools. Philosophy is the flowering of the individual's rational consciousness in its coming to know and take possession of itself. To that event, its traditional schools, its treatises, and its history are but contributions; and without that event they are stripped of real significance.[107]

Lonergan, then, would draw attention to three main differences between science and philosophy, and his purpose in doing so is to suggest that scientists may easily overlook these differences and may tend to reduce philosophy to science. The fact that philosophic method predetermines philosophic results may be understood by the scientist to mean that philosophy has no method of its own at all, and would do well to follow scientific procedures. Again, the absence of

163

II.

a precise technical language in philosophy may be taken by the scientist as testimony to the obtuseness of philosophers, who would do well by imitating the precision of scientific linguistic achievement. Finally, and as Lonergan suspects most likely, scientists will fail to grasp that philosophy is a matter of personal development and personal commitment; all too readily the scientist will be attracted by the recent philosophies associated with symbolic logic that offer an impersonal and automatic deductivism. Moreover, and perhaps of special relevance to my present topic, Lonergan notes that the scientist will hope for the integration of the sciences, not from an autonomous philosophy, but from within science itself; for Lonergan, this hope is in vain, for scientists are human and share the human lot of being involved in issues of knowledge, reality, and objectivity that simply cannot be resolved on scientific terms alone.

To conclude this lengthy section, allow me to recall what my purpose has been. The eventual aim is to understand Lonergan's understanding of theology in its new context, and this for the purpose of discovering the autonomous function of theology yet also its integration with other, non-theological specializations. Lonergan's proposal rests upon his understanding of the various developments in the medieval and modern periods that call for a reformulation of the function of theology as well. Hence, my first step has been to trace Lonergan's thought on those

164

developments in history, and so I have presented two
sections on the movement of philosophy towards autonomy and one section on the emergence of science as
autonomous. There remains a consideration of historical scholarship as a specialty and, in the final section, a discussion about the impact of that scholarship
on philosophy.

(4) The Autonomy of Scholarship

I have been tracing Lonergan's account of a number
of developments in medieval and modern Western culture
that have transformed this culture through a steady replacement of former views. In an initial move medieval
theology worked out its proper method by distinguishing
itself from philosophy. This led to a philosophy more
and more concerned to work out its own proper method,
and for a time it was able to assert its independence
from theology as well as its continuity with scientific
reflection. In a second move modern empirical science
gradually claimed its autonomy as a specialization in
its own right, breaking away from its philosophical
bonds and working out its own methods and aims. In a
third move the autonomy of modern science enabled philosophy to take another step towards formulating its
own purpose and method, resulting in a philosophy that
repudiated its ancient Greek heritage. In brief, the
first three topics have treated the separation of philosophy from theology, the gradual differentiation of
science from philosophy, and the movement from Renaissance to modern philosophy.

II.

For Lonergan, these developments were shifts within the cultural academic realm - within the reflective, objectifying understanding of the meaning of the world. There was not a modern discovery of science, but rather a shift from an Aristotelian to a modern notion of science. Philosophy was not an invention of modern times, but there was a notable shift from a Renaissance to a modern concept of philosophy. But besides these developments within the cultural academic realm, Lonergan would draw attention as well to another sort of development that involved a discipline in the ordinary realm of everyday culture applying for membership in the academic structure. Here he is referring to the fact of historical studies, that moved from being a rather naive assessment of the past to become a full-fledged and critical specialization, a quite distinct type of intellectual development on the academic level.

Before discussing this development, there is need to state more precisely just what Lonergan means by the term "scholarship." Generally, then, he has in mind the group of studies that are referred to as the cultural sciences or Geisteswissenschaften, such as philology, exegesis, history. These studies, as distinct from the natural sciences or Naturwissenschaften, are concerned with an understanding, not of nature, but of humanity. Further, the understanding of humanity sought by scholarship is not the generalizing sort of understanding that seeks a systematic grasp of mankind in terms of definitions, general truths, inferences,

166

such as in economics, psychology or sociology. Rather, scholarship is for Lonergan the search for an understanding of humanity's understanding of humanity; it seeks to study mankind as cultural, as expressing itself through acts of meaning, as historically conditioned. Scholarship, then, in the sense intended by Lonergan, is distinct from both natural science and the so-called behavioral sciences. And for Lonergan, it is distinct as well from philosophy, even though it cannot escape involvement in philosophical questions, just as modern science generally is involved in philosophic issues.[108]

Lonergan is aware that the notion of scholarship as an understanding of humanity's understanding of humanity is rather recent. If contemporary scholarship is dedicated to the reconstruction of the constructions of the human spirit in all their diversity and plurality, an earlier brand of historical studies was dedicated to propagating the uniqueness and superiority of a single culture, namely, the classicist. While this normative notion of culture as a permanent and universal achievement is often traced back to classical Greek philosophy, a more correct assessment attributes this non-critical historical view to the popularizers of philosophy in the Greek and Roman worlds, popularizers described by Lonergan as "the humanists, the orators, the school-teachers, . . . the men who simplified and watered down philosophic thought and then peddled it to give the slow-witted an exaggerated opinion of their wisdom and knowledge."[109] This assessment by Lonergan

resembles that by Bruno Snell. Snell writes that
against Plato, who strove to re-direct man's attention to the God who is the measure of all things,
Isocrates and the Sophists insisted that humanity is
the measure of all things; and it was this autonomy
of the commonsense, sophisticated, educated humanity
from any higher being that elevated classicist culture
to its normative status.[110]

However, Lonergan acknowledges that Greek philosophy itself played at least a negative role in this
canonization of classicist culture. So, in the previous section, I mentioned Lonergan's conviction that
Greek philosophy, while it distinguished itself from
commonsense thinking, offered nonetheless a notion of
science that was concerned with what is necessary, universal, eternal. The world of human affairs, then,
could be studied "scientifically" inasmuch as it par-
took in those qualities; and so there was a study, not
of human historicity, but of a human nature that remained constant for all people at all places and at all
times. In a word, Greek philosophy did not generally
encourage the study of what was merely of common sense,
merely contingent and passing. So Lonergan notes that
it was perhaps only to be expected that Greek humanism,
having no time for the subtleties of Plato and Aristotle, leapt to the conclusion that what philosophy did
not concern itself with was evident in all its splen-
dour before the eyes of common sense:

>It was on a rising tide of linguistic feed-
>back that logic and philosophy and early

science emerged. But such technical
achievements may repel rather than im-
press. One may be content to marvel at
the fact of language, the fact that makes
man unique among the animals. One may
with Isocrates trace cities and laws,
arts and skills and, indeed, all aspects
of culture to man's powers of speech and
persuasion. One may go on to urge one's
fellow townsmen to seek eloquence through
education and thereby to excel among men
in the very respect in which man excels
among the animals. So to be educated
linguistically and to become human are
found to be interchangeable. So there
emerged one strand of humanism that
spread from Greece to Rome and from
antiquity to the late middle ages.[111]

In a word, within the Aristotelian context especially, Lonergan interprets the study of mankind as
a well-rounded, closed, and past achievement, rather
than an ongoing discovery of human inventiveness. The
constant flux of historical process was viewed as
merely contingent and rather incidental to an understanding of mankind: for this was a matter of opinion,
practice, and prudence, excluded from science, theory,
and wisdom.[112]

As Lonergan mentioned, this classicist context
prevailed for centuries, was sometimes obscured, yet
received new life in the ideals of Renaissance humanism.
Yet even there, he notes that the seeds of its destruction had been planted in the sporadic yet impressive
achievements of Renaissance science. As mankind's control over nature gained ever further ground; as attention turned away from the spiritual to the worldly a-

169

chievement of the human spirit; as explorers encountered distant lands with strange people and very non-classicist cultures, it became increasingly obvious that classicism was not the whole story. It became clear to many that classicism was but one of many possible worldviews, that people past and present have been engaged in interpreting the world and themselves in different ways, that the path to the future would be for ourselves to go and do likewise, as best we can, and, while learning from the past, refusing to cling to past mistakes. So Lonergan contrasts the Renaissance classicist worldview with that of the modern pluralist worldview - a contrast between human nature and human historicity:

> The pluralist, then, differs from the classicist inasmuch as he acknowledges human historicity both in principle and in fact. Historicity means - very briefly - that human living is informed by meanings, that meanings are the product of intelligence, that human intelligence develops cumulatively over time, and that such cumulative development differs in different histories.
>
> Classicism itself is one very notable and, indeed, very noble instance of such cumulative development. It is not mistaken in its assumption that there is something substantial and common to human nature and human activity. Its oversight is its failure to grasp that something substantial and common also is something quite open. It may be expressed in the four transcendental precepts: Be attentive, Be intelligent, Be reasonable, Be responsible. But there is an almost endless manifold of

situations to which men successively
attend. There vary enormously the type
and degree of intellectual and moral development brought to deal with situations. The standard both for human reasonableness and for the strength and
delicacy of a man's conscience is satis-
fied only by a complete and life-long
devotion to human authenticity.[113]

This modern understanding of humanity clearly was
to have repercussions on those studies which sought
historical reconstruction of that understanding. Lonergan mentions the work of the historian Paul Hazard,
who showed that towards the end of the seventeenth
century, there emerged the beginnings of a new understanding of history. Initially, the rise of chronol-
ogy, archeological research, and philology served to
awaken scepticism about the assumptions and accounts
of previous historians. Their work, according to Lonergan, was increasingly judged to be an exercise in
rhetoric, rather than in historical exactitude, and was
meant to serve the interests of promoting classicist
norms and behavior, rather than to determine what in
fact had occurred in the past tradition. That previous work, in the terms of Lonergan, was a pre-critical history, advocating unquestioning belief in the
testimonies of past writers, and little concerned to
question the accuracy of what had been set forth by
the great figures of the past. The aim of such history had been the education of the masses, imparting
to them what Lonergan calls "a proper appreciation of
their heritage and a proper devotion to its preserva-

tion, development, dissemination."[114] This pre-critical history, then, was first and foremost intended to advance the interests of a group, whether social or cultural.[115]

But if there was a growing scepticism of the accuracy and procedures of pre-critical history, the new methods of historical investigation were themselves initially unable to hold out any credible promise that historical truth could ever be attained. These methods could more easily point out the errors in traditional views, than set scholars on a sure path to discovering the past; for the evidence available from that past was too fragmentary and the gaps in that evidence too numerous to reconstruct the actual course of events. Doubtless the fastest way to overcome the gaps was to disparage historical tradition itself and to start anew; and such a mentality is best associated with what Lonergan refers to as commonsense eclecticism, that I mentioned in the previous section. Perhaps inevitably in this break from pre-critical history scholars first invoked the principle of sound judgment and common sense in order to "objectively" assess past traditions and with equal "objectivity" reject those traditions as irrelevant to the pressing needs of the present. For it was now clear how modern humanity had far surpassed all its predecessors, making immense strides over the myths and stories clung to by less fortunate mortals. So for Lonergan, Enlightenment history at first came to be identified with continual progress towards further Enlightenment, Truth, and

172

Goodness; so he remarks that the great figures of the
French and German Enlightenment set forth successive
schemes of historical process and progress, that tended
generally to abstract from concrete historical events,
particularly those suggesting periods of decay and decline.[116]

If Enlightenment thinkers tended to view historical process abstractly, Lonergan adds that the idealist
tradition insisted on concrete particulars but as interpreted by a priori methods. Lonergan's interest here,
however, is not the philosophy of history, whether Enlightenment or idealist, but rather the work of historical scholars themselves. While such scholarship had a
small dose of empirical methodology in the seventeenth
and eighteenth centuries, the massive breakthrough of
critical history as a distinct discipline was the a-
chievement of German historians in the nineteenth century. So Lonergan, after noting the empirical approach
of modern science, describes a parallel development in
various human sciences, in philosophy, in hermeneutics,
and in critical history:

> This occurred in Germany and, as I cannot
> sketch the movement, I must be content to
> name a few of the originators. There was
> Friedrich Wolf who conceived classical
> philology to be a philosophico-historical
> study of human nature as exhibited in an-
> tiquity, and who brought together in his
> courses at Halle literature, antiquities,
> geography, art, numismatics, and the crit-
> ical spirit that produced his Prolegomena
> to Homer. There was Friedrich Schleier--
> macher who transformed hermeneutics from
> sets of rules of thumb followed by bibli-

cal or classical exegetes to a general
art of avoiding misunderstanding and misinterpretation. There was August Boeckh,
a pupil both of Wolf and of Schleiermacher, who conceived philology as the
reconstruction of the constructions of
the human spirit and wrote an Encyclopedia and Methodology of the Philologi-
cal Sciences. There was Leopold von
Ranke, who by his seminar and his writing
of history taught historians to keep the
passions of the present out of the facts
of the past, to base their facts on
strictly contemporary sources, and to
determine where the authors of the sources
got their information and how they used
it. There was Johann Gustav Droysen, who
lectured on the method of historical investigation and composed a text on the
subject. There was Wilhelm Dilthey who
endeavoured to work out the philosophical foundations for the new hermeneutics
and history.[117]

In similar vein as Lonergan, Bruno Snell notes that
it was this work that moved history from a pre-critical, classicist context into an empirical framework
concerned with setting forth the past as it was in
fact, and not as just a model of perfection to be imitated slavishly by all generations.[118]

In the lengthy passage just quoted from Lonergan, he distinguishes various levels of achievement
in the process that was the rise of critical historical scholarship.[119] Firstly, mention has already
been made of the early work of philologists, archeologists, and chronologists, and the grouping of this
and other work in the achievement of Friedrich Wolf
(1759-1824). According to Lonergan, Wolf envisioned

a comprehensive philology that would embrace philosophical criticism and empirical evidence from the
past.[120] In Wolf and others, then, Lonergan finds
a critical approach to the task of determining the
data from the past relevant to historical investigations, an approach that stood in contrast to both
a classicist canonization of past tradition and an
Enlightenment disregard of past tradition.

Secondly, Friedrich Schleiermacher (1768-1834)
was a theologian rather than a historian, yet Lonergan finds in Schleiermacher's work a fundamental
shift in historical methodology. Schleiermacher suggested that besides an understanding of the written
text and of that to which the text refers, the scholar
should also understand the author by striving to understand the succession of thoughts that led him or
her to write what in fact was written. Rather than
merely observe data, the scholar is to understand
both data and author, even if for Schleiermacher this
is mostly a matter of avoiding spontaneous misunder-
standings. Here, Lonergan finds in Schleiermacher's
work a refinement of the notion of Verstehen as operative in historical studies, a refinement that takes
the historian out of the closed circuit of both classicist and Enlightenment contentment with a thoroughly
non-academic understanding of the past.[121]

Thirdly, while Wolf, Schleiermacher, and Boeckh
were concerned mostly with the understanding of particular empirical evidence, other scholars sought to
generalize such hermeneutics in reference to an on-

going historical context. According to Lonergan
such generalization may be found in the work of Leopold von Ranke and Johann Droysen, although its formulation as a principle of historical investigation
occurs first in the work of Wilhelm Dilthey.[122]
Lonergan contends that while von Ranke's concept of
historical process is still under the influence of
idealism, Droysen sought a more precise analysis of
historical process by appealing to a critical dualism
of interacting thought and matter. For Droysen, "expression" has a broad meaning and can refer to the
objectifications, not just of individuals, but as
well of groups, nations, states, religions. Particularly in Droysen, then, Lonergan finds an emphasis
on critical historical judgment as relating historical
particulars in an account of what actually occurred
over time; and this clearly was a corrective to the
presumptuous and naive "sound judgment" approach urged
by both classicist and Enlightenment thinkers. Here,
Lonergan's interpretation resembles that of Gadamer,
who remarks that "by means of the concept of 'expression,' historical reality raises itself into the
sphere of meaning, and hence in Droysen's methodological self-analysis hermeneutics becomes master of the
study of history. 'The detail is understood within
the whole, and the whole from the detail.'"[123]

Accordingly, Lonergan concludes that it remained
only for Wilhelm Dilthey to indicate just what it was
that the historical document "expressed" and that the
scholar was attempting to understand. For Dilthey,

this is nothing else than human living as understood
by the authors of past documents, so that what exegetes and historians interpret is itself the product
of the understanding people have of themselves, their
situation, their role, the human condition: and such
for Lonergan is the meaning of Dilthey's phrase, Das
Leben selbst legt sich aus. As concerned with an understanding of mankind's understanding of itself,
Dilthey clearly distinguished the Geisteswissenschaften
from the natural sciences; these latter are concerned
simply with understanding nature, and not, obviously,
with understanding nature's understanding of itself.[124]

The foregoing is a brief outline of Lonergan's understanding of the development of historical studies
from being a pre-critical tool of a classicist or Enlightened common sense to becoming a critical specialization that sought a critical and empirical recovery
of the ordinary, commonsense living of the past.
Scholarship became the affair of a highly specialized
group of scholars who painstakingly and methodically
sought an accumulation of insights into the past that
would allow them to reconstruct, if only partially
and in passing fashion, the life and times of an earlier era. No longer was historical study the concern
of a cultured public seeking reinforcement of their
refinement and virtue. But neither was scholarship
reduced to theory in the manner of the natural sciences; for while Lonergan is aware that there are
scholars who view history in positivist terms as analogous to the natural sciences, he concurs with Col-

II.

lingwood's contention that such positivist views
are at least a century behind the times in their
ignorance of the crucial role of understanding in
the tasks of scholarship.[125]

Indeed, it is this role of understanding that
according to Lonergan introduces something of an
identity-crisis for scholars. Philologists, exegetes,
and historians do not generally offer detailed
accounts of cognitional theory, nor do they generally
offer to explain their epistemological principles
guiding their historical understanding. Rather,
scholars associate competence in their fields with
long and proved experience, submitted to their peers
for assessment and criticism. Still, Lonergan urges
that because understanding is crucial to their work,
some philosophy of interpretation and some philosophy
of history seem crucial to scholarly interpretations.[126]
And because historians and exegetes and philologists
themselves are generally silent on these issues, it
is not surprising to Lonergan that the rise of
critical scholarship attracted the attention of
the philosophical world. If philosophers had declared
their autonomy from theology, if the natural sciences
had declared their autonomy from philosophy, then
perhaps the role of philosophy could be defined in
reference to scholarship and to the notions of
Existenz and Geschichte upon which scholarly work
rested.

(5) The Autonomy of Philosophy: Part Three

Speaking of the rise of nineteenth-century German historical scholarship, Lonergan observes that the "background that gave this movement its sweep and profundity is to be traced to the French Enlightenment's dedication to human progress, it abhorred its abstract thinking. If it agreed with Hegel's insistence on concreteness and his concern with world history, it repudiated his a priori methods."[127] Now a guiding principle throughout this chapter is Lonergan's conviction that the rise of a specialization has repercussions on other specializations; and on the basis of this principle, we are led to expect an account by Lonergan of the impact of historical scholarship on philosophy especially, since it is the function of philosophy that Lonergan finds most in need of clarification.

Not unexpectedly, the initial emergence of critical scholarship was merged with a concern for philosophic issues that touched upon the work of scholars. So Lonergan's account of that emergence included mention of the philosophical contributions of Wolf, Schleiermacher, and Droysen to the clarification of scholarly methods. Nonetheless, as mentioned a moment ago, the concreteness of empirical historical research was clearly incompatible with both Enlightenment and Hegelian philosophical methods, the former being too abstract, and the latter being too restrictive in its a priori scheme of world history. Lonergan agrees with Kurt Frör, who found the rejection of idealism in scholarly circles to be accompanied by an

II.

increasing turn to positivism in the latter part of
the nineteenth century, leading to the crisis of historicism.[128] But historical scholars were by no means
alone in their rejection of idealism; philosophers
themselves had the beginnings of quite a new sort of
philosophical tradition in the work of Wolf, Schleiermacher, and Droysen, and the incompatibility of such
work with Hegelian a priori schemes became increasingly
evident in the course of the nineteenth century. As
Lonergan remarks in Insight, the Hegelian a priori neglect of facts was a restricted viewpoint that could
"topple outwards into the factualness of Marx or in-
wards into the factualness of Kierkegaard."[129]

For Lonergan, this concern for factualness characterizes the mainstream of philosophical thought from
Kierkegaard to the present day, and its varieties are
legion. Common to all varieties is the concern for
human deliberation, evaluation, decision, action.[130]
It is the recognition by philosophy of the primacy of
practical reason,[131] nor is it difficult to indicate
that Lonergan associates this turn to praxis as an
academic subject with the rise of critical scholarship. For that scholarship relativized the achievement of classicist culture, thereby putting an end
to what Lonergan calls "the age of innocence" - the
age that assumed the unblemished authenticity of Culture, and that identified this Culture exclusively
with the particular set of ideals propounded by both
classical and Renaissance humanists.[132] Against that
normative view, that held authenticity to reside auto-

matically in the Tradition, and that conceived personal authenticity as perfect conformity to that Tradition, critical scholarship uncovered a vast multiplicity of cultures and traditions, all of them very much man-made, and each of them a product, not only of human authenticity, but of human inauthenticity as well. This recognition of an ongoing dialectic of progress and decline within human cultures and traditions meant further that historical scholars themselves, standing within the horizon of these traditions and already shaped by them prior to their scholarly work, participated in this dialectic of authenticity and inauthenticity. And so Lonergan describes the end of an era when both cultural and personal authenticity could be taken for granted: speaking of the radical philosophic, ethical, and religious differences that can become traditional and that can infiltrate the process of socialization, acculturation, and education, he writes:

> Such radical and traditional differences put their stamp not only on the writings to be interpreted and the events to be narrated (in human studies - M. O'C.) but also upon the mindset, world view, horizon of exegetes and historians. In utopia, no doubt, everyone in all his words and deeds would be operating with the authenticity generated by meeting the exigencies of intelligence, reasonableness, responsibility. But our world is not utopia. Even if everyone manages to be perfectly authentic in all his own personal performance, still he cannot but

II.

> carry within himself the ballast of his
> tradition. And down the millenia in
> which that tradition developed, one can
> hardly exclude the possibility that un-
> authenticity entered in and remained to
> ferment the mass through the ages to
> come.
>
> So we come to the end of the age of in-
> nocence, the age that assumed that hu-
> man authenticity could be taken for
> granted. I do not mean that human wick-
> edness was denied. But it was felt it
> could be evaded. Truth was supposed to
> consist in the necessary conclusions de-
> duced from self-evident principles. Or
> it was thought that reality was already
> out there now, and that objectivity was
> the simple matter of taking a good look,
> seeing all that was there, and not see-
> ing what was not there. Or there was
> admitted the real existence of a criti-
> cal problem, but it was felt that a
> sound critical philosophy – such as
> Kant's or Comte's or some other – would
> solve it once for all.[133]

This priority of practical reason over speculative reason, of concrete existence within a community and tradition over inquiry and reflection into
the meaning and value of that community and tradition,
has for Lonergan been the theme most characteristic
of philosophy from Kierkegaard to the present day.
Lonergan finds this trend foreshadowed in the priority
of poetry that was proclaimed by Giambattista Vico
(1668-1744). Vico rejected the classical and Renaissance insistence that gave priority to the literal
meaning of words and phrases as set by human rationality, and that viewed figurative meaning as simply
an external garment, added to literal meaning to make

the latter more vivid or striking. For Vico, the
poetic, the figurative is basic meaning, and Lonergan interprets this as a fundamental insight into
the historicity of mankind: the triumph of logos
over myth and magic, of literal truth over figurative expression, of rhetoric over figures of speech,
all was necessary in the development of the human
mind, but Lonergan adds that the achievement can
solidify and easily obscure man's nature, constrict
his spontaneity, sap his vitality, and limit human
freedom. Hence when Lonergan asserts with Vico the
priority of poetry, Lonergan says he is proclaiming
that the human spirit expresses itself in symbols
before it knows, if ever it knows, what its symbols
literally mean. And here Lonergan notes the beginning of the effort to set aside the classical definition of person as rational animal, preparing the
way for cultural anthropologists' understanding of
person as symbolic animal, or for the personalists'
notion of person as incarnate spirit.[134]

It is especially in Kierkegaard's work that
Lonergan finds the beginnings of philosophic emphasis on human factualness, human existence, human
historicity, human praxis. If related to the rela-
tivization of classical and Renaissance Culture
that occurred with the rise of critical scholarship,
it was no less a reaction against a philosophic tradition that exploited the primacy of speculative intellect and that knowingly or unknowingly was the
spokesman for that particular and normative Culture.

II.

So Lonergan recalls Kierkegaard's complaint about
Hegelian insistence on logic; for Kierkegaard, what
is logical is also static, movement cannot be inserted
into a logic, and so Hegel's system has room, not for
existence (self-determining freedom), but only for
the idea of existence.[135]

To understand Lonergan's assessment of philosophy
in this, its latest stage, we can do no better than
consider the overview that he himself offers:

> It is only after the age of innocence
> that praxis becomes an academic sub-
> ject. A faculty psychology will give
> intellect precedence over will and
> thereby it will liberate the academic
> world from concern with the irrational
> in human life. The speculative intel-
> lect of the Aristotelians, the pure
> reason of the rationalists, the auto-
> matic progress anticipated by the lib-
> erals, all provided shelter for aca-
> demic serenity. But since the failure
> of the absolute idealists to encompass
> human history within the embrace of
> speculative reason, the issue of praxis
> has repeatedly come to the fore.
> Schopenhauer conceived the world in
> terms of will and representation.
> Kierkegaard insisted on faith. Newman
> toasted conscience. Marx was concerned
> not merely to know but principally to
> make history. Nietzsche proclaimed the
> will to power. Blondel strove for a
> philosophy of action. Paul Ricoeur has
> not yet completed his many-volumed
> philosophy of will, and Jürgen Habermas
> has set forth the involvement of human
> knowledge in human interests. Along
> with them have marched in varying ways
> pragmatists, personalists, and existen-
> tialists, while phenomenologists have

> supplanted faculty psychology with an
> intentionality analysis in which cog-
> nitional process is sublated by delib-
> eration, evaluation, decision, action.[136]

For Lonergan, then, the issue of modern philosophy in
its latest phase has quite correctly shifted to the
higher viewpoint that places rationality within the
broader horizon of praxis, freedom, liberty, responsibility, where the foundational concern is not necessary truth but human authenticity and human genuine-
ness. In this, Lonergan would agree with the general
direction in which philosophers are heading, and
would number himself among those concerned with promoting this trend.

At the same time, however, Lonergan would issue
a caveat regarding this philosophic attention to responsible subjectivity and existential intersubjectivity. He frequently acknowledges his debt to many of
the figures whom he mentions in the passage quoted a
moment ago, and has high praise, not just for the direction of their thinking, but also for the way in
which they have enriched contemporary thinking. Yet
he finds that many of them have leapt to the theme of
Existenz and Geschichte and Freiheit without bothering
to resolve the generally unresolved questions of cognitional theory, epistemology, and metaphysics,
thereby taking a turn to praxis that risks being inattentive, unintelligent, and unreasonable. For example, Lonergan expresses his reservations in the
following two passages:

I too hold for the primacy of conscience,
for the primacy of the questions that
lead to deliberation, evaluation, decision. Still, responsible answers to
those questions presuppose sound judgments of fact, of possibility, and of
probability. But such sound judgments,
in turn, presuppose that we have escaped
the clutches of naive realism, empiricism, critical and absolute idealism,
that we have succeeded in formulating a
critical realism.[137]

In the name of phenomenology, of existential self-understanding, of human encounter, of salvation history, there are
those that resentfully and disdainfully
brush aside the old questions of cognitional theory, epistemology, metaphysics.
I have no doubt, I never did doubt, that
the old answers were defective. But to
reject the questions as well is to refuse
to know what one is doing when one is
knowing; it is to refuse to know why doing that is knowing; it is to refuse to
set up a basic semantics by concluding
what one knows when one does it.[138]

Further, Lonergan finds in the all-too-frequent rejection of the questions concerning human rationality
the roots of the contemporary cult of the absurd that
has resulted in the alienated subject of present-day
cultures.[139] Here, I suspect that Lonergan is pointing to the fact that as "Enlightenment" can be invoked to so extol human rationality as to neglect human authenticity, so "Enlightenment" of a new kind
can be invoked to so extol human authenticity as to
neglect the rationality presupposed by such authenticity and a constitutive dimension of it.

It is worth mentioning that Lonergan himself

only rarely associated his <u>caveat</u> with specific philosophers or even philosophic trends of the past century. In <u>Insight</u>, Lonergan criticized Husserl for
his empiricist leanings, while in <u>Method</u> he offers
only very brief observations on the work of Dilthey,
Husserl, and Heidegger as contributing to the notion
of <u>Verstehen</u> in historical investigations. A more
extensive critique of "existentialism" was offered by
Lonergan at an institute in 1957, and passing references to that and related movements may be found scattered throughout his various writings.[140] I would
venture to say that Lonergan prefers to let the body
of his own work in <u>Insight</u> and <u>Method</u> be evaluated on
its own merits, and contrasted to the great figures
who have had such a profound effect on contemporary
philosophy. In a word, I think Lonergan's aim is dia-
logical, rather than polemical. At the same time I am
convinced that the basis of a critique of specific
philosophic views can be found in Lonergan's work, and
that conviction seems to be borne out by the secondary
literature on Lonergan referred to in my Introduction.[141]

As well, there is evidence that philosophers in
our own day are increasingly realizing the need to underpin their concern with praxis by a return to cognitional issues. But this, according to Lonergan,
easily can mean a return to the mistakes of the past,
rather than a purification of past mistakes. Empiricist positivism, an idealist critical rationalism, an
eclectic concern for ordinary language - all these and
other philosophic systems have returned to haunt the

II.

philosophic world. In the next chapter, I will outline Lonergan's suggestion for avoiding these pit-
falls, and here would note only that consensus among
philosophers seems a distant goal. So Lonergan writes,
in reference to philosophy as a "specialization":

> There remain the philosophers, a group apart
> if ever there was one, yet seemingly unsure
> of their function. Some identify their
> cause with that of common sense or ordinary
> language. Others assume the role of spokes-
> men for science. Still others switch their
> reflective concern to the hermeneutics of
> existence and the originality of Geschichte.
> Greeks of old sought to be universalist and
> autonomous by discoursing on being. A few
> moderns take their cue from the differen-
> tiation of horizons by specialization and,
> through an appeal to authentic subjectivity,
> seek to distinguish and evaluate the various
> orientations of the polymorphic conscious-
> ness of man.[142]

4. The New Study of Religion

In the previous section I discussed Lonergan's understanding of the process of specialization that has
resulted in a new context for theology. This process
was the gradual emergence of a modern science that repudiated its Aristotelian foundation; of a modern
scholarship that disengaged itself from servitude to
the classical and Renaissance promotion of Culture; of
a modern philosophy that has turned from a basis in
metaphysics in order to begin from the data of human
consciousness.

If theology was quite at home within the medieval

188

II.

context, it became very uneasy with the developments
that ushered in a new era. Natural science was crowned
the new queen, scholarship became the critical chron-
icler of the royal court, and philosophy, formerly considered the handmaid of theology, has (in the words of
Lonergan) for some centuries been going in for women's
liberation. And as each of these specializations
claimed its autonomy, theology too was challenged to
present its credentials and explain its presence and
function within this new cultural context.

In the present section I wish to indicate two
lines of development: (1) Lonergan's account of the
transition from medieval to classicist or dogmatic theology - a transition that tended to isolate theology
from its new context; and (2) his account of the rise
of empirical religious studies - a development that
tends to bring theology in touch with its cultural
context.

(1) From Medieval to Classicist Theology

If we turn from Lonergan's understanding of the
new cultural context to his understanding of theology
in this new context, we find Lonergan to be among the
many theologians urging a renewal of theology. He
contends that although theology was indeed a specialization in the medieval context, the emergence of a
new context demanded a renewal of theology. And although Lonergan is very much aware of the renewal that
has been going forward in recent times, and that I
described earlier in Chapter One, nevertheless he

189

II.

would also agree with those who admit that such renewal is not yet a common achievement and who continue
to ponder fundamental methodological issues. In
brief, Lonergan would maintain that contemporary theology has not yet clarified its status as a specialization in the modern context. This in turn implies
that theology in the post-medieval period failed to
keep pace with developments in science, scholarship,
and philosophy; and that the current flurry of activity in theological circles is an attempt to bring
theology up to date. Lonergan describes the situation in the following general terms:

> Any theology of renewal goes hand in hand
> with a renewal of theology. For "renewal"
> is being used in a novel sense. Usually
> in Catholic circles "renewal" has meant a
> return to the olden times of pristine vir-
> tue and deep wisdom. But good Pope John
> has made "renewal" mean "aggiornamento,"
> "bringing things up to date."

> Obviously, if theology is to be brought
> up to date, it must have fallen behind the
> times. Again, if we are to know what is
> to be done to bring theology up to date,
> we must ascertain when it began to fall
> behind the times, in what respects it got
> out of touch, in what respects it failed
> to meet the issues and effect the develop-
> ments that long ago were due and now are
> long overdue.[143]

According to Lonergan theology began to fall behind the times in the seventeenth century. More precisely, he notes that it was towards the end of that
century when theology retired into a dogmatic corner.
And for Lonergan it was no coincidence that this same

period witnessed the origins of modern science and
the beginnings of the Enlightenment.[144] It seems
that these events, far more than the Renaissance or
Reformation, profoundly affected theology's self-
understanding, for Lonergan draws attention to the
beginnings of a new "dogmatic" theology at the end
of the seventeenth century. In reference to Congar's
historical study of that period, Lonergan writes:

> It would be unfair to expect the theol-
> ogians of the end of the seventeenth cen-
> tury to have discerned the good and the
> evil in the great movements of their time.
> But at least we may record what in fact
> they did do. They introduced "dogmatic"
> theology. It is true that the word "dog-
> matic" had been previously applied to the-
> ology. But then it was used to denote a
> distinction from moral, or ethical, or
> historical theology. Now it was employed
> in a new sense, in opposition to scholas-
> tic theology. It replaced the inquiry of
> the quaestio by the pedagogy of the the-
> sis. It demoted the quest of faith for
> understanding to a desirable, but second-
> ary, and indeed, optional goal. It gave
> basic and central significance to the
> certitudes of faith, their presupposi-
> tions, and their consequences. It owed
> its mode of proof to Melchior Cano and,
> as that theologian was also a bishop and
> inquisitor, so the new dogmatic theology
> not only proved its theses, but also was
> supported by the teaching authority and
> the sanctions of the Church.[145]

While Lonergan would agree that dogmatic attitudes
assumed an emphatic role at the end of the seventeenth
century, he would add that the ground for such attitudes had been prepared by earlier decadence within

191

theology itself. The Augustinian-Aristotelian conflict that erupted at the end of the thirteenth century brought an overdose of logic to Scholasticism
and this undermined the quest for developing understanding that had characterized theology in the previous two centuries. So Lonergan is not surprised
that Scotist vocabularly dominated subsequent Scholasticism and that theologians wrote commentaries,
not on scriptural and patristic sources as gathered
in Lombard's Sentences, but rather on Aquinas' commentary on the Sentences or, worse, on Aquinas' systematic Summa. Lonergan observes that theology, becoming ever more removed from its vital sources in
scripture and tradition, seemed to be painting itself
into a corner.[146] He acknowledges that a new trend
was set with the Reformation and humanism, but adds
that Cano's De locis theologicis simply proposed a
notion of theology centered still in medieval doctrines to be proved by an appeal to tradition and
reason; hence the ancient fides quaerens intellectum
had been emptied of meaning.[147]

Lonergan asserts, however, that it was not
merely a question of a decadent Scholasticism that
presented difficulties for theologians at the end
of the seventeenth century. As well, the genuine
Scholasticism of the High Middle Ages was itself an
achievement with built-in limitations that would have
to be overcome with the emergence of new notions of
science, scholarship, and philosophy. To cling to
Scholastic views of science, scholarship, and philos-

ophy in a context when those views have been replaced by the new specializations discussed in the
previous section is, for Lonergan, to confine the
Catholic Church to a classicist mentality, thereby
keeping the Church out of the modern world and pro-
longing the already too long prolonged crisis within
the Church.[148]

I have already given Lonergan's account of the
main differences between the Aristotelian notion of
science and modern empirical science, between pre-
critical and critical history, between ancient/medi-
eval and modern philosophy. But these differences
are beyond the classicist horizon, and classicist
theology in particular failed to grasp both the limitations of Scholasticism and the defects in which
Aristotelian and Scholastic thinking were involved.
Accordingly, Lonergan offers a brief indication of
those characteristics of classicist theology that
stood in direct contrast to notions developed by
modern science, scholarship, and philosophy.

Firstly, Lonergan notes that the dogmatic theology developed towards the end of the seventeenth
century was grounded in a deductivist notion of science. The theses of theology were conclusions to be
proven from the premisses provided by Scripture and
Tradition.[149] Lonergan associates this exclusive
concern for deduction with an over-emphasis on truth
and certitude that in turn rests on the Aristotelian
notion of science as true and certain knowledge of
things through their causes. And though Aristotle

II.

and Aquinas gave at least equal attention to insight
and developing understanding, Lonergan finds the
classicist position to be ruled by abstract logic
that misinterpreted the ordo doctrinae in theology:

> . . . one misses the whole point of the
> ordo doctrinae if one mistakenly expects
> its syllogisms to offer not expressions
> of limited understanding but evidence
> for indisputable certitudes. There ex-
> ists certitude, but it is derived from
> the certitude of faith, and the deriva-
> tion is exhibited in the via inventionis.
> There is no additional certitude genera-
> ted by understanding itself, for our un-
> derstanding of the mysteries is imper-
> fect. To convey that imperfect under-
> standing is the function of the ordo
> doctrinae, and one only betrays one's
> incomprehension if, on the one hand,
> one pretends to find evidence for cer-
> titude where such evidence does not ex-
> ist or, on the other hand, one dismisses
> argumenta convenientiae as proofs that
> do not prove.[150]

Secondly, Lonergan says that classicist dogmatic
theology misconceived history on a classicist model,
and thought in terms of universality and permanence
rather than in terms of evolution and development.
So Lonergan refers to Vincent of Lerins claim that
God's truth was quod semper, quod ubique, quod ab om-
nibus and adds that this view remained unchallenged
in the grand siècle of French literature. On such
premisses, Lonergan observes that it was quite simple
to be an omnicompetent theologian, equally at home in
Scripture, patristics, medieval, Renaissance, and recent theologians, so that the dogmatic theologian

could range over whole centuries and discover the same fixed truths.[151] So Lonergan writes:

> More rapidly in the fields of patristic
> and medieval studies, more slowly in the
> field of Scripture, there gradually have
> been accepted and put into practice new
> techniques in investigating the course
> of history, new procedures in interpret-
> ing texts, new and more exacting require-
> ments in the study of languages. The re-
> sult of these innovations has been to
> eliminate the old style dogmatic theol-
> ogian. For the old style dogmatic the-
> ologian was expected: (1) to qualify his
> theses by appealing to papal and concil-
> iar documents from any period in church
> history and (2) to prove his thesis by
> arguing from the Old Testament and the
> New, from the Greek, Latin, and Syriac
> Fathers, from the Byzantine and medieval
> Scholastics, and from all the subsequent
> generations of theologians. But the new
> techniques in history, the new procedures
> in interpretation, the new requirements
> in the study of languages reveal the per-
> formance of the old style dogmatic theol-
> ogian to be simply out of date.[152]

Thirdly, classicist dogmatic theology employed a conceptual apparatus that, according to Lonergan, tended to ignore human historicity and Existenz by standardizing human reality. The standard followed was, of course, classicist Culture, and Lonergan notes that preaching the Gospel usually meant preaching the ideals and standards of classicist thought along with the Gospel. Such, of course, was in fact an imposition of an alien culture upon those commonly considered barbarians, and the imposition of a conceptual apparatus

II.

that was for the most part oblivious of the many differences among the peoples of the earth.[153] It was largely the result of a theology functioning within a church conceived as a societas perfecta: a theology more concerned with the mediation of past conceptual systems to all peoples, rather than with mediating between any given particular cultural matrix and the significance and role of Christianity within that matrix.[154] Lonergan concludes:

> The Gospel is to be preached to all nations, to every class of men in every culture. As long as classicist culture was accepted, it could be thought that there existed but a single culture and that the Gospel could be preached substantially through that culture, even though accidentally certain adaptations had to be made to reach the uncultured. Now that classicist culture is a thing of the past, we can no longer suppose that classicist assumptions could succeed in preaching the Gospel to all nations. We have to learn to express the Gospel message so that it can be grasped by the members of every class within each of the cultures of the world. A philosophy of culture can make a great contribution towards the fulfillment of that task.[155]

Particularly in the present century, these and other limitations and defects of the classicist brand of dogmatic theology have generally been recognized by theologians. There has occurred a gradual reception by theologians of the methods of critical scholarship, the conceptual apparatus of contemporary philosophies, the contingency of scientific under-

196

standing. Yet Lonergan and others are aware that
this reception has raised further and fundamental
issues that have to be faced if theology is to retain its specific identity while adapting to its own
purposes the gains of modern academic thought. To
date, there has occurred a disengagement from now
this, now that element of classicist theology, and
a turning to now this, now that element in modern
scholarship, philosophy, and science. There has not
yet occurred a transposition of theology of the sort
that enables theology to be identified as an integral
component of contemporary culture with its own specific contribution to make within this culture. Lonergan, however, would observe that the change which
has been going forward particularly in our own century points to the possibility that such a transposition of theology may be within our reach:

> In the present century, then, theology is
> undergoing a profound change. It is com-
> parable in magnitude to the change that
> occurred in the Middle Ages, that began
> with Anselm's speculative thrust, Aba-
> elard's hard-headed Sic et Non, the Lom-
> bard's Sentences, the technique of the
> Quaestio, and the fusion of these ele-
> ments in the ongoing process of commen-
> taries on the Sentences, Quaestiones dis-
> putatae, and the various Summae. Then,
> without any explicit advertence to the
> fact, theology operated on the basis of
> a method. For over a century it brought
> forth precious fruits. To theology as
> governed by method and as an ongoing pro-
> cess the present situation points. If
> that pointing is accurate and effective,
> then the contemporary revolution in the-

197

ology also will have the character of
a restoration.[156]

The "profound change" noted by Lonergan is of
course a reference to the reception by theology of
the methods of critical scholarship, of the insights
of modern philosophies, of the findings of human scientists. But Lonergan would also draw attention to a
further dimension of change, one that concerns the
move away from the assumptions of classicist dogmatic
theology, and not just from classicist methods. Those
assumptions took for granted the uniqueness and superiority of Christianity and Christian theology. But
the breakdown of classicist views and the recognition
by theologians of cultural pluralism is leading to a
reassessment of mankind's religions and human religiousness. In particular, theologians are becoming
aware of various approaches to the study of religion
that are inspired, not by theological convictions,
but by a concern to extend the methods of modern science, scholarship, and philosophy to the investigation of world religions and human religiousness. Besides, then, the stirrings currently taking place
within the theological world itself, there is being
raised the question of theology's relation to empirical religious studies. And while the full dimensions
of this problem must await discussion in later chapters, I wish to add a note regarding Lonergan's conviction that such religious studies are highly relevant to forming a contemporary notion of theology.

(2)   The Rise of Empirical Religious Studies

Earlier in this chapter I gave an account of
Lonergan's understanding of the new context provided by modern science, modern scholarship, and
modern philosophy. I then went on to outline Lonergan's view that the rise of classicist dogmatic
theology tended to isolate theology from its new
cultural context, but that classicist assumptions
and methods are rapidly disappearing in our own
age of renewal in theology. He finds the reason
for that renewal to lie principally in the reception by theology of the methods of critical historical scholarship, and so his initial concern
with empirical religious studies was very much from
the viewpoint of the impact of those studies on theology. This is clear from the following passage
from a lecture given in 1968 and published a year
later:

> . . . the modern science or discipline
> of religious studies has undercut the
> assumptions and antiquated the methods
> of a theology structured by Melchior
> Cano's De locis theologicis. Such a
> theology was classicist in its assump-
> tions. Truth is eternal. Principles
> are immutable. Change is accidental.
> But religious studies deal meticulously
> with endless matters of detail. They
> find that the expressions of truth and
> the enunciations of principles are
> neither eternal nor immutable. They
> concentrate on the historical process
> in which these changes occur. They
> bring to light whole ranges of inter-

esting facts and quite new types of
problems. In brief, religious studies
have stripped the old theology of its
very sources in Scripture, in patristic
writings, in medieval and subsequent
religious writers. They have done so
by subjecting the sources to a fuller
and more penetrating scrutiny than had
been attempted by earlier methods.[157]

There seems little doubt that Lonergan's initial
interest in religious studies was motivated by a concern to integrate the methods of critical scholarship
within a theological investigation of the past Christian tradition. For Lonergan, critical scholarship
is critical scholarship, and the methods of such
scholarship remain the same, whether one is studying
the past Christian tradition, the past Moslem tradition, or any other past tradition. I will discuss
this aspect of Lonergan's thought in later chapters.
At present, I would like to draw attention to a more
general interest of Lonergan in religious studies,
namely, that a contemporary theology has to operate
in conjunction with religious studies. Thus, it is
one thing for theology to borrow the methods of religious studies and employ these methods in investigating the Christian past; and it is something else for
theology to co-operate with religious studies in a
mutual enrichment that contributes to the understanding of religious traditions and to the promotion of
religious concerns. According to Lonergan, it is
precisely by such co-operation that theology can move
away from a classicist isolation from world religions,

and thereby take a stance that is truly open to the
social and cultural movements of our time.

In the present section I wish to discuss briefly
two points. Firstly, I shall summarize Lonergan's
reasons for wanting a notion of theology that situates
theology within the context of empirical religious
studies. Secondly, I shall outline a preliminary
notion of what Lonergan means by "empirical religious
studies." A more complete account of the methodological issues linking religious studies and theology
will be offered in the next chapter, and this will
prepare the way for Lonergan's account of the method
proper to theology.

Lonergan's basic conviction regarding the need
for a theology that operates within the context of
world religions and religious studies is similar to
the conviction expressed by such writers as Troeltsch,
Tillich, and Pannenberg.[158]   Lonergan offered a summary of the reasons motivating his own thought in a
1969 lecture entitled Theology and Man's Future.[159]
After speaking of the influence of modern historical
studies and of philosophy on theology, he turns to
the potential influence of religious studies:

> A third major influence is the field of
> religious studies: the phenomenology of
> religion, the psychology of religion,
> the sociology of religion, the history
> of religions, and the philosophy of re-
> ligion. I call this a major influence,
> not because the influence has been con-
> spicuous, but because of very signifi-

II.

cant and powerful contemporary trends.
The first stems from Vatican II, and it
consists in the Church's concern with e-
cumenism, with non-Christian religions,
and with the atheist negation of religion.
This fact requires the theologian to reflect on his religion, not in isolation
from all others, but in conjunction with
others. It requires him to attend, not
only to the differences separating his
religion from others, but also to the
similarities that connect them with one
another. To meet such requirements theology will be led into the field of religious studies and, indeed, while retaining its identity, to conceive itself as a
particular type of religious studies.
There is a second factor leading to the
same conclusion. I have already spoken
of the relations of theology with history
and with philosophy. But if it is to
take its place in contemporary culture,
it has also to be related to all the human sciences; and it is in the field of
religious studies, in the phenomenology
and psychology and sociology of religion,
that it will find models exhibiting what
can be done and accounts of what has
been tried and found unsatisfactory.
Finally, there is the theological doctrine that God grants all men sufficient
grace for their salvation. This doctrine is relevant to religious studies;
it makes them studies of the manifold
ways God's grace comes to men and operates as the seed that falls on rocks or
amidst thorns or by the wayside or on
good ground to bring forth fruit thirty
or sixty or a hundred fold.[160]

Such, for Lonergan, is the relevance of co-operation
between religious studies and theology: the promotion
of dialogue on religious matters, the more effective

202

communication of religious meaning and value in any
given culture, and the refinement of the criteria
for evaluating authentic and inauthentic expressions
of religious experience. In later chapters I will
discuss how these concerns are operative in Lonergan's own notion of theology that he has conceived
precisely along inter-disciplinary lines. For the
moment, I wish to note in preliminary fashion just
what Lonergan means by religious studies.

Generally, then, Lonergan has in mind those
studies of religion that are inspired by the methods
or aims of the three specializations discussed earlier
in this chapter. Corresponding to the methods of modern science are the various religious studies that
tend to pattern themselves on an analogy with the
methods and aims of modern science. These are the
generalizing, systematic types of study that employ
definitions, hypotheses, deductions - the so-called
behavioral sciences of religion such as the phenomenology of religion, the psychology of religion, the
sociology of religion. They tend to concentrate on
what is routine in human religious behavior and on
whatever is universal in the genesis, development,
and breakdown of routines.[161]

Secondly, corresponding to the methods of modern
scholarship, there are the scholarly studies of religion, such as the textual criticism and exegesis
of religious literature, the history of religious
movements, the comparative study of human religious

traditions. These disciplines are basically interpretative, and are simply applications of scholarly
methods to the data of human religions considered
as meaningful and historically constituted.[162]

Thirdly, corresponding to the rise of an autonomous philosophy, there is the philosophy of religion.
Its uniqueness will be discussed in the following
chapter, and for now I would note only that a
philosophy of religion presupposes especially the
scholarly studies of religion. For to the extent
that religious studies, whether systematizing or
scholarly, are not rigorously modelled on the
methods of natural science, to that extent do they
recognize the constitutive role of meaning in
human religions. And such recognition invariably
involves the scientist or scholar of religion in
philosophical issues.

I have offered here only a very preliminary
description of Lonergan's understanding of religious
studies, both to indicate their broad relevance
to theology and to note their concern for methods
derived from the autonomous specializations of
the modern context. To make more concrete the
similarities and differences between religious
studies and theology demands a reflection on these
religious studies and on the objects with which
they deal. And such reflection I include in the
next chapter within the framework of a philosophy
of religion.

5. Conclusion

In Chapter One I sketched three distinct notions of theology as set forth by Wolfhart Pannenberg, Karl Rahner, and Johann Metz. Each of these authors is very much concerned with the renewal of theology, and each of them has stressed a constitutive dimension of this renewed theology. Moreover, all three authors insist that a renewed theology is needed in order to take account critically of developments associated with the Enlightenment and Neuzeit. I suggested that Pannenberg interprets the Enlightenment as challenging theology to a renewed Wissenschaftlichkeit, that would put theology on a par with the modern empirically and historically-minded academic disciplines. For Karl Rahner, Enlightenment challenges theology to a renewed Kirchlichkeit, that would stress the proper and unique function of religion in human living and the distinct function of theology within the academic community. Johann Metz conceives Enlightenment as fundamentally challenging theology to a renewed Zeitoffenheit, that would stress the critical function of religion in human societal structures and the critical function of theology in academic circles.

Lonergan as well is concerned with the renewal of theology, and so the present chapter tried to find out about his interpretation of the developments in history that have demanded such renewal. As Pannenberg, Rahner, and Metz, so too Lonergan would point to developments in the cultural and social contexts that have undermined previous theological achievement. He finds in medieval theology a model for reconciling and integrating Wissenschaftlichkeit, Kirchlichkeit, and Zeitoffenheit. But at the same time he urges that it is a model that we today can follow only by shifting to a new key. The shift is demanded because the Enlightenment and Neuzeit provide a new context, a new framework, in which there is an autonomous empirical science, an autonomous historical scholarship, and an autonomous philosophy. Previously these disciplines could be called upon to serve theological aims; today, however, each has repudiated its former association with religion and theology and worked out, or is in the ongoing process of working out, its own identity on its own terms. Only belatedly has theology accepted a similar challenge, and so is engaged in a renewal that would again place theology squarely within the academic community, that would stress theology's unique reference to religion and religious living, and that would effectively and critically mediate this academic reference to religion to the societies and cultures of the present day.

Lonergan would not disagree that Wissenschaftlichkeit, Kirchlichkeit, and Zeitoffenheit are to be the characteristics of the renewed theology. To reconcile these concerns, however, he would suggest that theology has to shift to a new paradigm, a new level of systematic reflection. It is not enough for theology to come to terms only with modern science or only with modern scholarship or only with modern philosophy. <u>All</u> this is needed, in order for theology to work out its proper identity and method and purpose in the world of today, and so I think it is safe to say that Lonergan understands the Enlightenment challenge in terms of the need for theology to work out its own proper <u>method</u> in such a way as to be at once within the modern academic world, while retaining its reference to transcendent mystery. And just what this means for Lonergan will be discussed in the following chapters.

II.

III. FOUNDATIONAL UNITY: FROM RELIGIOUS
EXPERIENCE TO SPECIALIZED RELIGIOUS
KNOWLEDGE

> The real root and ground of unity is
> being in love with God - the fact that
> God's love has flooded our inmost
> hearts through the Holy Spirit he has
> given us (Rom. 5,5). The acceptance
> of this gift both constitutes reli-
> gious conversion and leads to moral
> and even intellectual conversion.[1]

In the previous chapter I discussed Lonergan's
understanding of the developments in recent centuries
that have brought about the need for renewal in theology. The emergence of a new notion of science, a
critical historical scholarship, and a philosophy
concerned with concrete human living has brought
home forcefully the limitations of a theology structured on Aristotelian presuppositions. Moreover,
the gradual reception by theology of these new developments has only served to highlight the inadequacy of the foundations upon which a classicist dogmatic theology rested. There has emerged a new sort
of reflection on Christianity and, indeed, a new approach to the study of humanity as religious. But,
according to Lonergan, all this novelty has raised
some very fundamental issues concerning the identity
of theology in the world of today. So it is that
Lonergan would attempt to clarify and resolve these
issues, thereby taking his place alongside such theologians as Pannenberg, Rahner, and Metz, whom I

III.

discussed in Chapter One.

Although there continues to be disagreement
among theologians about many aspects of the renewed
theology, it is nonetheless possible to discern in
many of them a concern for what generally is called
a theological anthropology.[2] I have no hesitation
in suggesting that this is precisely what Lonergan
has attempted to develop in his various writings,
and perhaps this fact will help the reader to understand the topics to be treated in this and the following chapters. A preliminary description of just
what he means by a theological anthropology is offered by Lonergan in a 1968 lecture,[3] wherein Lonergan notes his substantial agreement with Karl Rahner
on this matter. In a well-known article published
in 1967, Rahner argued that the dogmatic theology of
the past has to become a theological anthropology;
this means that all theological questions and answers
have to be matched by the transcendental questions
and answers that reveal in the human subject the conditions of the possibility of the theological answers.[4] Lonergan remarks that Rahner explicitly ex-
cludes a modernist interpretation of this proposal,
as if theological doctrines were to be viewed as
statements about merely human reality. Rather, Lonergan understands Rahner's position to be that man
is for God, that religion is intrinsic to an authentic humanism, that in theology theocentrism and an-
thropocentrism coincide; so it is that all theological statements are to be matched by statements of

210

their meaning in human terms. Lonergan concludes by
stressing Rahner's purpose in making this proposal:
Rahner does not want to water down theological truth
but rather to bring it to life; he does not want to
impose some alien method on theology, but instead
wants to exclude the risk of mythology by introducing
into theology rigorous controls.

In the Introduction to the present work I indicated the broad lines of Lonergan's interest in working out just such a notion of theology. Then, in the
previous chapter, I offered an account of Lonergan's
assessment of the historical developments that urge
a shift away from classicist assumptions and methods
to a theology that assimilates the categories of the
human subject as historical being and as incarnate
subject. This contemporary apprehension of the human
subject provides us with a wealth of new insights into
the meaning of "being human." And of particular interest here are the insights into the function of religion in human living, the historical development of
mankind's religious traditions, the recurrent patterns
in human religious behavior, and, theologically, the
literal meaning of human religious symbols.

It is my concern in the present chapter to prepare the way for a discussion of unity in theology by
presenting an account of what Lonergan means by the
turn to the human subject - die anthropologische
Wende - as relevant to an understanding of religious
living. In the first section I mention how Lonergan

211

III.

understands the increasing fact of specialization,
noted in Chapter Two, as contributing to the absence
of God in modern culture.   To convert that absence
into a presence, Lonergan suggests that we approach
religion and reflection on religion from a new starting point, a new foundation: the religious horizon
of the existential subject. There is discussed the
cultivation of religious experience by a religious
tradition, the relation of both religious experience
and religious traditions to human authenticity, and
finally, the core of religious experience in a loving,
inter-subjective commitment of the human subject to
God.

The second section moves from the fact of religious experience to the knowledge born of that experience - a knowledge identified by Lonergan as religious faith. This faith is described as the experienced fulfillment of our unrestricted thrust to
self-transcendence. It is an apprehension of transcendent value, that places vital, social, cultural,
and personal values in a new light.

The third section discusses how Lonergan relates
religious experience and faith to the acceptance of
the traditions of the religious community. Among the
values discerned by faith is the value of believing
the word of the religious community, and Lonergan sets
forth the process of coming to religious belief.

The fourth section turns from religious experience, faith, and belief to reflection on religion.

212

Mainly such reflection is a matter of giving an account of the reasonableness, intelligibility, and implications of one's religious commitment, faith, and belief. Lonergan first presents a sketch of ways in which systematic thinking may be structured. He finds neither a metaphysically-based system nor the theoretical systems of natural science to be adequate for a reflection on religion, and so he proposes a generalized reflection based on an intentionality analysis. Upon that basis Lonergan proceeds to ground the specific methods operative in reflection on human reality, including religious living: the methods of historical scholarship, dialectic, and praxis.

1. Religious Experience

(1) The Absence of God in Modern Culture

In the previous chapter I referred briefly to the new study of religion that Lonergan and many others are attempting to promote within the new cultural context. The task is far from easy, for the rise of modern science, modern scholarship, and modern philosophy all have focused attention on this world: on nature as well as on mankind, on mankind as historically conditioned as well as on mankind's responsibility for itself and its future. Nor is this attention confined to the academic world of scientists, scholars, and philosophers; it has filtered down to the everyday world of literature and factory and politics so that Lonergan can speak of the absence of God in modern

III.

culture, both in the academic and everyday components of that culture. Similarly, Walter Kasper writes that we find in modern times traces of ourselves rather than of God.[5]

The absence of God from academic specializations concerned with this world is only to be expected; it is a fact that makes the renewal of theology all the more urgent and that encourages us to develop a theology that can speak in a new way of God and of this world (including this world's academic disciplines) in relation to God. The urgency of the task becomes even more apparent when we consider the impact that the various "secular" academic disciplines have had on the everyday life and thought of people. On this everyday, more concrete level of ordinary living, Lonergan observes that there has taken place a reinterpretation of the human subject and this subject's world; a transformation of the control over nature and a subsequent reordering of society; and a shift in mankind's sense of power and responsibility.[6]

Firstly, the reinterpretation of the human subject in the world occurs mostly in academic circles, but through popularization and simplification it is transposed from technical expression to metaphors, images, narratives that can be more easily understood and practically applied. So it is that the modern concern for the things of this world and for human living in this world tends to stand opposed to a church and theology that seem exclusively other-worldly, quite uninterested in the discoveries of science and quite unconcerned with mankind's self-understanding as historically conditioned and ever subject to change. In the absence of due aggiornamento in theology and church structures, and in the presence of a cultural climate that went unchallenged in its proclamation of atheism and agnosticism, there resulted a distortion in mankind's self-understanding, devoid of a religious world of meaning. So Lonergan writes:

> Positivists, naturalists, behaviorists insist that human sciences have to be conducted on the same lines as the natural sciences. But the resultant apprehension of man, if not mechanistic, is theriomorphic. Nor is this view of man as a machine or as an animal confined to some rarified academic realm. It is applied. The applications reach out into all departments of thought and into all walks of life. They have the common feature of omitting advertence to human dignity and respect for human morality.[7]

Secondly, there has occurred a transformation of man's control over nature and this, in consequence, involves a reordering of society. Here, Lonergan points to the facts of technology, automation, built-in obsolescence, a population explosion, increasing longevity, detached relations among persons, universal education, increasing leisure and travel, instantaneous information, perpetually available entertainment. It is an ever changing scene in which God, if not totally absent, seems to be an intruder;

to speak of God seems irrelevant or meaningless.
National monetary policies are directed to non-
religious goals and secularism is the religion, or
anti-religion, by law established. Religious or-
ganizations are increasingly powerless to address
and heal concrete human living. So Lonergan notes
that perhaps Karl Rahner is correct in pointing to
the root difficulty in an integrism that believed
authority could resolve all problems by laying down
principles and deducing conclusions; for effective
solutions come only from familiarity with concrete
situations in their ongoing development or decline.
Ideals, principles, exhortations all are needed,
but they must be complemented by insights into the
concrete issues that are in need of analysis, encouragement, correction.[8]

Thirdly, there has taken hold in modern culture a new sense of power and responsibility. No
longer is the main concern simply to perpetuate the
wisdom of our ancestors and to hand on inherited
traditions. Rather, Lonergan points out a mentality
that understands the past as simply the springboard
to the future, that stresses individual responsibility and collective responsibility for the future
of mankind. Moreover, this concern is for the future of humanity in this world, and all too easily
it is pronounced by theologians or church authorities to be merely secular. Lonergan, however, would
urge the contrary; and in the following passage he
draws attention to the profoundly religious dimension

216

of this humanism - a dimension that can be cultivated
and that can lead to a reintegration of religion, religious studies, and theology within modern culture:

>Now this concern with the future of hu-
>manity is a concern for humanity in this
>world; so it has been thought to be purely
>secular. Such a conclusion is, I believe,
>mistaken. It is true that concern for the
>future is incompatible with a blind tra-
>ditionalism, but a blind traditionalism
>is not the essence of religion. It is
>true that concern for the future will work
>itself out by human means, by drawing on
>human experience, human intelligence, hu-
>man judgment, human decision, but again
>this is quite compatible with a profoundly
>religious attitude. It was St. Ignatius
>Loyola who gave the advice: act as though
>results depended exclusively on you, but
>await the results as though they depended
>entirely on God. What is false is that
>human concern for the future can generate
>a better future on the basis of individual
>and group egoism. For to know what is
>truly good and to effect it calls for a
>self-transcendence that seeks to benefit
>not self at the cost of the group, not the
>group at the cost of mankind, not present
>mankind at the cost of mankind's future.
>Concern for the future, if it is not just
>high-sounding hypocrisy, supposes rare
>moral attainment. It calls for what
>Christians name heroic charity. In the
>measure that Christians practise and ra-
>diate heroic charity they need not fear
>they will be superfluous either in the
>task of discerning man's true good in this
>life or in the task of bringing it about.[9]

I have presented Lonergan's assessment of the absence (and potential presence) of God in modern culture, for I believe that it helps us to appreciate

III.

Lonergan's starting-point for approaching religion, religious studies, and theology. To be avoided are classicist assumptions and methods that ignore the achievements of modern science, that uncritically promote past traditions, that isolate religion from individual and collective human historicity. In somewhat similar fashion, Walter Kasper urges a foundation that overcomes the limitations of notions that speak of religion "from without," that propose a god of the gaps to fill in the blanks of what mankind does not yet know, that reduce religion to a purely private affair of the heart or some existential decision that is irrelevant to concrete history, that speak only in abstraction without regard to human living. Against all such tendencies Kasper insists on a starting-point that is capable of bringing religious faith into a living and meaningful integration with concrete human experience:

> Eine der entscheidenden Aufgaben der
> Theologie ist es heute, dieses Verhältnis
> prinzipiell zu klären und - bevor sie die
> eigentlichen Aussagen von Schrift und
> Tradition über Gott interpretierend
> wiederholt - zuerst die Erfahrungs-
> Dimension wieder freizulegen, in der
> es sinnvoll und verständlich ist, von
> Gott zu reden. Bei allem Bewusstsein,
> dass es sich dabei um theologische
> Vorfragen und noch nicht um den eigenen
> Gegenstandsbereich der Theologie handelt,
> müssen diese hermeneutischen und funda-
> mental-theologischen Fragen heute doch
> im Vordergrund stehen.[10]

In this passage Kasper is appealing for a pre-theological" clarification of the experiential horizon of the human subject, for only on that basis will any discourse about God and religion be meaningful and intelligible. In similar fashion Lonergan criticizes his own philosophy of God that is found in the nineteenth chapter of Insight for its attempt to speak of God and his attributes in a purely objective fashion, without any appeal to the religious experience of the individual.[11] So Lonergan most recently is very much concerned to begin any discussion of religion with an account of the religious horizon of the individual human subject: is there any human experience that may be singled out as grounding the religious convictions of mankind? How can we understand the quite special involvement or engagement of people in the world of religious meaning, an involvement that is highly personal and quite distinct from particular traditions and beliefs? To what experience do religious symbols point, from what experience do they derive, what experience leads the symbols to be modified or changed?

The importance of these questions cannot be overlooked. To speak of the absence of God in modern culture is, for Lonergan, to speak of the failure of the institutional church and of theology to adjust to the changes that have been taking place in modern culture. Clearly, he is not suggesting that "modernity" means "goodness and authenticity," but on the contrary has often insisted that adaptation by the church and theology has to be done critically. Similar, then, to

III.

Pannenberg, Rahner, and Metz, Lonergan too would come
to terms with "Enlightenment" and modernity, where
coming to terms is a matter of discerning between
what is authentic and what is inauthentic, promoting
the former and reversing the latter.

(2) The Need to Begin from the Existential Subject

I have referred to the "God-problem" of modernity
- the absence of God from academic circles and from
ordinary, everyday living and thinking. I have noted
Lonergan's substantial agreement with such theologians
as Rahner and Kasper, who stress the need for a theological anthropology - an approach to theology that
links theological statements to the existential horizons of human subjects. And I have drawn attention
to Lonergan's more recent tendency to conceive religious experience as the origin of mankind's most fundamental search for knowledge of God. So Lonergan is
convinced that the task of promoting the presence of
God in modern culture demands a philosophy of religion,
religious studies, and theologies that find their basic
terms and relations in the religious consciousness of
the human subject. Just how these academic disciplines
are to carry out this task will be discussed later in
this chapter. For now, I would invite attention to the
meaning of religious consciousness and emphasize that
this consciousness or horizon is foundational to a
philosophy of religion, religious studies, and theology, at least as far as Lonergan is concerned.

220

Lonergan is aware that his readers may find it
difficult to conceive the foundation of academic
disciplines in terms of the human reality of those
engaged in those disciplines. For we spontaneously
seem to think of the foundations of a discipline
(whether theology, philosophy, science) in terms of
the basic doctrines, propositions, hypotheses, first
principles, from which academic reflection begins.
Somehow, we tend to forget about the human subject
who happens to be a theologian, philosopher, or scientist, and we think of an academic discipline in
terms of content or statements; so we spontaneously
think of the foundation of the discipline to lie in
the basic content or fundamental statements proper
to the discipline in question. Such thinking is
not wrong, but Lonergan suggests it is out of date
and quite inadequate to describe what modern disciplines in fact are all about. This point is of
fundamental importance to Lonergan's thought, and
I wish to illustrate it in reference to his search
for the foundation of theology.

Lonergan first notes that some foundation is
needed if theology is to be critical and discerning
in finding its place in modern culture. I doubt if
any contemporary theologian would disagree with
Lonergan's description of the need for a critical
foundation to theology:

> First, some foundation is needed. If
> change is to be improvement, if new
> tasks are to be accomplished fruitfully,
> discernment is needed and discrimination.

III.

> If we are to draw on contemporary psychol-
> ogy and sociology, if we are to revise
> scholastic categories and make our own the
> concepts worked out in historicist, per-
> sonalist, phenomenological, or existen-
> tialist circles, then we must be able to
> distinguish tinsel and silver, gilt and
> gold. No less important than a critique
> of notions and conclusions is a critique
> of methods. The new largely empirical
> approach to theology can too easily be
> made into a device for reducing doctrines
> to probable opinions. A hermeneutics can
> pretend to philosophic neutrality yet
> force the conclusion that the content of
> revelation is mostly myth. Scientific
> history can be so conceived that a study
> of the narrative of salvation will strip
> it of matters of fact. If our renewed
> theology is not to be the dupe of every
> fashion, it needs a firm basis and a
> critical stance.[12]

Next, Lonergan says that the old foundations will
no longer do, not because they are false, but because
they are inadequate and no longer appropriate. Here,
he recalls the biblical injunction against patching
an old cloak with new cloth or putting new wine in
old wineskins. He notes that one type of foundation
suits a theology that aims at being deductive, static,
abstract, universal, equally applicable to all places
and all times; here, Lonergan seems to have in mind a
notion of foundation conceived in terms of some authoritative doctrine, such as divine revelation, the inspiration of Scripture, the authority of the Church,
the consensus of patristic and theological writers,
the sensus fidelium, etc.[13] Such is the simple manner of conceiving foundations - as a set of premises

222

or logically first propositions, grounding a theology consisting in propositions about God; it is the
notion dominant in a Denzinger theology or conclusions
theology: and Lonergan describes its basic style:

> One must believe and accept whatever the
> bible or the true church or both believe
> and accept. But X is the bible or the
> true church or both. Therefore, one must
> believe and accept whatever X believes
> and accepts. Moreover, X believes and
> accepts a, b, c, d, ... Therefore,
> one must believe and accept a, b, c, d,
> . . . .[14]

Lonergan acknowledges that such a foundation suited a
classicist dogmatic theology, but he would insist
that a new foundation is needed when theology turns
from deductivism to an empirical approach, from the
static to the dynamic, from the abstract to the concrete, from the universal to the historical totality
of particulars, from invariable rules to intelligent
and ongoing adjustment and adaptation; and such a
theology is already operative in our own day, so that
one is led to inquire about the critical foundation
of this renewed theology - the problem I referred to
in Chapter One.[15]

According to Lonergan, if we understand theology
to be an ongoing, developing process - and most of us
do - then the foundation will be the immanent and operative set of norms that guides each forward step in
the process.[16] This means that we have to move out
of the static, deductivist style (which admits no

III.

conclusions that are not implicit in the premisses),
and into the methodical style (which aims at de-
creasing darkness and increasing light by adding
discovery to discovery).[17] In this latter style,
the key element is controlling the process, making
sure that theologians avoid entanglement in false
philosophies, free themselves from various forms of
bias, and in fact operate in virtue of their own religious experience.[18]

I think it is worth emphasizing what Lonergan
is proposing. He is trying to direct our attention
to the need for a dynamic, moving, methodical foundation to theology, religious studies, the philosophy
of religion. One may agree with him concerning the
absence of God from modern culture. One may further
agree on the need for a theological anthropology, as
the key to promoting the presence of God in modern
culture. But one would misunderstand Lonergan if it
were thought that he is trying to formulate a number
of theological statements about humanity or a number
of philosophical statements about theology. Behind
all statements he would insist on the stating subject, and thus would ask us to pay far more attention
than before to the existential horizon of those formulating the statements; for what is stated has meaning only in light of that horizon, and to neglect
that prior reality by attending only to what is
stated is to remain tied to a classicist and ultimately dogmatic mentality. Such, for Lonergan, is

the deepest meaning of the turn to the human subject,
die anthropologische Wende, wherein the realities of
the subject become primary, while metaphysical concepts become secondary and derivative:

> (The turn to the human subject - M. O'C.)
> is a turn from idealized objects, objects
> of infallible intuitions, of self-evident
> truths, of necessary conclusions. It is
> the turn to the actual reality of human
> subjects, to a community of men and women
> in a common attentiveness, in a common
> development of human understanding, in a
> common reflection on the validity of cur-
> rent achievement, in a common delibera-
> tion on the potentialities brought to
> light by that achievement. I cannot in-
> sist too much that this turn to the sub-
> ject is totally misconceived when it is
> thought to be a turn from the truly ob-
> jective to the merely subjective. Human
> subjects, their attention, their develop-
> ing understanding, their reflective scru-
> tiny, their responsible deliberations,
> are the objective reality. Infallible
> intuitions, self-evident premises, nec-
> essary conclusions are the merely sub-
> jective constructions that may have served
> their purpose in their day, but have been
> definitively swept aside by the science
> and scholarship of recent centuries.[19]

I have emphasized Lonergan's "starting-point" because it is of key importance in understanding his notion of the function of religion in human living, as
well as his notions of theology and religious studies.
The initial matter to be settled, then, is the meaning
of religious experience, religious consciousness, religious horizon. What precisely does Lonergan mean by

III.

these terms, in what sense can he speak of the a
priori openness of the human subject to religious
conversion, how does he describe the core of religious experience that is the a priori of religious
faith, religious belief, and reflection on religion?

(3) Religious Experience

It is worth mentioning that part of the difficulty in understanding what Lonergan is saying lies
in the ambiguity of the notion of "experience."[20]
He appeals to religious experience as constitutive
of the horizon of the human subject, and finds that
religious experience to be the foundation upon which
the contemporary philosophy of religion, religious
studies, and theologies should build. But what precisely is this religious experience to which he appeals? Is he suggesting that religious images or
religious feelings or religious concepts or religious
ideas or religious judgments are constitutive of the
horizon of the human subject? The answer is no. Lonergan indeed acknowledges that the word "experience"
most often is taken to mean a sort of practical knowledge resting on images, feelings, concepts, ideas,
judgments. But he would invite us to consider a more
technical meaning of the word "experience" that gets
behind this supra-structure of images, feelings, ideas,
etc., to the underlying component in this structure,
namely, that which gives rise to images, feelings,
ideas, etc.[21] Such, for Lonergan, is the given reality

226

of our own consciousness, simply as given, prior to all questioning and invariant regardless of images, feelings, answers that we happen to come up with in coming to know ourselves and our world.[22]

Experience, then, in this technical sense is neither knowledge nor self-knowledge, but rather is an infrastructure in human knowing. As such, experience is not perception of sense data, nor an introspection of the data of consciousness. Both perception and introspection pertain to a further level that presupposes the pure experience itself. In order to illustrate what Lonergan means, an example might be helpful. Firstly, let us consider the distinction between sensation and perception. Lonergan sometimes uses the example of a biologist who visits the zoo with his son. Whereas the son perceives a tall animal with long legs and long neck and calls it a giraffe, the father will perceive an animal with a tremendously complex set of biological systems and will call it Giraffa camelopardalis. Both father and son perceive the same data but their perceptions are quite different. Yet both manners of perceiving presuppose a prior element, namely, the sensation of the data as simply given, and such sensation is basically the same in father and son. Without the pure fact of sensation there would be nothing that the father would perceive as Giraffa camelopardalis or the son as giraffe. This outer experience of sensation is experience as an infrastructure in the knowing of both father and son. Such pure experience

227

III.

is not the knowing of either father or son, for their
knowing adds on to the sensation a whole supra-structure: for the father, the supra-structure of both ordinary and scientific language and knowledge; for the
son, the supra-structure of ordinary language and commonsense knowing. But behind these supra-structures,
and underpinning them, is the pure experience of sensation that is quite distinct from perception.

It is of course clear that religious experience
is not a matter of sensation or perception, but the
example perhaps helps to prepare for the meaning of
"inner experience," and this is highly relevant to
religion. Such inner experience, for Lonergan, is
consciousness as distinct from self-knowledge. Once
again, of course, we run into the problem of ambiguity, for "conscious" is commonly used to mean "knowledge." So, for example, we say that we are conscious
of the fact that it is raining, and we mean that we
know it is raining. But there is a more technical
meaning of "conscious," and perhaps the best way to
get at it is to ask, How do I know it is raining? I
may answer by appealing to sense experience and point
to the drops of rain. But this appeal presupposes a
rather significant fact, namely, that I'm awake, that
I'm not in a coma, that I'm conscious and capable of
sensation, perception, feelings, images, ideas, and a
host of other conscious and intentional operations.
Important here is to note that this consciousness is
not some extra operation or enjoys an existence apart

228

III.

from sensation, feeling, judging, etc. Lonergan,
then, speaks of religious experience in terms of religious consciousness, as a particular quality or
taste of consciousness that may or may not be attended
to, questioned, felt, imagined, conceived, known:

> To say that (religious experience - M. O'C.)
> is conscious is not to say that it is known.
> What is conscious, indeed, is experienced.
> But human knowing is not just experiencing.
> Human knowing includes experiencing but adds
> to it attention, scrutiny, inquiry, insight,
> conception, naming, reflecting, checking,
> judging. The whole problem of cognitional
> theory is to effect the transition from op-
> erations as experienced to operations as
> known. A great part of psychiatry is help-
> ing people to make the transition from con-
> scious feelings to known feelings. In like
> manner the gift of God's love ordinarily is
> not objectified in knowledge, but remains
> within subjectivity as a dynamic vector, a
> mysterious undertow, a fateful call to a
> dreaded holiness.23

Lonergan realizes that a distinction between consciousness and self-knowledge may seem strange and par-
adoxical, and so he clarifies what he means by drawing
attention to cognitional theory:

> We are all conscious of our sensing and
> our feeling, our inquiring and our under-
> standing, our deliberating and deciding.
> None of these activities occurs when one
> is in a coma or dreamless sleep. In that
> basic sense they are conscious. Still
> they are not yet properly known. They
> are just an infra-structure, a component
> within knowing that in large part remains
> merely potential. It is only when we
> heighten consciousness by adverting not

229

III.

only to objects but also to activities,
when we begin to sort out the activities,
to assign them their distinctive names,
to distinguish and to relate, only then
that we begin to move from the mere infra-
structure that is consciousness to the
compound of infra- and supra-structure
that is man's knowledge of his own cognitional process.[24]

Lonergan notes that a similar distinction between consciousness and self-knowledge may be found in the
client-centered therapy of Carl Rogers, that seeks to
help the patient come to an explicit knowledge of an
infra-structure of feelings that are just conscious
(and a source of turmoil or dismay) but not identified,
named, distinguished, known. Again, the work of Karen
Horney traces a deeper level of consciousness in which
a repressed impulse is present and "registers," though
we are not explicitly aware of it. Wilhelm Stekel
follows Klages in distinguishing between that which is
not thought about, and that which is present but not
recognized. Maslow discovered that peak experiences
were not rare but common; it is just that they pertain
to the conscious infra-structure, so that people are
simply unaware of the fact of their occurrence.[25]

But Lonergan would urge that we not only believe
the testimony of himself or others, but that we verify
the distinction for ourselves, from our own "experience." Think, for example, of an important decision
you are called upon to make; you find yourself a mass
of conflicts and opposed feelings, only some of which
you can identify and know.[26]

230

   The main reason why Lonergan offers this technical meaning of "experience" is, I think, to help us
in asking the right questions about religious experience and in understanding religious experience in
its tremendously diverse manifestations. More specifically, he is inviting our attention to that which is
symbolized by mankind's religious symbols and traditions, asking us to attend, not merely to the outward
data, but as well to the quality of consciousness
symbolized and expressed. It remains, of course, that
experience as an infra-structure easily goes unnoticed
until we explicitly advert to its reality and relate
it to a multitude of further elements that are already
understood and known. Nor is religious experience, religious consciousness, any exception. Lonergan stresses
at length the openness of the human subject for development, the plasticity and perfectibility of the human
person, the need for education and socialization by
which we master the network of symbolic systems available to us in our milieu.[27] So Lonergan notes that
religious experience, because merely conscious without
being known, needs cultivation. If we are to advert
explicitly to it, if its meaning is to surface and bud
forth and bear fruit by permeating our conscious living
and thinking, then cultivation is needed. To this end
there is available to us our symbolic context in which
we are born and that over time we assimilate. It is
most especially by the word, by linguistic symbols,
that we come to interpret ourselves to ourselves, and
of course the quality of the interpretation depends

III.

both on the words available to us as well as on our
responsiveness and attentiveness.

It is, expectedly, religious tradition that is
most directly concerned with nourishing and cultivating religious experience, and Lonergan distinguishes
various stages in the scope that such religious traditions may have.[28] In the earliest stage, the whole
of the universe and of human living pertains to the
realm of the sacred, so that all of mankind's conscious activity is colored by its reference to what
is beyond mankind and this world.[29] In a later stage
human symbols are differentiated and institutional-
ized, so that religion and religious symbols come to
take their place alongside other dimensions of human
living and thinking. What formerly pertained to a
sacralized universe becomes increasingly desacral-
ized, but a specifically religious realm remains;
it is localized through sacred places and buildings,
temporalized through sacred times and seasons, cultivated and promoted by individual mystics, prophets,
and priests who attempt to diffuse their own reference
to the sacred throughout an entire people or nation
and to integrate specifically religious concerns with
the rest of human living.[30] Finally, at least in the
contemporary Western world, the universe is desacral-
ized, institutional religions appear to be on the decline, and human living is secularized; religious experience tends to remain captive in mankind's conscious infra-structure, the institution of religion

becomes the custodian of a privatized religion, and in the absence of a theology rooted in transcendence there is proclaimed the death of god.[31]

But if the symbolic context is subject to such great shifts in its overt support and cultivation of religious experience, it remains, according to Lonergan, that the fundamental issue is not whether our symbolic context is or is not overtly religious. What commonly is referred to as the process of secularization is nothing more than the result of increasing specialization and differentiation in mankind's conscious living and thinking, particularly of the sort described earlier in Chapter Two; this process is really an opportunity for religion and theology to concentrate more fully on its own proper sphere and, through such concentration, to diffuse its reference to the transcendent throughout the whole of human affairs in the promotion of human authenticity.[32] So Lonergan insists that the main issue is not so much whether our symbolic contexts are explicitly "religious," but rather whether or not any symbolic context or tradition authentically mirrors and promotes what it means to be authentically human.

With this mention of human authenticity we are approaching something that is very fundamental to Lonergan's thought, and it might be well to pause and get our bearings. I have referred to the absence of God in modern culture - the dominant role of academic specializations that speak of this world and

233

III.

of what pertains to human experience, the increasing
inability of institutional religion and theology to
speak of God and of this world's reference to God. I
drew attention to attempts to reverse this trend by
working out a theological anthropology, the main concern of which is to begin from mankind's existential
horizon and human historicity in order to reveal the
native orientation of the human subject to God. I
mentioned that Lonergan places the ground of this orientation in human religious experience, but added that
this experience pertains to the infra-structure of
conscious living and, like all human experience, needs
cultivation and promotion by the human communities
into which each of us is born. Those communities and
their traditions may conceive themselves in exclusively
religious terms, as in primitive times; in both religious and secular terms, as occurred mostly from the
axial shift in human history between 800 and 200 B. C.,
down to about the seventeenth century; in secular and
often secularist terms in modernity. Finally, I noted
that Lonergan would direct our attention away from the
specifically religious cultivation of religious experience to the broader and, for him, much more fundamental
question of whether our contemporary human communities
and traditions, religious or secular, promote authentic
human existence. He points us in this direction in the
conviction that religion, religious studies, and theologies can play and must play a constitutive role in
promoting an authentic humanism: but this demands
that religion and religious traditions and theologies

234

themselves be authentic, and that religious meaning
and value is diffused throughout man's making of man,
contributing to the reversal of the decline that so
easily blinds human vision and corrupts human praxis.

The fundamental thing, then, is human authenticity
and the authenticity of the various symbolic contexts
or traditions that are available to us in interpreting
ourselves and our world. Here, there is no doubt in
my mind that Lonergan's turn to the question of human
authenticity is his "response" to the mentality associated with Enlightenment thought. He would acknowledge
the achievement of Enlightenment concern for a better
world brought about by human creativity; but he would
insist that the Enlightenment error was the assumption
that human progress was an automatic affair, that progress could result from individual and group egoism
that identifies progress with the overthrow of all
cultural and social and religious tradition. The Enlightenment failure was its inability to discriminate
authentic and inauthentic tradition, and thereby it
promoted the naive and erroneous view that "modernity"
is automatically authentic, while "tradition" is a
mere relic from an ignorant and unenlightened past.
Such was what Lonergan refers to as the age of innocence, that in our own day has come to an abrupt end.
The Enlightenment presumption of progress, sweetness,
and light has crumbled under the ongoing fact of decline, and, as Lonergan mentions in the following passages, people begin to question once again themselves
and their traditions:

III.

As Kierkegaard asked whether he was
really a Christian, so divers men can ask
themselves whether or not they are genuine
Catholics or Protestants, Moslems or Budd-
hists, Platonists or Aristotelians, Kant-
ians or Hegelians, artists or scientists,
and so forth. Now they may answer that
they are, and their answers may be correct. But they can also answer affirma-
tively and still be mistaken. In that
case there will exist a series of points
in which they are what the ideals of the
tradition demand, but there will be another
series in which there is a greater or less
divergence. These points of divergence are
overlooked from a selective inattention, or
from a failure to understand, or from an
undetected rationalization. What I am is
one thing, what a genuine Christian or
Buddhist is, is another, and I am unaware
of the difference. My unawareness is un-
expressed. I have no language to express
what I am, so I use the language of the
tradition I unauthentically appropriate,
and thereby I devaluate, distort, water
down, corrupt that language.

Such devaluation, distortion, corruption
may occur only in scattered individuals.
But it may occur on a more massive scale,
and then the words are repeated, but the
meaning is gone. The chair was still the
chair of Moses, but it was occupied by
the scribes and Pharisees. The theology
was still scholastic, but the scholasticism
was decadent. The religious order still
read out the rules, but one wonders whether
the home fires were still burning. The
sacred name of science may still be invoked
but, as Edmund Husserl has argued, all significant scientific ideals can vanish to be
replaced by the conventions of a clique.
So the unauthenticity of individuals becomes
the unauthenticity of a tradition. Then, in

236

the measure a subject takes the tradition, as it exists, for his standard, in that measure he can do no more than authentically realize unauthenticity.[33]

I find this passage to be of particular importance, for some may wonder how such a thing as "human authenticity,' so central to Lonergan's thought, can possibly be objectified and made a methodological norm. Behind this wonder lies the notion of authenticity as a purely private matter. And although it will be only in subsequent sections of this chapter that the full objective reality of authenticity will be clarified, I think that the passage quoted indicates rather well that authenticity, while always a private matter, inevitably has public overtones and is embodied, actualized, in communities and traditions. As mentioned earlier the "age of innocence," when one presumed both personal and community authenticity, cannot be affirmed by anyone except a classicist. The symbolic contexts that shape us, our religions and our sciences, our philosophies and our politics, all are susceptible to inauthenticity, so that we approach them, as Lonergan notes with Ricoeur, by a hermeneutic of suspicion as well as by a hermeneutic of recovery.[34] In other words, the authentic cultivation of human consciousness, including human consciousness in its orientation to God, is never to be considered an automatic and secure achievement. So Lonergan observes that the human subject is ever to be critical, not just of himself or herself, but of the tradition

237

III.

that nourishes him or her. And the needed cure, as
he often points out, is not the undoing or overthrow
of tradition, returning to a primitive state, but
rather the undoing of any given tradition's inauthenticity.[35]

In this task, Lonergan assigns a leadership role
to religion and theology, for human authenticity is
particularly of concern to the religions of mankind.
At its best, religion is human authenticity achieved.
Following the lead of W. C. Smith,[36] Lonergan asks
whether it is possible to get behind the tremendous
diversity in human religious symbols and traditions
and to identify some element common to all of them.
Basically, it is the "why?" question about religion,
that asks about the nature of the commitment involved
in living religiously. Smith had argued that such
religious living was not merely a matter of living
in the presence of certain religious symbols; as well
there was an involvement with these symbols or through
them in a quite special way -- a way that could lead
far beyond the symbols demanding the totality of a
person's response and affecting the person's relationship with himself or herself, with other people,
with the universe, what lay beyond the universe. So
Lonergan asks what it is that makes religion change,
transform, people's lives, what sort of conscious experience lies behind the religious symbols and is
striving to find expression through those symbols?

Lonergan's answer is in terms of the inner con-

238

viction of the fulfillment of one's own personal existence, the experience of the fullness of what it
means to be authentically human. Negatively, Lonergan notes that such religious commitment is absent
from the person who is just drifting through life,
content to do what everyone else is doing, to say
what everyone else is thinking, where the "everyone
else" is just drifting as well. Commitment occurs
when one freely and responsibly steps out of the
company of drifters to face the problem of personal
existence, _Existenz_, when one discovers that one has
to decide for oneself what one is to do with oneself
and one's life.[37] Such authentic existence commonly
is realized when one falls in love, and so it is that
Lonergan finds the core of religious experience, at
least in the religious traditions of the Middle East
and West,[38] to lie in the experience of unrestricted
loving. For besides the authenticity that is the
fruit of the love of intimacy and the love of one's
country, indeed underpinning those loves, is the love
of God:

> (To this love - M. O'C.) there testifies
> a great religious tradition that pro-
> claims: "Hear, O Israel: the Lord our
> God is the only Lord; love the Lord your
> God with all your heart, with all your
> soul, with all your mind, and with all
> your strength" (Mk 12,29f.). Of such
> love St. Paul spoke as God's love flood-
> ing our inmost heart through the Holy
> Spirit he has given us (Rom 5,5). To
> the power of that love the same apostle
> bore witness with the words:

239

III.

> " . . . there is nothing in death or
> life, in the realm of spirits or super-
> human powers, in the world as it is or
> the world as it shall be, in the forces
> of the universe, in heights or depths -
> nothing in all creation that can separate
> us from the love of God in Christ Jesus
> our Lord" (Rom 8,38f.).[39]

So Lonergan insists that the experience of being
in love with God is a human experience, in the technical meaning of "experience" that refers to a single
element, an infra-structure, in human knowing. Such
religious consciousness varies from individual to individual, for consciousness is like a polyphony and
religious experience may be a leading voice or a middle one or a low one; it may be dominant and recurrent, or it may be occasionally audible, or it may
be weak and barely noticeable; it may be in perfect
harmony with the rest of our conscious living, it may
be a dissonance that comes and goes, it may vanish
altogether or it may be so disruptive as to threaten
mental breakdown.[40] It is subject to development in
the lives of any of us, so that traditional spirituality distinguishes stages in the spiritual life
named the purgative, illuminative, and unitive ways.[41]
Finally, Lonergan notes that there are intricate relationships between religious development and moral
and intellectual development; most important here,
of course, is the question of the social, cultural,
and historical contexts within which any of us happens to live, for human development depends only
partly on our own creativity and is heavily dependent

on the resources available to us at any time or
place. Our contexts pre-determine our interests
and attention, language fixes the scope within
which we interpret ourselves to ourselves, all
symbols fix our commitments and direct our decisions.[42]

At this point the fact of religious experience
may be questioned as to its validity and objectivity.
The experiential objectivity of the experience as
simply given, as lived, but not yet questioned, not
yet known, becomes crucial especially in our own day
when its reality and validity and significance are
so massively denied or ignored. And so Lonergan invites us to consider the question of the possibility
of valid and objective religious knowledge.

2. Religious Faith

The present chapter has been described as an
attempt to set forth the broad lines of Lonergan's
theological anthropology. The main purpose in doing
this is to provide contemporary theology with a firm
basis in the world of human historicity and Existenz,
so that theology might become an integral dimension
in mankind's interpretation of itself and its world.
In the previous section I began with an account of
Lonergan's understanding of the human experience of
being in love with God as the commitment that holds
within itself the fullness of what it means to be
authentically human - a love that gives us an orien-

241

III.

tation within our universe and to our fellow human
subjects. As an experience that is conscious but
not known it is lived out in praxis before, if
ever, it becomes attended to, questioned, interpreted, affirmed, deliberately related to our moral
and cognitive development and to the social or cultural contexts in which we live.

In the present section I wish to sketch Lonergan's account of the impact of religious experience
on our conscious living. A first reflection will
indicate that religious experience generates in us
a conscious conviction and awareness of the fulfillment of our human thrust to self-transcendence. A
second reflection identifies this conviction more
specifically with a transvaluation of values, a new
sort of knowledge consequent upon the religious horizon of being in love with God; for Lonergan, that
new apprehension of transcendent value is faith.

(1)   The Normative Conviction of Authenticity

Inasmuch as religious experience is experience,
it is given immediately in consciousness; as simply
given it is indubitable and unquestionable, constitutive of the a priori existential reality of the
subject as subject so that to deny its reality would
be tantamount to denying one's own consciousness.
But inasmuch as religious experience is attended to
and questioned, further criteria of reality and objectivity come into play, the first of which is what

242

III.

Lonergan refers to as normative objectivity that is
simply the unfolding of the unrestricted thrust towards human authenticity.[43] It is opposed to the
mere subjectivity of wishful thinking, rash or ex-
cessively cautious judgments, allowing undue emotional
interference in the unfolding of our proper human development.[44] Within the present context it is awareness of authenticity - the inner assurance that I am
authentically appropriating an authentic religious
tradition.

In order to describe the manner in which this
inner conviction is operative, Lonergan discusses
the path of the authentic development of the human
subject. He refers to such authentic development as
the thrust of the human spirit to self-transcendence,
an orientation that becomes ever more explicit with
successively higher levels of conscious activity:

> . . . human authenticity is a matter of
> following the built-in law of the human
> spirit. Because we can experience, we
> should attend. Because we can under-
> stand, we should inquire. Because we
> can reach the truth, we should reflect
> and check. Because we can realize
> values in ourselves and promote them
> in others, we should deliberate. In
> the measure that we follow these pre-
> cepts, in the measure we fulfil these
> conditions of being human persons, we
> also achieve self-transcendence both
> in the field of knowledge and in the
> field of action.[45]

"Being human," then, is authentic inasmuch as

243

III.

each one of us strives to realize his or her potential. Such striving is a matter of following the open and unrestricted dynamism of our conscious and intentional operations, and, in this sense, cumulatively and progressively moving beyond the self as merely substance to the self as human subject.[46] Such moving beyond or self-transcendence (sich über-holen) is of qualitatively different kinds or of different tastes, just as there are qualitative differences in our conscious and intentional operations.

As unconscious, in deep sleep or in a coma, we are alive and human but our living is that of a substance rather than of a subject. We begin reaching beyond ourselves as substance and emerge if ever so fragmentarily as subject in our dreaming. Here Lonergan draws on the work of the existential analyst, Ludwig Binswanger, who distinguished between dreams of the night and those of the morning. Lonergan notes that the latter take us beyond our basic vital operations to consciousness and to conscious anticipation of our waking state, so that we begin obscurely to take a stance within our world, to possess a horizon.[47]

Upon awaking we end our dreaming and move into the world of our immediate experience - a world of sensations, feelings, movements, memories. The world of immediacy, in Lonergan's meaning of the word, is the world of the subject simply as experiencing, in the technical sense of "experiencing" explained ear-

244

lier. It is the subject simply as conscious, prior
to inquiring, understanding, conceiving, judging,
acting.[48]

Lonergan continues his analysis by noting that
we move beyond ourselves as confined to our immediate
surroundings when we try to grasp the meaning of
what is immediately experienced. We imagine and inquire, we draw upon our language to ask specific
questions, we exercise intelligence in trying to
answer these questions. So it is that our world of
immediate experience, though it remains, now becomes
just a tiny fragment of a vaster world that is our
symbolic context: a world constructed by imagina-
tion and intelligence, shaped by the experiences,
imaginations, intelligence of others, cultivated by
their languages, knowledge, and deeds. It is our
entry into a world that includes the past and future
as well as the present, the remote and distant as
well as that which is immediately given.[49]

But with the use of our intelligence, Lonergan
adds, we have not yet exhausted our talents and
abilities as human. In itself intelligence is un-
reliable: both myth and philosophy are products of
intelligence, as are science and myth, astronomy
and astrology, chemistry and alchemy, history and
legend. Yet philosophy, science, astronomy, history go beyond their counterparts to yield, not just
what is clever, bright, even insightful, but what
actually is so or can be reasonably affirmed or de-

nied. So Lonergan notes that critical judgment allows
us to take a critical stance in our symbolic world
mediated by meaning and to pronounce that world real
or imaginary, true or false. We move beyond ourselves,
for now we state not just what seems to be, appears to
be, what is likely, but rather what truly in fact is
so. [50]

It is one thing to know reality as independent
of ourselves, thereby achieving cognitional self-
transcendence, and quite another to determine what
we are to do, how we are to orientate ourselves existentially towards whatever is to be done. With
such deliberate decision we reach a further, moral
self-transcendence. Beyond questions for intelligence and questions for reflection, there are questions for deliberation; and beyond pleasures and
pains and moral feelings there are true values and
responsibility. So it is, according to Lonergan,
that we come to take responsible control over ourselves, to respond to the challenge of what psychologists describe as self-actualization, what spiritual
writers describe as self-mastery, what we experience
ourselves as self-sacrifice. With moral self-transcendence we are moved from consciousness to conscience. [51]

Moving closer to the theme at hand, Lonergan observes that this move from consciousness to conscience implies that there are differences in the
quality of our consciousness, in the experience we

have of ourselves at different levels of self-
transcendence. In a sense we are different people
at different times, as the self we experience is
the self relaxing in the world of sensitive spontaneity, the different self striving to understand
a problem, the further self arriving at a balanced
judgment, and the existential self at peace in the
experience that good decisions have been made. Yet,
far from being troubled at these differences, we
normally do not even advert to them, for they seem
to combine in a deep and fundamental unity that allows us to speak of our self in the singular. So
the experience we have of our conscious living is an
experience of wholeness, of continuity, of unity;
and there is abundant evidence to suggest that such
unity is characteristic, not just of our conscious
living, but of our unconscious as well.[52]

At this point Lonergan draws attention to the
intersubjective dimension of human development, the
dimension that is of particular importance in his
analysis of the normative conviction of authenticity.
The fundamental unity of the self-transcending subject can itself be experienced in its wholeness in
the experience of falling in love. A unitive bond
gathers individual subjects into a new creation, a
new synthesis, a new and deeper experience of wholeness and integration, and that bond is love. So it
is that beyond both cognitional and moral self-
transcendence there is the self-transcendence of the

247

person in love, a self-transcendence that may be
named affective or personal or unitive. The love
may be domestic, uniting husband and wife. It may
be the love that binds together a human group, nation, culture, the love of one's neighbor. It may
be the love that orientates us in the world and universe by drawing us to what is other-worldly, and
that commonly is named religious love. In each case
love is transforming and adds to the moral self-transcendence that is the product of our own authentic
knowing and choosing a higher self-transcendence that
is not chosen but to which we respond, and our response places us in a new world. Where before our human development, our self-transcendence, was a personal quest to move to ever greater understanding,
ever more accurate judgments, ever sharper discernment of value, now the power of love, while by no
means destroying that basis, transforms it entirely
by adding a development that comes, no longer from
ourselves alone, but from another or others. So
Lonergan draws here on Pascal, who commented that
the heart has reasons that reason does not know, a
comment that Lonergan interprets as follows:

> Such transforming love has its occasions,
> its conditions, its causes. But once it
> comes and as long as it lasts, it takes
> over. One no longer is one's own. More-
> over, in the measure that this transform-
> ation is effective, development becomes
> not merely from below upwards but more
> fundamentally from above downwards.
> There has begun a life in which the heart

has reasons which reason does not know.
There has been opened up a new world in
which the old adage, <u>nihil amatum nisi</u>
<u>prius cognitum</u>, yields to a new truth,
<u>nihil vere cognitum nisi prius amatum</u>.53

I have been presenting Lonergan's account of human authenticity as self-transcendence, and it remains
only to add a note on the meaning he attaches to inauthenticity. This latter is the fruit of a refusal
to follow the built-in dynamism of the human spirit,
a decision to remain closed-in on ourselves, a radical refusal to be open. Moreover, any of us easily is
inauthentic, for steady and unimpeded development is
rare, and our authenticity is ever a withdrawal from
inauthenticity. The key is an exercise of liberty,
wherein we respond consistently to truth, value, love;
but such response is dialectical, ever an acceptance
of the challenge to keep growing, developing, by overcoming mistakes, errors, selfishness, alienation. So
Lonergan maintains that for any one of us, being human
is the constant struggle between the self who is trans-
cending and the self to be transcended.54 Incessantly
we know ourselves to be called to leave the security
of our nest, our present surroundings, our present
horizons, our present selves, and to reach beyond whom
we are to the person we could become. Lonergan acknowledges it is a difficult task, and even its achievement in coming to truth, values, and love is an
achievement that is never secure or permanent; with
each advancement in truth we become more deeply aware
both of past errors and of the truth we do not yet

III.

know; each advancement in goodness reveals the mistakes of the past as well as the challenges of the future; and even the stability of love, that sets my universe unfolding as it should, provokes wonder at my previous lovelessness just as it casts a shadow over the stability in all that I experience love to be.[55]

Lonergan realizes that love, whether of intimacy, of neighbor, of God, is not unquestionable or indubitable in its permanency. Even the complete self-transcendence of being in love with God, while indubitable in its presence, nonetheless is a gift that is contained within fragile vessels, to the point even that the more deeply conscious we are of this gift, the greater the consciousness of the fragility of our own response and of the need for deeper commitment. Nonetheless, Lonergan insists that the conviction of authenticity, in one who is authentic, is both normative and unmistakable, while those who are evading the issue of self-realization are busy concealing the fact from themselves. From this Lonergan concludes that the inner conviction of the fullness of authenticity in religious commitment is so very much the inner dynamism of human reality itself that one cannot but be aware of its authenticity and of its vital role in human development, just as one cannot but hide the absence of such commitment when one is busy evading the abiding imperatives of what it is to be human.[56]

The dimensions of such other-worldly loving are many, and the many dimensions are differently stressed by the religious traditions of mankind. Yet Lonergan would draw attention to what he believes to be a common element in those traditions, namely, that this inner conviction of authenticity that is the fruit of religious loving is a conviction best described in terms of a transvaluation of values, a knowledge born of religious love, that Lonergan identifies as religious faith.

(2)   Faith as the Knowledge Born of Religious Love

Lonergan maintains that the major exception to the adage, <u>Nihil amatum nisi praecognitum</u>, is God's gift of his love flooding our hearts.[57] He concludes that in religious matters love precedes knowledge, and insists that the knowledge consequent upon such love is unique: "Faith is the knowledge born of religious love."[58]

To explain what he means by a knowledge born of love, Lonergan refers to Pascal's remark that the heart has reasons that reason does not know.   Lonergan interprets "reason" (in the singular) as the factual knowledge that we reach by our experiencing, understanding, verifying.   He interprets "heart" as the existential human subject who is in love.   He interprets the "heart's reasons" as the feelings of that subject as recognizing and discerning values.   So Lonergan concludes:

III.

> The meaning, then, of Pascal's remark
> would be that, besides the factual know-
> ledge reached by experiencing, under-
> standing, and verifying, there is another
> kind of knowledge reached through the
> discernment of value and the judgments of
> value of a person in love.[59]

Faith, then, is an apprehension of transcendent value, an apprehension generated by the experience of being in love with God, being in love without restrictions and without conditions. In terms that relate faith to the inner conviction of authenticity mentioned earlier in this section, Lonergan describes faith as the experienced fulfillment of our unrestricted thrust to self-transcendence, or as our actuated orientation towards the mystery of love and awe. For this reason he notes that this fulfillment is often objectified in terms that suggest various dimensions of our thrust to self-transcendence: to be human is to be intelligent, and faith is an apprehension of what is absolute in intelligence and intelligibility; to be human is to be reasonable, and faith is an apprehension of what is absolute in truth and reality; to be human is to be free and responsible, and faith is an apprehension of what is absolute in goodness and holiness.

Besides this recognition of transcendent value, Lonergan draws attention to the relative aspect of faith that places all other values in the light and shadow of transcendent value. Because transcendent value is supreme, it is preferred to all other values. But at the same time transcendent value places all other values in a new light: it transvalues them,

transforms them, makes them all the more worthwhile
and worthy of pursuit. So Lonergan contrasts the
vision of faith with the absence of that vision:
without faith, the source of values is man and the
goal of mankind's striving is the human good that
man can accomplish; but in faith, the source of value
is God and God's love, while the values chosen by man
now embrace the entire universe. So it is that the
human good now is taken up into a higher perspective
and given a higher finality, reaching beyond this
world to God and to God's world. Such a faith-appre-
hension grounds human worship, as well as human cooperation; it underpins man's striving for holiness,
as well as his struggle to develop and perfect skills
and virtues; it opens man's horizon to what lies beyond death, as well as motivating his ministry in and
to this world. In this way human authenticity consists fundamentally in being a mirror of God, in the
sense of being ourselves origins of true love and of
values.[60]

I think it is safe to say that Lonergan's understanding of faith as intimately related both to its
source in God's love as well as to human development
and progress is meant as a corrective to views that
either so stress transcendence as to ignore immanence,
or so stress immanence as to lose all reference to the
transcendent.[61] Most especially, perhaps, Lonergan
seems very concerned to link faith with human progress,
so that to promote authentic human development in any
sphere is to contribute to a climate of religious

III.

faith, just as the authentic promotion of religion
will invariably have repercussions on other areas of
man's social and cultural life. In particular, Lonergan understands the main role of faith in this regard to be the undoing of the decline that so easily
distorts human life and thought:

> Most of all, faith has the power of un-
> doing decline. Decline disrupts a cul-
> ture with conflicting ideologies. It
> inflicts on individuals the social, e-
> conomic, and psychological pressures
> that for human frailty amount to deter-
> minism. It multiplies and heaps up the
> abuses and absurdities that breed re-
> sentment, hatred, anger, violence. It
> is not propaganda and it is not argument
> but religious faith that will liberate
> human reasonableness from its ideologi-
> cal prisons. It is not the promises of
> men but religious hope that can enable
> men to resist the vast pressures of so-
> cial decay. If passions are to quiet
> down, if wrongs are to be not exacer-
> bated, not ignored, not merely palliated,
> but acknowledged and removed, then human
> possessiveness and human pride have to
> be replaced by religious charity, by the
> charity of the suffering servant, by
> self-sacrificing love. Men are sinners.
> If human progress is not to be ever dis-
> torted and destroyed by the inattention,
> oversights, irrationality, irresponsi-
> bility of decline, men have to be re-
> minded of their sinfulness. They have
> to acknowledge their real guilt and a-
> mend their ways. They have to learn
> with humility that religious development
> is dialectical, that the task of repent-
> ance and conversion is life-long.[62]

I think it is possible here to discern more

clearly the direction in which Lonergan's thought is moving. This chapter began by mentioning the absence of God in modern culture and Lonergan's conviction that the path to a renewed presence of God lies in exposing the fundamentally religious dimension of human living, especially the link between religious authenticity and individual, social, or cultural development. He is convinced that it is possible to speak of at least a potential presence of God, for there remains the indubitable fact of religious experience. Flowing from that experience is the knowledge of faith that is the apprehension of transcendent value and the transformation of all other values that places religion at the heart of genuine human progress and that assigns religion a dominant role in overcoming human decline. But if we agree with Lonergan and affirm with him the reality of religious experience and the fact of living faith, it remains that we are still a long way from giving an account of how such religious experience and faith in fact might come to bear the fruit that lies hidden within that experience and apprehension. At this point Lonergan invites our attention to further aspects of religious living. In the next section I shall discuss his understanding of the "faith-community," the religious tradition in history, whose expressions of religious meaning and value we are invited to believe. Then, in the fourth section, I'll discuss Lonergan's account of the reflection on itself by this community, as it seeks to give an account of the hope that informs its life and

III.

praxis.

3. Religious Belief

In his account of religious experience Lonergan
referred to the role of the religious tradition in
cultivating that experience. Because we are symbolic
animals, our development is ever a matter of adapting
to our historical milieu, of allowing ourselves to be
moulded and shaped according to the symbolic systems
made available to us in the processes variously named
socialization, acculturation, education.[63] Among
these symbolic systems in our own day is that system
or tradition explicitly concerned with expressions of
religious meaning and religious value. Lonergan
notes the uniqueness of this symbolic system, for
though its symbols are indeed human, expressing the
spirit of man, they nonetheless generally claim to
refer to what lies beyond man and beyond anything in
this world that can be observed by man.[64]

Such outward expressions intend, of course, to
capture the meaning and value of that prior word spoken to us in the immediate experience of God's love
flooding our hearts. The outward expressions attempt
to give a focus and clarity to what is conscious but
not known, and would promote an ever fuller knowledge
of what it means to be in love with God. In that
task, Lonergan would draw our attention especially to
the social dimension of religious experience, reli-

gious faith, and religious expression:

> For however personal and intimate is re-
> ligious experience, still it is not sol-
> itary. The same gift can be given to
> many, and the many can recognize in one
> another a common orientation in their
> living and feeling, in their criteria
> and their goals. From a common commun-
> ion with God, there springs a religious
> community.[65]

The religious community expresses itself in a variety
of manners and such expression becomes traditional as
the community endures and one generation succeeds another. There is built up a deposit of traditional
wisdom and learning, as each generation builds upon
the past and carries that past forward by virtue of
its own contribution to the common fund. And, as
Lonergan noted earlier, the authenticity of that tradition is the product of genuine faith resting in
turn upon genuine religious experience.

Lonergan described faith as an apprehension of
transcendent value and as a transformation of all
other values in light of transcendent value. He now
would add that among the values discerned by faith is
the value of believing the expressions of religious
meaning and value proposed by the religious community.
Those expressions are the judgments of fact and of
value common to the community and, indeed giving that
community its specific identity. Into such communities we are born, and from such communities we learn
the words that interpret us to ourselves. And the

III.

acceptance of such an interpretation, the acceptance
of the judgments of the community is, according to
Lonergan, largely a matter of belief. And that such
belief is worthwhile is something we know because of
our faith.[66]

Because belief plays such a large role in the
appropriation of our religious tradition, and in the
manner in which that tradition develops or changes
with successive generations, Lonergan gives considerable attention to the process of coming to believe
critically the outward expressions of religious meaning and value.[67] I think it is fair to say that
Lonergan's analysis of the structure of belief is an
effort to clarify the meaning of "tradition," a question that is all the more important in our post-Enlightenment era that tends to disparage tradition as
an impediment to true human progress; Lonergan would
point out the error of such a view by drawing our
attention to the key function of tradition in the
constitution of our humanity generally and of our
religiosity in particular.[68]

Lonergan's general analysis of belief begins
in the following way:

> To appropriate one's social, cultural,
> religious heritage is largely a matter
> of belief. There is, of course, much
> that one finds out for oneself, that
> one knows simply in virtue of one's
> own inner and outer experience, one's
> own insights, one's own judgments of
> fact and of value. But such immanently

generated knowledge is but a small
fraction of what any civilized man
considers himself to know. His immediate experience is filled out by
an enormous context constituted by
reports of the experience of other
men at other places and times. His
understanding rests not only on his
own but also on the experience of
others, and its development owes little indeed to his personal original-
ity, much to his repeating in himself
the acts of understanding first made
by others, and most of all to presuppositions that he has taken for granted, because they commonly are assumed
and, in any case, he has neither the
time nor the inclination nor, perhaps,
the ability to investigate for himself.
Finally, the judgments, by which he as-
sents to truths of fact and of value,
only rarely depend exclusively on his
immanently generated knowledge, for
such knowledge stands not by itself in
some separate compartment but in sym-
biotic fusion with a far larger context of beliefs.[69]

Such is the social character of human knowledge,
and Lonergan emphasizes it plays a key role in all
realms of human knowing. He notes that science is
often contrasted with belief, but insists that belief plays as great a role in science as in most
other areas of human knowing. Here, Lonergan has in
mind what generally is called "indirect verification":
the scientist, while he doubtless has an original contribution of his own to make, nonetheless invariably
builds upon the work of other scientists, presuming
its validity and confirming its validity indirectly by

III.

incorporating it successfully into his own work, without having to bother to repeat in detail the original contributions of others. Such is the indirect process of verification and falsification that is crucial to ongoing and cumulative scientific process; any other alternative would be primitivism, demanding that each scientist begin fresh from some total ignorance and work everything out for himself.

So Lonergan observes that human knowledge is not some individual possession but rather a common fund - from which each may draw by believing, to which each may contribute in the measure that he performs his cognitional operations properly and reports accurately their results. Through such communication and belief there are generated common sense, common knowledge, common science, common values, a common climate of opinion. Lonergan is aware that this public fund may suffer from blindspots and errors, but he adds that it's all we've got and that the remedy for its shortcomings is not the rejection of belief (thereby returning to primitivism), but rather the critical and selfless stance that purifies tradition by promoting progress and offsetting decline.[70]

Just what this critical and selfless stance is, is described by Lonergan in his account of the process whereby we can reasonably and responsibly come to believe our heritage or tradition. The very possibility of such a process lies in the objectivity of truth; truth is a public matter, something that

260

is the fruit of cognitional self-transcendence that pronounces this or that to be independent of myself and within reach, not of those who have eyes to see, but of those who ask questions and reach correct answers. So Lonergan writes:

> I cannot give another my eyes for him to see with, but I can truly report what I see, and he can believe. I cannot give another my understanding, but I can truly report what I have come to understand to be so, and he can believe. I cannot transfer to another my powers of judgment, but I can report what I affirm and what I deny, and he can believe me. Such is the first step. It is taken, not by the person that believes, but by the person whom he believes.[71]

The second step in the process of coming to believe is a general judgment of value that acknowledges and approves of the division of labor, both historically and socially, in the acquisition of knowledge. Such, for Lonergan, is the approval of the integral role that belief plays in human development - an approval which is critical, inasmuch as it realizes the possibility of error in this whole process.

Thirdly, there is a particular judgment of values. It is a matter of evaluating the various sources of what is proposed as worthy of belief, asking whether those sources were themselves critical and truly authentic. Such particular judgments often rest on the consensus of several witnesses, so that verification is of the indirect sort, particularly when it is generally accepted that the sources are indeed trustworthy and

III.

merit belief. Moreover, Lonergan notes that when
everything favors belief except one's own conviction
that a given statement is erroneous, the time has
come for the potential believer to question himself
in order to find out if the blockage to belief does
not in fact lie within his own error or limited horizon.

The fourth step is the decision to believe - a
deliberate choice that is consequent upon the general
and particular judgments of value. If believing generally is a good thing, if this particular statement
is worthy of belief, then I should believe it and in
fact choose to do so and my choice is reasonable.

The final step is the act of believing, whereby
I in my own mind judge to be true that judgment of
fact or value communicated to me. Lonergan notes that
the act of believing does not rest on immanently generated knowledge that is mine, but rather on the immanently generated knowledge of others.

Such is a sketch of Lonergan's account of the
process of coming to believe. As noted, he maintains
that religious belief has the very same structure, but
whereas non-religious belief rests on the basis of
factual knowledge, religious belief rests on the basis
of faith, the knowledge born of religious love.

It is worth mentioning that Lonergan relates this
matter of belief to the absence of God in modern culture.[72] In times of little social or cultural change,

262

beliefs are stable and generally are unquestioned, but in times of great social and cultural change, such as our own, beliefs too are changing; and because they are only beliefs, and not personally generated knowledge, such change in beliefs leaves people at a loss and quite bewildered. They are disoriented, feeling that everything they took for granted and cherished is now threatened. They may be tempted to disbelief or unbelief as a form of liberation, or they may conclude that unbelief is truly destructive of authentic human living. Such, Lonergan maintains, is the situation that is especially acute in Catholic circles, because up until Vatican II their beliefs were sheltered in secure isolation, whereas after the Council they have been exposed to the chill winds of modernity - of science, scholarship, philosophy, and of secular or secularist attitudes in everyday living.

It is precisely here that Lonergan raises the crucial issue of the restoration of belief in religious matters. He would urge that such a restoration, building on religious experience and faith, has to be truly creative and truly academic, demanding deep and thorough reflection by philosophers, scholars, and theologians on how to express meaningfully in our day the reality of religious experience, its meaning, its value, that to which it refers. Modern culture has to be known, assimilated, transformed, and such for Lonergan is the contemporary issue and challenge facing those who reflect on religion.

III.

4. Reflection on Religion

I have been outlining a few of the central elements in what might be called Lonergan's theological anthropology. The context of his thought is modern culture and the issue with which he is concerned is the absence of God in modern culture. At least in the Western world religion seems to have become a purely private affair, removed from the public sphere of cultural significance and pronounced an illusory comfort for weaker souls, an opium distributed by the rich to quiet the poor, a mythical projection into the sky of what really is mankind's own excellence.[73] I have mentioned Lonergan's conviction that the crisis is not due to an absence of religious experience; for there remains, not only a striving for human authenticity, but as well a depth of religious commitment that witnesses to the fact that such authenticity is an actual achievement and an integral component of the human horizon. I went on to add that Lonergan does not understand the crisis to be a crisis of faith; for there remains, not just the fact of religious experience, but as well an apprehension of transcendent value and a transformation of one's dedication to human values. In a further consideration it became apparent that Lonergan understands the present crisis to be a crisis of belief; among the values apprehended by faith is the value of believing the word of religion, of accepting the judgments of fact and of value proposed by the religious tradition. Yet in a time

of rapid social and cultural change, the beliefs
that underpin the religious tradition themselves
are changing as they come to be expressed in ever
new idioms, so that believers are at a loss in interpreting their religious commitment and faith to
themselves and their world. So Lonergan writes:

> . . . the analysis I am offering of our
> contemporary situation differs notably
> from simpler views that are more fre-
> quently heard. It is said that the
> Church had become a ghetto, that it had
> gone to excess in defensiveness and in
> rigidity, that it has to break away
> from its Byzantine and medieval trap-
> pings, that it has to speak to the peo-
> ple of today, and so forth.
>
> Now I do not think that these views are
> simply false, but I do think the truth
> they contain is expressed more politely,
> more accurately, and more helpfully, by
> noting that the Church, if it is to op-
> erate in the world, has to operate on
> the basis of the social order and cul-
> tural achievements of each time and
> place, that consequently its operation
> has to change with changes in its social
> and cultural context, that at present we
> have the task of a disengagement from
> classicist thought-forms and viewpoints,
> and, simultaneously, of a new involve-
> ment in modern culture.
>
> In brief, the contemporary issue is, not
> a new religion, not a new faith, but a
> belated social and cultural transition.[74]

It remains only to add that the challenge of
making the transpositions that will restore to religion an integral role in the societies and cultures

III.

of mankind is, for Lonergan, a highly complex task
demanding solidly academic reflection. For example,
in the introductory section to his 1964 treatise on
the Trinity, Lonergan mentions the opinion of some
that dogmas or academic reflection have little place
in religious matters, that we should stick to simplicity, common sense, feelings, emotions. Lonergan
opposes such views, and recalls that the function of
religion is to orientate and direct the whole of man's
living towards God. Accordingly, as human consciousness develops, so too must religion. He admits that
the simpler one's life-style, the simpler one's religion will be; but he adds that when human living
becomes highly diversified and highly specialised,
then to the many various aspects of such living there
correspond many and various functions of religion. So
Lonergan draws attention to the fact that religion may
be not just lived out in praxis but also judged and
evaluated by people who have achieved a more refined
and specialized type of intellectual development; to
exclude religion from such intellectual life would be
to serve the cause of secularism rather than the cause
of true religion. So Lonergan continues:

> But one may say, surely primitives and
> children can be genuinely religious, and
> just as surely, religious living does
> not consist in intellectual exercises.
> Quite true, but the argument simply mis-
> ses the point. For religion is not some
> eternal and immutable Platonic form,
> with but a single mode of participation
> for children and adults, for primitives

266

and highly-developed peoples alike. As
consciousness develops so too does religion, and so it is fallacious to infer
that what is appropriate for children
and for primitives constitutes the very
essence of religion, always and every-
where the same. Secondly, as we have
already said, with the development of
consciousness religion takes on many aspects and fulfills many functions; if
one particular aspect and function does
not constitute the whole of religion, it
does not follow that particular aspect
and function is therefore to be denied.75

In our own day, then, Lonergan urges a reflection
on religion that is as highly diversified and specialized as is the current stage of mankind's intellectual
reflection generally. He is quite aware that in fact
such reflection is taking place, both within theology
and in the disciplines that constitute religious studies. But he would again draw attention to the problem
of integration and unity, as well as to the more fundamental issues such as truth, value, and genuine religious commitment. He would point to the need for
authentic and methodological control of reflection on
religion, and just what he means by this may now be
sketched. Firstly, I shall indicate two manners in
which systematic reflection may be conceived, one
resting on a metaphysical basis, the other found in
modern empirical science. Lonergan finds both manners to be inadequate in dealing with religion, and
so he urges a new foundation based on intentionality
analysis. This is discussed in a second step under
the heading of a generalized reflection on religion.

III.

Finally, a third step indicates how such generalized reflection can ground the specialized methods that are most relevant to the investigation of religion - the methods of historical study, dialectical evaluation, and praxis. In my next chapter, I'll move on to the question of putting method and methods in theology.

(1)   Varieties of Systematic Reflection[76]

A moment ago I referred to Lonergan's contention that religion should develop as human consciousness itself develops and becomes ever more refined and specialized in its procedures. An infant is not an adult, nor is a pre-Socratic simply the same as a twentieth-century scientist. Consciousness develops both in the lifetime of the individual and in the history of mankind; thus Lonergan introduces his fundamental notion of differentiations or specializations of consciousness by stating that the human mind is ever the same, but the techniques it employs develop over time. Accordingly, although I presented Lonergan's notion of differentiation and specialization at the beginning of Chapter Two, it seems well here to review that notion and to add a few details that highlight the issue now under consideration. That issue is the sort of systematic reflection best suited to the study of religion in today's context.

A first differentiation of consciousness occurs when an infant learns to speak. Through language, the

infant no longer is restricted merely to his or her
immediate surroundings and feelings; rather, there
is as well a new world in which the infant lives, a
world of the absent, the past, the future, the possible, the ideal, the imaginary. It is a world of
meaning, and the meaning is mediated to the infant
by a language that reveals the memories of other people, the common sense of one's community, the heritage
of literature, the labors of scholars, the investigations of scientists, the experience of saints, the
meditations of philosophers and theologians. It is a
world to which we are related in a compound manner:
we are related immediately to the image, the word, the
symbol - to what carries the meaning; but we are related only mediately to what is represented, signified,
meant, symbolized.[77]

A second differentiation of consciousness occurs
when we add to our commonsense language the refinement
of a language rich and varied enough to portray mankind
in all its complexity. While this development of literary technique has significance in its own right, Lonergan urges attention to it for its role in preparing
for further differentiations of consciousness. It is
his conviction that such further techniques can be more
readily understood if we attend to the developments
that made them possible in the ongoing discovery of
mind; and because language plays such a central role
in this discovery, Lonergan invites our attention to
the genesis of language - to the manner in which com-

III.

monsense, literary, and technical languages become
originally meaningful. Nor, obviously, is this topic
foreign to the question concerning our reflection on
religion, for that reflection will employ language,
and it has already been pointed out that the crisis
of belief is in large part a crisis of language used
to express religious meaning and value.

With Ernst Cassirer, Lonergan stresses that some
sensible expression is intrinsic to our conscious living, so that motor disturbances resulting in aphasia
are accompanied by disturbances in perception, thought,
and action. With Gibson Winter, Lonergan notes that
the development of proportionate expression involves
certain key steps. Firstly, there is the discovery of
indicative signification, a pre-linguistic phase in
which one simply points to what is meant. Secondly,
there is a generalization whereby insight into the
schematic image of what is pointed to employs the pattern discerned in the image to guide bodily movements
including vocal articulation. Such movements might
be merely a matter of imitating the movements of another or of signifying the movements of the other by
our repetition; again, we may repeat the pattern but
with different movements, so that we advance to analogy. Thirdly, there is the development of language
itself; such is the work of the community of men and
women already in communication with one another through
intersubjective, indicative, mimetic, and analogical
expression, but who now endow vocal sounds with sig-

nification: words come to refer to data of experience, sentences to the various insights that shape
the experience, while the mood of the sentences
varies to express either assertions or commands or
wishes.[78]

Lonergan then employs that account of the genesis of language to explain the differentiation of
consciousness observable in the transition from a
primitive language to that of an ancient high civil-
ization and, again, from that language of practical
achievement to the language that has developed a high
literature. A primitive language easily expresses
all that can be pointed out or directly perceived or
directly represented; but only with great difficulty
can primitive language express the temporal, the
generic, the internal, the divine. Here, I wish to
note especially Lonergan's mention that such early
language is weak in expressing the human subject and
that subject's internal or psychological operations;
and the divine or godly, because it cannot be perceived
or imagined, can be associated with the object or event
or ritual that occasion religious experience, and there
arise the hierophanies that make religious experience
something determinate and distinct for human consciousness.[79]

Early language was a major tool in the constitution of mankind's social institutions and expressive
of the cultural significance of those institutions,
but Lonergan adds that such early language also of-

III.

fered an account of the world's shape and origin and
destiny and the result was myth. Again, he adds
that early language itself was endowed with a power
of its own and not just employed to direct human action, and the result was magic.[80] With Malinowski,
however, Lonergan adds that myth and magic did not
greatly interfere with the practical tasks of daily
living; and as such practical understanding evolved,
there emerged a corresponding enrichment of language
that lies behind the great achievement of the ancient
high civilizations that we find beginning around 700
B. C. Such was the context in which there occurred
the Greek discovery of mind, of the human spirit - a
development of high literature and of a demythologiza-
tion, a discovery of logos, to which Lonergan attaches
great importance:

> As technique advances, it reveals by con-
> trast the inefficacy of magic and turns
> man in his weakness from magical incanta-
> tion to religious supplication. However,
> if myth is to be broken, more is needed.
> Man must discover mind. He has to sort
> out and somehow detach from one another
> feeling and doing, knowing and deciding.
> He has to clarify just what it is to
> know and, in the light of that clarifica-
> tion, keep the cognitive function of
> meaning apart from its constitutive and
> efficient functions and from its role in
> the communication of feeling.[81]

The literary tradition that reflected on human
knowledge and that culminated in Heraclitus' insistence
on a logos, an intelligence, that guides human affairs

272

prepared the way for the third differentiation of consciousness. Plato's early dialogues tell of Socrates' interest in studying mankind and human behavior. Socrates is depicted, notes Lonergan, as one who is in search of universal definitions of what is familiar to everyone, yet seemed to possess no common meaning shared by all - things like temperance, courage, knowledge, justice. Socrates himself was unable to state just what that common meaning was, but before too long Aristotle was able to define all the virtues and to list the vices that sinned by excess and defect. The key question, according to Lonergan, is: what enabled Aristotle to succeed where Socrates and others had failed? Lonergan writes:

> To this the answer is a third differen-
> tiation of consciousness. Aristotle was
> able to define because he moved beyond
> the ordinary language of common sense
> and the refinements brought to it by
> literary development into systematic
> thinking. He scrutinized words, listed
> their several meanings, selected the
> meanings that meshed together to con-
> stitute a basic perspective, and made
> this interlocking group of meanings the
> primitive terms and relations that pro-
> vided the basis for derived definitions.[82]

For Lonergan, the notable characteristic of this development lies in the fact that the linguistic process itself becomes an object of reflex study, so that human language mediates, objectifies, examines human languages. There are developed controls over languages

273

III.

through alphabets, dictionaries, grammars, literary
criticism, logics, hermeneutics, philosophies.[83]

There results a commonsense realm of meaning and
a quite distinct systematic realm - two distinct ap-
prehensions of the same reality. On the basis of common sense, one can know the meaning of words but one
is quite unable to define that meaning. Such systematic definition becomes possible only when a precise
set of univocal and interlocking meanings has been
selected, clarified, and determined.[84] Further, Lonergan adds that one may usually approach the systematic realm by beginning with the available commonsense
meanings, but nonetheless the systematic realm places
one eventually in a whole new world. He illustrates
this by saying that all of us have had experience of
heat and cold, but this experience does not coincide
with what is meant by the systematic term, "tempera-
ture." So Lonergan writes, in terms reminiscent of
the specialization discussed in Chapter Two:

> To move into the systematic differentia-
> tion of consciousness does not merely in-
> volve the employment of a new set of
> technical meanings. It involves a new
> method of inquiry, a new style of under-
> standing, a different mode of conception,
> a more rigorous manner of verification,
> and an unprecedented type of social group
> that can speak to one another in the new
> way.[85]

I do not think that many members of the academic
community would disagree with Lonergan's account of
the distinction between commonsense and systematic

274

meaning. However, what many of us might find surprising and novel is the fact that Lonergan then distinguishes three distinct manners in which such systematic thinking can be done. Two of these manners
result in worlds of systematic theory that are totally
different from the world of common sense. The third
manner results in a world of systematic interiority,
from which one returns to the worlds of common sense
and theory, critically grounding the procedures of
each.

Lonergan's notion of systematic interiority will
be discussed in the next section. For the moment I
shall talk about the other two manners of systematic
reflection, both of which are most likely familiar to
the reader. Basically, our problem is to come up
with the sort of systematic reflection that can yield
an understanding of religion and that can guide the
procedures or methods employed by those who study religion. And if there are three distinct manners in
which systematic reflection can be done, then our
question is, To which manner should we turn?

For Lonergan, the first alternative for systematic thinking is the Aristotelian type based on a
metaphysics.[86] The idea was to set up a system based
on what was necessarily and eternally true, a system
that would be permanent and forever valid. The basic
terms and relations were rooted in metaphysics as the
most general "science," while such disciplines as
physics, psychology, and biology were simply to be

III.

further determinations of the basic terms and relations defined in metaphysics. Its main tool was
logic, so that science was conceived as a deduction
from first principles. Lonergan observes that the
systematic metaphysics of Aristotle resulted not so
much in a world of theory contrasted to a world of
common sense, but rather in a world of episteme,
sophia, and necessity contrasted to a world of doxa,
phronēsis, and contingence.[87] The limitations of
systematic thinking based on a metaphysics were discussed in Chapter Two; by and large such an approach
is today abandoned, and attention is focused on the
second manner of systematic thinking based on empirical science.

This type of systematic thinking also was discussed in the previous chapter. There is abandoned
any notion that systematic thinking is to be an expression of necessary and eternal truths and first
principles; instead, systematic thinking is conceived
as an ongoing process that aims indeed at the attainment of truth but that proceeds by an ever fuller and
exacter understanding of all relevant data. There is
a distinct world of scientific theory that is a specialization of advancing understanding. The sciences
find their basic terms and relations, not in metaphysics, but in sensible data. The main tool is no
longer logic, though logic remains, but methods of appealing to the data of sense for verification. Such
empirical systematic thinking is theory, and the theory stands in sharp contrast, not so much to praxis

276

as to common sense. So Lonergan employs an example
that I referred to earlier:

> If a biologist takes his young son to
> the zoo and both pause to look at a
> giraffe, the boy will wonder whether
> it bites or kicks, but the father will
> see another manner in which skeletal,
> locomotive, digestive, vascular, and
> nervous systems combine and interlock.
>
> There are then a realm of common sense
> and a realm of theory. We use differ-
> ent languages to speak of them. The
> difference in the languages involves
> social differences: specialists can
> speak to their wives about many things
> but not about their specialties. Fi-
> nally, what gives rise to these quite
> different standpoints, methods of com-
> ing to know, languages, communities,
> is the systematic exigence.88

Such is systematic thinking based on empirical
science, and the question arises, Could not reflection on religion be this sort of systematic thinking,
at least in some analogous sense? It is an important
question. For if one happens to reject the type of
systematic thinking based on a metaphysics, then one
most likely will try to come to terms with the systematic thinking found in empirical science, assuming
that this is the one and only alternative to Aristotelian views. Accordingly, one is likely to move
in one of two directions: either one will try to incorporate empirical systematic thinking at least analogously into reflection on religion; or one will
reject such systematic thinking as inadequate to re-

III.

flection on religion. If one chooses this latter
alternative, then one most likely will identify reflection on religion with simple commonsense thinking or with the specialization of commonsense thinking that is historical scholarship. But regardless
of the direction one takes, one meets what seems to
be insoluble problems. If one chooses to follow the
lead of scientific systematic thinking, one encoun-
ters tremendous difficulty in dealing with the truth
claims of religion and with the historicity of religious expression. If one chooses to opt for common
sense, one easily finds oneself in the midst of a
relativism of conflicting views that cry out for a
truly academic treatment that can resolve what lies
beyond the competency of common sense to resolve.
If one turns to historical scholarship alone, then
one gains tremendous insights into religious traditions, but one is at a loss to resolve systematically
the conflicts in that tradition and to transpose that
tradition systematically into the world of the present
and future.

Lonergan is convinced that the question of truth,
so vital to religion, cannot be resolved by an appeal
to common sense; already I have referred to his conviction that reflection on religion has to be systematic. But Lonergan would urge as well that attempts
to model reflection on religion according to the systematic thinking of empirical science are mostly a
waste of time and energy. He would be the first to
acknowledge that the systematic thinking conspicuous

278

in empirical science provides a preliminary notion
of the sort of reflection needed to understand religion and religions; this shall be explained in the
following section. But he would urge that philosophers and theologians put an end to their endless
critiques of positivism and their tendency to imitate
slavishly scientific systematic thinking. He would
suggest that we leave the world of theory to the empirical scientists, and that we work out a philosophy
based neither in common sense nor in theory but in
human interiority. And he would encourage a reflection on religion and religions that takes its stand
on that interiority as brought to fulfillment by religious experience. So it is that Lonergan proposes
a third manner of systematic thinking - one that in
his opinion is most suitable for reflection on religion, one that has the potential of relating religious
transcendence to the world of common sense, whether
past or present, and to the world of scientific theory.
It begins, neither from a metaphysics nor from an epistemology of science, but rather from human conscious
intentionality and a cognitional theory. And to its
consideration we may now turn.

(2) Generalized Reflection on Religion

Lonergan has been moving us from the fact of religious experience to the apprehension of transcendent
value that is faith, from faith to the further value
of believing the judgments of fact and value proposed

III.

by the religious tradition, from belief to the need
for critical reflection on religion and religious
traditions. I have noted his dissatisfaction with
the sort of systematic reflection based on a metaphysics. I have indicated his conviction that the
sort of systematic reflection found in modern empirical science, because it yields at best an ever
more probable understanding of things and not objective truth, is quite inadequate to a reflection on
religion that would be, not just systematic, but
critical and dialectical as well. I have mentioned
that Lonergan thus proposes a third manner of systematic thinking that _is_ critical, and I wish in
this section to indicate the broad lines of his proposal.

It might be well to begin by observing that
Lonergan identifies this third manner of systematic
thinking as the proper function of "philosophy."
This is evident in the following passage, that serves
well to introduce the discussion which will follow:

> Now the emergence of the autonomous sci-
> ences has repercussions on philosophy.
> Since the sciences between them under-
> take the explanation of all sensible
> data, one may conclude with the posi-
> tivists that the function of philosophy
> is to announce that philosophy has no-
> thing to say. Since philosophy has no
> theoretic function, one may conclude
> with the linguistic analysts that the
> function of philosophy is to work out a
> hermeneutics for the clarification of
> the local variety of everyday language.

> But there remains the possibility - and
> it is our option - that philosophy is
> neither a theory in the manner of sci-
> ence nor a somewhat technical form of
> common sense, nor even a reversal to
> Presocratic wisdom. Philosophy finds
> its proper data in intentional con-
> sciousness. Its primary function is
> to promote the self-appropriation that
> cuts to the root of philosophic differ-
> ences and incomprehensions. It has
> further, secondary functions in dis-
> tinguishing, relating, grounding the
> methods of the sciences and so promot-
> ing their unification.[89]

Inasmuch as philosophy is to find its proper
data in intentional consciousness, Lonergan is asking us to turn from the outer realms of common sense
and theory to the appropriation or grasp of our own
interiority, our subjectivity, our operations, their
structure, their norms, their potentialities. Basically, it is an invitation to find out for ourselves
if common sense is just primitive ignorance that must
give way to the scientific dawn of intelligence and
reason. It is an invitation to find out for ourselves
if science is merely of pragmatic value in controlling
nature while failing to reveal to us what nature is.
It is an invitation to get behind the claims of both
common sense and science and to resolve the more fundamental issue of discovering what our human knowing is
all about. It is an invitation to be "critical" in
the deepest sense of that word, by answering the three
basic questions confronting the human subject: What
am I doing when I am knowing? (cognitional theory);

III.

Why is doing that knowing? (epistemology); What do
I know when I do it? (metaphysics). In answering
these questions, one turns from both common sense
and theory to a heightening of one's own intentional
consciousness, whereby we attend both to objects and
to ourselves as intending subject.[90]

Such, in barest outline, is the third manner of
doing systematic thinking. Its basic terms are not
borrowed from metaphysics nor are its basic terms derived from the data of sense, as in empirical science.
Rather, the basic terms are the data of consciousness
- the conscious and intentional operations that occur
in human knowing. And its basic relations, notes Lonergan, denote the conscious dynamism that leads from
some operations to others. Further, its derived terms
and relations are simply the procedures operative in
common sense, mathematicians, empirical scientists,
interpreters and historians, philosophers and theologians. To clarify this third manner of systematic
thinking even further, Lonergan contrasts it precisely
to the other two varieties:

> It differs from Aristotelian system inas-
> much as its basic terms and relations are
> not metaphysical but cognitional. It re-
> sembles modern science inasmuch as its
> basic terms and relations are not given
> to sense, but differs from modern science
> inasmuch as its basic terms and relations
> are given to consciousness. Unlike Aris-
> totle and like modern science, its basic
> truths are not necessities but verified
> possibilities. Like modern science, its
> positions can be revised in the sense

282

that they can be refined and filled out indefinitely; but unlike modern science, its basic structures are not open to radical revision, for they contain the conditions of any possible revision and, unless those conditions are fulfilled, revision cannot occur.[91]

Such is a general description of what Lonergan is suggesting as a third manner of systematic thinking. Several aspects of his suggestion need clarification, and while I must refer the reader to Insight and Method in Theology for the full account, I nonetheless will attempt to explain a few key issues.

Lonergan, then, understands his proposal as a modification rather than a rejection of Aristotelian philosophy, as going beyond Aristotelian thought yet remaining in traditional continuity with it. Here, Lonergan has in mind the Aristotelian ideal of a universalist and autonomous philosophy that took as its field the whole of being. Similarly, Lonergan would urge a universalist and autonomous philosophy that would appeal to authentic subjectivity in order to distinguish and evaluate the many different orientations or specializations or differentiations of human consciousness. It would, then, be distinct from such specializations as science and scholarship, but at the same time it would underpin and distinguish and critically evaluate the procedures operative in any specialization of consciousness. It can do so because as Lonergan mentioned earlier, though the techniques employed by the human mind develop over time,

III.

the human mind is ever the same normative pattern of related and recurrent operations.[92]

More specifically, Lonergan explains that the transition from Aristotle to his own proposal is a transition from logic to method.[93] He recalls that Aristotle himself would restrict the logic of his Posterior Analytics to the field of mathematics. Similarly, Lonergan observes that modern empirical science relies on empirical method, and does not base itself on any logical principles or laws, all of which are open to revision on the basis of method. Again, the non-logical character of modern historical scholarship is well-known: Lonergan describes it as a matter of increasing familiarity with the data, advancing understanding of what the data mean, a complete openness to revision when contrary data or a fuller understanding comes to light. Modern science and modern scholarship are best conceived in terms of method, not of logic. And Lonergan maintains that method is quite central as well to the performance and concerns of both Aristotle and Aquinas.[94] He conceived his own work, Insight, as a study of methods generally, as preparatory to writing on method in theology; and what Insight does is set forth a generalized empirical method that operates principally on the data of consciousness to work out a cognitional theory, an epistemology, and a metaphysics.

Lonergan continues by pointing out that a shift from logic to method is a change in structure rather

than in content. By this he means that there is a
reversal of priorities in the constructing of systematic thinking. For logic, premises are first, and
the first among the premises are those that are most
universal. These, of course, regard being, so that
metaphysics is the first and fundamental science. It
follows that psychology (that considers the mental
operations of the subject) will be a faculty psychology employing metaphysical terms and speaking of po-
tencies and habits, intellects and wills, souls and
substances. Such terms are not among the immediate
data of consciousness. And the relations among those
terms are by efficient and final causality, not intentionality. Finally, Lonergan adds that because metaphysics is first, primacy goes to the speculative intellect concerned with metaphysical reflection.

Method reverses such priorities. It begins from
principles, but now the principles are concrete realities, namely, sensitively, intellectually, rationally,
and morally conscious subjects;[95] it does not begin
from logical propositions. It proceeds, not by demonstrating necessary truths, but by a self-appropriation
of one's conscious intentionality, by a discovery and
acknowledgement of human authenticity and inauthenticity, by a personal decision for authenticity and thus
for a normative and critical philosophic foundation.
Intentionality analysis replaces a faculty psychology.
Finally, speculative intellect remains but its operations are sublated by the existential deliberations
of the human subject that determine what the subject

III.

existentially is; by the interpersonal deliberations
of the human subject that determine his relations
with others; by the practical deliberations of the
human subject by which the subject makes this world
a better or worse place in which to live. So Lonergan notes that this existential horizon of freedom
and responsibility gives to cognitional reflection a
higher objective while preserving those operations
in their integrity, refining their performance, extending their relevance, and enriching their significance. Accordingly, Lonergan understands the shift
from logic to method to be a true enrichment. It is
a concern for concrete subjects and not abstract premisses. By rooting itself in cognitional theory it
does not negate metaphysics but instead establishes
a critically structured metaphysics. It removes the
ambiguity and narrowness of talk about intellect and
will by offering a wealth of systematic thinking on
the constitution and development of human subjects.
It acknowledges the primacy of conscience over speculative intellect, thereby avoiding speculative in-
tellectualism while according full power to intellectual life.

Lonergan adds a further consideration. Method
acknowledges the autonomy of science and scholarship
and has no desire to determine in advance the basic
terms and relations of those specific fields. It
would, however, contribute to the grounding and clarification of procedures operative in those autonomous

disciplines; and it would oppose any efforts on the part of scientists or scholars to reject tradition by rejecting an autonomous philosophy.

It remains to add only that a shift from logic to method does not mean the abandonment of logic. Priority moves to the non-logical operations such as discovery and verification, but logical operations such as defining terms, formulating hypotheses, working out presuppositions and inferring conclusions - all these are still needed to provide clarity and rigor at any stage of development without at all precluding the possibility of further development.

In the search for a manner of systematic thinking appropriate to reflection on religion, Lonergan has directed us away from a basis either in metaphysics or in scientific epistemology to that which in fact underpins both metaphysics and epistemology, namely, the human mind in its conscious and intentional operations. Inasmuch as the mind is constituted by operations, it is method and so Lonergan has described the shift from Aristotelian thought as a shift from the priority of logic to that of method. It is a matter of coming to learn what our conscious and intentional operations are, singly and in their relationships, and of employing that basis as a critical, dialectical, and systematic norm which grounds and guides reflective inquiry in any cognitional enterprise.

Lonergan, then, is suggesting that we can dis-

III.

cover a third manner of systematic reflection by
discovering the systematic structure of our own
knowing. The discovery is to be made, not by reading a book about human mental activities, but rather
by heightening our own conscious activities - a process of self-appropriation that normally takes considerable time and effort. Nor is this process an
end in itself - sort of a mystical vision contem-
plating the wonders of my interior life; rather, the
process at each phase is solidly linked to the world
in which one lives, whether that world is the world
of common sense, of mathematics, of empirical science,
of interpretation and history, of philosophy and theology. Accordingly, Lonergan urges attention to the
world of our interiority precisely in order to "return" to the various worlds in which our interiority
functions, but now we are equipped with the tools for
an analysis, not just of commonsense procedures, but
also of the differences and methods of specific sciences or disciplines.[96] So Lonergan summarizes the
positive content of Insight as follows:

> Thoroughly understand what it is to un-
> derstand, and not only will you under-
> stand the broad lines of all there is
> to be understood but also you will pos-
> sess a fixed base, an invariant pattern,
> opening upon all further developments of
> understanding.[97]

It is quite beyond the scope of my present work
to present Lonergan's account of the normative pattern
of related and recurrent operations that constitute

288

III.

human conscious intentionality and that contain within
themselves the abiding, transcultural, transhistorical
imperatives of what it means to be human and to develop
authentically as human. His major account is Insight,
and summary accounts are offered both in his article,
Cognitional Structure, as well as in the first chapter
of Method in Theology. My aim is restricted to drawing attention to the fact that Lonergan is suggesting
a third manner of systematic reflection, one which he
insists is normative, critical, dialectical, and foundational, and thus one which is eminently suited to systematic reflection on religion. If commonsense thinking alone is not adequate to the task of setting forth
the meaning and value of religion in our highly specialized world; if a systematic reflection that begins
from a metaphysics is inadequate to the task of relating religion and religions to human Existenz and Geschichte; if the systematic reflection operative in
modern empirical science can yield only verified possibilities but not truth; then the alternative, for
Lonergan, is to develop a systematic manner of thinking that is as well critical and capable of critically
grounding specialized methods of reflecting on religion. And while I cannot offer here a full account of
Lonergan's thought, nor answer the multitude of questions or objections that might arise concerning his
proposal, I think that some further clarity will emerge
if I offer Lonergan's own summary of what he means by
"generalized empirical method," which is what he calls
this third manner of systematic reflection.[98]

289

III.

Generalized empirical method is a method. By method, Lonergan means a normative pattern of related and recurrent operations that yield ongoing and cumulative results.[99] Method, then, is not a list of operations, but the operations themselves, the activities involved in human knowing and deciding and acting. It is not a set of rules on how to know, decide, act, but rather the operations involved in knowing, deciding, acting. The operations are recurrent and can be repeated over and over again indefinitely. Further, by repeating the operations one attains results that are cumulative and ongoing, not static and ever the same. And the pattern of operations is normative, for the results attained set a standard, the operations meet that standard, and so the pattern of operations is the right way of doing the job.

Generalized empirical method envisages all data:

> The natural sciences confine themselves to the data of sense. Hermeneutics and historical studies turn mainly to data that are expressions of meaning. Clinical psychology finds in meanings the symptoms of conflicts between conscious and preconscious or unconscious activities. Generalized empirical method operates on a combination of both the data of sense and the data of consciousness: it does not treat of objects without taking into account the corresponding operations of the subject; it does not treat of the subject's operations without taking into account the corresponding objects.[100]

290

Lonergan continues by noting that "generalized" refers not just to data but also to method. The experimental method of the natural sciences is different than the methods of hermeneutics and history. Generalized empirical method would get behind this diversity, not by inventing some extra or "neutral" method, but rather by discovering the core of operations common to both scientific methods and scholarly methods, thereby preparing the way for integrated studies. Inasmuch as man is regarded as an animal, he is object for the natural sciences. Inasmuch as he is regarded as logical or symbolic or self-completing, he is object for hermeneutic or historical studies. So Lonergan asks: What is the common core of related and recurrent operations that may be discerned both in natural science and in human studies?

The key operation or event in natural science is discovery, the emergence of something new. Similarly, in hermeneutics the key event or operation is understanding, pinpointed by Schleiermacher. Similarly, in history the key is understanding peoples' expression of themselves, a point made by Droysen. Similarly, in common sense the key event is understanding, catching on to the concrete and particular meaning of things.

But discovery or understanding alone, while the key event in human knowledge, is not the whole of knowledge but simply one element that must combine with further elements in order for human knowing to

III.

occur. Understanding presupposes data, whether of
sense or of consciousness, into which some insight
is sought, some intelligible relationship or meaning. Besides data, understanding presupposes the
spirit of inquiry that searches restlessly to piece
together into some intelligible whole that which is
not yet understood. Nor is discovery or understanding the terminal point, for it demands adequate expression in word or deed. Such expression would ap-
proximate what in fact is given in the data and understood, and so there follows a cool and detached
process of checking and reflection that weighs the
evidence and tests it before discovery is claimed.

These operations of experiencing, understanding, and reflective judgment are for Lonergan the
core normative pattern of related and recurrent operations that yield ongoing and cumulative results
in natural science, in hermeneutics, in history, in
common sense. He draws our attention to the fact
that all these operations are conscious, and none of
them occurs in dreamless sleep. Further, he invites
us to notice the dynamism that moves one operation
along to the next: the spontaneity of sense; the
spirit of intelligent inquiry searching for understanding, and, once we have understood, the further
intelligence with which we formulate what we have
grasped; the reasonableness with which we reflect on
our formulations in order to check them out and pronounce on them in light of the available evidence

292

and data. Hence, both the operations and the relations uniting them in a dynamic normative pattern
are given in consciousness.

To say that the operations and the relations
uniting them are conscious is not to say that they
are known. Neither scientists, scholars, commonsense people usually advert to their conscious and
intentional operations, but are content simply to
give their entire attention to that into which some
understanding is sought. And, as already mentioned,
Lonergan conceives the task of philosophy to lie
precisely in promoting the self-appropriation of intentional consciousness, discovering its pattern and
procedures, and grounding the different manners in
which the operations proceed towards goals - the
manner of common sense, of the sciences, of interiority and philosophy, of the life of prayer and theology.[101] Such philosophy is really a matter of each
of us heightening our consciousness, so that the operations and the relations uniting them are not just
experienced but also understood, known, and chosen
deliberately.

To come to know ourselves, then, demands first
that I attend to my attending - noting its spontaneity,
recalling its development and sharpening over the
years, all the while conscious of the delights and
dangers that fix our attention. Secondly, I have to
advert to my intelligence, its awareness of a failure to understand, its dissatisfaction with explana-

III.

tions that do not quite explain, its puzzled search for the right question to ask that will clear matters up, its delight over a solution, its concern to express well and precisely just what has been understood. In attending to my own intelligence, then, I discover a basic meaning of "normative": for my intelligence prompts us to seek understanding, to be dissatisfied with merely partial understanding, to keep searching for an ever fuller grasp, to express with accuracy just what we have thus far attained. Thirdly, by attending to my reasonableness I discover an equally basic but complementary type of normativeness. For my ideas may be fine, but they are not enough. My practical bent wants to know if the ideas will work, my theoretical bent wonders if they are true. So I test them in their inner coherence, compare them with what I consider to be already established; I work out the implications of my ideas, perhaps devise experiments to verify those implications and, if all goes well, I will state that my ideas are, not true, but certainly probable. Finally, there is the normativeness of my deliberations. Because we are free, we are also responsible and in attending to my responsibility I may discern what Lonergan calls the reasonableness of action. Just as I cannot be reasonable if I pass judgment beyond or against the evidence, so too I cannot be responsible if I fail to advert to what is right and what is wrong, if I fail to enjoy the peace of a good conscience in choosing what is right, if I fail to suffer the disquiet of an unhappy conscience in choosing what is wrong.

I think there is a sense, then, in which Lonergan's proposal is quite a homely affair. He is inviting us to find out in and for ourselves what it means to be attentive, intelligent, reasonable, and responsible. He is inviting us to be ruled and guided by the inner norms that constitute the meaning of what it is to be an authentic human person, by choosing those norms deliberately and committing ourselves to the fulfillment of their imperatives. In some such manner, we move towards the conviction that objective knowledge means, not that which is public, out there for everybody to see, but rather that which is the fruit of being attentive, of striving to understand, of verifying my understanding, of acting responsibly.

Although Lonergan's proposal is fairly simple and straightforward, he is aware that the actual achievement of self-knowledge generally demands a prolonged effort. I think the main reason for this lies in the fact that we are called upon the break the habit of attending only to the external world of data and problems and events and to broaden our horizon, and even move to a totally new horizon, by attending to ourselves as well as to objects. It is far easier to identify truth with that which lies plainly before our eyes and everyone else's eyes, than to set up different sets of criteria for

III.

assessing the validity and objectivity of knowledge.
Again, it is far easier to conceive of systematic
reflection as a matter of learning to use technical
terms properly, struggling to keep up to date on the
latest technical publications, reaching forth for
some insight into a particular and burning issue,
than to conceive systematic reflections as doing all
that, but from a basis in our own intentional consciousness. Finally, most will readily admit the
need for attentiveness, intelligence, reasonableness,
and responsibility; but surprisingly few take a cue
from Socrates and ask precisely what it is to be attentive, intelligent, reasonable and responsible.
Lonergan has attempted that task and is convinced of
the fact of a normative pattern or system or structure linking those activities, a pattern which informs and permeates human knowledge and action whenever humans think and act, a pattern that easily can
be overlooked whenever humans are inattentive, stupid,
unreasonable, and irresponsible, but a pattern as well
that can be objectified, brought to light, and made
the basis of a systematic and critical approach to
human thought and action in all fields at all times,
past, present or future.

   That such operations, and the relations uniting
them, actually exist and can be objectified by self-
appropriation is something that we can verify only
by taking the trouble to heighten our own intentional
consciousness. Lonergan offers an account of things
that we can employ in that exercise, but he insists

III.

that it is up to ourselves to do the actual work and
thereby to offer our own refinements and insights to
the sort of thing he is proposing.

I have been presenting Lonergan's suggestion for
a third manner of doing systematic thinking, and my
specific aim has been to relate that systematic thinking to reflection on religion. In order to indicate
that relationship, I wish now to discuss briefly what
Lonergan states are the functions of generalized empirical method.[102] Firstly, there is the normative
function. This has already been indicated by noting
that all human knowing and doing, all specific methods operative in various fields, consist in making
determinate the normative precepts, Be attentive, Be
intelligent, Be reasonable, Be responsible. Such precepts are formulations, expressions, but what they express has a prior existence and reality in the spontaneous, structured dynamism of human consciousness.
So it is that advertence to the difference between attention and inattention, intelligence and stupidity,
reasonableness and unreasonableness, responsibility
and irresponsibility, will be the normative and ultimate basis for all transcendental and categorial
precepts. Here, Lonergan is simply referring to the
normative role of human authenticity in all spheres
of human reflection and action.

Secondly, there is the critical function. Agreement on scientific questions is common, but Lonergan
adds that men tend to disagree in the most outrageous

297

III.

fashion on basic philosophic issues. There is disagreement about the activities named knowing and
about the relation of those activities to reality,
and about reality itself; this, I think, is clear
from the discussion of the autonomy of philosophy
in the previous chapter. But Lonergan notes that
disagreements about reality (metaphysics) can be
reduced to, or found to lie in, disagreements about
objectivity and knowledge. Differences concerning
the meaning of objectivity can be traced to different
views on cognitional theory and knowledge. And Lonergan is convinced that differences on cognitional
theory can be met by a process of self-appropriation
that reveals actual performance to be often quite
different from philosophic accounts of that performance.

Thirdly, there is the dialectical function.
Later I shall treat more fully Lonergan's meaning of
"dialectical," and here would note only that Lonergan conceives dialectic as a method of objectifying
fundamentally opposed views on knowledge, morality,
and religion, and of promoting religious, moral, and
intellectual conversion. To assign a dialectical
function to generalized empirical method is to employ this generalized method critically in bringing
to light every mistaken cognitional theory whether
expressed with philosophic generality or presupposed
by a particular method of hermeneutics, of historical investigation, of theology, or of demythologiza-
tion. Further, such use can extend to questions of

epistemology and metaphysics.

Fourthly, there is the systematic function. Indeed, I introduced Lonergan's notion of generalized empirical method as a third manner of doing systematic thinking, as pertaining to the systematic differentiation of consciousness but as then proceeding to a further differentiation that, far from losing a systematic function, grounds that function normatively, critically, and dialectically. So generalized empirical method reveals a set, a system, of basic terms and relations, where the terms refer to the operations of cognitional process and the relations are the links uniting one operation to another. Such terms and relations are formulated in a cognitional theory that not only grounds an epistemology but as well a metaphysics: for the terms and relations are isomorphic with the terms and relations denoting the ontological structure of any reality proportionate to human cognitional process.[103]

At this juncture, I wish to express my own conviction that current discussions of Wissenschafts- and Handlungstheorie are moving in the right direction, inasmuch as they have turned from metaphysics to epistemology. But I would suggest that the "critical problem," the problem of truth, can be handled only by making the further move from an epistemology to a cognitional theory. It goes without saying that the problem of truth and value-judgments is central to reflection on religion. Thus, Walter Kasper has

III.

observed correctly, I believe, that the fundamental
issue facing contemporary theology is not the relation between dogma and history, but rather the more
basic issue of truth.[104]

Fifthly, generalized empirical method is systematic in the further sense of assuring continuity
without imposing rigidity. The continuity is provided by the fact that generalized method takes its
stand on human cognitional process that is ever the
same in structure, though varying in its techniques
or manners of achieving results. Rigidity would result if cognitional operations were seen as logical
premisses of static deductive systems. But Lonergan
clearly indicates that cognitional operations are not
premisses but operations or activities that underpin
all methods, whether deductive or inductive. Moreover, Lonergan readily admits the need of refinement
to his own account of cognitional process, but is
convinced that such refinement will result, not in a
radical revision of his proposal (which would demand
a new human consciousness, period), but rather in a
fuller and more exact determination of basic terms
and relations.

Sixthly, there is the heuristic function. It
has been said that "method" is the way or path to
truth, and this Aristotelian view is quite in accord
with Lonergan's generalized empirical method. Every
inquiry that we make aims at transforming some unknown into a known, so that inquiry itself is some-

thing between ignorance and knowledge. It is less than knowledge, for there is need of inquiry. It is more than sheer ignorance for it reveals the fact of ignorance and strives to replace it with knowledge. So it is that our inquiry intends an unknown that is to be known. Method is basically the exploitation of that intending, outlining the steps to be taken if one is to move from the initial intending of the question to the eventual knowing of what has been intended all along. Within method, the use of heuristic devices is fundamental, for reflection presupposes understanding, understanding presupposes inquiry, and inquiry intends insight into what is indeed given in sense or in consciousness, but which is not yet known. Generalized empirical method reveals the very nature of this heuristic function by objectifying the activity of intending and that which is intended, the unknown. Finally, it settles the identity of the unknown as an object that is to be known by the basic operations of experiencing, understanding, and judging.

Seventhly, there is the foundational function. There are special methods proper to specific fields of inquiry, and these derive their proper norms from the experience of investigators in the tradition of those fields. But Lonergan would recall the existence of common norms, mentioned a moment ago, and adds that besides the methods proper to each field, there are interdisciplinary problems. Lonergan feels that to the extent that special methods acknowledge their com-

III.

mon core in generalized empirical method, to that extent will the various special methods find a common
normativity, a firm basis for attacking interdisciplinary problems, and a common orientation towards a
higher unity of vocabulary, thought, and purpose.

I have been presenting Lonergan's account of the
functions of generalized empirical method as that account is found in Method. He adds there several further functions indicating especially the relevance of
generalized empirical method to theology. I would
like to extend that relevance to include both theology and other disciplines concerned with reflection
on religion. The relevance of generalized empirical
method, that promotes the self-appropriation of the
subject, to religion is indicated by Lonergan in the
tenth chapter of Method:

> What I have referred to as the gift of
> God's love, spontaneously reveals itself
> in love, joy, peace, patience, kindness,
> goodness, fidelity, gentleness, and self-
> control. In undifferentiated conscious-
> ness it will express its reference to the
> transcendent both through sacred objects,
> places, times, and actions, and through
> the sacred offices of the shaman, the
> prophet, the lawgiver, the apostle, the
> priest, the preacher, the monk, the teacher.
> As consciousness differentiates into the
> two realms of common sense and theory, it
> will give rise to special theoretical ques-
> tions concerning divinity, the order of the
> universe, the destiny of mankind, and the
> lot of each individual. When these three
> realms of common sense, theory, and inter-
> iority are differentiated, the self-approp-

riation of the subject leads not only to
the objectification of experiencing, understanding, judging, and deciding, but
also of religious experience.[105]

Here, Lonergan is merely making more explicit his
contention that, as human consciousness develops, so
too must religion. I have already mentioned Lonergan's
account of the Greek discovery of mind, when human consciousness differentiated into the two realms of common
sense and theory; in that stage, one could express one's
religious experience in the mode of a commonsense reference to concrete and particular places, times, actions
objects, people; or, if one also had achieved expertise
in theoretical matters, one could not only feel religious compunction but also define it, one could not
only please the Trinity but also discourse learnedly
upon it, one could, in other words, theorize about religion, divinity, transcendence. But Lonergan would
insist that stage, wherein thinking was either commonsense or theoretical, is now giving way to a new stage
wherein common sense remains, theoretical reflection
is left to the empirical sciences, scholarly reflection reconstructs the commonsense meanings and values
of another place and time, and philosophic reflection,
by a heightening of consciousness, reflects on human
development, whether scholarly, scientific, religious,
commonsense, or prelinguistic - assigning to each its
proper competence and relating each to the others.[106]

In this new stage, then, I think that Lonergan
would distinguish three main types of thinking about

III.

religion . Commonsense thinking is characterized
mainly by its spontaneity and will express its reference to the transcendent by drawing upon ordinary
language or by employing literary language and narrative that communicate both understanding and feelings; moreover, its "thinking" will be as much, if
not more, a matter of deeds and actions as of words.
Secondly, scholarly reflection will aim at a Horizont-
verschmelzung, whereby the scholar retains his own
common sense, while developing the common sense of
another place and time,[107] attending particularly to
the reconstructions of the human spirit as religious.
Philosophic reflection, finally, will transpose the
former generalized theoretical reflection on religion
(mostly referred to as "natural theology") to a new
key: the self-appropriation of the subject will include the objectification of religious experience as
well as the conditions of the possibility of valid
and objective religious knowledge; it thereby would
provide the basic terms and relations of reflection
on religion and, without at all determining the categorial objects proper to specific fields (empirical
religious studies and theologies), would nonetheless
ground the special methods operative in those fields.

It is important here to note that Lonergan is
not at all denying that there are methods proper to
theologies and religious studies. He is merely trying to point out that those special methods invariably are the work of human minds performing the same

304

basic operations in the same basic relations as are
found in other special methods. Generalized empirical method is thus a constituent part of the special
method of theology, of the special methods of empirical religious studies, of the special methods involved
in commonsense thinking about religion:

> However true it is that one attends, un-
> derstands, judges, decides differently
> in the natural sciences, in the human
> sciences, and in theology, still these
> differences in no way imply or suggest
> a transition from attention to inatten-
> tion, from intelligence to stupidity,
> from reasonableness to silliness, from
> responsibility to irresponsibility.[108]

As it happens, I have employed this third manner
of reflecting on religion in developing this present
chapter. More correctly, perhaps, I have provided
merely a very inadequate sketch of what should be involved in such a reflection - one that begins neither
from common sense nor from theory (neither metaphysical nor scientific) but instead from the religious
experience of the human subject. The task is to
heighten that experience by bringing to light its often hidden presence in human consciousness, its need
of intersubjective cultivation within a religious tradition, its immanent meaning and value as other-worldly
commitment yielding inner-worldly authenticity. From
there one moves on to ground the knowledge born of religious loving: the knowledge that is faith, the eye
of love, apprehending transcendent value and transforming human values; the knowledge that is belief in

305

III.

the word of the religious tradition. To express that
belief adequately is to express it on the cultural
level of the day, and when that level is a compound
of commonsense thinking and reflective study, then
religion too has to learn to speak to differentiated
as well as to undifferentiated consciousness. Such
speech was primarily theoretical, but in this latest
stage is called to seek a grounding in human religious
interiority and from that ground to return to the
worlds of common sense and theory.

In the previous section I gave an account of Lonergan's generalized empirical method that he proposes
as this new manner of systematic thinking. It is a
generalized method, for it does not attempt to solve
particular issues in any of mankind's religious traditions but would instead bring to light the issues and
general categories relevant to all religious traditions
and common to them in their constitution and historical
development. So generalized empirical method clarifies
the meaning of religious experience, religious faith,
the structure of religious belief, the variety of manners of thinking about religion and reflecting upon
it. Lonergan acknowledges that his clarification is
formulated or expressed at times in terms of the specifically Christian tradition; but he draws on this
tradition more to point to the realities expressed by
it than to canonize the expression itself. I think
this is a legitimate manner of proceeding, for the
process or self-appropriation does not occur in some

vacuum removed from history, but has to draw on
the language available at any given place or time.
The transcultural or transhistorical aspect of generalized empirical method is not the formulation or
expression of that method, but the human subject in
his or her conscious interiority and religious experience.[109]

Besides generalized reflection there is specialized reflection on religion, specialized methods
of investigating religious phenomena, meaning, value,
behavior. Chronologically, indeed, one might say
that such special methods of study precede generalized reflection, for performance precedes reflection
on that performance and, for Lonergan, reflection on
performance is what generalized empirical method is
all about. It remains, however, that among the functions of generalized empirical method Lonergan noted
the foundational function. This means that generalized empirical method can provide norms common to
special methods, without at all pretending to establish the proper norms of each method. It means that
generalized empirical method can account for the development of specialized methods and provide the ultimate basis for appropriate methods of investigation, thereby justifying or criticizing currently-
accepted procedures.[110]

(3) Specialized Reflection on Religion

In my own personal study of Lonergan's thought I
have found it very useful to keep in mind that which

has motivated him throughout his entire life to the
present day. It is his conviction, mentioned earlier,
that as human consciousness develops so too must religion. It is a conviction, I believe, that is shared
by anyone who takes seriously the meaning of aggiornamento or Heutigwerden or renewal. Lonergan's approach
to this renewal, further, seems to be eminently reasonable: first study the various developments and specializations of human consciousness that have occurred
in history, then locate the core of conscious and intentional operations common to and underpinning all
those developments, and finally, on this basis, objectifying the function of religion in human living,
noting the many aspects and developments of that function in the past that allowed religion to be on the
social and cultural level of each time and place, pin-
pointing when and why religious thinking fell behind
the times, setting forth the way or method that could
lead to the needed development and renewal.

For Lonergan, the needed development and renewal
of reflection on religion is in fact occurring in many
different ways. There is a new study of religion employing a number of specialized methods of investigation. But Lonergan feels that despite the richness of
current reflection, there remain some fundamental
problems. On the performative level there is the
problem of integrating the many methods of investigation and the many results of those investigations.
On a more fundamental level there is the problem of

dealing with opposed convictions regarding religion, morality, and philosophy. Lonergan is convinced that the way of dealing with both these problems is to develop a manner of systematic thinking that transposes the former theoretical approach to religion. That transposition, for Lonergan, is to a reflection on religion that finds its basic terms and relations in human interiority and religious experience. It is a solid basis or foundation, for such interiority and experience are ever the same, though the manner in which it is formulated, expressed, lived-out varies in each society and culture over time.

Lonergan would suggest that specialized reflection on religion within the current context has three main dimensions, each employing distinct methods yet each related to the other two. The first of these, historical reflection on religion, is well-known and is a particular application of an autonomous historical scholarship. The other two specialized methods are operative in current reflection on religion, but are in need of a clearer delineation and distinction; these are the methods of dialectical evaluation of radical and traditional differences present in thinking and reflecting about religion, and of practical implementation or promotion of religious meaning and religious value. In the following pages I wish to indicate briefly Lonergan's account of the relevance of generalized empirical method to the three specialized methods operative in human studies generally and

III.

in studies of religion particularly.

    (a) Historical Investigations[111]

    Earlier I referred to Lonergan's conviction that
the transition from a classicist to a modern culture
was a transition from a normative and monolithic interpretation of man and the world to a historically-
minded and pluralistic interpretation. It was a recognition of the constitutive role of meaning in human
living: that acts of meaning inform human living, that
such acts proceed from a free and responsible incarnate
subject, that the meaning given to human living differs
from nation to nation, from culture to culture, that
over time meanings develop and go astray. It is the
recognition that besides the meanings by which we apprehend and transform nature, there are the meanings
by which we figure out the possibilities of our own
living and make our choice among them.[112]

    Again, Lonergan has noted that human development
is a matter of moving from a prelinguistic existence,
wherein we are confined to a world of immediate experience, towards a far vaster world of meaning that is
to be known, not by feeling it or touching it or seeing
it, but by asking questions and reaching correct answers. It is our symbolic world to which we are introduced by a process of education whereby we slowly learn
to master the various symbolic traditions at our disposal.

    Moreover, Lonergan adverted to the fact that our

III.

symbolic traditions, our worlds of meaning, themselves are a product of other peoples' striving to
understand and express themselves and their world.
And it was the explicit recognition of this constitutive role of meaning in the formation of human traditions that was the achievement of critical scholarship in nineteenth century Germany, and that led Dilthey to reflect on the difference between human studies
and natural science, between the Geistes- and the Naturwissenschaften. Lonergan himself sums up the difference
in the following way:

> Both the scientist and the historian would
> understand: the scientist would under-
> stand nature; the historian would under-
> stand man. But when the scientist under-
> stands nature, he is not grasping nature's
> understanding of itself; for though nature
> is intelligible, it is not intelligent.
> But when the historian understands man,
> his understanding is a recapturing of
> man's understanding of himself. This re-
> capturing is interpretation. It differs
> from the understanding that it recaptures,
> for it makes thematic, puts in words, an
> understanding that was not thematized but
> lived. Yet in another fashion it corres-
> ponds to what it recaptures, for it envis-
> ages an earlier situation and recounts how
> an individual or group understood that
> situation and revealed themselves by their
> understanding of it.[113]

Scholarship, then, is concerned to thematize or interpret the self-understanding of a people distant in
place or in time. Generally, this need for thematization arises in order to understand, not what the people
themselves thematized, but what was simply lived out in

311

III.

their everyday human affairs. So I noted Lonergan's
earlier reference to Vico's claim of the priority of
poetry, that Lonergan interprets to mean that the human mind expresses itself in symbols before it knows,
if ever it knows, what its symbols literally mean.
Again, Lonergan refers to Dilthey's conviction that
the self-understanding of a people is found precisely
in their living, in the tremendous diversity of their
everyday dealings and concerns; and for Lonergan, the
task of scholarship is to reconstruct these everyday,
ordinary constructions of the human spirit.[114]

Lonergan offers his own methodological account
of the key tasks of scholarship in Method, but I wish
to restrict my comments to the broad relevance of his
generalized empirical method to historical studies of
religions. Firstly, then, generalized reflection on
religion provides an a priori scheme that is capable
of synthesizing any possible set of historical data
irrespective of their place and time. This of course
does not mean that the details or results of historical investigation are determined in advance, but rather
that historians and interpreters may find in such generalized reflection the heuristic structures that guide
them in their inductive historical inquiries. In particular, the account of religious commitment in terms
of authenticity can provide investigators with a valuable tool in the interpretation of outward religious
behavior as well as one the inner meaning and value
attached by people to their religious behavior and
expressions.[115]

III.

A further relevance of generalized reflection to
historical studies is indicated by Lonergan's use of
Gadamer's notion that scholarship involves a Horizont-
verschmelzung, a merging or fusion of horizons.[116]
Commonsense understanding is constitutive of ordinary
language and enters into the fabric of human invention
and human praxis; it is constitutive of the symbolic
world that is the object of historical investigations.[117]
So it is that the scholar would enter the symbolic
world of another place and time, and such entry is
described by Lonergan in terms borrowed from Gadamer:

> To use the language of Prof. Gadamer in
> his great work, Wahrheit und Methode,
> scholarship is a matter of Horizontver-
> schmelzung, of merging or fusing hori-
> zons. It is a matter of retaining the
> common sense that guides one's own speak-
> ing and acting and that interprets the
> words and deeds of other people, real or
> fictitious, of another, often remote,
> place and time. For the scholar, as it
> were, lives in two worlds, possesses two
> horizons. He is not an anachronist read-
> ing contemporary common sense into the
> past; and he is not an archaist employing
> an ancient common sense in contemporary
> speech and action. To be neither, neither
> an anachronist nor an archaist, he must
> both retain the common sense of his own
> place and time and, as well, develop the
> common sense of another place and time.[118]

To the extent, then, that generalized reflection on religion succeeds in clarifying the relation of religious
experience to commonsense expressions of that experience, to that extent will generalized reflection clar-

313

III.

ify the sort of understanding sought by historians
of religions.

Finally, just as generalized reflection can provide historical scholarship with a heuristic scheme
in which data receive an initial interpretation; just
as it can clarify the sort of understanding sought by
scholars; so too it can help scholars to weigh the results of their investigations. As Lonergan points
out, generalized empirical method reveals the conditions to be fulfilled in arriving at sound judgment
in any field of human inquiry, for such method is
critical. And he observes that scholars are concerned
with the truth of their interpretations and historical
judgments, and wish their findings to be as accurate
as possible. So Lonergan notes that while the conditions for pronouncing results to be certain are indeed
stringent, still, this stringency will serve both as
an encouragement to modesty in communicating results,
as well as a guide that reveals when one's investigations have reached a point that exhausts at least
present questions on a given topic.[119]

Such, very schematically, is the relevance of
generalized reflection on religion to historical reflections on religions. The full relevance is indicated by Lonergan in the chapters of Method that deal
with research, interpretation, history, history and
historians, to which account I must refer the reader
desiring a more detailed explanation of things.

(b) Dialectical Evaluation

314

In the present section I am giving a sketch of specialized methods of reflection in human studies, bearing in mind especially those studies concerned with reflecting on religions. The first sort of specialized reflection noted by Lonergan was historical reflection, something that in our own day is a fully specialized manner of investigation. The second specialized method discussed by Lonergan is dialectic. Although it is operative in current reflection, its precise meaning is still in the process of being worked out. Accordingly, Lonergan would make a contribution to that clarification by extending the dialectical function of generalized reflection on religion to the work of those concerned specifically with sorting out the conflicts that arise in human studies.[120]

That conflicts arise is something that Lonergan attributes to the growing tendency within human studies to stop imitating the methods of empirical science and to develop methods that can deal with the human world of meaning and value. Lonergan would by no means discourage this tendency, but would add that a concern for meaning and value, while avoiding the troubles associated with Historicism, nonetheless involves investigators in philosophic, ethical, and religious issues. That involvement is a source of conflict, for philosophies are many and contradictory, ethics can emphasize mere satisfactions as opposed to authentic values, and religions can embody inauthen-

III.

ticity as well as authenticity leading to distinct
and even disparate religious traditions.

Lonergan observes that such differences are
both radical and traditional: radical, in the sense
that they are at the root of dialectically opposed
horizons; traditional, in the sense that such differences accumulate to infiltrate a tradition, and,
by that fact, become the common fund that each of us
must draw from as we are educated, socialized, ac-
culturized. Such is the problem of authenticity, discussed earlier with specific reference to the cultivation of religious experience, but applicable to any
cultivation of human conscious living. Here, however,
Lonergan would draw attention to the problem that this
creates for scholars, for those concerned with research,
interpretation and hermeneutics, history:

> Such radical and traditional differences
> put their stamp not only on the writings
> to be interpreted and the events to be
> narrated but also upon the mind-set, world
> view, horizon of exegetes and historians.
> In utopia, no doubt, everyone in all his
> words and deeds would be operating with
> the authenticity generated by meeting the
> exigences of intelligence, reasonableness,
> responsibility. But our world is not u-
> topia. Even if anyone manages to be per-
> fectly authentic in all his own personal
> performance, still he cannot but carry
> within himself the ballast of his tradi-
> tion. And down the millennia in which
> that tradition developed, one can hardly
> exclude the possibility that unauthentic-
> ity entered in and remained to ferment
> the mass through ages to come.[121]

316

I have already referred to this point in mentioning Lonergan's critique of Enlightenment ideals and classicist norms; such was the "age of innocence" that assumed the authenticity of (one's own) tradition and places unbounded confidence in the ability of a philosophy or reason to resolve all questions. The end of that age is a fact, and Lonergan means that human studies have to deal with the complexity that recognizes the data to be a possible mixture of authenticity and inauthenticity, and that the investigators themselves may corrupt their own investigations with their personal or inherited inauthenticity.[12]

To deal with this complexity, Lonergan proposes a specifically dialectical procedure or method. It differs from the methods employed in scholarly studies, for it is one thing to reconstruct the constructions of the human spirit, but quite another to bring into sharp focus and reduce to their radical origins the conflicts that such reconstruction reveals. Clearly, the method of dialectic will rely on the methods of scholarly investigation, but it will attempt to go beyond those methods by confronting the problem of inauthenticity in human life and by providing a technique for distinguishing between authenticity and inauthenticity. And while the precise functioning of this method is to be worked out in light of the experience and knowledge of experts in each field, it remains that generalized reflection on religion can extend its dialectical function to specific dialectic.

III.

Here, I think that Lonergan has in mind especially
the ability of generalized reflection to offer a
rather comprehensive account of the meaning of authenticity and inauthenticity, and of the way of promoting movement from the latter to the former. Already I have given Lonergan's account of authenticity,
and it remains only to add his understanding of conversion that is a movement from inauthenticity to authenticity.[123]

Lonergan distinguishes three distinct kinds of
conversion: intellectual, moral, and religious. Intellectual conversion refers to the authenticity of
the human subject as knower; moral conversion is the
authenticity of the subject as responsible; and religious conversion is the authenticity of the subject
as self-transcending through being in love with God.
Before discussing each of these, it is worth noting
that conversion, as authenticity, is obviously more
than an isolated event in the life of an individual;
rather, it is an orientation of the life of the subject to truth, value, God.[124]

Perhaps the best way to introduce Lonergan's
notion of intellectual conversion is to recall his
distinction between knowledge gained by immediate
experience and knowledge gained by asking and answering questions. To acknowledge that distinction
and to assign distinct criteria of validity and objectivity to each, is intellectual conversion. Lonergan writes:

Intellectual conversion is a radical clarification and, consequently, the elimination of an exceedingly stubborn and mis-
leading myth concerning reality, objectivity, and human knowledge. The myth is that
knowing is like looking, that objectivity
is seeing what is there to be seen and not
seeing what is not there, and that the
real is what is out there now to be looked
at. Now this myth overlooks the distinction between the world of immediacy, say,
the world of the infant and, on the other
hand, the world mediated by meaning. The
world of immediacy is the sum of what is
seen, heard, touched, tasted, smelt, felt.
It conforms well enough to the myth's view
of reality, objectivity, knowledge. But
it is but a tiny fragment of the world mediated by meaning. For the world mediated
by meaning is a world known not by the
sense experience of an individual but by
the external and internal experience of a
cultural community, and by the continuously
checked and rechecked judgments of the community. Knowing, accordingly, is not just
seeing; it is experiencing, understanding,
judging, and believing. The criteria of
objectivity are not just the criteria of
ocular vision; they are the compounded
criteria of experiencing, of understanding,
of judging, and of believing. The reality
known is not just looked at; it is given
in experience, organized and extrapolated
by understanding, posited by judgment and
belief.[125]

This passage merely brings together a number of points

that are uncovered in the self-appropriation of the

subject. Briefly, the authenticity of the subject as

knower is a matter of self-transcendence: of moving

beyond ourselves as sure of the earth upon which we

III.

tread, to the self who is certain that the earth is indeed firm and will not give way under his tread.[126]

Besides intellectual there is moral conversion. Besides the authenticity of the subject as knower - as attentive, intelligent, and reasonable - there is the further authenticity of the responsible subject, the existential subject, the subject as one who deliberates, evaluates, chooses, and acts.[127] It is the subject in a world regulated by value, as well as mediated by meaning, a world in which our knowing is set within the larger context of our deciding and acting and doing.[128]

Generalized empirical method is the self-appropriation of the human subject as correlative both to the world mediated by meaning and to the world regulated by value. Lonergan here is insisting that morality exists and is operative in the Lebenswelt, and that it is by reflecting on this functioning of morality that the subject comes to know the meaning of value.[129] He observes that this is just another way of explaining Aristotle's refusal to speak of ethics apart from the ethical reality of good men, or of stressing the fact that it is only in light of one's own moral authenticity that the individual or the society can distinguish good from evil. Lonergan explains this correlation of the subject and his or her world of value in the following way:

> Just as the notion of being functions in
> one's knowing and it is by reflecting on

320

that functioning that one comes to know
what the notion of being is, so also the
notion or intention of the good functions
within one's human acting and it is by
reflection on that functioning that one
comes to know what the notion of good is.
Again, just as the functioning of the notion of being brings about our limited
knowledge of being, so too the functioning of the notion of the good brings about
our limited achievement of the good. Finally, as our knowledge of being is, not
knowledge of essence, but only knowledge
of this and that and other beings, so too
the only good to which we have firsthand
access is found in instances of the good
realized in themselves or produced beyond
themselves by good men.[130]

Lonergan understands freedom or liberty, not as
some neutral or value-free potential for choosing from
a number of options or values that are lined up and
listed by some external authority, but rather as self-
determination. Thus he notes that we experience our
liberty as the active thrust terminating the process
of deliberation by settling on one of the possible
courses of action and proceeding to execute it.[131]
He adds that such execution obviously changes the
world of objects, but the more important change that
occurs in the exercise of liberty is the change that
occurs in the human subject himself or herself: we
build up our character or destroy it, we achieve or
fail to achieve our personality.[132]

The existential moment is when we realize this
fact, when we grasp that it is a matter of my personal

III.

decision as to what I shall make of myself, and that
my personal decisions are precisely the making of myself. It is this that reveals the possibility of
moral conversion, of an exercise in what Lonergan
names vertical freedom, whereby we choose what is
truly good by opting for value against satisfaction,
when the two conflict.[133] Moreover, I have already
noted Lonergan's account of the insecurity of the existential subject and of the ongoing need to root out
the inauthenticity generated by bias. Such bias,
generally, is a clinging to satisfaction over value;
it is being rooted in the spontaneous immediacy of a
practical present, with a corresponding disregard for
a seemingly unreal and vague world of value, the world
in which we function and exist but refuse to acknowledge.[134]

Besides intellectual and moral there is religious
conversion, identified by Lonergan as other-worldly
falling in love, or as being grasped by ultimate concern, a phrase borrowed from Paul Tillich. It is conversion in the sense that it is the replacement of
the heart of stone by a heart of flesh, a conversion
to a total being-in-love as the efficacious ground of
self-transcendence, whether in the pursuit of truth,
or in the realization of human values, or in the orientation we adopt to the universe, its ground, its
goal.[135] Its further characteristics were described
earlier in discussing religious experience.

I have been offering only a hint of the problem

322

to be confronted by dialectical method in human
studies. Lonergan realizes its enormous complexity,
but at the same time would suggest that an account
of human authenticity and conversion can clarify
things considerably. He suggests that it is an account that can be applied methodically to problems
of interpretation as well as to historical issues -
whether the general issues of progress, decline, recovery, or the specific issues that arise when historians are in radical disagreement. Its further contribution lies in promoting dialogue among those of
differing traditions, who can discern beneath those
differences a common foundation in authenticity.[136]

(c) Praxis

I have been considering the relevance of generalized reflection on religion to the specialized reflection that is characteristic of our own day. In
each case Lonergan understands the specialized method
to be a further determination of generalized method,
a derivation from generalized method. I have indicated his notion of method as historical reflection
and as dialectical evaluation, and it remains only to
discuss his notion of method as praxis.[137] He writes:

> Experimental method reveals nature. His-
> torical method reveals man, the self-
> completing animal, in the manifold variety
> of his concrete existing. Dialectic con-
> fronts us with the problem of the irrat-
> ional in human life and, as well, provides
> a technique for distinguishing between
> authentic and unauthentic evaluations, de-

III.

> cisions, actions. Praxis, finally, raises
> the final issue: What are you to do about
> it? What use are you to make of your know-
> ledge of nature, of your knowledge of man,
> of your awareness of the radical conflict
> between man's aspiration to self-transcen-
> dence and, on the other hand, the wayward-
> ness that may distort his traditional her-
> itage and even his own personal life?[138]

I wish to observe initially that this notion of
praxis, suggested by Lonergan, is an understanding of
praxis as an academic discipline or specialization,
and that it stands within the context of other disciplines, namely, empirical science, history, and dialectic. It is academic, however, in the sense proper to
Lonergan's account of the "third" meaning of reflection or systematic thinking. Accordingly, praxis as
an academic subject is not to be conceived in terms
of the practical conclusions that follow from metaphysical premises or in terms of the practical achievements to which empirical science is orientated. Rather,
Lonergan understands praxis as an academic subject in
the sense of the process of making the reflective and
practical judgments of value that promote authenticity
in one's cultural and social contexts.[139]

Further, praxis as an academic discipline stands
within the context of other academic disciplines and
presupposes them. Here, Lonergan refers especially
to the dialectical dimension of contemporary human
studies, a dimension that objectifies all too clearly
the element of the irrational in human life and human

324

tradition. It is a dimension that reveals our traditions to be a compound of inauthentic as well as of
authentic elements, a product of human failure as well
as of genuine achievement. That dialectical dimension
of contemporary human studies, noted by Lonergan, is
almost taken for granted in most circles today, but it
tended to be overlooked or minimized in past academic
reflection. The primacy of speculative intellect or
pure reason or automatic progress sheltered the academic world from concern with the irrational; but Lonergan notes that following the failure of the absolute
idealists to encompass human history within the embrace of speculative reason, there has occurred an
ever more explicit and thematic awareness in academic
disciplines that authenticity is never to be taken
for granted. But if this dialectical dimension confronts us with the problem of the irrational in human
living, it also has the result of raising the further
question asked by Lonergan in the passage quoted a
moment ago: What are you to do about it? What use
are you to make of your knowledge of nature, of your
knowledge of man, of your awareness of the radical
conflict between man's aspiration to self-transcendence
and, on the other hand, the waywardness that may distort his traditional heritage and even his own personal
life?

The method of answering those questions is the
method of praxis. As mentioned, Lonergan conceives it
as the process of making the reflective and practical

III.

judgments of value that promote authenticity in
one's cultural and social contexts. If method as
dialectic reveals the values and disvalues operative in these contexts, method as praxis is concerned with the task of taking a stand towards the
present and future by promoting authentic values
and thereby undoing the forces of decline. The
values chosen as authentic are not one's own values but rather the values of the tradition as set
forth by dialectic; but the praxis, the choosing,
will be authentic to the extent that the reflective
and practical judgments proceed from authentic subjects: from subjects who have made a deliberate
decision for, and commitment to, truth, human values, and transcendent value. Praxis rests on that
decision, and is a matter of objectifying that decision by promoting what is genuine in the tradition.

Lonergan's notion of method as praxis, then,
is critically grounded inasmuch as it occurs within
the tradition revealed by dialectic and is the work
of subjects who are intellectually, morally, and
religiously authentic.[140] It is the work of critical intelligence making reflective and practical
judgments of value, and thereby is distinguished,
not just from other systematic notions that lack
this critical function, but as well from spontaneous
commonsense intelligence. Commonsense thinking is
highly relevant to the practical judgments made by

326

III.

praxis, but that relevance comes only after one has
secured a foundation in that which can purify common
sense from its propensity to common nonsense, and
that foundation is religious interiority.[141]

5. Conclusion

     In the present chapter I have tried to indicate
Lonergan's approach to some of the topics generally
associated with a "theological anthropology." Like
other theologians at the present time Lonergan is
convinced that theological reflection and expression
will be all the more meaningful and effective the
more it is correlative to the horizon of incarnate
human subjects in history.

     The point of departure was the "God-problem" of
modernity - the absence of God from modern culture,
from mankind's interpretation of itself and its world.
Lonergan acknowledges the roots of that absence can
be found in the fact of specialization, discussed in
Chapter Two: it was a process of increasing autonomy
from religion and theology by disciplines once integrated within a religious view of mankind and the universe. In itself that process is not to be lamented,
but Lonergan adds that it should have been accompanied
by a corresponding renewal in theology and religious
living that kept pace with those developments and that
continued to mediate religious meaning and value in
the new cultural context, without at all interfering

327

III.

with the autonomy claimed by the new science and the
new scholarship. Such renewal of theology did not
in fact occur, however, and without that renewal the
autonomous spirit of modernity was not always accompanied by a concern for human authenticity - something that is at the heart of religion and theology
in a special way, but that demands a religion and
theology on the level of the day.

If God is absent from human social structures
and cultural channels, this means for Lonergan that
human religious development remains confined largely
to a prelinguistic level, barely audible to the individual, unable to be communicated effectively among
one's fellow humans, unable to ignite and inspire a
religious community, unable to be technically reflected upon and expressed in such a way as to reveal
the world's deepest meaning and highest value amidst
other disciplines that explore the meaning and value
of natural and human reality. Lonergan, with other
theologians, would return to the concrete reality
of the subject in the world and would pinpoint precisely the level at which this breakdown in communication occurs. To that extent Lonergan joins the
company of those concerned with the linguistic expression of religious conviction. But I think that
he parts company with many of those concerned with
religious language by directing attention, in the
first instance, to the immanent context of religious
experience in the consciousness of the human subject.

Religion has a prelinguistic dimension, and Lonergan would insist that religious expression has to mirror that dimension as accurately as is possible by drawing on human language and other carriers of meaning and value. Accordingly, the initial section of this chapter included Lonergan's account of religious experience, the religious horizon of the human subject, in the conviction that reflection on God and on the world as orientated to God is meaningful only within such a horizon. If the human subject is not for God, then religion and reflection on religion, far from being intrinsic to an authentic humanism, is nothing more than an impediment to genuine human development.

For Lonergan, then, the challenge is the liberation of religious experience: bringing such experience from a prelinguistic, barely audible level to become a dominant voice in man's personal, social, and cultural living. The potential of such liberation is to be found both in the fact of religious experience as well as in the faith that apprehends transcendent value and that transvalues human values. But the human horizon, constituted by religious experience and orientated by the knowledge of faith, is a historically-conditioned horizon. It relies on the word of religion, especially on the interpretations stated by a religious tradition, in order to interpret itself to itself and to its world. Such reliance, for Lonergan, is belief and the value of believing the religious tradition is a value appre-

III.

hended by faith. Still, in a time of rapid social
and cultural change, expressions of belief too are
subject to change and ongoing reinterpretation. Such
change is characteristic of modernity, and its fact
imposes upon the religious tradition the monumental
task of re-casting its interpretation in such a way
as preserve the truth and value of religious expression, while at the same time developing an expression that is an integral dimension of man's understanding of himself and his world.

That task, for Lonergan and many others, demands
truly academic, technical reflection, not just on the
truth of revelation, but more fundamentally on the
truth of the human subject in the world as historically conditioned - a world that is insecure, a combination of authenticity and inauthenticity, a world
orientated indeed to God but seemingly unaware of the
fact, if not militantly opposed to it. In our own
day there is a choice of foundations for such reflective thinking. It can imitate medieval achievement
and turn to a metaphysically or ontologically grounded
philosophy, but this just raises more fundamental issues concerning human historicity and human responsibility. It can turn to the successful example of systematic thinking in our own day embodied by empirical
science, but this just raises more fundamental issues
concerning religious truth. Indeed, both of those alternatives tend only to accentuate the disparity between ordinary religious living and thinking and, on

the other hand, a theoretical superstructure that
is simply another world, removed from the existential horizon of incarnate human subjects in history.
Lonergan, then, would recommend that we leave "theorizing" in the new sense to empirical science, that
we recognize the autonomy of quite a distinct type
of intellectual development in historical scholarship, and that we get behind this diversity in order
to uncover the system that grounds both science and
scholarship, as well as everyday commonsense thinking. This will uncover a basic method, a basic and
normative pattern of related and recurrent operations that is the common core of all human thinking
and doing. From there, one can proceed to distinguish and relate the several different manners of
thinking and reflecting that characterize humanity
in the world of today, including the manners in
which we think and reflect about our religious living.

Reflection on religion, then, is to employ a
variety of distinct methods, each of which is ultimately rooted in the transcultural and transhistorical structure of the human mind, yet each of
which represents a specialization of that mind.
Moreover, these specializations, this variety of
methods, can be employed regardless of the context
of one's own work. Generalized empirical method,
as well as the specialized methods of history, dialectic, and praxis are relevant to theologians as

well as to scientists, philosophers, scholars of
religion.   This does not mean that Lonergan simply
identifies theology with empirical religious studies; it will be clear that such is not the case
from my discussion in the next chapter.   Theology
has the task of discerning the literal meaning of
religious symbols, and for that task there is needed
a distinct theological method; empirical religious
studies are concerned with the meaning of religious
symbols as constructions of the human spirit, and
must leave to theologians the further task of clarifying the meaning of the other-worldly reality to
which those symbols point.   But despite these differences, Lonergan would insist that because the
religious symbols studied by theologians are constructions of the human spirit, theologians will
benefit by employing those methods outlined in this
chapter, methods that are operative in empirical
religious studies generally.   Here, Lonergan is
really pointing out and clarifying what in fact has
happened, as theologians in our own day draw on
modern science, modern scholarship, and modern
philosophy.

It remains that theology has a dimension of
its own.   To a consideration of that dimension we
may now turn, but it is worth noting that a theology which is a reflection on a religion in the
sense in which both generalized and specialized reflection have been here presented, will be a theol-

ogy with a correlation to the horizon of the incarnate human subject in history.

III.

IV. THEOLOGICAL UNITY:
METHOD AND METHODS IN THEOLOGY

> Let us now turn from deriving general
> theological categories to deriving
> special theological categories. In
> this task we have a model in the the-
> oretical theology developed in the
> middle ages. But it is a model that
> can be imitated only by shifting to a
> new key. For the categories we want
> will pertain, not to a theoretical
> theology, but to a methodical theol-
> ogy.[1]

In the previous chapter I gave an account of
both generalized and specialized reflection on religion and religions. Generalized reflection on
religion is a matter of bringing to light the function of religion in human living. Specialized reflection on religions is a matter of bringing to
light either the many religious constructions of
the human spirit (history), or the radical conflicts
in those constructions and their interpretations
(dialectic), or the foundation of authentic religious constructions in the present and future (praxis).

In the present chapter I shall indicate the
relevance of generalized and specialized methods of
reflection to theology. Firstly, I shall describe
various notions of specialization, in order to find
out in what sense theology today might possibly be
considered an academic specialization. Secondly,
because available notions of specialization tend to

335

IV.

be inadequate, Lonergan offers a brief description
of current theological work in terms of distinct
theological tasks, in order to prepare the way for
a notion of specialization based on the function
and functions of theology. Thirdly, these various
tasks are further defined in light of generalized
and specialized reflection on religion. Fourthly,
there is offered an account of the unity of theology, where the unity is conceived dynamically as
the interacting of the various tasks. A brief conclusion relates this chapter to the next, where I
shall consider the function of theology itself
within the broader contexts of the church and of
human living.

1. Specialization in Theology

Earlier, in Chapter Two, I traced the broad
lines of the movement from medieval theology to
the new study of religion. I pointed out that medieval theology can be conceived as a distinct specialization or horizon within the religious community. It was an effort to reflect systematically on
the meaning of the community - an attempt to work
out in an explicit manner the literal meaning of
the many symbolic expressions whereby the community
had come to an understanding of itself in history.[2]

The shift from a medieval to a modern context,
and the rise of new ways of reflecting on religion

and religions, does not mean that theology should
now disappear or that theologians no longer have a
meaningful contribution to make to the modern world.
True, there are those who claim that medieval theology has been quite adequately replaced by the various modern specializations of science, scholarship,
and philosophy, especially inasmuch as these specializations happen to be concerned with human religious behavior. In such a view, theology is likely
to be associated with naive, prescientific, non-
critical, superstitious, mythical thought that perhaps once served a purpose but that is quite out of
place in a world come of age.

The demise of medieval theology as a specialization, however, does not mean the demise of theology as a specialization. For Lonergan, modern
science, scholarship, and philosophy do not make
theology obsolete, but rather provide a new context
in which theology is to work out a new self-understanding of its function in history. But in order
to understand in what sense theology might possibly
be considered a specialization in this modern context; in order to determine how theology is both
distinct from and related to other disciplines, Lonergan invites us to reflect on different meanings of
"specialization."[3]

Firstly, there is what can be called a commonsense notion of specialization, one quite easy to
understand. It is a matter of dividing and sub-

IV.

dividing the field of data to be investigated.[4]
Thus, for example, "mankind" is the data investigated by human studies, religious studies, Christian studies, and Roman Catholic studies; but each
of these differs from the others inasmuch as an
ever narrower field of data is selected as relevant.[5] Again, each of those sub-divisions can itself be sub-divided; thus, Christian studies might
include scriptural, patristic, medieval, reformation, and modern studies. Further sub-divisions
may be made, so that one specializes, not just in
the New Testament but in the gospels, not just in
the gospels but in the gospel of John, not merely
in the gospel of John but in the Prologue to this
gospel. Such specialization is "a concentration
on one field to the neglect of all others, . . .
an increasing concentration of attention in that
one field so that, as people say, one comes to know
more and more about less and less."[6]

In this sense, Christian studies are distinguished from religious studies inasmuch as the former concentrate on a narrower field of data than
the latter; Christian studies are really just a
more specialized brand of religious studies. Generally, however, it is urged that Christian studies
are to be distinguished from religious studies, not
merely on the basis of more specific data, but as
well because the data of Christian studies are revealed truths while the data of religious studies

338

are of human origin. So it is that we are encouraged to think of Christian studies, not so much in
terms of field specialization, but more along the
lines of subject-matter: Christian studies are distinct from other studies because the former deal with
revealed truths, while other disciplines deal with
purely human topics; and even when Christian studies
seem also to deal with human topics, they do so under
the light of revelation and faith.[7]

In this latter view, the significant distinction
is not between empirical religious studies and empirical Christian studies, but between Christian theology and a mere philosophy of religion. The difference between the two, it is claimed, lies in the fact
that theology is concerned with the revealed God and
with what God has revealed, while philosophy of religion is concerned with humanity and with human efforts to know God. In other words, where field specialization tends to reduce Christian studies to just
a more specialized form of empirical religious studies, a classification according to specific subject-
matter (subject specialization) clearly would result
in a discipline, Christian theology, that is quite
distinct from all other disciplines. Such areas as
language studies, exegesis, history, empirical science, and philosophy may and should serve the theological cause, but they remain auxiliary disciplines,
Hilfswissenschaften, quite separate from theology as
such.[8]

IV.

This conceptual classification into different
subjects is something that is most familiar to us,
for it is the basis of the divisions among faculties
and departments of universities and colleges, just
as it is the ground for organizing different courses
within a given faculty. On the surface, such conceptual classification seems quite in line with the
Aristotelian division of the sciences in terms of
material and formal objects: the field of a discipline is defined by that discipline's material object, and the specific approach to the material object or field is defined by the formal object. So
theology conceives itself as the science about God
and about all other things in their relation to God,
studied under the light of revelation and faith.
And because theology has both a material and a formal object, it at once is distinguished from other
sciences with other material or formal objects yet
is assured of scientific status and a place in the
university.[9]

In fact, however, the framework has shifted.
There are still universities and colleges, with
their faculties, departments, and courses. There
is still a classification of subject-matter that
organizes the results of investigations for assimilation by students. But there is a profound difference in the investigations that lie behind the
classification. Not only is there a material difference in the sheer amount of data to be investi-

gated and classified; more significantly, there is
a formal difference in the whole approach to the investigation of data. The Aristotelian framework has
been repudiated, and the various sciences no longer
are distinguished according to particular spheres of
being studied under particular attributes of being.
Instead of material objects, one speaks of data; and
instead of formal objects, one simply applies to the
data the operations that are prescribed by the particular method of the science in question.[10]

This shift of framework or context has not gone
unnoticed by theologians, who generally are quite
aware of the demise of the Aristotelian notion of
science. Further, such theologians are aware of the
need to justify their continuing presence at universities and colleges. Logically, then, theologians
have been attempting to re-define their science in
terms provided by the conspicuously successful model
of the new science, namely, the natural sciences
that continue to dominate university faculties and
budgets. With a measure of success, theology too
has become largely empirical, resting on data uncovered by empirical Christian studies. With far
less success has theology been able to articulate
its specific approach to the data that would distinguish it from empirical religious studies yet
leave its scientific status intact. The former appeal to revealed truths is ruled out of court as an
uncritical dogmatism and authoritarianism. So one

IV.

is forced to take a stand on empirical reality,
and because this reality also is studied by the
various particular sciences, theology conceives
its role as the science that reveals the ultimate
meaning, not just of this or that reality, but of
reality as such, both natural and especially human.
As such, theology tends to be identified with the
philosophy of religion: but a difference is claimed,
inasmuch as theology presupposes divine reality as
revealing the ultimate meaning of reality as such,
while philosophy, technically speaking, can prescind
from or bracket questions of God's existence as
factual.[11]

The main problem with these modern attempts to
conceive the distinctness of theology on the basis
of distinct subject-matter is the fact that such an
approach remains essentially deductive. It envisions
some permanently valid concept of God or of universal history that theologians apply to the current
state of natural and human affairs in order to judge
the worth of actually functioning history and, in a
practical moment, to suggest where improvements might
be made. Just who is to determine this permanently
valid concept is unclear, as is the manner in which
such determination is to be done. One fears, as a
minimal consequence, a revival of positivism or, in
the extreme, a relativism and subjectivism.

It is to avoid such dangers that Lonergan has
suggested a notion of theology that rests, not on

342

field specialization, nor on a classicist subject
specialization, but rather on the sort of specialization that underpins empirical subject specialization. That underpinning is, of course, the distinction of sciences according to distinct methods of investigation, rather than according to differences of
data or differences in the viewpoints from which the
same data are considered. If Lonergan turns to the
natural sciences, he does so, not in the hope of
constructing a theology on the analogy of natural
scientific method, but in order to get a clue as to
what "method" itself might possibly be.[11a] From
natural science he turns to common sense, to discover if behind the procedures of commonsense knowing the same basic operations are at work as in the
natural sciences or mathematics. From there he turns
to the work of theologians; again, a plurality of
methods are operative, yet common to each he discovers the same core of related and recurrent operations at work in the many different stages of theological investigation and classification and communication. So it is that theology shares an empirical
foundation with the various spheres of human knowing - a foundation in generalized empirical method;
yet theology is not reduced to empirical science or
philosophy or common sense because there is a method
that is specifically theological.

Just what this method is, I hope to outline in
the present chapter. It is a notion of theology that

343

IV.

rests, not on field specialization, nor on subject
specialization, but on methodical or functional
specialization. It is a matter of dividing up
different investigative processes and of stages
within each process whereby data are investigated
and results communicated. It is a notion of theology
that rests, not on common sense, nor on science,
but on method - generalized empirical method.

It should be noted that Lonergan is not inventing a new theology, nor is he demanding an abandonment of scholarly Christian studies. Both field
specialization and subject specialization will
continue to be operative, but their operation will
be under the control of method that will guide the
work of each specialist in each field or subject,
as well as relate the work of each to what others
are doing both within theology and in other spheres
also. Lonergan is asking us to reflect on current
theological performance, to note what we are doing
as we actually function as exegetes or historians
or systematic or pastoral theologians. Accordingly,
to indicate this link with current theological
performance, Lonergan offers a brief description
of eight distinct functions or tasks of theology,
in order to give us an initial taste of things by
drawing our attention to what is already more or
less familiar and common.

2. The Basic Pattern of Specialties

I have been asking about the meaning of theology in a contemporary context, and began by noting that it is first necessary to clarify just in what sense theology might be considered a specialization. In the contemporary world, the model of specialization is provided by the natural sciences, although there is as well the quite distinct model of the scholarly sciences. I have mentioned that theological work at the present time is most likely to be fashioned after one or the other of these models, but that Lonergan, for reasons to be outlined later, has suggested a quite distinct model or notion of specialization. Finally, I noted that Lonergan's suggestion is not to be understood as sheer novelty, but that it is rather a refinement and clarification of theological performance presently being carried out. In order now to move a step further in our investigations, Lonergan invites us to an examination of field and subject specializations in contemporary theology. In this regard, there follows a description of eight distinct tasks, most of which will be familiar to us, and, in the following section, I shall with Lonergan objectify the grounding and interrelationship of these various tasks by generalized empirical method. Firstly, then, a simple description of what is happening in contemporary theology, and then, in the next section, an exercise in generalized empirical method that will conceive these tasks in terms, not of field or subject specialization, but of functional specialization.

IV.

The basic pattern of theological specialties
that have been developed in contemporary theology
are research, interpretation, history, dialectic,
foundations, doctrines, systematics, and communications.

(1) Research - Research is the task of uncovering and making available the data relevant to theological investigation.[12] Lonergan distinguishes
two kinds of research, both of which are quite familiar to us. Special research assembles the data relevant to a particular question or problem; so a doctoral student patiently or otherwise spends long
hours plowing through library card systems and book-
shelves in the search for materials that might be
relevant to a dissertation on the notion of theology
in the thought of Bernard Lonergan. General research
is more ambitious, in that the questions or problems
are of a more general nature, so that the researcher
commonly is associated with the fields of epigraphy,
papyrology, paleography, diplomatics, sigillography,
archeology, genealogy and heraldry: tasks that demand skills in such areas as statistics, demography,
microphotography and oral recording, as well as long
and extensive use of archives and libraries.[13]

(2) Interpretation - In the contemporary context, a distinction generally is made between "hermeneutics," concerned with the principles of interpretation, and "exegesis," concerned with applying

these principles to a given task.[14] Both the methodical principles and the methodical application of principles are aimed at reaching an understanding of whatever data is made available to theologians:

> While research makes available what was written, interpretation understands what was meant. It grasps that meaning in its proper historical context, in accord with its proper mode and level of thought and expression, in the light of the circumstances and intention of the writer. Its product is the commentary or monograph.[15]

As was the case with research, so too with interpretation: it is highly relevant to contemporary theological investigations. For now, this simple fact is all that I wish to indicate, since my concern in the present section is merely to draw attention to the things that present-day theologians are doing. In simple terms, I am drawing attention to the fact that the doctoral student cannot be content with amassing a bibliography, but also has to read and understand what he or she has amassed; similarly, a critical edition of the writings of Bultmann may decorate one's library, but it also may be the subject of investigation as one tries to understand this or that dimension of Bultmann's thought.

(3) History - Among the ingredients of modern theology, critical historical studies have come to play a dominant role. Familiar enough are the studies in basic history that concern themselves with the geo-

IV.

graphic and temporal dimensions of human affairs, as
well as the more special histories of cultural and
institutional movements.[16] The less familiar, more
difficult, yet crucial special history that deals
with the development of Christian teachings and of
theology is receiving ever more attention in our own
day, and is providing the basis for a more general
or universal historical viewpoint from which can be
increasingly understood the differences and similarities among religious groups within world history.[17]

(4) Dialectic - while research, interpretation,
and history are readily acknowledged to be concerns
of modern theology, the task of dialectic is less
familiar, perhaps because of the many different manners in which the word "dialectic" may be used. Still,
from my comments in Chapters One and Three, the reader
should have little difficulty in associating Lonergan's
meaning of dialectic with current theological practice.[18]

> By dialectic, then, is understood a gen-
> eralized apologetic conducted in an ecu-
> menical spirit, aiming ultimately at a
> comprehensive viewpoint, and proceeding
> towards that goal by acknowledging dif-
> ferences, seeking their grounds real and
> apparent, and eliminating superfluous
> oppositions.[19]

The presence of conflicts within the Christian tradition, and among those whose task it is to reflect on
that tradition, is a fact that, if once possible to
ignore, now has entered into the heart of theological

work. This work in part has to get behind the fact
of conflicts to their reasons; it has to line up
contrary and opposed positions, and critically reveal instances of misunderstanding, faulty reasoning,
or undue ambitions that resulted in the conflicts.
Nor is such work unknown in contemporary theology,
even though its methodical grounding has not been
worked out in any detail. One has only to think of
the ongoing debates among theologians of the same
tradition in such questions as infallibility, situation ethics, dehellenization of doctrine; or of ecumenical dialogues that strive to confront the basic
differences in such questions as eucharist, ministry,
or church structures; or of commissions that relate
Christian churches to non-Christian religions and to
those dialectically opposed to any religion.

(5) Foundations - It is generally acknowledged
that the traditional fundamental theology, at least
in Catholic circles, is undergoing a process of transformation.[20] In very broad terms, this process is a
shift from religious doctrines (on the true church,
the true religion, etc.) to the human horizon in which
religious doctrines are apprehended as meaningful. So
it is that one of the tasks of a contemporary theology
is the objectification of the horizon within which the
meaning of religious doctrines can be affirmed, understood, and communicated. This task is foundational,
for it brings to light the dimensions of religious,

IV.

moral, and cognitional authenticity that are needed
both to resolve the conflicts uncovered by dialectic
and to guide the working out of theological categories. To say this means, of course, that theology is
not restricted to the scholarly study of the past
Christian tradition, but has the function as well of
passing this tradition on to the present and the future. But as has been mentioned, both tradition itself and the investigation of tradition are involved
in a dialectic of inauthenticity and authenticity.
There is need, then, for thematizing the conversion
whereby one moves from inauthenticity to authenticity,
in order that this may serve as a principle for determining what is in fact authentic tradition, and to
provide the basis for authentically transposing that
tradition to the world of the present and future.
Prior to stating what is authentic doctrine, prior
to an attempt to understand that doctrine or effectively communicate it, there is needed an account of
the horizon within which such statements, understanding, and communication are meaningful. To offer such
an account is the task of foundational theology.

    (6) Doctrines - It has been mentioned that the-
ology has a function in service to Christian truth.
So theologians are called upon to make the judgments
of fact and of value about expressions of truth in
the Christian tradition. It is a matter of stating
what the truths of the Christian tradition are, and

IV.

of setting forth clearly the beliefs of the Christian community. Such doctrines may be dogmas, but as well there are the teachings of moralists, ascetics, mystics, preachers, teachers, pastors, not to mention the sensus fidelium.[21] Theology is to be ecclesial, not just in the sense that it speaks from within a particular ecclesial tradition, but also in the sense that it establishes what is authentic in that tradition by an appeal to religious, moral, and intellectual conversion. The doctrinal theologian, then, is not just a Denzingertheologe, but has an autonomous function in service to the entire ecclesial community.

(7) Systematics - That which is affirmed to be authentic teaching may or may not be readily intelligible to a given mentality in a given age. For doctrines commonly take on the coloring of the age in which they are formulated, and such contexts are subject to change, development, and decline in history. What is quite intelligible in one context becomes obscure or even suspect of error in another, as times change, and words shift in meaning or even disappear from usage. So it was that medieval theologians sought to resolve apparent contradictions in Church teachings by working out a systematic understanding of these teachings that went beyond their symbolic expression to their literal meaning. So it is that modern theology abounds with systematic ef-

351

IV.

forts to understand and organize Christian teaching
by drawing on the resources of contemporary philosophies and sciences. Such is the systematic task
of theologians, described by Lonergan in the following way:

> It is concerned to work out appropriate
> systems of conceptualization, to remove
> apparent inconsistencies, to move towards
> some grasp of spiritual matters both from
> their own inner coherence and from the
> analogies offered by more familiar human
> experience.[22]

(8) Communications - Yet a further dimension
of current theological work is the effort to communicate effectively the Christian message to those
within the Christian community and through them to
the larger context of human history. It is a dimension that is currently receiving extensive attention, as the limitations of a classicist theology
are recognized. Within a classicist framework, it
was presupposed that the one Christian teaching
could be preached to the one world in one uniform
manner. But the empirical notion of culture has
revealed tremendous diversity among the peoples of
the world, challenging theologians to overcome the
limitations, not just of classicist thinking, but
of any thinking that stems from a culture different
from the one in which they happen to be operating.
In response to this challenge, theologians have
shifted concerns to the relation of Christian teach-

352

ing to dominant ideologies, to other sciences outside the theological framework, to the multitudinous
needs of people in their ordinary symbolic living.

3. From Theological Methods to Method in Theology

I have been sketching a number of tasks that
are of concern to the contemporary theological community. I should add at once that this sketch is intended to be a pedagogical tool in helping the reader
to make the transition from accustomed notions of
theology to Lonergan's notion of theology as a functional specialization. I suspect that most of us
think of theology in terms of field and subject
specializations. We are used to thinking of theology in terms of the subjects offered us at colleges
and universities, and quite readily grant the title
of "scholar" to the men and women who teach us or who
are involved in a variety of research activities.
The traditional divisions are well-implanted in our
minds and in our catalogues: biblical languages, Old
and New Testament exegesis and theology, dogmatic or
systematic theology, moral theology or ethics, pastoral or practical theology, church history, church
law. The actual designations may vary from place to
place, nor is there unanimous agreement on the scope
and procedures of any one of the areas listed. Nevertheless, it is both familiar and easily understood to
think of theology in terms of the field of data or

353

IV.

the subject-matter that is studied.

What I offered in the previous section was a description of theology in terms, not of the areas or subjects that form the content of theological investigation, but rather in terms of the methods that guide investigation into any area. In this way, Lonergan is inviting the reader to shift attention away from the objects studied to the people who are doing the studying and teaching. He is inviting the reader to reflect on theology as a many-staged process of investigation, rather than as a discipline concerned with Christianity in its origins, development, and current teachings. In a word, attention should shift from data and results to operators and operations that are the sources of investigations into data and of the communication of results. Generally, it is an invitation to reflect on the conditions of the possibility of current field and subject specialization, in an attempt to discover what theology is as a whole and in its many parts, and to carry out whatever re-organization of field and subject specialization may be called for.

This shift to a notion of theology in terms of method rather than in terms of data or results has been noted by Heinrich Ott:

> It is particularly necessary for theol-
> ogy to give an account of its own proper
> thought-process. For in theology there
> is a primacy of method: it cannot for-
> get its method or let it remain unre-

> flected upon, sticking to results alone.
> Theology needs to exhibit no experimen-
> tal or statistical results which have
> been proven and are simply valid. The
> result without the way leading to it,
> without the method then, simply does not
> exist for theology. Hence, the method,
> the way, is to some degree implicit in
> each theological insight and its articu-
> lation. And only in the measure that
> method is so entailed can there be talk
> about a 'truth' of insight.[23]

As Ott remarks, method is to some degree implicit in
each theological insight; what Lonergan is suggesting
is that method become the explicit grounding of all
theological insights. In somewhat similar fashion,
Gadamer has urged us to go beyond an epistemology of
interpretation, in order to relate history and consciousness to each other on the basic level where the
human subject is subject, and not object;[24] and such
objectification of the subject as subject is Lonergan's meaning of generalized empirical method, just
as the objectification of the operations of the theologian as theologian is the specific method in theology. Those operations, in their principal features,
were indicated in the eight tasks listed in the previous section, and now the time has come to indicate
the grounds of these tasks in generalized empirical
method.[25]

Lonergan first distinguishes the two phases of
theological reflection. Because Christianity is a
reality in the world mediated by meaning, the sym-

IV.

bolic world of outwardly expressed meaning, the external or historical world, it follows that an initial phase of theology is concerned with the assimilation of the past meaning of the tradition, while a second phase aims at making this tradition meaningful in the present and future historical context. Neither the Christian religion nor Christian theology are brand new inventions; there is a past tradition, and the tradition may be neglected only at the price of cutting oneself off from the roots that identify who one is. But if study of the past tradition cannot be neglected, no less can the responsibility of carrying this tradition forward be evaded, if Christianity is truly to promote human progress and undo the elements of human decline. Such, then, is the initial basis of specialization in theology:

> The first principle of the division is
> that theological operations occur in
> two basic phases. If one is to harken
> to the word, one must also bear witness
> to it. If one engages in lectio divina,
> there come to mind quaestiones. If one
> assimilates tradition, one learns that
> one should pass it on. If one encoun-
> ters the past, one also has to take
> one's stand toward the future. In
> brief, there is a theology in oratione
> obliqua that tells what Paul and John,
> Augustine and Aquinas, and anyone else
> had to say about God and the economy of
> salvation. But there is also a theol-
> ogy in oratione recta in which the the-
> ologian, enlightened by the past, con-
> fronts the problems of his own day.26

The division of phases arises inasmuch as Christianity

356

is a reality in the world mediated by meaning and is
a reality that is constitutive of the world mediated
by meaning. In other words, because Christianity is
a reality in the world mediated by meaning, the theologian has to reflect on this meaning in its origins
and development; and because Christianity is constitutive of the world mediated by meaning, because it
would reveal the ultimate meaning of that world, the
theologian has also to mediate this meaning into the
whole of human affairs and thereby influence the contemporary cultural context.[27] If the Christian tradition is not to stagnate or die, if it is to remain a
living tradition, then more must be done than simply
study what this tradition is and how it arose; besides
finding out how others expressed their religious experience as God's love in Christ Jesus, formulated according to the resources of their own day, theologians
also have to take a stand and state clearly, intelli-
gibly and forcefully just what Christianity means today, in the present cultural contexts.

This division of phases is, of course, quite familiar to theologians, whether with the classicist
one speaks of positive and speculative theology, or
with the contemporary one speaks of reconstruction of
the past and construction of the present and future.
What is novel in the work of Lonergan is the unity
between these phases that comes to light in a methodical objectification of the precise tasks within each
phase. Just what this means has now to be clarified.

357

IV.

   Commonly, then, modern theologians are aware of
the general division of labor indicated by the two
phases of theological reflection. Again, most are
not content to identify themselves with one or the
other phase, but consider themselves as specialists
within either. As mentioned, such specialization is,
in the first phase, a matter of concentrating on a
given part of the field of data; no one person can
master the whole of the past Christian tradition, so
one specializes in scripture, another in patristics,
others in medieval or modern history. In the second
phase, specialization occurs along different lines,
but generally the division of labor has specialists
that thematize the tradition along existentialist
(moral), theoretical (dogmatics/systematics), or
practical (pastoral) classifications. Moreover,
these second-phase specialists usually draw heavily
upon historical investigations, so that there is
considerable overlapping of the phases.

   For Lonergan, however, sub-divisions within
each phase can be clarified considerably by introducing a second principle of division that rests,
not on dividing up the field of data, nor on thematizing and classifying subject matter, but rather
on dividing the process of theological reflection
itself: distinguishing different stages in the investigative process, where the tradition is assimilated in different reflective techniques and mediated in different techniques. To get some general

idea of this second principle of division, I would
refer the reader to the quotation from Lonergan
given a moment ago. Commonly, the difference between
attending to the word and bearing witness to the word
is a difference that is readily understood. But does
the reader note any difference among the following
operations: attending to the word, lectio divina,
assimilating tradition, encountering the past? Or is
there any difference between the operations of witnessing to the word, posing quaestiones, passing tradition on, taking one's stand toward the future? On
a first reading, we are likely to think that Lonergan is simply describing the same task with different
words. So attending to the word, lectio divina, assimilating tradition, encountering the past seem
merely to be different ways of describing the one job
of reflecting on the past Christian tradition. And
witnessing, quaestiones, passing tradition on, taking
one's stand toward the future, all seem to refer to
the one job of reflecting on what the tradition means
today, in the present context. In fact, however,
what Lonergan has done is indicate, in a descriptive
way, eight quite distinct types of conscious operation, eight distinct stages in the process of finding
out what the Christian tradition is, and what this
tradition means in the present cultural situation.

So, for example, he mentions that the theologian
is to harken to the word, and is to engage in lectio
divina. Lonergan seems to be saying the same thing,

but in different ways. But if we reflect for a moment, perhaps a subtle difference between these operations will be noted, and perhaps what is first thought subtle will, upon yet further reflection, become quite an obvious difference. I do not deny that our commonsense thinking is able to lump together the tasks of harkening to the word and engaging in a lectio divina. But what is here demanded is to find a distinction that common sense commonly overlooks. For it is one thing to be attentive to the word, to see exactly what is written in a text, and quite another to understand what the printing means. One can have a very critical edition of Lonergan's writings, yet fail to grasp what Lonergan means. Yet, to edit a critical edition of Lonergan's writings, and to interpret what Lonergan means, are clearly two distinct tasks involving different methods that aim at quite different goals. I do not deny that one person can do both tasks, for that is what I have done in composing the present work; but in doing basic and special research on the texts of Lonergan, in finding out which were early drafts and which were eventually published, I was doing something quite different than attempting to interpret what Lonergan meant in the published text.

It is in realizing this distinction of operations or tasks that the reader will begin to understand what Lonergan means by functional specialties. We are asked to shift our attention from exclusive

IV.

concern with the data or results of theological investigation to the theologian who, in his or her operations, is correlative to these data and results: to the theologian as conscious subject, whose conscious operations occur on four distinct levels:

> The second principle of division is derived from the fact that our conscious and intentional operations occur on four distinct levels and that each level has its own proper achievement and end. So the proper achievement and end of the first level, experiencing, is the apprehension of data; that of the second level, understanding, is insight into the apprehended data; that of the third level, judgment, is the acceptance or rejection of the hypotheses and theories put forward by understanding to account for the data; that of the fourth level, decision, the acknowledgment of values and the selection of the methods or other means that lead to their realization.[28]

It is, of course, one thing to describe conscious operations as occurring on four levels, or to read that in the present work; and it is quite another to verify for oneself these qualitative differences in our conscious intentionality. Such verification is Lonergan's generalized empirical method, described in the previous chapter. It is a matter of self-appropriation of ourselves as conscious in one way as experiencing, in another as striving to understand what is experienced, in yet another as rationally affirming as true, false, or probable our understanding of the data, and in yet another as responsibly ack-

361

IV.

nowledging values and acting towards their realization.

As Lonergan notes, to distinguish differences
in the qualities of one's conscious operations, to
know what one is doing when one is experiencing, understanding, judging, and deciding, and to realize
that one's doing in each case is different: all this
is not something that comes easily, that is easily
understood, that is familiar to us. All of us are
ordinary, commonsense folk, and our everyday commonsense thinking and doing seems to be so simple that
it defies complicated analysis.

> Now in everyday, commonsense performance,
> all four levels are employed continuously
> without any explicit distinction between
> them. In that case no functional spe-
> cialization arises, for what is sought is
> not the end of any particular level but
> the cumulative, composite resultant of
> the ends of all four levels.[29]

On the other hand, specialization arises inasmuch as
self-appropriation of our conscious and intentional
operations reveals four distinct and related levels
of operation, with four distinct and related goals
or ends, and we proceed to operate on all four levels,
but in order to achieve the end proper to some particular level:

> It follows that the very structure of hu-
> man inquiry results in four functional
> specializations and, since in theology
> there are two distinct phases, we are led
> to expect eight functional specializations

in theology. In the first phase of theology _in oratione obliqua_ there are research, interpretation, history, and dialectic. In the second phase of theology
in oratione recta there are foundations,
doctrines, systematics, and communications.[30]

Once again, at this point, I fear that the brevity of
my presentation will lead to a failure to communicate
this second principle of division within theology; I
can but recommend that the reader study Chapters One
to Five of Method in Theology and accept the challenge
there issued. What Lonergan is proposing, however,
should be appreciated in its simplicity, as well as in
the complexity that seems to frighten away a goodly
number of otherwise interested readers. This simplicity lies in the fact that Lonergan wishes to make explicit and thematic something that is quite present in
contemporary thought, but only in an implicit and un-
thematized, unmethodical manner. I refer to the fact
that current academic disciplines, whether one considers theology, philosophy, or the natural and social
sciences, all are characterized more by their methods
than by their fields.[31] For example, the distinction
between empirical religious sciences and theology cannot be justified simply by stating that the former
treats of humanity while the latter treats of God;
rather, greater clarity is achieved by distinguishing
the different methods of investigation in each discipline, methods which in their own ways treat both humanity and God. Again, the process of specialization

IV.

described in Chapter Two was fundamentally a process of ever-greater refinement of old and new methods, and was not just a matter of dividing up some
field of data, but treating it in basically the same
way. Theology, philosophy, natural science, scholarship, and even common sense are specializations, distinct horizons, precisely inasmuch as they each operate with particular methods to achieve particular
goals. What Lonergan wishes us to do is to make explicit these various methods, to trace their common
ground in the generalized empirical method that is
the human mind conscious and knowledgeable of its
basic conscious operations, and to use that basis as
the principle of ongoing and cumulative work in all
particular fields.

     This is, clearly, the foundation of specializa-
tion. I have already mentioned that the absence of
an explicit distinction among the various levels of
conscious and intentional operations is a characteristic of our commonsense performance. Perhaps it is
worth adding that the absence of such distinctions
is characteristic of current manners of dividing up
theology. Theologians usually manage to get beyond
commonsense thinking in their work; they recognize
the utility of specialization, once theology has
reached a certain stage of development and it becomes obvious that things are getting too extensive
and too complex for any one person to master and
communicate. But when specialization is effected,

it most likely will be simply an extension of commonsense thinking into the discipline, rather than a
methodical effort to ground specialties in human cognitional and existential performance. Nor is this to
be lamented, for performance precedes reflection on
that performance, and the variety of theological tasks
have to be actually functioning, before one has the
challenge to step back and ask precisely what is being
done, and if it could be done more effectively. So it
is, that initially at least, specialization is a
straightforward matter of dividing the work load, and
letting each specialist choose whatever field or subject happens to interest him or her. At a latter
stage, bolder spirits may choose the scientific model
that radiates success and endless results, so that
theology strives to imitate the accuracy of scientific investigation, while clinging to what it considers a specific theological principle in a religious object, whether material or formal. Lonergan,
however, urges attention to modern science, not with
a view to emulating its methods, but with a view to
understanding what modern scientific method is; and
he urges us to do the same for the procedures of common sense, for the same reason. And what is discovered in each case is the rock, the basic pattern of
conscious and intentional operations that form the
core of all particular methods, including that in
theology.[32]

Hence, it is one thing to do theology. It is
quite another to know what one is doing when one is

IV.

doing theology. Functional specialization is intended, not to introduce new methods into theology,
but to provide a clear delineation of what currently
operative methods are, how they operate, what they
intend. Accordingly, I wish now to offer a slightly
fuller account of the eight tasks of theology described in the previous section. None of the tasks,
of course, is operative in some cultural vacuum, but
only in correlation to a particular religious tradition. And because the religious tradition that is
of concern in the present work is Christianity, my
account will be of method in Christian theology.[33]
Firstly, I shall outline the method in mediating theology. Secondly, to clarify the transition from mediating to mediated theology, I shall discuss the
specifically theological principle. Thirdly, I shall
outline the method in mediated theology whereby that
principle is objectified, affirmed, partially understood, and effectively communicated.

(1) Method in Mediating Theology

    In investigating the meaning and value of the
past Christian tradition, theologians should be attentive, intelligent, reasonable, and responsible.
In functional specialization, each of these stages
in the process of coming to know and evaluate the
tradition becomes a specialized concern. So it is,
that operations on all levels of consciousness are
directed towards the goals intended by attentiveness

(research), by intelligence (interpretation), by reasonableness (history), and by responsibility (dialectic). What is intended is the Christian tradition, and it is considered in correspondingly different ways: as data for research, as data that possess and convey a meaning to be determined by interpretation, as data whose meaning factually constitute an ongoing process to be affirmed by historians, and as data whose history manifests the values and disvalues brought about by various persons: values and disvalues to be catalogued and compared in dialectics.[34] Taken together, these four specialties constitute mediating theology: theology that mediates to us an encounter with persons witnessing to Christ.[35]

The research scholar directs his or her attentiveness, intelligence, reasonableness, and responsibility to the goal intended by the operations of attentiveness. This goal is the apprehension of whatever data might be relevant to theological reflection. The greater the scholar's depth of perception, the broader the experience, the more refined the sensibility, the weightier will be the contribution of the researcher in the task of making available the materials that shed light on the Christian tradition. Still, while a specialist in attentiveness, the researcher clearly needs other qualities as well, and so places intelligence, reasonableness, and responsibility at the service of

IV.

attentiveness. Intelligence gives the researcher an
understanding of just what attentiveness means in
this or that situation. Reasonableness allows the
researcher to judge the direction in which attentiveness is going, as well as the results of research
work. Responsibility encourages the researcher to
select the proper methods demanded by attentiveness
in a given situation, and to communicate findings
in the most effective manner to specialists in other
fields.[36]

The interpreter directs his or her attentiveness,
intelligence, reasonableness, and responsibility to
the goal intended by the operations of intelligence.
This goal is insight into the apprehended data, an
understanding of the meaning of the data. The meaning to be understood is the meaning intended, not by
the interpreter, but by the people who are the source
of the data apprehended by researchers. The interpreter has to grasp that meaning in its historical
context, in the manner and level of thought and expression of the writer, and in the light of the particular circumstances and intention that the writer
had in mind.[37] To this end, the interpreter specializes in three basic exegetical operations: "(1) understanding the text; (2) judging how correct one's
understanding of the text is; and (3) stating what
one judges to be the correct understanding of the
text."[38] Just what is involved in each of these operations is discussed by Lonergan in Method in The-

ology, to which the reader is referred.[39] Here, I
wish simply to stress that the central operation of
the interpreter is that of understanding the text
or data, to which task all conscious and intentional
operations are directed. Thus, attentiveness demands
that the interpreter apprehend accurately just what
it is that is to be interpreted. Reasonableness is
needed so that the interpreter may judge the accuracy
of interpretation. And responsibility is directed to
the selection of the proper methods to employ in arriving at an understanding of the text, as well as in
communicating results to specialists in other fields.[40]

While research is related principally to experiencing and attentiveness, while interpretation is related principally to understanding and intelligence,
history is related principally to judging and reasonableness. For many, this relation of history to judgment in Lonergan's methodology has been questioned on
various grounds and subjected to extensive criticism.[41]
Rather than attempt a refutation of the critics, I wish
instead to indicate briefly what Lonergan affirms in
his presentation of historical operations, and perhaps
prepare the way for criticisms that rest on a fuller
understanding of things. The historical scholar, then,
directs his or her attentiveness, intelligence, reasonableness, and responsibility to the goal intended by
the operations of reasonableness. This goal is "the
acceptance or rejection of the hypotheses and theories
put forward by understanding to account for the data."[42]

IV.

In the first phase of theology, the hypotheses and
theories in question are the meanings expressed by
individuals in their efforts to come to an understanding of themselves as Christian. These meanings have been reconstructed, with greater or lesser success, by interpreters; but it is one thing
to determine what individuals meant or intended in
their religious expressions, and quite another to
reconstruct the historical process by determining
what in fact occurred in specific times and places:
to determine what actually was the prior, contemporary, and subsequent context of religious meaning.
Granted, there have been those who suggest that history is just a matter of stringing together a series
of interpretations of individual people; in this
case, there would be no real difference between interpretation and history. But Lonergan is of a
different opinion, and I think the reason may best
be given by drawing attention to the constitutive
function of meaning in human living.

> Just as language is constituted by ar-
> ticulate sound and meaning, so social
> institutions and human cultures have
> meanings as intrinsic components. Re-
> ligions and art-forms, languages and
> literatures, sciences, philosophies,
> histories, all are inextricably in-
> volved in acts of meaning. What is
> true of cultural achievement, no less
> is true of social institutions. The
> family, the state, the law, the econ-
> omy are not fixed and immutable enti-
> ties. They adapt to changing circum-

IV.

stances; they can be reconceived in
the light of new ideas; they can be
subjected to revolutionary change.
But all such change involves change
of meaning - a change of idea or concept, a change of judgment or evaluation, a change of the order or re-
quest.[43]

Meaning, then, is an integral component of cultures and societies. Such cultural and societal
meaning is the context from which the individual
draws in giving expression to what he or she experiences, understands, affirms, decides. It follows
that it is one thing to determine what an individual
meant by any given expression, and another to determine the context in which individuals express themselves and from which they draw and to which they in
turn contribute. In the former instance, I am attempting to reconstruct the factual context in which
such understanding occurred. So it is, that the task
of the historian is to determine, not what was meant
or intended by such and such an expression, but rather
the context actually constituted by the meaningful
acts and deeds, reflections and judgments, inquiries
and understanding, attending and experiencing of people of another time and place. It is an effort to
state what in fact occurred (Ranke), or, in the words
of Lonergan, what in fact was going forward at any
given place or time.

Without doubt, there is an interdependence of
interpretation and history. Without doubt, the inter-

371

IV.

preter can understand what the data mean only in
light of the broader historical process. Without
doubt, the historian can state what the historical
process is only in the light of understood data.
But the point here is not the interdependence of interpretation and history, but the fact that two distinct goals are intended, and the distinction of
goals calls for distinct methods of investigation.
It is one thing to strive for an understanding of
what Aquinas meant in his various writings; and it
is quite another to strive for a reconstruction of
the actual context within which Aquinas stood and
of the actual context that resulted from his presence in history. To put it another way, it is one
thing to understand what a series of individuals
meant by their various expressions; but it is a
separate task to affirm critically what these expressions meant in light of what actually was taking
place over time. Critical history, then, adds to
interpretations the element of judgment, a judgment
that states interpretations to be correct or erroneous in light of what in fact occurred, in light of
what the facts really are.

To stress the role of rational judgments as
central to the historian's work is not to say that
other conscious operations are not at work. Historical judgment presupposes historical experience
and historical understanding.[44] The historian,
then, is to be attentive to the data uncovered by

research and, indeed, to rather broad accumulations of that data. Such data constitutes the existential or lived experience that is the tradition of a group.[45] For this tradition to be methodically apprehended, there are needed researchers. For it to be methodically understood, there is the work of interpreters. Upon all such work the historian depends if he wishes history to be critical, and not merely the instrument promoting the aims of a given group.[46] However, as noted, historical work, historical knowledge, is more than a matter of compiling the data of researchers and the theories of interpreters. Rather, historical knowledge is a grasp of what was going forward in the group, "what, for the most part, contemporaries did not know," but which the historian can know.[47] To determine this, the historian draws on his or her historical knowledge as data, and asks questions for historical intelligence. When insights follow, and seem to fit the data, there emerges an understanding of one's sources. An intelligent use of these sources may allow one to arrive at an understanding of the objects to which the sources refer. And in the absence of further relevant questions on the topic, the historian is in a position to make a reflective judgment on the process referred to - a judgment that admittedly remains open to revision, in light of ongoing historical investigations, or in light of later events that shed light on the earlier.[48] This possibility of revision will lead the historian to a responsibility that communicates results in a modest fashion and that

373

IV.

continually prods the historian to the refinement
of methods employed in historical studies.

Dialectical method, finally, is the direction
of attentiveness, intelligence, reasonableness, and
responsibility to the goal intended by responsibility.
This goal is "the acknowledgment of values and the
selection of the methods or other means that lead to
their realization."[49] The values to be acknowledged
are not, of course, the values held by the one doing
dialectics, but rather the values discerned in the
various witnesses to Christ Jesus, as these witnesses
(made available by research) have expressed themselves
in their words (understood by interpreters) and in
their deeds (narrated by historians). This witness
has been carried out in a vast variety of manners, so
that one might wonder if it is at all possible to
speak of the Christian tradition: are there not instead Christian traditions? Such multiplicity is revealed by historical studies, and there is needed a
dialectic to discover just what sort of multiplicity
exists. The traditions may be genetic, a matter of
different stages in the one process of development.
The differences may be complementary, due to the variety of commonsense traditions that have highly different ways of describing the same reality. The different traditions, finally, may be dialectical, the
fundamentally opposed horizons that result from contrary views on knowledge, values, and religion. It
is with these fundamental conflicts that the func-

374

tional specialty, dialectic, is concerned, and such
dialectic will operate to bring these conflicts to
light and to provide a technique that will objectify
subjective differences and promote conversion.[50]

As values are operative as exercises of responsibility, so the discernment of values in dialectical
method is an exercise of the investigator's responsibility. Just as the work of the researcher depends
on the keenness and openness of his or her attentiveness; just as the interpretation of the interpreter
depends on the clarity of the exegete's own understanding; just as the narratives of the historian depend on the historian's sharpness of judgment: so
the evaluations of the person in dialectics will depend on what that person discerns as value. This is
not to say that the dialectician is one who knowingly
imposes his or her own values on the past tradition,
but simply to affirm that the horizon of the dialectician mediates an encounter with the horizons, the
values, existent in the tradition. But because the
dialectician mediates what he or she considers instances of authentic tradition, as well as instances
of inauthenticity in the tradition, the way is opened
to the further methods that will take their stand on
authenticity as something to be objectified and realized in the present, in the second phase of theological reflection.

I note, finally, that the dialectician, while a
specialist in the operations and goal of responsibility,

nonetheless needs and presupposes attentiveness, intelligence, and reasonableness in the service of this responsibility. Such qualities are involved in the determination of the materials of dialectic.[51] Attentiveness demands accurate assembly both of the carriers of the tradition and of the investigative work done on them. Understanding is needed to promote insights into what is of value or disvalue, to examine and compare instances that manifest the same values or set forth different values, and to reduce these affinities and differences to their underlying roots. Judgment is needed to determine which affinities and oppositions result from dialectically opposed horizons. And, to come to the specialty considered in itself, responsibility selects "the affinities and oppositions grounded in dialectically opposed horizons and dismisses other affinities and oppositions."[52]

To understand the specialties of the first phase of theology in terms of functional specialization, with emphasis on conscious intentionality, rather than in terms of field specialization, with emphasis on what is to be investigated by conscious intentionality, will most likely seem a bit strange to the reader. I think it will be useful, therefore, to conclude this brief section with a lengthy quotation wherein Lonergan summarizes his own thought on the matter, in hopes that such a summary, when studied carefully, will give the reader at least an initial insight into what we are saying.

> So in assimilating the past, first, there
> is research that uncovers and makes avail-
> able the data, secondly, there is inter-
> pretation that understands their meaning,
> thirdly, there is history that judges and
> narrates what occurred and, fourthly, there
> is dialectic that endeavors to unravel the
> conflicts concerning values, facts, mean-
> ings, and experiences. The first four func-
> tional specialties, then, seek the ends
> proper respectively to experiencing, under-
> standing, judging, and deciding; and, of
> course, each one does so by employing not
> some one but all four of the levels of con-
> scious and intentional operations.
>
> This fourfold specialization corresponds to
> the four dimensions of the Christian message
> and the Christian tradition. For that mes-
> sage and tradition, first of all, are a
> range of data. Secondly, the data purport
> to convey not the phenomena of things, as in
> the natural sciences, but the meanings en-
> tertained and communicated by minds, as in
> the human sciences. Thirdly, these meanings
> were uttered at given times and places and
> transmitted through determinate channels
> and under sundry vicissitudes. Fourthly,
> the utterance and the transmission were the
> work of persons bearing witness to Christ
> Jesus and, by their words and deeds, bring-
> ing about the present religious situation.[53]

The cumulative work of those engaged in research, interpretation, history, and dialectic mediates to us an encounter with persons witnessing to Christ. Such work illuminates and objectifies the Christian message and the Christian tradition, and thereby mediates to us the present situation in Christianity by tracing

IV.

its origins and development down the centuries to
the present day. This first phase work, moreover,
objectifies the Christian message and tradition in
all its complexity and pluralism. Research and interpretation make known to us the tremendous variety
of commonsense mentalities in which the message and
tradition have been expressed; and this leaves us
wondering if there is any way of understanding systematically this message and tradition, in order to
promote its effective communication to the current
brands of common sense. History makes known to us
the various specialized manners of expressing the
message and tradition, whether the successive brands
of common sense or successive technical expressions
that build on a metaphysics, on modern science, on
modern philosophies, on faith, on ordinary languages;
and this leaves us wondering if there is possibly any
way of affirming normatively the continuity of expression as it moves through different stages of development, so that pluralism here is just the genetic
succession of specialized manners in which the one
message and tradition may come to be formulated. Dialectic, finally, makes known to us the variety of
diametrically opposed horizons in which the message
and tradition have been expressed, and leaves us wondering if there is possibly any way for ourselves to
decide responsibly and freely amidst such conflicting
views on the meaning, value, and source of what is
supposed to be a simple message and simple tradition:

so that we at least can take a stand that is authentic, and thereby undo the dialectical pluralism that
splits the Christian community asunder and renders
it powerless in human history.[54]

(2) From Mediating to Mediated Theology

Lonergan has distinguished four distinct tasks
that cumulatively aim at the evaluative reconstruction
of the Christian tradition. Such tasks obviously are
an integral dimension of theology, for the end of the
age of innocence means that such evaluative reconstruction is always needed before theologians can pronounce
which elements of the tradition are true, how these
traditional truths may be reconciled with one another
and with the conclusions of science, philosophy, history, and how these truths can be communicated ap-
propriately to the members of each class in every culture.[55] It remains, of course, that evaluative reconstruction is not the whole of theology. Research, interpretation, history, and dialectic mediate to us an
encounter with the past, but theology would also take
a stand towards the future. It would be archeological
in its evaluative reconstruction, but also teleological
or eschatological in its evaluative construction of the
present and future. That construction or praxis is a
matter of pronouncing which elements of the tradition
are true, how they can be reconciled with one another
and with the conclusions of science, philosophy, history, and how the truths of tradition can be communi-

IV.

cated effectively to the members of each class in
every culture.

At this point, however, there occurs something
of a dilemma for the theological community. The
broad lines of the dilemma were sketched in Chapter
One. Basically, it is the problem associated with
moving from evaluative reconstruction of the Christian tradition to pronouncing what that tradition
means in the world today. On what basis, on what
foundation, is theology to take a stand in order to
state what is true in the tradition? It is one thing
to reconstruct and evaluate the Christian tradition;
it is something else for theology to translate that
tradition and to influence the cultural context by
projecting that tradition into new mentalities and
new situations.[56]

The need, then, is for a theology that is not
only historical and dialectical but also critically
practical. Lonergan of course acknowledges that
this critical function of theology must include a
foundation in history and dialectic; theology will
be all the more critical, the more that it rests
solidly on an evaluative reconstruction of the Christian tradition.[57] But he would add that this evaluative reconstruction of the Christian tradition cannot
provide the whole foundation for a theology that
would be critically practical. Theology needs an
added foundation in order to move from the evaluative
reconstruction of the convictions and opinions ex-

pressed in the Christian tradition to the constructive or direct discourse that states what is so.[58]

This added foundation is needed, then, inasmuch
as the dialectical evaluation of the Christian tradition does no more than reveal the deep and irreconcilable oppositions present within the tradition.
As such, it at once sets forth an evaluative reconstruction of the tradition, and also challenges to a
decision. It challenges theologians to take sides,
to take a stand regarding the tradition - in a word,
to be critical regarding the tradition, deliberately
choosing what is authentic Christian tradition and
proceeding to transpose that tradition to the world
today. In terms borrowed from Chapter Three, it is
the question of theological praxis; as Lonergan
writes:

> Dialectic confronts us with the problem
> of the irrational in human life and, as
> well, provides a technique for distin-
> guishing between authentic and unauthen-
> tic evaluations, decisions, actions.
> Praxis, finally, raises the final issue:
> What are you to do about it? What use
> are you to make of your knowledge of na-
> ture, of your knowledge of man, of your
> awareness of the radical conflict between
> man's aspiration to self-transcendence
> and, on the other hand, the waywardness
> that may distort his traditional heritage
> and even his own personal life?[59]

Here, the crucial question concerns the critical
principle. To what does the theologian appeal in order to ground his or her particular stand vis-à-vis

IV.

the Christian tradition? For Lonergan, that appeal
cannot be to divine revelation, to the inspiration of
Scripture, to the authority of the Church, to the consensus of patristic and theological writers, to the
sensus fidelium, etc. All of these are doctrines, and
what is required is the critical principle whereby
these or other doctrines are selected as true by theologians.[60] And so Lonergan urges that the foundation
of critical theology objectively is found in the evaluative reconstruction revealed by dialectic, but sub-
jectively is found in the religious, moral, and intellectual authenticity of the theologian. The critical
principle, then, is conversion. It is in light of, in
the horizon of, one's own authenticity that one is to
pronounce which doctrines are true, how they are to be
reconciled with one another and with the conclusions
of science, philosophy, history, and how they are to
be communicated effectively to the members of each
class in every culture.

In theology's initial phase, the four specialties
of research, interpretation, history, and dialectic
yield an evaluative reconstruction of the Christian
tradition. For Lonergan, conversion is not a prerequisite for specialists doing work in the first phase;
the methods of research, interpretation, history, and
dialectic are the same for both believers and non-be-
lievers.[61] Lonergan is of the opinion that such openness to all comers is vital to a theology or any other
discipline not wishing to box itself up in an a priori

determination of results.[62] At the same time, however, he is aware that though believers and non-be-
lievers follow the same methods in the first phase,
they will not reach the same results; whether or not
the specialists of the first phase are authentically
Christian, is something that will show up in the work
that they do. This is a rather well-known fact, and
it lies behind the claim of some that exegetes and
historians should have a Vorverständnis, even an em-
pathy and commitment, rooted in religious experience
and faith if accurate exegetical and historical work
is to be done. Lonergan agrees that the presence or
absence of conversion in first-phase specialists will
affect results of investigations, but again urges
that these radical differences will come to light in
dialectic and will be resolved to the extent that theology in its second phase takes a stand on what is
authentic both in the tradition and in the investigation of the tradition. So Lonergan writes:

> Neither the converted nor the unconverted
> are to be excluded from research, inter-
> pretation, history, or dialectic. Neither
> the converted nor the unconverted are to
> follow different methods in these functional
> specialties. But one's interpetation of
> others is affected by one's understanding
> of oneself, and the converted have a self
> to understand that is quite different from
> the self that the unconverted have to under-
> stand. Again, the history one writes de-
> pends on the horizon within which one is
> attempting to understand the past; the con-
> verted and the unconverted have radically
> different horizons; and so they will write

> different histories. Such different
> histories, different interpretations, and
> their underlying different styles in re-
> search become the center of attention in
> dialectic. There they will be reduced
> to their roots. But the reduction itself
> will only reveal the converted with one
> set of roots and the unconverted with a
> number of different sets. Conversion is
> a matter of moving from one set of roots
> to another. It is a process that does
> not occur in the marketplace. It is a
> process that may be occasioned by scien-
> tific inquiry. But it occurs only inas-
> much as a man discovers what is unauthen-
> tic in himself and turns away from it,
> inasmuch as he discovers what the fulness
> of human authenticity can be and embraces
> it with his whole being. It is something
> very cognate to the Christian gospel,
> which cries out: Repent! The kingdom of
> God is at hand.63

I have been attempting to present Lonergan's understanding of the critical principle in theology,
that allows theology to move from evaluative reconstruction of the Christian tradition to constructing
that tradition in today's world. Besides evaluative
reconstruction of the past, then, there was added the
reality of conversion upon which theology in its second phase is grounded. Theologians in the second
phase are to employ the touchstone of their own authenticity in order to state the truths of the tradition, to work towards some partial understanding of
those truths in light of the present historical context, and to communicate those truths effectively to
all people. This does not mean, of course, that the-

ologians are to impose their own values on the tradition; rather, it means that theologians in the
second phase are to select the values and meanings
that are authentic in the tradition, and this demands
that theologians themselves be authentic. Just how
this occurs may now be outlined.

(3)   Method in Mediated Theology

To put method in the second phase of theology is
to conceive theology, not in terms cf material and
formal objects, but in terms of the operations of human subjects, the theologians who happen to be working
in this second phase. As such, theclogy in the second
phase is the method of praxis. It presupposes the ongoing evaluative reconstruction of the Christian tradition, and so is a praxis linked to historical and
dialectical theology. It is a praxis that is consequent upon a decision - the decisior to embrace religious, moral, and intellectual authenticity. And this
decision is the critical principle whereby theologians
in the second phase bring the value and meaning of
Christian truth fully to bear on the world of today.[64]

In order to distinguish the distinct tasks involved in theology as praxis, Lonergan again appeals
to generalized empirical method. Just as that method
allows us to distinguish four distinct tasks in the
first phase of theology, so too it yields a fourfold
distinction in the meaning of theology as praxis.
Generally, I do not think that this fourfold distinc-

385

tion is hard to understand. Lonergan draws attention to current theological praxis that roughly is
already divided into four specialties – fundamental,
dogmatic, speculative, and pastoral/practical theology.[65] But he would suggest that generalized empirical method can shed a great deal of light on these
specialties. There can be highlighted the key operation in each, so that these specialties can become
more aware of their precise function, as well as of
the unity among them.

Such, for Lonergan, is functional specialization
in the second phase of theology. Within this phase,
"being responsible" means deliberately selecting the
horizon that is normative and critical in their work;
so the key task of "fundamental theology" (for Lonergan: foundations) is the thematizing of the authentic
Christian horizon, in light of the choices revealed by
dialectic and in virtue of one's own authenticity.
"Being reasonable" means pronouncing which elements in
the Christian tradition are true; so the key task in
"dogmatic theology" (for Lonergan: doctrines) is to
affirm the truths of the tradition, thereby pronouncing
on the alternatives set forth in dialectic. "Being intelligent" means striving for some partial understanding of the truths affirmed in doctrines; so the key
task of "speculative theology" (for Lonergan: systematics) is to strive for a reconciliation of Christian
truths among themselves and with the conclusions of
science, philosophy, history. "Being attentive" means

IV.

communicating the truths effectively to the members
of each class in every culture; so the key task of
"pastoral/practical theology" (for Lonergan: <u>commun-
ications</u>) is to effect the transpositions needed if
Christian truth is to reach the minds and hearts of
all people in all cultures. Hence, theology in its
second phase is praxis as academic, in the best sense
of "academic": it is the mediation into the whole of
human affairs of the Christian message and the Christian tradition, whose value is apprehended in foundations, whose truth is affirmed in doctrines, whose
meaning is understood by systematics and transposed
by communications.

Such is the general scheme, and now I wish to
describe briefly how Lonergan understands each of
these specialties.[66] The foundational theologian
directs attentiveness, intelligence, reasonableness,
and responsibility to the goal intended by responsibility. This goal is "the acknowledgment of values
and the selection of the methods or other means that
lead to their realization."[67] The values to be acknowledged are the values manifest in the evaluative
reconstruction of the Christian tradition, as studied
in history and dialectic. The acknowledgment occurs
in virtue of the self-appropriation by the foundational theologian of religious experience. Indeed,
such self-appropriation crystallizes the apprehension of transcendent and human values in faith. Such
faith is not a list of doctrines, but a horizon, and

387

IV.

it is the task of foundations to objectify that
horizon and to express it in terms of the Christian tradition, in specifically Christian categories. Hence, it is inasmuch as Christian conversion is made thematic and explicitly objectified that there emerges the functional specialty
of foundations. Accordingly, it is the concern
of foundations to present, not the doctrines of
the Christian community, but rather the horizon
within which the meaning of those doctrines can
be grasped.[68] So Lonergan writes:

> At its real root, then, foundations
> occurs on the fourth level of human
> consciousness, on the level of de-
> liberation, evaluation, decision. It
> is a decision about whom and what you
> are for and, again, whom and what you
> are against. It is a decision illum-
> inated by the manifold possibilities
> exhibited in dialectic. It is a ful-
> ly conscious decision about one's
> horizon, one's outlook, one's world-
> view. It deliberately selects the
> framework, in which doctrines have
> their meaning, in which systematics
> reconciles, in which communications
> are effective.[69]

The objectification of conversion, besides
involving a deliberate acknowledgment of values,
includes as well deliberate control over the various manners in which these values may in fact be
realized. This control is among the chief bene-
fits of a methodical theology, for it assures the

IV.

acceptance of authentic positions and the rejection of inauthentic counter-positions.[70] Such control is exercised in the process whereby the foundational theologian derives, purifies, and utilizes the various categories that in various manners direct and guide the investigations of theologians. These categories are controls in the sense that they are models, paradigmata, interlocking sets of terms and relations, that may be useful "in guiding investigations, in framing hypotheses, and in writing descriptions."[71]

The derivation of the categories is a matter of "the human and Christian subject effecting self-appropriation and employing this heightened consciousness both as a basis for methodical control in doing theology and, as well, as an *a priori* whence he can understand other men, their social relations, their history, their religion, their rituals, their destiny."[72]

For Lonergan, then, human and Christian authenticity is the foundation of mediated theology, and the thematization of this authenticity, through self-appropriation, is the task of the foundational theologian. Such thematization provides the horizon for theological work in the second phase. It is to be noted that the fully conscious decision to select one horizon and reject others, to choose true values and reject disvalues, does not occur in some vacuum.

389

IV.

Foundations is not the first functional specialty,
but the fifth. For horizon to be responsible and
critical, it not only has to proceed from a responsible and virtuous subject, but proceeds from this
subject as correlative to the Lebenswelt. So it
is, that the horizon selected is not some private
theory of a fundamental theologian about what Christianity should be; on the contrary, horizon selection is a decision made following a comprehensive
assimilation of the various horizons of the Christian Lebenswelt, made available by the specialties
of the first phase.[73]

While the foundational theologian directs his
or her operations to the apprehension of values,
there is need as well for the foundational theologian to be reasonable, intelligent, and attentive.
Indeed, the categories developed by the foundational
theologian will be all the more useful as models to
the extent they build on these qualities. Thus,
the foundational theologian wishes the categories
to be relevant to the work of doctrinal theologians,
who determine the true and false teachings uncovered
by dialectic; the categories, then, should themselves
possess a high degree of validity and be conspicuous
in their accuracy. Again, the categories should be
useful to systematic theologians as they frame hypotheses that will promote an understanding of doctrines, and so categories should be of the kind
that lend themselves easily to adaptation by sys-

390

tematic understanding. Finally, the categories
should be useful to the description and communication that is the task of those concerned with the
fruit of theological reflection; to the degree
that categories facilitate linguistically the transpositions involved in dealing with extremely concrete situations, to that degree will the work of
transposition and communication be all the more effective.[74]

The doctrinal theologian directs attentiveness,
intelligence, reasonableness, and responsibility to
the goal intended by the operations of reasonableness. This goal is "the acceptance or rejection of
the hypotheses and theories put forward by understanding to account for the data."[75] The hypotheses
and theories are the conflicts assembled by dialectical understanding in the first phase of theology.
The horizon within which such conflicts are to be
resolved, the horizon of faith, is objectified in
foundations. The acceptance of truth and the rejection of error is the task of doctrines:

> . . . the functional specialty, dialec-
> tic, deploys both the truth reached and
> the errors disseminated in the past.
> The functional specialty, foundations,
> discriminates between truth and error
> by appealing to the foundational reality
> of intellectual, moral, and religious
> conversion. The result of such discrim-
> ination is the functional specialty,
> doctrines, and so doctrines, based on
> conversion, are opposed to the aberra-
> tions that result from the lack of con-

IV.

version.[76]

Accordingly, doctrines as a functional specialty
is to be distinguished from other kinds of doctrines.[77]
There may indeed be one fundamental Christian stance,
one grounding horizon, but it may be mediated, objectified, in various ways and this gives rise to different types of doctrine.[78] Firstly, there is the mediation of the Christian horizon in the realm of transcendence, in the linguistic and incarnate meaning of
Jesus Christ; the inner word of God's love is interpreted by the outer Word that also is from God - the
Word who is Christ Jesus, who is transcendence incarnate in the world mediated by meaning. This is the
primary source of doctrine, both as the original message of Christ himself and as this message came to be
formulated and proclaimed by original witnesses.
Secondly, there is the mediation of the Christian
horizon in the realm of common sense, of community,
of church; and such mediation results in church doctrines, that are the common judgments of value and
of fact that bring the meaning of the original message into the ongoing succession of social infra-
structures. Thirdly, there is the mediation of the
Christian horizon in the realm of theory, and such
mediation yields theological doctrines of the classicist variety, that bring the meaning of the original
message into a cultural superstructure that is classicist. Fourthly, there is the mediation of the Christian horizon in the realm of interiority, and such

mediation results in two further types of doctrines:
there are methodological doctrines that ground theology as such by confronting basic philosophical issues, by thematizing Christian religious experience,
by accounting for the historicity of expressions and
witness by clarifying the diversity of human cultures
and the differentiations of human consciousness; and,
besides the methodological doctrines that ground theology as such, there are the theological doctrines
grounded in this methodology as a distinct functional
specialty.

As primarily concerned with reasonable affirmations, doctrines exercise a normative function inasmuch as they are based on conversion and thereby reveal the aberrations of the errors uncovered by dialectic.[79] Moreover, to the extent that doctrines
have a grounding in method, to that extent will it
be possible for this functional specialty to affirm
the continuity of doctrines amidst the pluralism of
religious language in which such doctrines may be
expressed; without such an account, this pluralism
will be simply unintelligible to the lesser educated
and will only block efforts to pass authentic teaching on to the present and future.[80]

The doctrinal theologian, while concerned primarily with matters of truth and error, nevertheless
is to be responsible, intelligent, and attentive.
Responsibility reveals the horizon within which the
doctrinal theologian functions, and leads to the se-

lection of the specific methods demanded in carrying out doctrinal tasks. Intelligence brings to light the variations in doctrinal expressions due to different interpretations in different cultural contexts. Attentiveness allows the doctrinal theologian to be sensitive to the many levels of consciousness that may be sources of doctrine and to which authentic doctrine is to be communicated.

The systematic theologian directs attentiveness, intelligence, reasonableness, and responsibility to the goal intended by the operations of intelligence. This goal is "insight into the apprehended data."[81] The apprehended data into which insight is sought are doctrines:

> The seventh functional specialty, systematics, is concerned with promoting and understanding of the realities affirmed in the previous specialty, doctrines.[82]

The aim, then, of systematics is not to evaluate, nor to judge, nor to communicate, but to understand. That which the systematic theologian seeks to understand are the mysteries of faith affirmed in doctrines:

> The aim of systematics is not to increase certitude but to promote understanding. It does not seek to establish the facts. It strives for some inkling of how it could possibly be that the facts are what they are. Its task is to take over the facts, established in doctrines, and to attempt to

work them into an assimilable whole.[83]

Systematics aims at the promotion of understanding, but it is worth noting that such understanding occurs within a profoundly religious horizon. It is the work of one in love with God, of one who operates within the horizon that is faith, of one who believes the truths of the tradition to be truths that liberate the human spirit. In a word, systematic theology is not just a brand of philosophy, without any religious significance.[84] On the other hand, systematic theology should be integrated with the procedures and aims that, in recent centuries, have been separated from theology and assigned to some natural theology or natural philosophy; for systematic theology is properly the Christian prolongation of that which humanity can begin to know by its native powers.[85] Such integration, indeed, is demanded by the unity of human consciousness, and it can be achieved by preserving the distinction between the knowledge that is "from above downwards," from faith, and the knowledge that is from below, that is reached by experiencing, understanding, and verifying. To separate these two types of knowledge and to treat them in isolation from each other may be done only to the detriment of both.[86]

Earlier, it was mentioned that the task of systematics is an understanding of the realities affirmed in the previous specialty, doctrines. This implies that those realities may be lacking to some degree in intelligibility, that they may be facts and

IV.

values that, because lacking in clarity, give rise
to questions for intelligence. The reason for this
is the fact that transcendent mystery, while with-
drawing us in adoration from the world mediated by
meaning, nevertheless is also objectified in the
world mediated by meaning: primarily in the mystery
of Christ, and secondarily in the witness of word
and deed that we give to the mystery of Christ. So
it is, that besides a negative theology, content to
say what God is not, there also is an affirmative
theology that is concerned with the entry of God into
history, into man's making of man, into the world
mediated by meaning. Such entry is religious expression, and the expressions have meaning only within
some cultural context, and contexts change. Hence
the function of systematics:

> Accordingly, while mystery is not to be
> confused with problem, the ongoing con-
> texts within which mystery is adored and
> adoration is explained are anything but
> free from problems. Least of all at the
> present time is the existence of prob-
> lems to be ignored. For now problems
> are so numerous that many do not know
> what to believe. They are not unwilling
> to believe. They know what church doc-
> trines are. But they want to know what
> church doctrines could possibly mean.
> Their question is the question to be met
> by systematic theology.[87]

Systematics, then, is a specialty concerned with
the goal of the operations of understanding. The procedure is a matter of asking and answering questions,

through which understanding develops to a point
where further questions and answers yield diminish-
ing returns. Yet a further exercise of intelligence
is involved in the proper ordering of the questions
and answers, beginning with the issues whose solution does not presuppose the solution to other issues. It is further to be noted, that the understanding sought by systematics is bound to be imperfect, analogous, probable; yet such understanding, however imperfect, has to be on the level of
its times, and today this means being at home in
modern science, scholarship, and philosophy.[88]

The systematic theologian needs to put his or
her attentiveness, reasonableness, and responsibility at the service of understanding. Responsibility
demands that systematic work be done within the horizon of faith, in response to transcendent value
and in response to social and cultural values. Reasonableness demands a knowledge of the community's
confession of transcendent mystery, into which the
systematic theologian seeks insights. Attentiveness
demands that systematic work provide the basis for
the final specialty, communications, through a sensitivity to the complexity of the contexts in which
systematic understanding is to bear fruit.[89]

The final specialty, communications, is concerned with theology in its external relations.[90]
Attentiveness, intelligence, reasonableness, and
responsibility are directed to the goal intended by

397

IV.

the operations of attentiveness. This goal is the
apprehension of data.[91] Communications, then, is
concerned to apprehend the significance of data, of
doctrines and the understanding of doctrines, within
the contexts of the day. It is a concern to transpose the truths and understanding for the varieties
of common sense within the Christian community and
within human history as a whole. Such communication
is not just a repetition of the doctrinal formulae;
it is not just a matter of repeating the insights of
systematic theologians for the general public; rather,
it is a transposition of religious meaning and religious value from the context of academic theology to
the contexts of Christian and human history. Nor can
such transpositions be limited to the forum of common
sense, for theology has to speak to other disciplines
in the cultural superstructure, that have a subtle
yet profound influence on common sense. And such
speech, whether to the superstructure or infrastructure, has to be creative, making imaginative use of
the available resources of communication.[92]

It goes without saying that the task of communications has a profound theological significance.
Lonergan links this significance to the dialectic of
authenticity and inauthenticity in human affairs, a
dialectic that is a breakdown of communication at
the deepest level possible:

> It affects community for, just as common
> meaning is constitutive of community, so

dialectic divides community into radically opposed groups. It affects
action for, just as conversion leads
to intelligent, reasonable, responsible action, so dialectic adds division, conflict, oppression. It
affects the situation, for situations are the cumulative product of
previous actions and, when previous
actions have been guided by the
light and darkness of dialectic,
the resulting situation is not some
intelligible whole but rather a set
of misshapen, poorly proportioned,
and incoherent fragments.[93]

Such is the imperfect community that is embodied in
human society, and such is the need for an ongoing
effort to bind society together through overcoming
decline and promoting the conversion that yields
common meaning as the basis of the human community.
In this light, it is possible to understand the
function of the Christian church in human history,
and it is in service to this church that the functional specialty, communications, operates.[94]

The specialist in communications needs responsibility, reasonableness, and intelligence at the
service of attentiveness. Responsibility locates
attentiveness within the authentic horizon of faith,
and bestows on communications the values to be promoted within human history. Reasonableness brings
to communications the truth that will liberate humanity from its inauthentic prisons. Intelligence
relates communications to the whole theological en-

IV.

terprise and makes available the insights that form
the basis of meaningful transpositions. But besides
these qualities, there is the specialty itself that
in its operations relates the Christian message and
the Christian tradition to the concrete policies of
the Christian churches, and to these policies I shall
devote Chapter Five.

4. The Function of Method in Theology

There would be little point in urging a renewal
of theology if such renewal were not in fact needed.
And so we come to what may be considered the central
issue of the present work, namely, the question of
whether or not Lonergan's method in theology is
really worthwhile, really serves a purpose, really
meets a need. This is the question of the function
of method in theology, and that function has been
described by Lonergan in the following way:

> Just as theology reflects on revelation
> and church doctrines, so methodology re-
> flects on theology and theologies. Be-
> cause it reflects on theology and theol-
> ogies, it has to mention both the reve-
> lation and the church doctrines on which
> the theologies reflect. But though it
> mentions them, it does not attempt to
> determine their content. That task it
> leaves to the church authorities and to
> the theologians. It is concerned to de-
> termine how theologians might or should
> operate. It is not concerned to prede-
> termine the specific results all future
> generations must obtain.95

400

IV.

Now I do not think anyone would disagree with
the statement that the function of methodology is
to reflect on theology and theologies. The disagreement arises over the meaning of "reflect," and this
disagreement results in different notions of the
function of methodology in theology. Distinguish,
then, method as a theory of theology, method as the
art of doing theology, and method as the operations
that theologians perform.

For some, method is a matter of theorizing a-
bout theology. Thus, reflection on theology means
the attempt to determine more precisely the specific
objects with which theology is concerned and the
specific manner in which theology is concerned with
these objects. In this view, methodology is usually
identified with at least a substantial part of fundamental theology, or with a theological hermeneutics,
or with a theory of theology, or with a metatheology,
or with a philosophical theology. While there are
differences among these disciplines, they seem to have
in common that they are doctrines about theological
doctrine, where theology is conceived as the subject
or science that deals with God and with all things related to God.[96]

For others, method is a more homely affair. It
is really just the art of doing theology in a correct
manner, so that one speaks about the method of theology rather than about method in theology. Clearly,
too, theology has at its disposal many different meth-

ods, so that one speaks further about the methods of
dogmatic theology, the methods of fundamental theology, the methods of practical theology, the methods
of biblical theology, the methods of biblical exegesis and of historical theology, the methods of church
history. Further, the art of doing theology demands
of the theologian the use of other methods as well,
drawn from anthropology, psychology, sociology, history, philosophy, and even natural science. The general rule is that the theologian should use whatever
resources may be useful tools in understanding the
Christian tradition and in communicating that understanding to different audiences. Just what tools or
methods should be used cannot really be determined
in advance, but is more a question of acquiring experience in one's specialty, of ongoing learning
through study and dialogue, of getting feedback on
the success of one's work. Here, too, theology is
conceived as the subject or science that deals with
God and with all things as related to God, and the
methods of theology are the guides along the way
that help us to an understanding of divine truth.[97]

Most theologians, I suspect, would acknowledge
the validity of both these notions of method. There
is needed both a theory of theology as such, and
there are needed critical and effective procedures
within theology in its many subjects. Moreover, I
would add my own agreement to that of theologians
who concur on the need for a reflection on theology

and for correct procedures within theology. But I
would urge that a theory of theology presupposes
the priority of the speculative intellect and to
operate on such a presupposition is to leave theology isolated in its contemporary context. Again,
I too would urge the need of critical and correct
procedures in theology's reflection on Christian
truth, and would encourage a variety of methods.
But I would add my own agreement to that of theologians who concur on the need to relate to one another the contemporary plurality of fields, subjects, and methods that leave theology in fragments and theologians in little boxes.[98]

It was to resolve these basic problems of interdependence, unity, and continuity that Lonergan
has developed a quite distinct notion of methodological reflection and of theology. For Lonergan,
reflection on theology and theologies is a matter
of conceiving theology as a set of related and recurrent operations cumulatively advancing towards
an ideal goal; and because contemporary theology
is specialized, it is to be conceived, not as some
single set of related operations, but as a series
of sets.[99] Methodology, then, as noted a moment
ago, is concerned to determine how theologians
might or should operate. It is not methodology
in the sense of a set of rules that theologians
should follow in their teaching and learning.
Rather, it is methodology in the sense of that

which is the principle of development, the method, of the theology that is to be taught and learned. Hence, it is not methodology in the sense of a logic that will guide theologians to expressions of the eternally valid Christian truth. Rather, it is method in the sense of an ongoing process of ever-increasing understanding that guides theologians to expressions of what is the best available theological opinion on the meaning and value of the Christian message and the Christian tradition.

This ongoing process of ever-increasing understanding has been conceived as a series of sets of related and recurrent operations, where each set is a distinct functional specialty. Eight such functional specialties were described and explained, and the question that now arises is the question of the interdependence and unity of these sets. It is clearly an important question. If the sets are not interdependent, if each functional specialty stands in isolation from the others, then Lonergan could be accused of merely introducing further complexity to an already complicated situation. In this case, one would be inclined to favor the practice of those who simply juxtapose traditional and modern methods, for two isolated methods would be better than eight. In fact, however, the eight sets are interdependent, and it is precisely this interdependence that allows Lonergan to integrate both traditional and modern

404

views in a higher unity, and thereby "to ease the
tensions in theology between exegetes and historians
on the one hand and doctrinal and systematic theologians on the other."[100]

In order to indicate the functional unity of
theology, Lonergan first draws attention to the
meaning of "unity," and then proceeds to discuss the
unity of mediating theology, the unity of mediated
theology, and the unity between mediating and mediated theology.

As to the meaning of unity, the basic distinction is between static unity and dynamic unity,
where static unity is the ideal of logic and dynamic
unity is the product of method. To clarify this distinction, I would refer the reader to Lonergan's Insight and his discussion of the truth of interpretation.[101] To relate this discussion to the present
topic, I would draw attention to the fact that theology, considered as a whole, is a matter of interpretation: it wishes to reach an understanding of
the Christian message and tradition, and such understanding is clearly a matter of interpretation if
one is not merely to repeat the latest Greek version
of the New Testament. Moreover, this theological interpretation should possess a unity, for the Christian message and tradition is one, and this means it
has but one meaning, one interpretation.

This one interpretation may be approached from

IV.

the viewpoint of logic. Logic aims at an interpretation that will be valid for all times, and so con-
structs an interpretative expression that rests on
fixed terms, accurately and immutably formulated ax-
ioms, and an absolutely rigorous deduction of all
possible conclusions:[102] a static classification,
that will result in a perennial theology rooted in
the perennial philosophy. The unity of theology is
the unity of a closed system, and the development of
theology is merely a matter of re-applying the same
logical premises to whatever question happens to a-
rise.

There are, however, limitations to logic and to
the ideal of logical, static unity.[103]

> A little learning is a dangerous thing,
> and the adage has, perhaps, its most a-
> bundant illustrations from the applica-
> tion of logic to the tasks of interpre-
> tation. A familiarity with the elements
> of logic can be obtained by a very modest
> effort and in a very short time. Until
> one has made notable progress in cogni-
> tional analysis, one is constantly temp-
> ted to mistake the rules of logic for the
> laws of thought. And as all reading in-
> volves interpreting, there follows auto-
> matically the imposition upon documents
> of meanings and implications that 'logi-
> cally' they must possess but in fact do
> not bear.[104]

Lonergan goes on to note the limitations of the treatise, where treatise is an expression of logic. These
limitations are evident in the logic itself, that has

406

to introduce the treatise, not in technical terms,
but in an ordinary language that introduces the topic
to a particular audience. Again, the limitations of
logic have appeared in mathematics, with Gödel's the-
orem on the limits of a given mathematical system;
and in the natural sciences, where similar limits
have been traced to the involvement of the inquiring
observer in scientific method. Yet further limitations become evident, when we turn to dynamic systems
that are on the move, developing, ongoing. And basic
to Lonergan's thought is the following:

> Unfortunately, treatises cannot move; def-
> initions and postulates have the eternal
> quality of Plato's ideas; their implica-
> tions are perpetually the same; but the
> growth of an organism or the development
> of a psyche is a movement from a generic,
> rudimentary, undifferentiated system to a
> specific, expert, differentiated system;
> and the proper concern of the scientist
> in the field of genetics is not the sev-
> eral stages of the dynamic system but
> rather the operators that bring about the
> successive transformations from each
> stage to the next. Nor is one to enter-
> tain the hope that some day when such op-
> erators are well known there may be de-
> veloped a more complicated logic that
> will handle the operators with the exac-
> titude, the rigour, and the automatic
> security that now is enjoyed by the math-
> ematical treatises. For neither the or-
> ganism nor the psyche develops exactly,
> rigourously, and securely; it advances
> tentatively; it adapts to a non-systema-
> tic manifold of circumstance; it is what
> it is because exactitude, rigour, and

407

IV.

>   automatic security are irrelevant to the
>   problems that are to be solved only vi-
>   tally and by consciousness.[105]

From this, one may easily conclude that the
limitations of logic lead to disunity and chaos, and
that it is far better to live with the limitations
than to invite the confusion that is sure to arise
with the introduction of non-logical elements into
interpretations. Such a conclusion seems to permeate
much of theological thought; and when theology strives
to break the bonds of logic, it easily is accused of
heresy, bad faith, or idolatry by those for whom logic
is the guarantee of orthodoxy.

I would quite readily grant that the abandonment
of logic is inauthentic, and that the introduction of
non-logical elements into theology may be instances
of heresy, bad faith, or idolatry. But what Lonergan
is urging is a shift from the priority of logic to
the priority of method, to human consciousness in its
logical but also non-logical operations. Nor does
this imply chaos and disunity, for the control is to
be provided now by method instead of by logical technique. The meaning of such methodical control was
indicated in Chapter Three: it is a matter of a
heightening of consciousness, of coming to know our
logical and non-logical conscious operations both
singly and in their interrelationship, and of proceeding to operate in accord with the imperatives,
Be attentive, Be intelligent, Be reasonable, and Be
responsible.

408

The need for a shift from logic to method a-
rises inasmuch as human knowledge is in process of
development, is on the move, and also because the
objects of human knowledge, to a notable extent, also
are in process of development. Logic is invaluable
in consolidating and classifying knowledge at any
given stage of its development; but logic as a technique is quite incapable of promoting development,
of keeping human knowledge an ongoing and developing
reality.[106]

There is, then, logical unity. But as well
there is dynamic unity, the unity of a subject in
process of development. Such dynamic unity is characteristic of a methodical theology. At its root,
dynamic unity is the unity of human consciousness itself; it is the unity that is the pattern, the interlocking set, of conscious and intentional operations,
and this unity, this pattern, is not something that
we impose a posteriori on our conscious living, but
rather is the a priori unity of our consciousness
simply as given:

> . . . we do not experience the operations
> in isolation and then, by a process of
> inquiry and discovery, arrive at the pat-
> tern of relations that link them together.
> On the contrary, the unity of consciousness
> is itself given; the pattern of the opera-
> tions is part of the experience of the op-
> erations; and inquiry and discovery are
> needed, not to effect the synthesis of a
> manifold that, as given, is unrelated, but
> to analyze a functional and functioning

409

IV.

unity.[107]

If this is the case, then such dynamic unity will be
mediated by the particular instances of the human mind
in action, whether in commonsense knowing, theoretical
knowing, philosophic knowing, or even religious knowing: the unity of knowing will itself be given, will
be operative in each case. This is an important point
in the understanding of Lonergan's thought. It means
that there is a unity to theology as already given,
already operative, in the work of theologians. And
what Lonergan is advocating is that we inquire into
and discover this functional and functioning unity in
current theological practice. It is a reflection on
theology and theologies, not as these might exist in
some future world, but as they are currently functioning in the present world.[108]

It is, then, a reflection that aims at making explicit a unity that presently is only implicit: that
is given to current theological consciousness, but
that is not adverted to, not understood, not affirmed,
and not made the deliberate basis for ongoing collaboration among theologians. Because such unity remains
implicit, because this methodical, dynamic unity is
not adverted to, there remains a tension within the
theological community between practitioners of different particular methods of theological inquiry. As
most theology students would be only too willing to
corroborate, the unity of modern theology is anything
but conspicuous, and one wonders just how the many

different fields and subjects might possibly fit
together. Attempts to construct a logical unity,
by attending to the objects of theological investigations and trying to work them into a well-defined
whole, are doomed to failure for results are ever increasing and logical classifications do no more than
highlight present tensions. What is needed is a turn
to theological subjects themselves, to the theologians
in their various operations whereby they proceed towards an understanding of the Christian message and
the Christian tradition. It is not a turn away from
the message and tradition, for one cannot discover
what theologians are concretely doing without also
mentioning the objects they are investigating. But
unity will be uncovered only by attending to the conscious pattern of operations that guide all theological work, by discovering the unity already operative
in that work, and by going on to a discovery of the
unity in the message and tradition intended by that
work. [109]

Lonergan's notion of functional specialization
is precisely this objectification of dynamic unity in
theology. It is making explicit a unity that is
merely implicit, and just how this is so may now be
explained. [110]

There is, then, theology in a first phase, in
oratione obliqua, concerned with the reconstruction
of the Christian past. It is a major concern of contemporary theology, and it engages an impressive num-

411

IV.

ber of specialists, Nor are these specialists all
of the same kind, for there is a division of labor
within this phase. For the most part, these sub-
divisions are divisions of the field of data, so
that one specialist is responsible for the data provided by scripture, another for the data provided in
patristic writings, and so on. This responsibility
imposes a heavy burden on each specialist, for it demands of each specialist an expertise in several methods - in the techniques of textual criticism, of interpretation, of history, of evaluative judgments of
what is investigated and on the degree of accuracy
of the investigations. Generally, the specialist is
spontaneously aware of the different methods, but is
not explicitly knowledgeable of the precise differences in these methods and does not advert to the particular goals of each method. Instead, what is intended is the composite result of all methods, namely,
the reconstruction of the Christian situation in the
period under investigation.[111]

Functional specialization, on the other hand, is
the result of explicit advertence to the different
methods and to the particular ends intended by each
method. And by such explicit advertence, there is uncovered the dynamic unity of the first phase. No
longer are there endless divisions of data into ever-
smaller and isolated unities, but rather there is a
specialized yet integrated process of investigation
yielding a cumulative understanding of the Christian

past: it is a dynamic unity of several distinct levels of conscious operation that together for the
compound yet single process of coming to know, and it
is the dynamic unity of several distinct known objects
that together form the compound object that is increasingly understood by the first phase.

> The unity of this first phase is manifestly
> not static but dynamic. The four special-
> ties stand to one another, not in some log-
> ical relationship of premiss to conclusion,
> of particular to universal, or anything of
> the sort, but as successive partial objects
> in the cumulative process that inquiry pro-
> motes from experiencing to understanding,
> that reflection promotes from understanding
> to judging, that deliberation promotes from
> judging to deciding. Such a structure is
> essentially open. Experience is open to
> further data. Understanding to a fuller
> and more penetrating grasp. Judgment to
> acknowledgment of new and more adequate
> perspectives, of more nuanced pronounce-
> ments, of more detailed information. De-
> cision, finally, is reached only partially
> by dialectic, which tends to eliminate
> evidently foolish oppositions and so nar-
> rows down issues, but is not to be expec-
> ted to go to the roots of all conflict for,
> ultimately, conflicts have their ground in
> the heart of man.[112]

In other words, the data is the object intended by
four distinct operations, and by attending to the distinction of operations, each with its own methodical
precepts and goal, investigators will have a clear and
distinct idea of what they are doing and of how the
quite different tasks come together in a dynamic u-
nity.[113] That which is uncovered by research according

IV.

to the methods proper to research becomes that which
is understood according to the methods of interpretation; that which is uncovered by an array of research
work with a corresponding series of interpretations
becomes that which is worked together into a historical narrative according to the methods proper to historical scholarship; that which is uncovered by research, understood by interpretation, and narrated by
history becomes that which is evaluated by the methods
proper to dialectic.

Moreover, as Lonergan notes, there is a reciprocal dependence.[114] The movement is not just in one
direction, but there is as well an interaction of the
specialties. So an interpretation obviously depends
on the availability of a text, but also the researcher
will be guided as to which texts are relevant by interpretations already carried out. Similarly, both
research and interpretation are performed in and enlightened by the broader historical context; and dialectic can bestow on the previous three specialties
the universal viewpoint of authenticity that provides
these specialties with an ongoing critique of procedures and aims.[115]

If now we turn attention to the second phase:
this is theology in oratione recta, concerned with
mediating the Christian message and tradition to the
present and future. This too is a major concern of
contemporary theology, and it engages an equally impressive number of specialists. Nor are these spe-

cialists all of the same kind, for there is a division of labor within this second phase. For the most part, these sub-divisions are conceptual classifications of the results made available by those working in the first phase. The aim of such classification is, of course, communication, for the Christian message and tradition are to be mediated in a coherent and intelligible manner to people living today. Accordingly, the sub-divisions of the second phase are based on different kinds of results to be communicated. One specialist is responsible for communicating the principles underlying the existential human, Christian, and theological horizons, as in a fundamental theology; another for communicating the truths of the Christian tradition and some insight into these truths, as in a dogmatic or systematic theology. One specialist is responsible for communicating the moral principles contained in the Christian tradition, as in a moral theology, while another is responsible for communicating the guidelines for effective witness to the tradition in daily life, as in church law and in practical or pastoral theology. This responsibility imposes a heavy burden on each specialist, for it demands of each specialist an expertise in several methods: he or she needs basic research techniques and familiarity with exegesis and history, but also a competency in philosophy and perhaps even in anthropology, psychology, and sociology, along with the gift of effective communication whe-

415

ther to fellow theologians, students, or the general
public. Generally, the specialist is spontaneously
aware of these different methods, but is not explicitly knowledgeable of the precise differences in
these methods and does not advert to the particular
goals of each method. Instead, what is intended is
the composite result of all methods, namely, the effective communication of the Christian message and
tradition to the present and future world.[115a]

Functional specialization, on the other hand,
is the result of explicit advertence to the different methods and to the particular ends intended by
each method in the composite task of mediating the
Christian message and tradition to the present and
future. And by such explicit advertence, there is
uncovered the dynamic unity of the second phase.
No longer are there endless divisions of results
among more and more specialists doing their work in
much the same way, but rather there is a specialized
yet integrated process of mediation yielding a cumulative communication of the Christian present, in
light of a cumulative understanding of the Christian
past. It is a dynamic unity of several distinct levels of conscious operation that together form the
compound yet single process of communication, and it
is the dynamic unity of several distinct communicated objects that together form the compound object
that is increasingly communicated by the second
phase.

>As the first phase rises from the almost
>endless multiplicity of data first to an
>interpretative, then to a narrative, and
>then to a dialectical unity, the second
>phase descends from the unity of a
>grounding horizon towards the almost
>endlessly varied sensibilities, inter-
>ests, and tastes of mankind.
>
>The descent is, not properly a deduction,
>but rather a succession of transpositions
>to ever more determinate contexts. Foun-
>dations provides a basic orientation.
>This orientation, when applied to the
>conflicts of dialectic and to the ambig-
>uities of history, becomes a principle of
>selection of doctrines. But doctrines
>tend to be regarded as mere verbal for-
>mulae, unless their ultimate meaning is
>worked out and their possible coherence
>revealed by systematics. Nor is such ul-
>timate clarification enough. It fixes
>the substance of what there is to be com-
>municated. But there remains both the
>problem of created use of the available
>media and the task of finding the ap-
>propriate approach and procedure to con-
>vey the message to people of different
>classes and cultures.[116]

In other words, the object intended is the compound object intended by four distinct operations,
and by attending to the distinction of operations,
each with its own methodical precepts and goal, specialists in the second phase[117] will have a clear
and distinct idea of what they are doing and of how
the quite different tasks come together in a dynamic
unity. That which is objectified in foundations according to the methods proper to foundations becomes

IV.

the horizon in which doctrines are to be selected according to the methods proper to doctrines; that which is affirmed in doctrines becomes that which is partially understood in systematics, and what is understood in systematics becomes that which is to be transposed in communications.

Again, the dependence is reciprocal. The problems encountered in communications may give rise to new questions to be settled in systematics; systematics may continue to influence the manner in which doctrines are expressed; doctrines may clarify the categories worked out in foundations.[118]

There remains the question of the interdependence of the two phases. That the second phase depends upon the first is evident, for it is only in light of the past that theology can confront the present and the future: we bear witness to what we have heard, we raise questions about what we have interpreted, we pass on a tradition that we first have assimilated. To attempt to make the second phase independent from the first is to cut off theology from its sources in past Christian witness of word and deed, and to advocate a theology that is identified with spiritual experience and without words to constitute a historical bond with the incarnate Christ.[119]

The more difficult question concerns the dependence of the first phase on the second. Lonergan concedes that there is such a dependence, but before lo-

cating it precisely, he notes mistaken notions of
this dependence are to be avoided. These mistaken
notions are to the effect, that it is theology in
its second phase that predetermines the results to
be achieved in the first phase or that sets the methodical procedures to be followed in the first phase.
Such undue interference is just a more subtle, yet
equally effective manner of cutting theology off from
its sources by stating in advance what those are.[120]
Still, to the degree that the second phase is theological, and is an exercise of theological method
within the framework of authentic theological autonomy from undue influence from church authorities, undue interference from the second phase, when it occurs, has the elements of an irenic solution in the
procedures of dialectic.[121]

The dependence of the first phase on the second
is located principally in the interdependence of doctrines and doctrinal history, and of foundations and
dialectic. I think the dependence of doctrinal history on doctrines is clear enough: to write the history of a given doctrine, one first has to have a
grasp of the meaning of a doctrine, in order to determine what is or is not significant in the historical development. Similarly, dialectic aims at giving
an account of instances of authenticity and inauthenticity; in this task, it will be helped immeasurably
by accounts of genuine conversion, as offered in
foundations: such accounts, no matter how much they

IV.

differ in emphases, no matter how many questions
they leave unresolved or how personal and univocal
the expressions seem to be, still can shed light
on instances of authentic behavior in the Christian
past, and will result in a dialectic that in its
openness promotes true ecumenism.[122]

The interdependence and unity of the functional
specialties would be most evident when one theologian
worked towards the eight particular goals by employing eight distinct methods. The complexity of things,
however - whether we consider the data to be investigated, the procedures to be followed, the results to
be classified and communicated - seems to imply that
the most a single theologian can hope for is a degree
of mastery in one particular specialty. This is not
to be lamented, for, as mentioned, there is a unity
to the specialties that consciously and knowingly
promotes collaboration among the specialties.

Perhaps I could add the observation that Lonergan's notion of functional specialization is not a
pedagogical tool. It does not call for the abolish-
ment of current departments of theology or radical
revisions to course offerings. It has a pedagogical
relevance, inasmuch as the aim of theological instruction would be, not the imparting of all theological knowledge, but an introduction into the various methods employed in theological investigations;
such an introduction, clearly, cannot but mention the
central truths investigated and the witness to those

truths by Christians down the centuries. But for
the moment, the value of Lonergan's methodology is
perhaps propaedeutic: if its presentation is the occasion for theologians to pause and examine what they
are doing when they are doing theology, then the re-
organization implied in functional specialization will
result, not from a priori interference, but from the a
posteriori reflection on things which have been tried,
judged, and evaluated by specialists in each discipline.

> Such, then, is in outline the dynamic unity
> of theology. It is a unity of interdepen-
> dent parts, each adjusting to changes in
> the others, and the whole developing as a
> result of such changes and adjustments.
> Further, this internal process and inter-
> action has its external relations. For
> theology as a whole functions within the
> larger context of Christian living, and
> Christian living within the still larger
> process of human history.[123]

5. Conclusion

In our own day, the study of religion is conducted by various academic disciplines, employing distinct methods of investigation. Most notable among
these are the empirical religious studies, that would
examine all the religions of mankind in their observable expressions of religious behavior. Less notable
but of equal significance is philosophy, that would
complement the strictly empirical methods of the religious sciences with a philosophic reflection on the

IV.

conditions of the possibility of such sciences and
of the behavior studied by these sciences. Finally,
least notably, and seemingly of lesser significance,
there was posed the question of the function and worth
of theology within the modern context. For it would
seem that once religious studies and philosophy have
had their say, there would be little room left for any
theological discourse that did not have a foundation
in empirical data or a basis in philosophic reflection.

What Lonergan has done, I believe, is to provide
theology with such a foundation and basis. The empirical foundation is the initial phase of theology, and
the basis in philosophic reflection is the transformation that, through generalized empirical method, sub-
lates the empirical reality of the initial phase into
a theological praxis of the second phase. It is, further, this transformation that is distinctive of theology and that promotes theology to a level that goes
beyond, yet does not invalidate, the work of empirical
studies and of philosophy. For in its second phase,
theology takes a stand on authenticity. It critically
objectifies the reality of authenticity, and proceeds
to mediate that reality to the world of today. Moreover, it does so, not on the foundation of a cognitional
and moral authenticity alone, but on the foundation of
religious authenticity; and, in the case of Christian
theology, the very interpretation of such religious
living is itself a gift from God, incarnate in the
person and teachings of Jesus Christ our Lord.

To investigate this interpretation in Christ Jesus, and to communicate it effectively to the world of today, theology has been conceived as a series of interrelated specialties, where the interrelationship and unity is knowingly promoted through methodical practice of each specialty. As such, theology is a withdrawal from the world of ordinary Christian living - an attempt to thematize what is already a part of Christian living, as die Wendung zur Idee within Christianity.[124] Clearly, such thematization is not an end in itself, an effort to escape from the world of everyday living in order to take refuge in an ivory tower. If theology is to serve the Christian religion by mediating the meaning and value of that religion to the world; if this mediation is to reveal the ultimate meaning and the deepest value of the world; if theology as such is truly directed to the communication of the Christian message and the Christian tradition to the present and to the future: then the withdrawal of theology from Christian history and from human history into the realm of interiority and religious experience is not an end in itself, but rather is a withdrawal that always intends a return and, in its ultimate stage of communications, effects such a return.[125] It is with this return of theology to the worlds of common sense and of theory that we shall be concerned in the next and final chapter.

IV.

V. CONTEXTUAL UNITY;
FROM THEOLOGY TO THE CHURCH IN SOCIETY

My reflections have come full circle.
Not only does the cultural context influence theology to undo its past a-
chievements, but theology is also called
upon to influence the cultural context,
to translate the word of God and so project it into new mentalities and new
situations. So a contemporary Catholic
theology has to be not only Catholic but
also ecumenist. Its concern must reach
not only Christians but also non-Christians and atheists. It has to learn to
draw not only on the modern philosophies
but also on the relatively new sciences
of religion, psychology, sociology, and
the new techniques of the communication
arts.[1]

Lonergan has conceived theology as die Wendung
zur Idee, the shift towards system, that occurs with
the Christian community. Theology arises out of the
questioning by the Christian community about its origins, its various conflicts, its present function in
history. For Lonergan, theological reflection occurs
in two basic phases. In an initial phase, theology
works towards an evaluative reconstruction of the
Christian tradition. In a second phase, theology
works to construct that tradition in a given culture.

Theology, then, presupposes Christian living and
makes thematic what is an element in that living; such
thematization is a withdrawal from Christian living,
in order to reflect on it. Still, it is clear that

425

V.

the withdrawal is never total and, indeed, occurs
with the intention of mediating ever more effectively
the meaning of God into the whole of human living.
This intention guides all theology, and in the final
functional specialty, communications, such mediation
is effectively realized. Communications, accordingly,
is theological witness. It is the re-integration of
theology into the life of the religious community, it
is theology bearing fruit in a unique contribution to
that life.

To say that theology becomes integrated with
Christian witness implies that such witness involves
dimensions that are non-theological. Theology has a
unique contribution to make to the life of the Christian community, but it is a contribution that stands
within the context of the mission of the church as a
whole; and this mission, in turn, stands within the
larger context of human history.[2] Theological witness, then, will be all the more effective to the extent that it merges or becomes integrated with the
horizon of the Christian community in history. Without such integration, theology and theologians would
occupy an ivory tower, quite removed from the mission
of the church and from the destiny of mankind.

In the present chapter, I wish to focus attention
on the functional specialty, communications, and examine Lonergan's understanding of the manner in which
theology effectively is to be integrated within the
life of the Christian community, as this community

strives to fulfill its mission in meeting the challenges presented by human living, Firstly, I shall
draw attention to different views on the meaning of
a pastoral theology. Secondly, I shall offer an account of the meaning of community, in order to understand these different views. Thirdly, there shall be
affirmed a methodical notion of pastoral theology that
is integrated with the life of the Christian church.
Finally, I shall discuss the method whereby theology
might be integrated with other human studies in promoting the integration of the Christian church with
the world of today.

1. Varieties of Pastoral Theology

Different views on the meaning and function of
theology as a whole give rise to different opinions
on the meaning and function of a pastoral or practical
theology. It follows, that shifts in the understanding of theology will involve a succession of changing
views on the meaning and function of pastoral theology.

In a context wherein theology is conceived as the
sort of systematic reflection associated with a metaphysics, then pastoral theology is most likely to be
understood simply as the art of communicating doctrine.
Such communication is to be a matter of applying general teachings to particular situations, where the
teachings in question are conceived normatively, valid
for all times regardless of concrete circumstances.

V.

Orthodoxy is the source of orthopraxis, just as theory is higher than praxis and contemplation superior
to action.[3]

In a context wherein theology is conceived as
the sort of systematic reflection associated with
empirical science, then pastoral theology is most
likely to be understood as the theory of Christian
praxis. Most often it will be referred to, not as
pastoral theology, but as practical theology. It is
to be a thoroughly academic subject, where "academic"
means theoretical as opposed to praxis, so that practical theology is conceived as either the theory of
praxis, or as the theory of the theory-praxis-mediation.[4] It would be a speculative discipline, resting
on clearly defined terms borrowed from existentialist
philosophies or the behavioral sciences. It is assigned a normative and critical function, both towards other theological disciplines as well as towards the church and society. It is to be an "existential ecclesiology,"[5] that conceptualizes what is
to be done or understood here and now by groups in
the church or by the church as a whole.[6]

In a context, finally, wherein theology is conceived as the sort of systematic reflection associated
with an intentionality analysis, then pastoral theology is most likely to be understood as the effective
communication of Christ's message.[7] It resembles the
first variety of pastoral theology in its concern to
communicate Christ's message. It differs from the

428

first variety and resembles the second inasmuch as
it is an integral dimension of a solidly academic
theology. But it differs from the second inasmuch
as it is academic, not in the sense of theory as opposed to praxis, but in the sense of method as praxis
in its communicative function. This latter variety
is suggested by Lonergan. It would not so much be
understood as something totally new, but rather would
seek to incorporate the legitimate concerns of the
other two varieties, giving those concerns a new
grounding and a new efficaciousness. Just what this
means may now be sketched.[8]

2. The Notion of Community

I have said that different notions of theology
give rise to different views on pastoral theology.
In saying this, I wish merely to indicate a relationship, without settling matters of causal relationship.
It could happen, that a theologian carefully works out
a theory of theology, and on the basis of that theory
concludes to the meaning of pastoral theology. But I
suspect that the more common procedure is less sophisticated. It probably would be more accurate to say
that certain needs or problems or pastoral concerns
arise in the life of the Christian community; and to
keep the community together, to help it towards a
self-understanding on the level of its time, to meet
the pastoral concerns, there occurs a shift towards
systematic thinking, that is first and foremost in-

V.

tended to be pastoral, in service to the community.
So Lonergan writes:

> As we have seen, the principal part of
> human living is constituted by meaning,
> and so the principal part of human move-
> ments is concerned with meaning. It fol-
> lows more or less inevitably that the
> further any movement spreads and the
> longer it lasts, the more it is forced
> to reflect on its own proper meaning, to
> distinguish itself from other meanings,
> to guard itself against aberration.
> Moreover, as rivals come and go, as cir-
> cumstances and problems change, as is-
> sues are driven back to their presup-
> positions and decisions to their ulti-
> mate consequences, there emerges the
> shift towards system, which was named
> by Georg Simmel, die Wendung zur Idee.
> But what is true of movements generally,
> also is true of Christianity. The mir-
> ror in which it reflects itself is the-
> ology.[9]

To say that theology is a reflection on Christian living that is carried out in service to that
living is to say that human reflection, human thinking, human meaning are constitutive of human living.
It is to point to the fact that human living must
not be reduced to a materialistic succession of stim-
ulus-response movements. It is to insist that meaning is constitutive of the reality of my life, of my
identity as a person. No less it is to insist that
meaning is constitutive of community living. A theology, then, that is pastoral is a theology that
somehow is constitutive of Christian community, is

430

meaning that binds together in community those who
otherwise would be a mere collection of individuals.[10]

If, then, theological reflection is to be constitutive of the Christian community in some dimension
of that community's living, then it is clear that a
notion of community is central to a pastoral theology.
I shall outline Lonergan's meaning of community, and
then employ that meaning to contrast the variety of
pastoral theologies noted in the previous section.

> Community is not just an aggregate of in-
> dividuals within a frontier, for that over-
> looks its formal constituent, which is com-
> mon meaning. Such common meaning calls for
> a common field of experience and, when that
> is lacking, people get out of touch. It
> calls for common or complementary ways of
> understanding and, when they are lacking,
> people begin to misunderstand, to distrust,
> to suspect, to fear, to resort to violence.
> It calls for common judgments and, when
> they are lacking, people reside in differ-
> ent worlds. It calls for common values,
> goals, policies and, when they are lacking,
> people operate at cross-purposes.[11]

Community, then, is not a static but a dynamic
reality. It is the achievement of common meaning between or among human subjects, who are one in their experience, understanding, judgment, and deciding. In-
versely, the absence of such common meaning divides
community. The absence may be due to cultural differences, that rest on different brands of common sense;
so the community is divided, but the division is experienced as complementary and generally tolerable

431

manners of understanding the same world. Again,
the absence of common meaning occurs with differentiated consciousness, that results in classes of
specialists in various fields and subjects, and an
isolation of specialists in one field from those in
another, along with an isolation of all specialists
from the non-specialists; but again, such diversifi-
cation, while it divides community, does so in a
manner that meets the need for an increasingly more
complex division of labor and an ever more refined
control over human achievement. The radical division of community occurs with the presence and absence of intellectual, moral, and religious conversion. For, at their deepest root, common meaning
and community are achievements of self-transcending
subjects: of subjects who are striving for authenticity in knowledge, action, and orientation within
the world and universe. Here, the togetherness of
subjects is the togetherness of truth, of value,
and of total loving, while error, bias, and idolatry is the alienation of the subject, not just
from community, but from himself or herself as human.[12]

This notion of community is highly relevant
to an understanding of the varieties of pastoral
theology discussed in the previous section. Community is constituted by common meaning, and theology obviously is to play a role in bringing about
that common meaning. For those who conceive theol-

ogy in terms of theory, and practical theology in
terms of the theory of praxis, Christian community
will function all the more effectively, the more
there is a withdrawal from commonsense spontaneity
and a turn to solidly reflective controls articu-
lated in theoretical terms. The legitimate insight
in this notion of pastoral theology is its conviction regarding the limitations of commonsense thinking and acting, manifest especially in the short-
range vision and tendency to bias that characterize
common sense. But perhaps the dilemma facing such
practical theologians in our own day is the sort of
reflective thinking needed to guide and control the
church in its mission. Metaphysics has been repudiated as a foundation; the type of theorizing common to empirical science can be applied analogously
to theological reflection, but although this yields
useful practical or applied insights, it also tends
to sharpen the gap between theology and the everyday, commonsense living of the community.[13]

At present, I think that the theoretical notion of practical theology most often is combined
with previous views of pastoral theology as an art,
rather than a science. This latter notion also has
its legitimate insight, and it too can contribute
to the constitution of Christian community. Conceived as an art, pastoral theology would meet concrete needs with concrete solutions. Nor can the
achievements of such a kerygmatic or catechetical

433

notion of theology be denied. But at the same time,
there is need of solidly reflective work if preaching and teaching and ministering is to reach all levels in any culture, and thereby to deal with the
complexity of church and societal living in our day.
So once again we are confronted with the tension
between common sense and theory, and all too easily
one simply opts for one or the other.[14]

That there is a tension between these two different notions of practical theology is not to be
denied. The tension, of course, is the familiar
one of theory versus common sense. Both notions
are very much concerned with effective practice,
with building up the Christian community. For the
one, such effective practice presupposes the guiding light of sound reason, for action without reflection is irresponsible. For the other, worthwhile reflection presupposes effective practice,
for reflection not rooted in action is ideology.

There is, however, a third alternative. While
some would urge a practical theology that is to be
the study of how to relate Christian theory and
Christian practice; while others would urge a practical theology that is to be the practice of Christianity to be theorized by other brances of theology, Lonergan would seek to ease the tension by
thinking of practical theology, not in terms of
theories, nor in terms of deeds, but rather in
terms of theologians performing the task of relat-

ing theological meaning to some non-theological
context. The meaning to be transposed is the
meaning determined by the systematic theologian.
The context to which such meaning is to be transposed is the broader context of human history or
the narrower context of Christian living and Christian community. The manner in which such transposition is to be made is a matter of adapting theological meaning to the various carriers of embodi-
ments of meaning that are operative in the given
context.

Just what this all means will be sketched
briefly in the following sections. At once, however, I would draw attention to the merits of this
alternative. On the one hand, the practical theologian is very much a person that is practical,
engaged in the actual task of communication in the
countless manners that this can occur. On the other
hand, the practical theologian is solidly academic,
for what he or she communicates is not a series of
spontaneous and bright ideas, but rather the understanding of the Christian message and the Christian
tradition that is the fruit of the seven previous
functional specialties. Moreover, the process is
not a one-way street, for effective communication
is constitutive: it results in ever new situations
within the various contexts, and these in turn give
rise to questioning, the sort of questioning that
is ever new, never to be excluded on a priori

grounds, but rather to be met head-on as it arises. And while the communicator, the practical theologian, is the one who first hears the question, who reads the signs of the times and who notes trouble-spots or genuine needs, still it remains that the answer to the questions and needs may demand resources that the practical theologian does not have. It is then that recourse must be had once again to the other specialties in theology, so that again a withdrawal occurs from the engagement with other contexts, but with the ultimate purpose of re-engagement with fresh insights, new and sound theories, and informed proposals for concrete action.

There is need, finally, for this third alternative. Theories about effective communication, about how to relate Christian doctrine and Christian living, have their rightful place, but that place is in the minds of systematic theologians in touch with communication specialists in various non-theological disciplines. Concrete action and involvement is to be praised, indeed, it is the stuff that gives rise to theological reflection; but if such involvement is not to be haphazard, misinformed, so caught up in the moment that the overall, long-range vision is lost, then there is need for intelligent practice that not only can suffer with those who suffer, and rejoice with those who rejoice, but that can as well work to eliminate the sources of suffering by overcoming evil with the

V.

wisdom and strength and self-sacrificing love of
Christ Jesus.

3. The Christian Church and Practical Theology

I have drawn attention to different notions of
pastoral theology and attempted to account for the
differences by relating these notions to an understanding of community. The main conclusion was that
community is a complex reality, and that two of the
different pastoral theologies, each in its own way,
tend to overlook this complexity. The oversight may
result from the assumption that pastoral concerns
are to be met exclusively by some doctrine or some
theory being applied to community living; or from
the assumption that pastoral concerns are to be met
exclusively by some past or present brand of common
sense being applied to community living.

For Lonergan practical theology is to be neither the logical application of doctrine or theory
nor an exercise of commonsense intelligence. Rather,
it is to be the methodical communication of Christ's
message. Because grounded in method and not in
logic, practical theology is very much concerned
with those who are to communicate Christ's message,
and not simply with the message itself. Because
grounded in method and not in common sense, practical
theology is very much concerned with communicating
the message itself, and not simply with the message

437

V.

as it has been formulated in one's own cultural
brand of common sense.

Firstly, then, practical theology is very much
concerned with those who are to communicate Christ's
message. This is simply the turn to the human subject described in Chapter Three and now mediated by
the special method of communications. Generally,
communication is a matter of leading another to
share meaning that one possesses. The meaning that
here is of interest is the meaning of the message of
Christ, and Lonergan notes that this meaning is cognitive, inasmuch as it tells what is to be believed;
it is constitutive meaning, inasmuch as Christ's
message joins together in community those who believe the message to interpret the love of God in
their hearts; it is effective meaning, inasmuch as
Christ's message prescribes the ministry Christians
are to exercise in society in realizing the rule of
God.[15] It follows, that those concerned with practical theology have first to be constituted by the
meaning they wish to communicate. This is stressed
by Lonergan in the following way:

> To communicate the Christian message is
> to lead another to share in one's cog-
> nitive, constitutive, effective meaning.
> Those, then, that would communicate the
> cognitive meaning of the message, first
> of all, must know it. At their service,
> then, are the seven previous functional
> specialties. Next, those that would
> communicate the constitutive meaning of
> the Christian message, first of all,

438

> must live it. For without living the
> Christian message one does not possess
> its constitutive meaning; and one can-
> not lead another to share what one
> oneself does not possess. Finally,
> those that communicate the effective
> meaning of the Christian message, must
> practise it. For actions speak louder
> than words, while preaching what one
> does not practise recalls sounding
> brass and tinkling cymbal.[16]

I think that this turn to the human subject, who
is communicating the Christian message, is worth emphasizing. Lonergan is not merely listing a number
of qualities that are desirable in those charged with
communicating the gospel; rather, he is indicating
the conditions of the possibility of effective communication on the part of the human subject. Traditional pastoral theology tended to ignore the fact
of this dependence on the human subject for effective
communication; nor, to my knowledge, is the human
subject as communicator methodically and explicitly
integrated within the newer forms of pastoral theology, which have much to say on what is to be communicated and to whom one communicates, but little or nothing on the prerequisite constitution of the subject
doing the teaching or preaching.

Secondly, practical theology is very much concerned with communicating the message itself, and not
simply the message as it has been formulated in one's
own cultural brand of common sense. This fact is
widely recognized by contemporary theologians,[17] and

439

is part of the movement from a classicist to an empirical notion of culture, described earlier in
Chapter One. The classicist knows of only one culture, his or her own, that is normative for the
whole of humanity; preaching the gospel is identified with preaching the gospel as formulated with
the resources of classicist culture. The more contemporary understanding is empirical and pluralistic, recognizing a diversity of cultures and communicating the message within the resources of any
given particular culture:

> The Christian message is to be communi-
> cated to all nations. Such communica-
> tion presupposes that preachers and tea-
> chers enlarge their horizons to include
> an accurate and intimate understanding
> of the culture and the language of the
> people they address. They must grasp
> the virtual resources of that culture
> and that language, and they must use
> those virtual resources creatively so
> that the Christian message becomes,
> not disruptive of the culture, not an
> alien patch superimposed upon it, but
> a line of development within the cul-
> ture.[18]

To the extent that communication is effective
there is constituted community, just as community
constitutes and perfects itself through communication.[19] Accordingly, a methodical practical theology, as outlined, will result in a community, rather
than simply an aggregate of individuals, and this
community will dynamically fulfill its proper func-

V.

tion, will perfect itself, inasmuch as practical
theology is authentically methodical. It is this
methodical practical theology that underpins the
currently accepted understanding of the Christian
church as a process of self-constitution, a Selbst-
vollzug, occurring within human society.[20] As
such, it is an organization, a structure, and
clearly strives for the promotion of authentic human and religious living in its members;[21] but of
special interest here is the church as an out-going
process, existing not just for itself but for all
of humanity. It is this fact especially that demands of Christians that their self-understanding
as Christian be integrated with a self-understanding
of the human reality generally, as uncovered within
the non-theological human studies, and to the method
of this integration we may now turn.

4. The Christian Church, Theology, and Human Studies

     Inasmuch as the church is an out-going process,
it works to meet the needs of its own members so that
these in turn may transfer their witness, fellowship,
and service to all mankind. As such, the church also
is a redemptive process, on behalf both of its own
members and mankind generally: for as was stressed
in Chapter Three, human development is dialectical,
and the possibility of authenticity comes only through
a withdrawal from inauthenticity.

441

V.

> The Church is a redemptive process. The
> Christian message, incarnate in Christ
> scourged and crucified, dead and risen,
> tells not only of God's love but also of
> man's sin. Sin is alienation from man's
> authentic being, which is self-transcen-
> dence, and sin justifies itself by ideol-
> ogy. As alienation and ideology are de-
> structive of community, so the self-sac-
> rificing love that is Christian charity
> reconciles alienated man to his true be-
> ing, and undoes the mischief initiated
> by alienation and consolidated by ideol-
> ogy.[22]

The actual exercise of this redemptive process
is, of course, a highly concrete matter, involving
the existential reality that is the church at any
given time in history. As an existential concern,
it will involve the selection of ends and the determination of priorities, and, in light of the
priorities selected, the assembling of appropriate
resources, the investigating of the concrete con-·
textual conditions, the formulating of plans and
policies that utilize the resources optimally under
the given conditions, and the coordinating of all
such plans through a process of communication and
feedback.[23]

This exercise, as outlined, is clearly methodical. But it is to be noted, that no one of the
operations described can be methodically implemen-
ted unless theology is integrated with human studies, and, indeed, in a methodical manner. The selection of ends and the determination of priorities,

V.

the gathering of resources, the investigation of
contexts, the formulation of policies, the coordinating of the entire procedure: all of these presuppose a church enlightened, not only by its own
theology, but as well by the knowledge and wisdom
of all disciplines concerned in any way with humanity in the world. And this, in turn, presupposes a theology integrated with these disciplines,
in a manner that enriches both theology and the
disciplines in question.

Before discussing the broad outline of what
would be demanded in such methodical integration,
I would like to draw attention to the importance
that Lonergan attaches to such integrated studies.
This is significant, for although theologians are
normally aware of the need for some collaboration,
there remains considerable hesitation to undertake
experimentation in this area - a hesitation due,
perhaps, to a feeling of inferiority in the presence of sciences and disciplines which have en-
joyed conspicuous success in our own day.[24]

In the article, Theology and Understanding,
published in 1954,[25] Lonergan described the issue
as the relation between speculative theology and
the empirical human sciences. The former treats
of God and all things in their relation to God,
and hence is considered the queen of sciences.
Generally, the queen has delegated the exercise
of her functions to philosophy, which handled

443

V.

quite adequately and quite abstractly all considerations of the human condition. But the novelty
of our own day lies in the fact that the empirical
human sciences treat of people, not abstractly in
terms of some unchanging human nature, but concretely
and pluralistically, as they are in fact in history.
But what people are in the present order of things is
a strictly theological topic, inasmuch as they suffer
from the effects of sin and are concretely in need of
redemption in order to realize their human potential.
To pretend that such concrete facts of sin and redemption can be relegated to an abstract system of philosophical understanding for their ultimate interpretation and solution is absurd. Hence, the dilemma is
clear. The empirical human sciences study people concretely existing in history. Such concrete existence
demands a theology for its full interpretation. But
such a theology has to be built on a philosophy which
is not fundamentally an abstract system. Hence, the
need for a new philosophy, grounding a methodical
theology that can collaborate with the empirical human sciences in interpreting the meaning of human existence.

In Insight, Lonergan repeats and expands upon
his earlier remarks.[26] After noting the need for
theology and the human sciences to complement one another, he goes on to point out that it was this very
problem that in large measure determined the structure of Insight. For if the Catholic thinker is com-
mitted to the universal relevance of theology, it re-

444

mains that human reason has spheres of independent
inquiry that can reach valid conclusions out of
their own resources. Hence, Lonergan wrote the
first eighteen chapters of Insight "solely in the
light of human intelligence and reasonableness and
without any presupposition of God's existence,
without any appeal to the authority of the Church,
and without any explicit reference to the genius of
St. Thomas Aquinas."[27] In other words, the reconciliation of the universality of theology and the
independence of other fields rests on the inner dynamism of human inquiry itself.

For while other fields alone are competent to
answer their own proper questions, still in fact
there exists human bias that, if it is to be overcome, demands the raising of ever further questions
from ever further fields. Nor is it possible to
overlook such bias, as if we lived in an age of
deep religious faith or even of infallibly valid
human reason. On the contrary, Lonergan recalls
Sorokin's phrase that we live in the midst of a
sensate culture:

> . . . to employ Prof. Sorokin's phrase,
> we live in the midst of a sensate cul-
> ture, in which very many men, in so far
> as they acknowledge any hegemony of
> truth, give their allegiance not to a
> divine revelation, not to a theology,
> not to a philosophy, nor even to an in-
> tellectualist science, but to science
> interpreted in a positivistic and prag-
> matic fashion.[28]

445

V.

Lonergan goes on to indicate the relevance of theology to empirical human science, and the relevance of empirical human science to theology. To this point I shall return in a moment. For the present, it might be opportune to mention Insight's description of the tension or disunity created by an absence of interdisciplinary labors. Here, the matter of the correct interpretation of the results of the empirical human sciences is a central issue. For if these sciences reveal the evil, as well as the good, in the human situation, still the remedy for the evil cannot be the product of human understanding, but rather rests on the initiative of God providing a solution. Because of this, a systematic understanding of the solution is the work, not of the empirical human sciences, but of a theology resting on faith:

> In a word, empirical human sciences can become practical only through theology, and the relentless modern drift to social engineering and totalitarian controls is the fruit of man's effort to make human science practical though he prescinds from God and from the solution God provides for man's problems.[29]

Again, while stressing the need for theology, one must also acknowledge that theology can be no substitute for the work carried out in the empirical human sciences. Theology can provide neither their theory, nor the concrete relevance of this theory to actual circumstances. The theologian as such has always to

be aware of this fact, for otherwise theology becomes simply identified with one or the other theoretical science, or with tasks proper to techni-
cians, consultants, social workers. Instead, the
theologian's role in this regard is to encourage
scientists to complete fidelity in their calling,
for inasmuch as fidelity exists there is an orientation of their work to ultimate value. As well,
the theologian can teach non-scientists the high office of the scientific spirit, and provide not only
the societal context which will support fundamental
research, but as well will help to ease the pres-
sures exerted by so-called practicality in projects
that have little significance. Most importantly,
theologians can work towards development of theological theory, rooted in the human thirst for God
and relevant to questions raised in other fields
and disciplines.

Such, then, is the significance of interdisciplinary work for theology. Without an integral
and dynamic relationship to the human sciences,
philosophy, and history, theology can easily lapse
into an abstract system, without any concern for
the concrete life of people in the world, and
without serious efforts to reveal the sacred in
the human condition. Religion and theology would
be, at best, rigidly confined to other-worldly
matters, or at least without influence on the various sectors of human life in this world. At the

447

V.

same time, merely to identify theology with one of
the human sciences would be to eliminate the ultimate orientation that each of these sciences should
have, and would result in a theology that is hardly
more than a secularist scheme for heaven on earth.[30]

Turning now to Method in Theology, Lonergan
there offers but a few hints on the direction of interdisciplinary work, and on the methodical principles
that should guide it.[31] To help the reader understand
these hints, perhaps I could note that collaboration
may occur in any of three manners.

Firstly, there is spontaneous or commonsense cooperation. Theologians may become aware of developments in other fields that seem to bear some relevance
to theological reflection, and these developments become part of the data considered by the theologian.
For example, political theorists may develop a set of
hypotheses that interpret the rights of the state as
related to the rights of individuals; such hypotheses
are of considerable interest to moral theologians,
and become data to be scrutinized and evaluated in
the light of moral principles. Such is the most common form of interdisciplinary interest, and while it
shall always have a value, it goes without saying
that it leaves theologians in a "catch-up" position,
one of response rather than of control.

Secondly, cooperation may be systematic in the
theoretical sense that the results of theological investigations are logically integrated with the re-

448

sults of scholarly or scientific investigations.
Unfortunately, such cooperation is usually no more
than a juxtaposition of findings, whose chief ad-
vantage lies in the fact that it may encourage study
on a deeper level. For example, an ecclesiologist
may find it highly desirable to complement studies
on the church with sociological insights on the dynamics of human development and change. In this
case, there is a potential for control, but the potential is generally thwarted through the incompatibility of defined terms and relations.

Thirdly, cooperation may be systematic in the
methodical sense that it rests neither on data alone
nor on results alone, but on the cognitional and
evaluative process leading from data to results.
Here, the basic notion is meaning. Meaning is constitutive of the human world, and, as such, is the
common element in what is studied or intended by all
human studies. Again, behind all special methods by
which the various human studies and theology work
towards specific goals, there is the generalized empirical method that identifies the common core and
ground of all such special methods in the pattern of
operations common to all conscious human subjects.
Accordingly, in the very dynamism of human inquiry,
there is a basis for interdisciplinary collaboration:

> . . . transcendental method offers a key
> to unified science. The immobility of
> the Aristotelian ideal conflicts with

449

> developing natural science, developing
> human science, developing dogma, and
> developing theology. In harmony with
> all development is the human mind itself
> which effects the developments. In unity
> with all fields, however disparate, is
> again the human mind that operates in all
> fields and in radically the same fashion
> in each. Through the self-knowledge, the
> self-appropriation, the self-possession
> that result from making explicit the ba-
> sic normative pattern of the recurrent
> and related operations of human cogni-
> tional process, it becomes possible to
> envisage a future in which all workers
> in all fields can find in transcendental
> method common norms, foundations, system-
> atics, and common critical, dialectical,
> and heuristic procedures.[32]

What Lonergan is advocating, then, is a thematic
attempt to integrate theology with human studies by
beginning, not with the data of human studies and
theology, not with the results of the investigations
in these various fields and disciplines, but with the
method whereby any data are investigated and any results classified and communicated. This means, for
example, that the work of a sociologist of religion
and a theologian find their basis of integration, not
in the data investigated or in the results reached,
but in the complementarity of methods employed: the
data viewed from different methodological perspectives, studied by different methods, becomes better
known than this data investigated by just one special
method. This is not to deny that a given field may
have "privileged" data, peculiar to the field in

question; but the uniqueness of the science lies,
not in this privileged data, but in the specific
method whereby this or any other data is investigated.[33]

The broad dimensions of such integrated studies may be noted briefly. Firstly, scholarly
studies of any field can be methodically grounded
in the functional specialties of research, interpretation, and history; in this way, the opportun-
ities for collaboration between such studies and
theological scholarship would surface as investigations are carried out and results communicated.
With regard to the systematizing human studies,
such as the psychology and sociology of religion,
these studies may be methodically conceived as
processes of experiencing, understanding what is
experienced, and affirming the meaning of what is
understood and experienced by formulating classical and statistical laws of human behavior.[34] And
inasmuch as theological research, interpretation,
and history also are conceived as a process of experiencing, understanding, and affirming, there
would seem to be possibilities of collaboration
between the systematizing human studies and theological scholarship. For example, Gibson Winter
has drawn attention to the interdependence between
social science and historical scholarship,[35] so
that it is quite conceivable that empirical religious studies of the systematizing variety could

be methodically integrated with theological scholarship. To mention but a pair of examples: the interpretation of religious documents could benefit
immensely from the insights uncovered by a psychology of religion, just as a psychology of religion
could profit from the work of exegetes and interpreters; similarly, the work of historians may in-
teract with that of sociologists of religion, in a
manner that brings the novelties and regularities
in a religious tradition into a more comprehensive
whole.[36]

Again, an account was given of the functional
specialty, dialectic, and in Chapter Three a similar dialectic was urged for empirical religious
studies. One could extend this need for dialectic
to all historical and empirical human studies, in
order to deal with the disagreements and conflicts
that arise within these fields. But besides the
collaboration that would thereby be encouraged among
dialecticians in various disciplines and fields, the
foundational theologian could illuminate the radically authentic positions and thereby discourage
ideological tendencies among investigators in the
historical and empirical human studies.[37]

Inasmuch as dialectic is invoked, not just to
deal with conflicts among investigators, but with
conflicts in what is studied by investigators - the
social process itself - a deeper level of integration is possible. Historical studies will offer

accounts of the concrete historical process in which
ideology has played a part; and empirical studies
will catalogue the effects of such ideology in the
actual social situation. This prepares the way for
policy makers, who "will devise procedures both for
the liquidation of the evil effects and for remedy-
ing the alienation that is their source."[38]

The policy making, planning, and executing of
the plans, that is carried out by various social
groups have a point of integration with theology in
doctrines (policy making), systematics (planning),
and communications (execution of the plans).[39] The
obvious benefit of collaboration in these dimensions
is that the policies of the various groups would be
explicitly guided by the values uncovered by the
different historical and empirical human studies,
values that receive their grounding in a generalized
philosophy and their orientation from a theology.
Moreover, the process is not merely cumulative but
also recurrent, so that policies decided upon may be
examined and criticized in the light of their implementation, which implementation becomes the data for
the historical and empirical studies.[40]

To the extent that theology achieves integration
with historical and empirical human studies, and is
constitutive in the formulation of Church policies,
to that extent will theology promote a fully-deliber-
ate redemptive role of the Church in human society.
But, as Lonergan notes, the exercise of this redemp-

V.

tive role presupposes genuine scientific advance,
the acceptance of this advance by responsible authorities, and the communication of such acceptance, and its implications for policies, planning,
and execution, to local authorities responsible for
constructive action on various levels. And, because authenticity can never be assumed, it is to
be expected that progress will be slow and that dialectic, conducted hopefully in dialogue, will play
a central role. Still, even the realization that
methodically integrated studies are a possibility
leads us to work towards their realization, however
arduous and slow:

> In conclusion, let me say that such in-
> tegrated studies correspond to a profound
> exigence in the contemporary situation.
> For ours is a time of ever increasing
> change due to an ever increasing expan-
> sion of knowledge. To operate on the le-
> vel of our day is to apply the best avail-
> able knowledge and the most efficient
> techniques to coordinated group action.
> But to meet this contemporary exigence
> will also set the church on a course of
> continual renewal. It will remove from
> its action the widespread impression of
> complacent irrelevance and futility. It
> will bring theologians into close contact
> with experts in very many different
> fields. It will bring scientists and
> scholars into close contact with policy
> makers and planners and, through them
> with clerical and lay workers engaged in
> applying solutions to the problems and
> finding ways to meet the needs both of
> Christians and of all mankind.[41]

5. Conclusion

The brevity of the present chapter has been demanded by the concreteness of the subject matter. On matters that are concrete, one is faced with composing an ever unfinished encyclopedia or with being content to indicate a few principles whereby such concrete matters might be considered.

In the main, my concern has been to draw attention to the fact that theology occurs within the context of the Christian church, and that this church exercises a function in and on behalf of humanity itself. To say that theology occurs within the context of the Christian church has been understood in a methodical sense: not only is theology one of the things that occurs within the Christian church, but as well a methodical theology is constitutive of a dimension of this church's meaning and role within the human community. It can play a significant role in the formulation of church policy, and will do so all the more effectively the more it is integrated with historical and empirical human studies of all kinds.

The mention of these empirical studies brings us back to Chapter Two. Yet the return is not some closed circle, but rather a deeper understanding of the meaning of theology in the context of empirical religious studies.[42] Quite readily, then, can we grant the priority of empirical studies in our mod-

455

V.

ern era. Yet equally can we affirm this priority
to be relative, and that such studies call for
their sublation into the higher unities of a philosophy of religion, a theology, and an effective
praxis that mediates religious meaning and value
to the present world.

Although criticism was levelled at both traditional and modern varieties of pastoral theology,
my aim was constructive. It was to affirm the valid
concerns manifest in these varieties, and to suggest
a method that a new pastoral theology might find
useful in coordinating the massive amount of work
currently being carried out. Praxis has come into
its own in our day, and it is hoped that such praxis
will be all the more effective because set within
the context of empirical religious studies, a philosophy of religion, and Christian theology.

CONCLUDING REMARKS

Chapter One of this work included a brief discussion of the notions of theology proposed by Wolfhart Pannenberg, Karl Rahner, and Johann Metz. It was implied that these three authors, though they disagree among themselves on many theological questions, nevertheless tend to be methodologically complementary. In order to illustrate this, subsequent chapters treated the work of Bernard Lonergan. Ideally, the procedure should have been to provide an ongoing dialogue between Lonergan and those three theologians, comparing and contrasting their thought on such central issues as the interpretation of Enlightenment, religious experience, religious faith, religious tradition and belief, the various manners of reflecting on religion, the way in which these manners differ from one another, the uniqueness of theology, the role of theology in church and world. But while such a procedure would have been ideal, its adequate realization would have demanded far more space than was here available.

It remains, however, that this present work cannot be concluded without offering some account of the methodological complementarity of Pannenberg, Rahner, and Metz. Accordingly, this concluding section will first offer a note on Lonergan's distinction between methodology and theology. Secondly, Pannenberg's work will be discussed in terms of method as history and as dialectic. Thirdly, Rahner's work will be presented in terms of method as praxis and, specifically, as concerned with the foundations of praxis. Fourthly, the theology of Metz will be related to praxis as communicative. And fifthly, some critical comments will be made on the work of Lonergan himself.

1. Methodology and Theology

In his Summa, I, q. 1, a.7, Aquinas states: "Theologia tractat de Deo et de aliis quae ad Deum ordinantur." Such is a notion of theology in terms

457

of the object of theology, and is a notion that continues to be repeated or imitated by theologians in
our own day. Lonergan, however, has proposed a notion of theology in terms of method, and he would
maintain that such a notion is more comprehensive:
it includes, indeed, the objects of theological reflection, but it adds a consideration of the conscious and intentional operations of the theologians
as reflecting on those objects. As mentioned earlier in this work, this means that Lonergan speaks,
not of material objects, but of data; and not of
formal objects, but rather of the application to the
data of the operations prescribed by the specific
method. So it is that while Aquinas describes theology as the science about God, Lonergan considers
theology to be reflection on the significance and
value of a religion in a culture. Further, Lonergan
is aware that such reflection in our own day is
highly specialized, and he lists eight basic specialties as distinct but integrated components of a
methodical theology. Finally, he would insist that
none of the eight is his own invention, but rather
that all are presently operative in theology and
that he has merely made methodically explicit what
currently is operative in theological reflection.

While Lonergan would stress the continuity between a notion of theology in terms of material and
formal objects, and a notion of theology in terms of
method, it remains that the continuity can be understood only by shifting to a new key. Some of the
questions that arise in making this shift will be
discussed later in reference to the work of Karl
Rahner. First, however, it seems important to stress
that Lonergan's proposal results in an explicit distinction (though not separation) between "theology"
and "method in theology." So Lonergan writes in
Method:

> Just as theology reflects on revelation
> and church doctrines, so methodology re-
> flects on theology and theologies. Be-
> cause it reflects on theology and theol-
> ogies, it has to mention both the revel-

ation and the church doctrines on which
theologians reflect. But though it mentions them, it does not attempt to determine their content. That task it
leaves to the church authorities and to
the theologians. It is concerned to determine how theologians might or should
operate. It is not concerned to predetermine the specific results all future
generations must obtain.[1]

Lonergan, then, is not <u>directly</u> concerned with
the objects of theology. Instead, he is concerned
with the way (method) that theologians can reach some
idea of what those objects are, what they have meant
to people in the past, and what meaning they have for
people today. This point is so important in understanding Lonergan's work that I wish to quote extensively from his <u>Method in Theology</u>, listing some of
the passages wherein Lonergan stresses this distinction between theology and methodology.

If I hope many readers will find in themselves the dynamic structure of which I
write, others perhaps will not. Let me
beg them not to be scandalized because I
quote scripture, the ecumenical councils,
papal encyclicals, other theologians so
rarely and sparingly. I am writing not
theology but method in theology. I am
concerned not with the objects that theologians expound but with the operations
that theologians perform.[2]

Later, in the chapter on "Religion," Lonergan is discussing religious belief. He has noted the community
dimension of religious commitment and the historical
character of religious communities, in the sense that
they exist over time. He adds that there is a far
deeper sense, however, in which religion is historical, inasmuch as there is a personal entrance of God
into history, a communication of God, the advent of
God's word into the world of religious expression, as
in the religion of Israel and in Christianity. Here,

459

CONC

to the gift of God's love there is added the outer
word of the religious tradition that also comes
from God and, in a privileged area, is the word
who is God. With these comments, Lonergan admits
he is leaving strictly methodological considerations
and raising theological issues:

> So we come to questions that are not meth-
> odological but theological, questions con-
> cerning revelation and inspiration, scrip-
> ture and tradition, development and au-
> thority, schisms and heresies. To the
> theologians we must leave them, though
> something will be said on the method of
> resolving them in our later chapters on
> Dialectic and on Foundations.[3]

In Chapter Six on "Research," Lonergan notes that doing research is much more a matter of practice than
of theory. It is a concrete task that is guided, not
by abstract generalities, but by the practical intelligence generated by the self-correcting process of
learning. He continues:

> But if we do not propose to give instruc-
> tion on the procedures of research, we
> may be expected to indicate the areas
> that theological research is to investi-
> gate. Such an indication we are prepared
> to offer, but it will settle not theolog-
> ical but only methodical issues.[4]

In Chapter Ten on "Dialectic," Lonergan has presented
an account of the sort of radical conflicts and op-
posing horizons with which dialectic is concerned.
He introduced his discussion of conflicting notions
of "method" and of philosophy by saying:

> Now the task of dealing with these con-
> flicts pertains, not to the methodologists,
> but to theologians occupied in the fourth
> functional specialty. . . . It remains
> that the methodologist cannot totally ig-
> nore the conflict of philosophies or meth-

ods. Especially is this so when there
are widely held views that imply that
his own procedures are mistaken and
even wrong-headed.[5]

Chapter Eleven discusses the functional specialty,
"Foundations." A central function of this specialty
is the determination of the general and special categories employed in theology. Lonergan writes:

> While the transcendental notions make
> questions and answers possible, categor-
> ies make them determinate. Theological
> categories are either general or special.
> General categories regard objects that
> come within the purview of other discip-
> lines as well as theology. Special cat-
> egories regard the objects proper to the-
> ology. The task of working out general
> and special categories pertains, not to
> the methodologist, but to the theologian
> engaged in this fifth functional spe-
> cialty. The methodologist's task is the
> preliminary one of indicating what qual-
> ities are desirable in the theological
> categories, what measure of validity is
> to be demanded of them, and how are the
> categories with the desired qualities
> and validity to be obtained.[6]

In this same section, when discussing the validity
to be expected of general and special theological
categories, Lonergan states:

> First, such categories will form a set
> of interlocking terms and relations and,
> accordingly, they will possess the util-
> ity of models. Further, these models
> will be built up from basic terms and
> relations that refer to transcultural
> components in human living and operation
> and, accordingly, at their roots they
> will possess quite exceptional validity.

461

> Finally, whether they are to be considered more than models with exceptional foundational validity, is not a methodological but a theological question. In other words, it is up to the theologian to decide whether any model is to become an hypothesis or to be taken as a description.[7]

Similarly, in sketching the broad lines of special theological categories, Lonergan concludes:

> So much for a sketch of general and special theological categories. As already noted, the task of the methodologist is to sketch the derivation of such categories, but it is up to the theologian working in the fifth funtional specialty to determine in detail what the general and special categories are to be.[8]

Chapter Twelve is on the functional specialty, "Doctrines." Already I have referred to the passage wherein Lonergan speaks of the distinction of methodology from theology, with the former charged with the task of reflecting on the latter. In this same chapter Lonergan discusses the permanence of the meaning of dogmas and concludes that section as follows:

> Such I believe is the doctrine of Vatican I on the permanence of the meaning of dogmas. It presupposes (1) that there exist mysteries hidden in God that man could not know unless they were revealed, (2) that they have been revealed, and (3) that the church has infallibly declared the meaning of what has been revealed. These presuppositions also are church doctrines. Their exposition and defence are tasks, not of a methodologist, but of a theologian.[9]

Later in the chapter, Lonergan is writing of the
proper autonomy of the theologian within the church;
he emphasizes the openness of his method to theologians of all persuasions:

> Though a Roman Catholic with quite con-
> servative views on religious and church
> doctrines, I have written a chapter on
> doctrines without subscribing to any
> but the doctrine about doctrine set forth
> in the first Vatican council. I have
> done so deliberately, and my purpose has
> been ecumenical. I desire it to be as
> simple as possible for theologians of
> different allegiance to adapt my method
> to their uses. Even though theologians
> start from different church confessions,
> even though their methods are analogous
> rather than similar, still that analogy
> will help all to discover how much they
> have in common and it will tend to bring
> to light how greater agreement might be
> achieved.[10]

In Chapter Thirteen on the functional specialty,
"Systematics," Lonergan concludes the chapter with
a note on the relation of revelation and doctrinal
development:

> Even though fundamentally current the-
> ological revision is just an adaptation
> to cultural change, there remains the
> possibility that these adaptations will
> in turn imply still further revisions.
> Thus the shift from a predominantly log-
> ical to a basically methodical viewpoint
> may involve a revision of the view that
> doctrinal developments were "implicitly"
> revealed. Again, just as the Alexandrian
> school refused to take literally the an-
> thropomorphisms of the bible to bring a-
> bout a philosophically based demytholog-
> ization, so it may be asked whether mod-

463

ern scholarship may not bring about
further demythologizations on exegetical or historical grounds. Such questions, of course, are very large indeed. Unmistakably they are theological. They accordingly lie outside the
scope of the present work on method.[11]

In the final chapter, on the functional specialty,
"Communications," Lonergan begins by speaking of its
importance, but then adds:

Having insisted on the great importance
of this final specialty, I must at once
recall the distinction between the methodologist and the theologian. It is up
to the theologians to carry out both the
first seven specialties and no less the
eighth. The methodologist has the far
lighter task of indicating what the various tasks of theologians are and how
each presupposes or complements the
others.[12]

I have quoted at length from Lonergan because
the distinction between the methodologist and theologian, in the sense intended by Lonergan, is something of a novelty. As indicated by him in the last-
quoted passage, the methodologist has the task of indicating what the various tasks of theologians are
and how each presupposes or complements the others.
In other words, methodology is a matter of reflecting
on theology and theologies, with the purpose of promoting greater clarity concerning the function of theology in any given context, of contributing to cooperation among theologians, and of helping to objectify
and clarify the resolution of radical conflicts within
the theological community, thereby contributing to the
foundational unity of that community.

It is with this distinction in mind that we may
discuss the methodological complementarity of Pannenberg, Rahner, and Metz. If methodology is a reflec-

tion on theologies, then we are led to believe that
a reflection on the work of those authors might reveal points of complementarity. The following pages
will stress this fact, and prescind from the far
more complex task of resolving areas of theological
disagreement.

2. Pannenberg, Wissenschaftlichkeit, and Method

Bearing in mind the distinction between methodology and theology, and presupposing the presentation
in Chapter One, it is possible to discern in the work
of Wolfhart Pannenberg a notion of theology more or
less coextensive with what Lonergan refers to as the
first phase of theology - theology in oratione obliqua. "Coextensive," of course, does not mean "iden-
tical." Pannenberg should not be forced into some a
priori Lonerganian context, nor should Lonergan's
first phase of theology simply be equated with Panen-
berg's Offenbarung als Geschichte. Rather, all that
is claimed is a certain similarity between Pannenberg's notion of theology, and Lonergan's understanding of theological method in its historical and dialectical functions.

For Pannenberg, then, theology is rooted in historical knowledge:

> Theologie erwies sich uns als Wissenschaft
> von Gott, die sich aber ihrem Gegenstand
> nur indirekt, durch das Studium der Reli-
> gionen, zuwenden kann. Einerseits nämlich
> ist Gottes Wirklichkeit keiner direkten
> Beobachtung zugänglich, andererseits ist
> sie in den Religionen immer schon themat-
> isch geworden als machtvoller Grund der
> menschlichen Lebenswelt und als Quelle der
> Überwindung der in ihr auftretenden Erfah-
> rungen von Bosheit und Leid. Solche Them-
> atisierung der göttlichen Wirklichkeit hat
> jeweils geschichtlich bestimmte Gestalt.
> Auch die Unmittelbarkeit gegenwärtiger re-
> ligiöser Erfahrung erweist sich der Re-
> flexion als bestimmt und vermittelt durch

> ihren geschichtlichen Ort und als in der
> einen oder anderen Weise bezogen auf vo-
> gegebene religiöse Überlieferung. Der
> Stoff der Theologie - und zwar nicht nur
> der christlichen Theologie oder der The-
> ologie des Christentums - ist also immer
> schon geschichtlich geprägt.[13]

For this reason Pannenberg maintains that the methods of critical scholarship are not just theological Hilfswissenschaften, but rather are truly theological methods. To borrow a phrase commonly used by Loner-gan, an indispensable dimension of theology itself is the reconstruction of the past religious tradition as historical.[14]

But Pannenberg is quite aware that such recon-struction is not the whole of theology. Accordingly, he proceeds to delineate the other dimension of the-ological work, and it is here that there is a similar-ity with Lonergan's notion of method as dialectic. As Lonergan would add to the historical reconstruction of the past an evaluative reconstruction of the past tra-dition, so Pannenberg maintains such an evaluative function to be the key task of a "systematic" theol-ogy. Clearly, Pannenberg's meaning of "systematic" thereby is not the same as that meant by Lonergan in the latter's seventh functional specialty. What Pan-nenberg means is much closer to Lonergan's notion of "dialectic," charged with evaluating the past tradi-tion and sorting out the truth and falsity of that tradition:

> Theologie kann nicht nur historich sein;
> denn sie hat es nicht nur mit religiösen
> Erfahrungen, Überzeugungen und Institu-
> tionen vergangener Zeiten zu tun, sondern
> mit der Frage nach ihrer Wahrheit, also
> mit der Frage nach der Wirklichkeit Got-
> tes. Diese Frage nach der Wahrheit einer
> religiösen Überlieferung stellt sich im
> Falle einer ungebrochenen, wenn auch viel-
> fältig aufgesplittert, von ihren Ursprün-

gen bis in die Gegenwart reichenden Tradition wie der christlichen mit besonderer
aktueller Dringlichkeit, zumal im engeren
kulturellen Wirkungsbereich dieser Tradition, nämlich in den aus dem Zusammenhang
christlicher Überlieferung hervorgegangenen
Gesellschaften. Die Frage nach der Wahrheit ist ihrer Natur nach systematisch;
denn sie fragt notwendig nach der Zusammen-
stimmung der verschiedenen Inhalte der
Überlieferung untereinander und mit der
jeweiligen gegenwärtigen Wirklichkeitser-
fahrung.[15]

Here, note than Pannenberg's "systematic" function of theology remains focused on the past religious
tradition, and would uncover the truth and falsity of
that tradition. Clearly, this is also very much an
indispensable component in theology, so that Lonergan,
too, urges precisely an evaluative reconstruction of
the tradition in order to complete the first phase of
theology. The difference between Pannenberg and Lonergan, then, lies in the fact that Pannenberg has
chosen to concentrate on the function of theology in
oratione obliqua, while Lonergan would draw attention
to the additional function of theology as praxis - in
oratione recta. Pannenberg conceives of theology as
an evaluative mediation of the past into the present;
Lonergan would agree, but would ask as well for a
theology that critically mediates the present into
the future. That Pannenberg himself has not (yet)
developed this further dimension of theology should
not be taken as a criticism of Pannenberg's thought.
One cannot expect a single theologian to do everything, and it seems far better to understand Pannenberg's work as contributing extensively to a notion
of theology as history and dialectic. The value of
Lonergan's methodology, then, lies in the fact that
it gives us an appreciation of what Pannenberg has
in fact accomplished, while also directing our attention to the need to complement Pannenberg's work with
that of theologians such as Rahner and Metz, both of
whom are concerned, not so much with mediating the
past into the present, as with mediating present

CONC

Christian truth into the future.

Indeed, in light of Pannenberg's recent Wissenschaftstheorie . . . , it seems possible to conclude that Pannenberg himself is moving in precisely this direction. His comments on "praktische Theologie" and praxis are indeed few, and occur within the context of his evaluative historical foundation. Yet he seems to be moving to a notion of praxis that is grounded, not just on the past Christian tradition, but as well on the "living faith" of the present Christian community. With M. Theunissen, Pannenberg agrees,

> . . . dass Theorie nicht nur auf die noch
> offene Zukunft einer geschichtlich be-
> griffenen Welt und so auf Praxis bezogen,
> sondern dass sie auch "ihrerseits in den
> Strom einer Praxis eingebettet ist, der
> auch noch durch sie hindurchfliesst."
> Dabei kann freilich für christliches Den-
> ken die endgültige Vollendung nicht
> schlechthin als in der gegenwärtigen
> Welt noch ausstehend gelten, so dass im
> Lichte erhoffter Vollendung die gegen-
> wärtige Welt nur kritisch ihrer Unmensch-
> lichkeit zu überführen und ihre radikale
> Veränderung zu fordern wäre. Vielmehr
> ist für das Bewusstsein des christlichen
> Glaubens das Endgültige durch Jesus
> Christus schon in dieser vorhandenen
> Welt trotz Ungerechtigkeit, Leid und Tod
> gegenwärtig, und ihre noch ausstehende
> Vollendung kann nur die geschichtliche
> Verwirklichung der von Jesus Christus
> her schon in der Welt gegenwärtigen und
> wirksamen Versöhnung zum Inhalt haben.
> Dieser im christlichen Glauben selbst
> angelegten Verhältnisbestimmung von The-
> orie und Praxis kann eine praktische The-
> ologie nur so entsprechen, dass sie den
> in der Geschichte Jesu Christi begründe-
> ten und in der Geschichte des Christen-
> tums weiterwirkenden, teilweise auch ge-

hemmten Praxisbezug des christlichen
Glaubens thematisiert und die gegenwärtige Praxis der Kirchen aus dem Zusammenhang der christlichen Versöhnungs-
geschichte begreift und kritisch beleuch-
tet, um so zur Entwicklung von Modellen
gegenwärtiger kirchlicher Praxis zu ge-
langen.[16]

Pannenberg, then, refers explicitly to the living faith experience of the present Christian community as "praxis." And he assigns to theology the
function of thematizing this praxis in a critical
manner. His notion of theology as history and as
dialectic, then, seems quite open to further development towards theology as praxis. In this regard,
the methodological reflection of Lonergan concerning
theology in its second phase as praxis might serve
as a guideline. Equally important, however, is to
examine the example of theologians actually promoting a notion of theology as praxis, and so we may
now consider briefly the work of Karl Rahner and
Johann Metz.

3. Rahner, Kirchlichkeit, and Method

After an account of method in mediating theology (research, interpretation, history, and dialectic), Lonergan makes the transition from mediating
to mediated theology - from theology in oratione
obliqua to theology in oratione recta. This second
phase of theology is a matter of theologians, enlightened by the past, taking a stand towards the
future; and the question is, on what basis or foundation is that stance to be taken? For Lonergan,
part of the foundation (its objective dimension)
lies of course in the past tradition as evaluatively
reconstructed in dialectic; dialectic reveals the
religious situation, the religious tradition, to
which theologians in the second phase are correlative. Such, however, is not a sufficient foundation,
for that religious situation is a compound of authenticity and inauthenticity. As such, it challenges

469

theologians to a decision: the decision to pronounce what is true in the tradition, to reconcile
various truths among themselves and with the conclusions reached in non-theological adademic circles, and to communicate Christian truth effectively
to the members of all classes in every culture. The
sufficient foundation of theology in its second
phase, then, will be the religious, moral, and intellectual authenticity of theologians that enables
them to take an authentic stance towards the Christian tradition and mediate that tradition authentically in the present and future. This is just another way of saying that, for Lonergan, foundational
reality is conversion. It is conversion that will
enable theologians to pronounce on the truth of tradition; it is conversion that gives to theologians
the horizon that enables them to state the truth in
the various sources of Christian tradition.

Accordingly, the fifth functional specialty is
foundations. It is pivotal, for it builds the bridge
between the evaluative reconstruction of the Christian past, and the praxis that mediates authentic
Christian tradition to the present and future. As a
functional specialty, foundations is a matter of objectifying the horizon or foundation of this praxis.
For Lonergan, it is the self-appropriation by the
theologian of his or her religious interiority, and
this is formulated in both general categories and in
specifically theological categories - the latter
made available in the specialty of dialectic. So,
writing in Method in Theology, Lonergan notes:

> The derivation of the categories is a
> matter of the human and the Christian
> subject effecting self-appropriation and
> employing this heightened consciousness
> both as a basis for methodical control
> in doing theology and, as well, as an a
> priori whence he can understand other
> men, their social relations, their his-
> tory, their religion, their rituals,
> their destiny.[17]

As methodologist, Lonergan is concerned principally with the task of indicating the qualities
desirable in theological categories, the validity
to be demanded of these categories, and the manner
in which such categories are to be obtained. He
readily acknowledges that the task of actually
working out the general and special categories pertains, not to the methodologist, but the the theologian working in the functional specialty of "foundations."[18] Here, Karl Rahner may be considered
just such a theologian. If the assessment of Rahner's project is accurate, then he has been principally concerned with the derivation of the categories relevant to a specifically Christian theology. Rahner, of course, has gone beyond such derivation to the other specialties that Lonergan calls
"doctrines," "systematics," and "communications";
but the presentation in Chapter One focused, not on
these further aspects of Rahner's thought, but on
his unique achievement in working out the categories
foundational to Christian theology. Two aspects of
this achievement merit repetition: the manner of
self-appropriation, whereby Rahner derives theological categories; and the eminent usefulness of the
categories suggested by Rahner.

Firstly, then, Rahner operates in the manner of
a self-appropriation of his Christian religious experience. His first level of reflection (erste Reflexionsstufe) is a matter of heightening consciousness, of bringing to light an experience that is
simply experienced but not adverted to, not questioned, not interpreted, and not known. Accordingly,
Rahner's erste Reflexionsstufe is remarkably similar
to the sort of reflection that Lonergan names generalized empirical method. Probably the main difference between the two types of reflective thinking
lies in the fact that Lonergan's method is in fact
generalized, while Rahner's erste Reflexionsstufe
is formulated in specifically religious and theological categories. To put this in another way, Lonergan's generalized empirical method is the work of
a methodologist, uncovering the core of conscious
and intentional operations common to all human in-

quiry including theological reflection; Rahner's
erste Reflexionsstufe is the work of a theologian,
objectifying conscious intentionality in specifically religious and theological categories. For
this reason Rahner may be considered an example of
what it means to be engaged in the functional specialty, "foundations." Rahner is concerned with
theological method as praxis and, indeed, as praxis
in its foundational function.

Secondly, the categories derived by Rahner for
Christian theology seem to be eminently useful and
comprehensive. One has only to study the massive
extent of Rahner's writings over the years to con-
firm this fact and to find the categorial structures of a Christian theology that is truly a theological anthropology. Moreover, Rahner himself
has given this structure a coordinated integration
in his Grundkurs des Glaubens, that moves from human religious experience to the other-worldly
source of that experience, to the revealed Word of
Jesus Christ interpreting the experience, and to
the togetherness in community of those bearing witness to Christ in the world. All this provides
Christian theology with a solid core of foundational
categories that will help theologians to take a
stand on what is authentic in the Christian tradition and to mediate this tradition to the whole of
human affairs.

It is suggested, then, that Rahner's first level of reflection is coextensive with Lonergan's
notion of the functional specialty, "foundations."
I should perhaps add that "foundations," as a functional specialty, stands within the context of
method as history and method as dialectic. It
seems to follow, then, that Rahner's work might
eventually be understood as complementary to that
of theologians concerned with factual and evaluative history. This would allow Rahner's first level of reflection to be situated methodically
within the context of the Christian tradition - a
need that has been indicated by many commentators
of Rahner's thought.

In light of these admittedly brief and incomplete remarks, it is possible to resolve some of the problems that Rahner has with Lonergan's notion of method in theology.[19] Rahner's criticism was occasioned by the publication in Gregorianum of Lonergan's chapter from Method in Theology on "functional specialties."[20] This occurred prior to the appearance of Method in Theology, and the article was accompanied by a note to the effect that "functional specialties" was to be the second chapter of Lonergan's book, following an initial chapter on "method" as generalized. This led Rahner to wonder about the specifically religious, Christian, and theological dimensions of Lonergan's theological method; for Lonergan to "leap" directly from generalized empirical method to the structural organization of theology into functional specialties left unanswered the crucial question about the proprium of theology and, secondly, about the proprium of Christian theology.

After the appearance of his article in Gregorianum, and prior to the publication of Method in Theology, Lonergan seems to have acknowledged the legitimacy of such criticism. To highlight the proprium of theology, Lonergan made the chapter on "functional specialties" the fifth chapter of Method in Theology, preceded now by chapters on generalized empirical method, the human good, meaning, and religion. Thus, the relevance of generalized method to theology is clarified by formulating a notion of method in theology in terms of reflection on religion, thereby highlighting the proprium of theology amidst the various academic disciplines. Lonergan himself clarified this further in an interview in which he directly referred to the criticism of Rahner. I wish to quote this clarification at some length for it treats, not only the proprium of theology, but also the crucial distinction, mentioned earlier, between methodology and theology:

> To the question whether Method in Theology was restricted to theology or to a particular theology Fr. Lonergan replied:

473

"Karl Rahner, in his paper, remarked he thought it could be applied to any human science that was fully conscious of itself as depending on the past and looking towards the future. I think that's true. But I'm not working it out in those terms. I'm working it out in terms of a theology. That chapter on functional specializations is not going to be chapter two (as was said a year and a half ago when I sent this paper to Gregorianum) it's chapter five now. The four background chapters are: 'Method,' 'The Human Good,' 'Meaning,' and 'Religion.' So it's a theology because it's a reflection on religion, as said in Functional Specialties.

"Now it is doing method in theology; it is not doing theology. It aims at avoiding settling any theological question. Is it the Koran? Or the Old Testament? Or the Old and the New? Or the Old and the New and the Fathers? Or does it include the whole Christian tradition? Those are questions that theologians have to settle. I'm not going to settle them. So it's a structure, and you can have an analogy to it in Piaget's Le Structuralisme - a very thin little book in which he conceives this structuralism as a matter of interdependent, self-regulating, ongoing process.

"The eight functional specialties are a set of self-regulative, ongoing, interdependent processes. They're not stages such that you do one and then you do the next. Rather you have different people at all eight and interacting. And the interaction is not logical. It's attentive, intelligent, reasonable, responsible, and religious. The responsibility includes

474

the element not only of morality but
also of religion. I conceive religion
as total commitment."[21]

Lonergan, then, says that his notion of functional specialization, as set forth in the finished
version of Method in Theology, is theological inasmuch as the various specialties are integral com-
ponenets in the process of reflecting on religion.
In light of Chapter Three of the present work, it
is possible to relate Lonergan's notion of "religion"
to Rahner's demand for a theological method - a method
that takes account of the "formal object" that distinguishes theology as properly "discourse about God
as such." According to Lonergan, the specifically
theological principle is fundamentally religious conversion - the gift of God's love resulting in the free
and total commitment of a person. It is what Rahner
names "mystery," and it is what both Lonergan and
Rahner understand to be the source and goal of reflection on religion.

It would seem, then, that there is a fundamental
agreement between Lonergan and Rahner concerning the
meaning of a method that is specifically theological.
Both agree that when one conceives theology in terms
of material and formal objects, a discipline is
"theological" when it treats of God and of all things
in relation to God. But Lonergan would add that when
one shifts to a new key, attending both to objects
and to reflecting subjects, then the religious dimension of a theologian's horizon has to be taken into
account. Accordingly, a discipline will be theological, not just because it reflects on God, but also
because the theologian is operating on the basis of
religious conversion - something that makes reflection on God profoundly meaningful. Nor is it likely
that Rahner himself would disagree with this attention to the theologian as religious subject, for his
erste Reflexionsstufe is simply the effort of a religious subject to articulate his or her own existential reality, in light of a given religious tradition.

475

CONC

This mention of religious tradition, however, raises the second criticism by Rahner of Lonergan's theological method. For Rahner, theology has a specifically Christian dimension, centered on a unique relationship to the concrete person of Jesus Christ as a proper "material object" in theology.

In this regard, Rahner is quite correct in designating the chapter on "functional specialties" as not specifically concerned with the proprium of Christian theology. Lonergan's self-understanding is that of a methodologist, and not that of a theologian. Accordingly, the various functional specialties could be applied to reflection on any of mankind's religious traditions to the extent that these traditions sought an understanding of their past in order to guide their future. Again, even the published Method in Theology, that was not available when Rahner wrote his criticism, cannot be said to be centered on the proprium of Christian theology; rather, Lonergan is very much concerned to present a notion of theology that stresses, and builds on, what is common to the great religions of mankind, thereby paving the way for dialogue among these religions and among their theologians.

The question, then, as to the proprium of specifically Christian theology is a question that is not answered by Lonergan in any explicit fashion in his Method in Theology. It would, however, be wrong to draw the conclusion that Lonergan denies a proprium to Christian theology. Lonergan readily acknowledges that there is a distinctive dimension to Christianity, not found in other world religions; that distinctive component is not some original philosophy of life, nor is it some original ethical code, but rather the fact that God's grace is given in Christ Jesus - something that Karl Rahner has stressed in his work.[22] This means, for Lonergan, that the religious experience of the Christian is specifically distinct from religious experience generally, inasmuch as Christian religious experience is intersubjective with Christ Jesus apprehended as God.[23] For Lonergan, accordingly, Christian theology is distinct from non-Christian theologies to the extent that the former is a reflection on specifically Christian religious experience from within the specifically Christian religious tradition. But Lonergan himself has not given a great deal of attention, in his formal publications, to the derivation of the categories appropriate to specifically Christian theology. Hence, in discussing specifically theological categories, he refers to a first set of categories being derived from religious experience, and does not refer explicitly to that specific religious experience intersubjective with Christ Jesus. He mentions a second set of categories that is concerned with the togetherness of the religious community, but does not explicitly advert to the Christian church. In noting a third set of categories, concerned with the God who is the source of religious experience, Lonergan explicitly mentions that he is drawing on the Christian tradition by identifying this source in trinitarian terms.[24] Other examples could be given, but Lonergan's intention is obvious. Without at all denying the proprium of Christian theology, and urging the need for specifically Christian theological categories, he quite simply has written about a notion of theology that would first establish a basis of dialogue and cooperation, before moving into the properly theological issues of what is unique in each religious tradition.

I have been discussing two aspects of the criticism voiced by Rahner about Lonergan's notion of method in theology. On the one hand, such criticism was perhaps unavoidable and to some degree legitimate in light of the ambiguity surrounding the placement of Lonergan's chapter on "functional specialties" within his Method in Theology. On the other hand, Lonergan in fact understands his method to be specifically theological, inasmuch as it is a reflection on religion. Further, there is the possibility, not worked out by Lonergan, of working out the categories appropriate to a specifically methodical and Christian theology - drawing upon the

477

CONC

Christian tradition and upon specifically Christian
religious experience. Finally, it was noted that
this latter task is assigned by Lonergan to Christian theologians, and it has been suggested that
Karl Rahner might be considered paradigmatic among
those theologians concerned with working out the
categories central to a specifically Christian theology.

In Rahner, then, there seems to be an example
of what Lonergan means by a theologian who takes a
methodical stance on religious, moral, and cognitional authenticity, and who objectifies this horizon, employing it as the normative and critical
foundation for mediating the Christian tradition to
the world of today. It is clear, however, that Rahner is chiefly concerned with the foundations of
theology as praxis - as concentrating on constructing the Christian tradition in the world of the
present. It is a key element in contemporary theology, yet it is but one of many theological tasks.
One of the main advantages of a methodological notion of theology is precisely to highlight the
uniqueness of each task, yet its need for further
completion. Not only does "foundations" presuppose
history and dialectic; as well, it is followed by
further specialties that relate theological praxis
to its concrete historical and cultural contexts.
This relatedness seems to dominate the thought of
Johann Metz, whom we may now briefly consider.

4. Metz, Zeitoffenheit, and Method

Johann Metz is not unaware of critical scholarship, or of evaluative reconstruction of the Christian tradition, or of religious experience and religious faith. Moreover, he perhaps is indebted to
his theological mentor, Karl Rahner, precisely for
his concern for a theology that truly is praxis.
To come immediately to what seems to be the main
difference between Metz and Rahner: the latter is
concerned especially with working out the foundations
of theology as praxis, while the former is concerned
especially with working out the communicative func-

tion of theology as praxis.

The distinction between "foundational" and "communicative" dimensions of praxis is adapted from Lonergan's methodology, and seems very useful in understanding the distinct concerns of Rahner and Metz. Both are concerned with praxis. Rahner tends to give attention to the Christian horizon that is the foundation of genuine Christian praxis in history; and, inevitably, Rahner finds himself involved as well in the doctrinal and systematic explicitation of the fundamental horizon. Metz, on the other hand, tends to operate in the opposite direction. He tends to give attention to the fact of concrete Christian praxis now functioning in history and society (his recent book is entitled "Faith in History and Society"); and inevitably Metz finds himself involved as well in the systematic, doctrinal, and foundational issues presupposed by such praxis.

This should not be taken to imply that Metz, any more than Pannenberg or Rahner, should be forced into some Lonerganian framework. At issue is the simple fact of three theologians all concerned with the same ingredients of a Christian theology, yet each choosing to stress one of these ingredients as "central." Lonergan's methodology tends to sharpen the concerns of each, while also indicating how history, evaluative dialectic, foundations, and communications might be integrated. Indeed, such integration is hinted by Rahner himself, in reference to the relation of his own work to that of Metz.[25]

To become more specific, Metz is a theological activist in the good sense of that phrase. He wants a theology that is concerned to make the concrete judgments of fact and of value that will constitute human history, that will undo its perennial bias towards inauthenticity, that will mediate the truth who is Christ to the concrete level of human societal living, even though this often means a theology in radical opposition to existing societal structures. But Metz is not only an activist. As

479

well, he is aware that societal living is greatly
influenced by what goes on in academic circles;
he knows that significant improvement on the level
of societal living, aiming at the Subjektwerden of
all mankind, demands as well a theology in touch
with those academic circles, in interdisciplinary
collaboration with science, scholarship, philosophy.
He is aware that traditional notions of theology,
and traditional theological language, are inadequate
in this context. And so he appeals for a renewal of
theology, along the lines sketched in Chapter One.

It is my own personal conviction that Metz has
concretized the meaning of Lonergan's functional
specialty, "communications," giving to that specialty a scope that goes far beyond Lonergan's own
brief methodological considerations. But Metz himself is quite aware of the need for a solidly "academic" approach to that which is presupposed by his
notion of theology. Lonergan himself will not be of
much use in contributing to a clarification of Erinnerung, Erzählung, Handeln, or Leiden in specifically
Christian categories. But Lonergan's work seems extremely relevant in pointing out the direction that
an academic grounding of Metz' work might take.
Metz' gefährliche Erinnerung is to be constituted by
the evaluative reconstruction of the Christian tradition, perhaps along the lines suggested by Wolfhart
Pannenberg. Metz' appeal to Nachfolge, Umkehr, Exodus, Metanoia, might receive its basic clarification
and foundation in the work of a Karl Rahner. The
content of Erzählung is to be determined by doctrinal
theologians and transposed by systematic theologians
in a manner that reveals at once the one truth who
is Christ and the plurality of manners in which this
one truth might legitimately be formulated.

Such is the basic challenge, and Lonergan has
contributed extensively to its basic clarification.
There seems to be a possibility, however remote,
that the apparent conflicts among theologians may be
more easily reconciled, while the real conflicts may

be at least brought to light. It remains, however, that Lonergan's proposal seems to contain a built-in impediment - one that may delay its acceptance for an almost indefinite period. The impediment centers on the ambiguity of the expression given by Lonergan to generalized empirical method, and to this topic we may turn in a final observation.

5. Some Final Observations

     I introduced the thought of Bernard Lonergan by relating his work to the current renewal of theology and, specifically, to the fundamental methodological questions being raised in this age of renewal. This was made more precise in Chapter One: the problem of pluralism in the mission of the church, the further pluralism of various specialties within theology, and the more fundamental pluralism of notions of theology itself. To illustrate this third type of pluralism, there was offered a very brief account of the meaning of theology for Wolfhart Pannenberg, Karl Rahner, and Johann Metz. In order to relate the concerns of these three theologians, there was a turn to the methodology of Lonergan, not in order to resolve theological questions, but in order to discover a systematic way of resolving theological questions. This implies that former ways of doing theology are inadequate; this is generally admitted in this age of renewal, but there are different opinions on just why this is so. Accordingly, Chapter Two considered Lonergan's account of the medieval theological achievement and of subsequent developments associated with Enlightenment and Neuzeit that called forth further development in theological reflection. Such development was not forthcoming, and so Chapter Three tried to present Lonergan's notion of the foundations upon which reflection on religion might occur in this new context. At root, such reflection will be a matter of clarifying the function of religion and religions in human living, and so there was mentioned the meaning of religious experience, religious faith, religious tradition and belief. Further, there was outlined Lonergan's notion of gener-

481

CONC

alized reflection on religion, whereby the human
subject comes to know himself or herself as religious. And finally in Chapter Three, attention
turned to the related specialized manners of reflecting on religion - the methods of history, of
dialectic, and of praxis.

Chapter Four offered Lonergan's account of
what these various methods might mean for theology.
Theology has its proper objects of investigation,
of course, but Lonergan suggests that a notion of
theology in terms of method, and not just in terms
of objects, will help theology to deal with the various types of pluralism that all too often leave
theologians working in isolation from one another,
if not also in fundamental disagreement with each
other. Lonergan, then, invited us to consider theology in terms of method and methods. This consideration enables us to distinguish further the various tasks of method as history, and Lonergan proposes that we understand these tasks as research,
interpretation, and history. To these was added
method as dialectic, that enables theologians to
carry out an evaluative reconstruction of the
Christian tradition. Such is theology in its first
phase, but Lonergan also would help theology in its
second phase of praxis. Such praxis is already a
concern of doctrinal, systematic, and pastoral theologians. But the difficult question in our own day
is the question of the foundation of such praxis.
We are to take a stand on the past Christian tradition, but that tradition is a mixture of inauthenticity and authenticity. To appeal to various doctrines such as the inspiration of Scripture, the
fact of revelation, or the infallible teaching of
the church is only to beg the question and to raise
the more fundamental issue of the basis or foundation on which such appeals are made. For Lonergan,
the answer lies in appealing to religious, moral,
and cognitional authenticity; here, Lonergan recalls
the word of St. Paul:

A man who is not spiritual refuses what
belongs to the Spirit of God; it is folly

482

to him; he cannot grasp it, because it
needs to be judged in the light of the
Spirit. A man gifted with the Spirit
can judge the worth of everything, but
is not himself subject to judgement by
his fellow-men.[26]

The functional specialty, foundations, is concerned with objectifying this spiritual horizon
that grounds and justifies one's choice of some doctrines and the rejection of others. For Lonergan,
this is theological method as praxis in its foundational function. And on those foundations Lonergan
proceeds to distinguish further dimensions of theology as praxis in its doctrinal, systematic, and
communicative functions. In this fashion, Lonergan
draws attention to the actual methodological unity
of theological reflection, and Chapter Four concluded by discussing various aspects of this unity.
Finally, the concluding chapter gave explicit attention to theology in its communicative function,
in order to relate theological reflection to the
broader contexts of church and society.

As noted in the Introduction, the aim of the
present work is a systematic presentation of Lonergan's thought. It has tried to set forth in an
ordered manner the main lines of Lonergan's proposal for a methodological notion of theology.
Without doubt, there is a further need for a truly
critical evaluation of Lonergan's project, both in
its general features as well as in specific elements.
Such critical work lies beyond the scope of the present dissertation, but perhaps it would be useful
to suggest lines along which such evaluation might
occur. Accordingly, there will be discussed here
three interrelated topics: (1) Lonergan and the
philosophic tradition; (2) the language of "interiority"; and (3) the notions of "authenticity" and
"conversion." In the fourth section, there will be
added a note suggesting the further development of
Lonergan's proposal by working out a symbolic intentionality.

(1) Lonergan and the Philosophic Tradition

Chapter Two of the present work included an account of Lonergan's understanding of the historical background to the problem of pluralism in contemporary theology. Lonergan maintains that there has been taking place a process of increasing specialization: disciplines once integrated within a metaphysically-grounded system have become autonomous and, in addition, a pre-critical notion of history has been largely replaced by an autonomous critical scholarship. Lonergan offers this notion as a model, hopefully useful in interpreting the actual course of events in academic circles, especially since the medieval period. As such, the theme of "specialization," and its underlying grounding in an increasingly differentiated consciousness, is indeed useful in interpreting the contemporary isolation of academic disciplines from one another – a fact that forms the background of the identity-problems currently experienced by theology.

More specifically, Lonergan's account of the autonomy of empirical science and the autonomy of historical scholarship is highly useful in interpreting the reasons for the fragmented worldview of our twentieth century. With regard, however, to Lonergan's account of the autonomy of philosophy, there is need for a brief observation.

In the main, one can agree with Lonergan's account of the dilemma faced by modern philosophy as both empirical science and critical historical scholarship moved towards an autonomy explicitly repudiating reliance on metaphysical principles. Further, Lonergan's own "critique" of modern philosophy chose to concentrate on the single issue of cognitional theory, thereby prescinding from other issues discussed in the modern philosophic heritage. Again, Lonergan acknowledges his debt to this heritage – not just for a clarification of the philosophic problems, but as well for the conceptual apparatus made available by philosophers

484

in recent centuries.

It remains, however, that despite this acknowledgement by Lonergan of his debt to the philosophic
heritage, there is apparently no explicit acknowledgement by Lonergan of his debt precisely in the realm
of cognitional theory. He gives due recognition to
the critical realism of Aquinas; he offers a keen
analysis of the breakdown of that realism in concep-
tualist, empiricist, and idealist philosophies; but
there is missing in Lonergan's writings an account
of the "genuine" philosophic heritage that embodied
critical realism from Aquinas to the present. Without such an account, one easily might get the impression of total discontinuity between Aquinas and Lonergan. But had such an account been offered, Lonergan's own work would be both enriched and more readily intelligible to contemporary philosophers and
theologians.

At issue here is simply an appeal for a more
nuanced understanding of the movement referred to
by Lonergan as the search by philosophy for its
proper function in modern thought. Lonergan is correct in his contention that there is not a philosophic "tradition" in the same sense in which there
is a scientific tradition: philosophy is always to
be grounded more in personally generated knowledge
than in the indirect verification of belief, so that
one properly speaks of a philosophic heritage rather
than of a philosophic tradition. At the same time,
however, Lonergan's own understanding of philosophy
in terms of generalized empirical method would
likely be more readily discussed and debated if it
could be more closely set in some sort of continuity
with post-medieval philosophy. As it is, Lonergan's
notion of philosophy all too easily can have the
appearance of sheer novelty - continuous perhaps
with the genius of Aquinas, but dialectically opposed to the entirety of modern cognitional theory.
Such in fact is not the case, but the element of
continuity has yet to be shown.

CONC

(2)   The Language of Interiority

Chapter Three of the present work drew attention to Lonergan's conviction that both the type of
systematic thinking based on a metaphysics as well
as the type found in modern empirical science are
inadequate to ground the sort of systematic thinking that should characterize philosophy and theology. Lonergan thus proposes a generalized empirical method as a third manner of systematic thinking,
wherein the basic terms denote the conscious and intentional operations that occur in human knowing,
and the basic relations denote the conscious dynamism that leads from some operations to others. The
basic terms and relations, then, are not metaphysical but cognitional.

Lonergan acknowledges that his own formulation
of this third manner of systematic thinking has un-
dergone a transition. In an earlier stage he employed the terminology proper to a faculty psychology; more recently he employs the terminology proper
to an intentionality analysis. Whereas a faculty
psychology tends to presuppose a grounding in metaphysics, an intentionality analysis is grounded
squarely in the data of consciousness - in what Lonergan refers to as the realm of interiority. Lonergan offers an example of this shift to interiority
in reference to the manner in which an older and a
newer theology speak of inner experience or of God·

> Where we distinguish four realms of
> meaning, namely, common sense, theory,
> interiority, and transcendence, an older
> theology distinguished only two, common
> sense and theory, under the Aristotelian
> designation of the priora quoad nos and
> priora quoad se. Hence, the older the-
> ology, when it spoke of inner experience
> or of God, either did so within the
> realm of common sense - and then its
> speech was shot through with figure and
> symbol - or else it did so in the realm

> of theory -- and then its speech was bas-
> ically metaphysical. One consequence of
> this difference has already been noted.
> The older theology conceived sanctifying
> grace as an entitative habit, absolutely
> supernatural, infused into the essence
> of the soul. On the other hand, because
> we acknowledge interiority as a distinct
> realm of meaning, we can begin with a
> description of religious experience, ack-
> nowledge a dynamic state of being in love
> without restrictions, and later identify
> this state with the state of sanctifying
> grace.[27]

The problem with this shift to interiority is
not with the shift itself but with the language employed by Lonergan to denote this shift. A shift
to a new realm of meaning would seem to call for
the development of a new linguistic structure. To
leave the realm of theory (as tied to the data of
sense) and to move to the realm of interiority (as
tied to the data of consciousness) may of course
occur by giving a new "interior" meaning to current
"theoretical" terms, but such a procedure seems to
invite endless ambiguity. In a word, a shift to interiority, as advocated by Lonergan and others, needs
a new technical language. For Lonergan, this means
a properly philosophic language, corresponding to
the realm of conscious interiority with which philosophy is concerned.

Lonergan himself acknowledges the existence of
this problem,[28] and readily grants that such a technical language, even if available, would have to be
constantly shifting and changing, in order to adapt
to the changing mentality of successive generations.
In the absence of such a technical language, Lonergan has sought to draw on more literary terms, being careful to state precisely what he means by the
terms employed and the new meaning that he has given
to these terms. To take but a single example, referred to in the passage quoted a moment ago, Loner-

CONC

gan begins with a discussion of "religious experience," and proceeds to identify this with a dynamic
state of being in love without restrictions. And,
from the presentation in Chapter Three, it is clear
that Lonergan assigns a very technical meaning to
the word "experience" - a meaning very much rooted
in conscious interiority.

Lonergan's procedure is perhaps inevitable,
given the absence of a "language of interiority"
that is clearly distinguished from the language employed by common sense and by metaphysical or scientific theory. Again, once the reader has "mastered" Lonergan's conceptual system; once the reader
has effected in himself or herself the self-appropriation that gives old words new meanings; then the
consistency of Lonergan's own terminology is apparent. But nevertheless the limitations of such an
approach have to be emphasized. Perhaps the best
way of putting this is to pose the question concerning the conditions of the possibility of the shift
to interiority, of self-appropriation, of a "heightening of consciousness." To answer what Lonergan
says is the fundamental question, "What am I doing
when I am knowing?" demands a linguistic structure;
one can accept the structure suggested by Lonergan,
that tends to give familiar words new meanings, but
invariably this approach must be but the preliminary (and perhaps necessary) stage in the development of a language of interiority.

I mention this problem, not only because such
phrases as "religious experience" are highly ambiguous in the English language, but also because
of the enormous difficulties encountered in trying
to explain Lonergan's thought to a non-English-
speaking cultural community. For an illustration
of this, it is enough to compare the English and
German versions of the same passage from Lonergan's
writings: the former is readily intelligible to a
reader who is both Anglo-Saxon and versed in Lonergan's thought; the latter is so replete with philosophic overtones as to invite incomprehension.

For example, compare the following passages:

> Human knowing, then, is not experience alone, not understanding alone, not judgment alone; it is not a combination of only experience and understanding, or of only experience and judgment, or of only understanding and judgment; finally, it is not something totally apart from experience, understanding, and judgment. Inevitably, one has to regard an instance of human knowing, not as this or that operation, but as a whole whose parts are operations. It is a structure and, indeed, a materially dynamic structure.[29]

> Das menschliche Erkennen ist also nicht nur Erfahrung, nicht nur Verstehen, nicht nur Urteil; es ist keine Verbindung nur aus Erfahrung und Verstehen oder nur aus Erfahrung und Urteil oder nur aus Verstehen und Urteil; und schliesslich ist es nicht etwas, das völlig abgesondert von Erfahrung, Verstehen und Urteil liegt. Der Vorgang des menschlichen Erkennens ist also notwendigerweise nicht als diese oder jene Handlung zu betrachten, sondern als ein Ganzes, dessen einzelne Teile Handlungen sind. Er ist eine Struktur, genauer: eine materielldynamische Struktur.[30]

In order to overcome the limitations of a direct translation of Lonergan's writings from English to another language, there would be needed expressions of self-appropriation that begin from (utilize) these other linguistic worlds; instead of translation, Lonergan's project should be transposed by thinkers from various cultural backgrounds. But this seems to be just a second-best solution, and in any case would only serve to highlight further the need for a technical language of philosophic interiority. Lonergan

cannot be criticized for failing to invent such a
language, but one might have expected from him a
fuller account of the need for such language if
the realm of interiority is to be indeed the basic
source of terms and relations in philosophy and
theology.

The ambiguity of such words as "experience,"
"understanding," and "judgment" tends to clarify
the reasons why thinkers like Lonergan and Rahner,
who begin from the realm of philosophic and religious interiority, often are accused of "subjectivism." To take but a single example, Pannenberg
criticizes Lonergan's combination of "authority
and subjective decision."[31] A careful reading of
Pannenberg's remarks, however, reveals the main
problem to be terminological, inasmuch as the commonsense meaning of "experience," "understanding,"
and "judgment" is in fact heavily "subjective" and
quite arbitrary. Chapter Three of the present
work indicated that Lonergan employs those terms
in a technical sense, and manages quite well to
get beyond the arbitrary world of privatized subject. Nonetheless, although Lonergan has employed
ordinary language in a technical sense, rooted in
intentionality analysis, there remains the probability that such language will be assumed to have
a commonsense meaning and, on the basis of that
assumption, to be both arbitrary and subjective.

The need, then, seems to be for a new philosophic Begrifflichkeit. As well, however, there
is a similar problem in Lonergan's discussion of
moral consciousness, and to this problem we may
now turn.

(3) "Authenticity" and "Conversion"

Despite the linguistic limitations of Lonergan's thought, there is a persuasive validity in
his shift to interiority and in his insistence on
the cognitional, moral, and religious authenticity
of philosophers and theologians. Specifically,

"authenticity" is indispensable to theology: both
the authenticity of one's inherited tradition, as
well as the authenticity of those responsible for
reflecting on this tradition and carrying it forward. Chapter Four sketched Lonergan's notion of
theology, and tried to highlight his concern for a
theology that includes both a dialectical evaluation of the Christian tradition as well as a foundational stance on personal authenticity. As functional specialties, both dialectic and foundations
are indeed structurally integrated within Lonergan's
method in theology; perhaps one of Lonergan's main
achievements is his effort to articulate explicitly
the methodological operations central to both dialectic and foundations. However, one wonders to
what extent the formulation of these operations in
terms of "authenticity" and "conversion" actually
obscures the reality behind these terms.

Both "authenticity" and "conversion," as explained and employed by Lonergan, are notions that
enrich philosophic and theological reflection.
Again, while both are drawn from ordinary language,
Lonergan has given them a technical precision that
avoids commonsense moralizing, spiritualizing, or
mysticizing. It remains, however, that both notions are somewhat removed from the modern phil--
osophic heritage - a heritage that Lonergan himself
understands to be most recently concerned especially
with the meaning of moral consciousness. Lonergan
has chosen to express his own concern in a language
that speaks of authenticity and conversion, and he
is careful to explain what he means by these terms;
such is a legitimate procedure, but it has the result of isolating Lonergan's thought from the mainstream of contemporary philosophic and theological
reflection. That reflection is focused on the notion of "autonomy," a notion that has technical
meaning, even if it lacks technical precision. One
may choose to abandon the notion of "autonomy" because it is so tied to erroneous philosophic views,
and so one turns to notions like "authenticity" and
"conversion." But perhaps the happier procedure is

to set the notion of autonomy within the context of a critical realism, and then move on to show how that notion demands, not atheism or agnosticism, but religion and theology. Such seems to be the intention, for example, of theologians recently striving to develop an autonome Moral.

(4) Symbolic Intentionality

These concluding observations have, with the greatest brevity, been drawing attention to the difficulty of relating Lonergan's thought to current philosophy and theology. The main problem seems to lie in Lonergan's linguistic structure. He is advocating a shift to a new realm of meaning (philosophic interiority) yet, in the absence of a technical philosophic language and given the overt inadequacy of faculty psychology, Lonergan is forced to rely on a somewhat literary language that is all too often ambiguous. Lonergan indeed is careful to state precisely what he means by his technical use of literary terms; but this procedure tends to set up something of a "closed Lonerganian system": ordinary language is given a new technical meaning, but the technical meaning is obvious only to those who have begun from a basis in the words chosen by Lonergan from the ordinary language. Such a threat of a closed system is certainly contrary to Lonergan's own intentions. He would be the first to insist on the priority of mental operations as the reality behind the original meaningfulness of any language, whether ordinary or technical. But for Lonergan to formulate conscious intentionality in linguistic terms that already possess an ordinary or semi-technical meaning is to invite endless ambiguity and misinterpretation. In a word, it is quite possible to acknowledge the soundness of Lonergan's basic project, but for this project to prosper and bear fruit, there is needed far more attention to the manner in which generalized empirical method is formulated. To put the problem in its simplest terms: Lonergan distinguishes cognitional theory, epistemology, and metaphysics; he holds (correctly)

that the fundamental discipline is cognitional theory; he has repudiated the terminology of a metaphysical faculty psychology; but has he not beeh
forced to express his cognitional theory in basically epistemological terms, admittedly giving those
terms a new meaning? Perhaps Lonergan had no alternative in this regard, but it seems that it is here
that we meet the limitations of his achievement.
Until those limitations are overcome, until there
is a language appropriate to human conscious and
intentional operations, Lonergan's project will not
bear the fruit it deserves.

The problem is immense. To build a new language is the work, not of the individual in isolation,
but of a community in communication. Nor is the direction of a solution at all evident. Lonergan himself seems aware of the need for a distinct and unambiguous language of interiority, but he is equally
aware of the philosophic errors that so easily infiltrate human thought and twist the meaning of human words. Nonetheless, it should be mentioned that
in recent years Lonergan has turned increasingly to
the symbolic dimension of human living, perhaps in
order to ground the needed linguistic structure for
conscious intentionality. If a faculty psychology
tends to rely on a metaphysical system, the language
of intentionality analysis seems wedded to epistemological reflection. Perhaps for this reason Lonergan, in his post-Method in Theology phase, has tended
to complement intentionality analysis with what could
be called an explicit symbolic intentionality. He
has not yet offered any extensive account of this interest in the symbolic dimension of human living and
thinking, but perhaps a few remarks could here be
made on certain dimensions of what is involved.[32]

Firstly, it should be noted that such explicit
symbolic intentionality is to be distinguished from
the symbolic apprehension and expression native to
common sense. The latter is spontaneous, while explicit symbolic intentionality is "an academic subject" - a deliberate and reflexive effort to con-

CONC

struct a symbolic world appropriate to the realm
of conscious interiority.

Secondly, one is tempted to direct attention
to the work of Johann Metz. Perhaps Metz is trying to formulate linguistically the broad lines of
just such a symbolic intentionality. One senses
that this underpins Metz' project for a fundamental
theology, but Metz' specific proposals are in need
of careful study and further refinement.

Thirdly, it seems important to distinguish
three distinct aspects of symbolic intentionality.
There is the literal intentionality of symbol, corresponding to the pre-linguistic pointing to what
is signified: this is often called the signatic
intentionality of symbols, their traditional or
conventional meaning. There is an ideological intentionality that is the spontaneous, commonsense
interpretation of conventional or traditional symbols. Finally, there is a teleological ("eschatological") intentionality that in some way already
is given or promised in the actual presence of what
is symbolized - something very close to what the
Christian tradition refers to as anamnesis.

Fourthly, the notion of symbolic intentionality as teleologic tends to move linguistic expression from an epistemological to a cognitional context. This means that expression is not "from below" - from attentiveness to inquiry and judgment
- but "from above": from an all-encompassing context that we do not choose but that tends rather
to choose us. The symbols relevant to human living are "pre-given": to them we respond, and our
response is what Lonergan and W. C. Smith describe
in terms of total conviction. This is just another
way of stating that, prior to belief, there is the
existential horizon of the believer who expresses
himself or herself in symbols before, if ever, he
or she knows what the symbols literally mean.

Finally, and in summary, a turn to symbolic

494

intentionality in its teleological dimension would seem to provide the basis for a language of interiority, as demanded by Lonergan's assertion that we are entering a third stage of meaning. Admittedly, we are only at the threshold of developing such symbolic intentionality, but there exists the hope that it will eventually provide a conceptual apparatus that at once preserves yet goes beyond the achievement both of a faculty psychology and of an intentionality analysis.

To the extent that the foregoing critical observations are accurate, and to the extent that they lead to refinements in what Lonergan is suggesting, to that extent will Lonergan's basic project be furthered. His attempt to shift theology to a new key - to the realms of interiority and of transcendence - yields a vastly enriched account of the human person and of the person's approach to God. It is a shift that can give new life to theological reflection by revealing the person's native orientation to the divine and by grounding a theology that takes its stand on the reality of this orientation. In some such manner theology can work to make the potential presence of God in modern culture a palpable reality.

INTRODUCTION

FOOTNOTES

(Numbers in parentheses refer to my bibliography)

1   See Geffré (128).

2   See Lonergan (6e), p.63. Also Kasper (163b), pp.1-10.

3   Kasper (167), p.258. A longer assessment of the Tübingen
     School is offered by Kasper (161), pp.9-32. A standard
     work on the subject remains Geiselmann (129). Most
     recently, Reinhardt (236).

4   A representative figure of this phase is Joseph Kleutgen;
     see his five-volume work, Die Theologie der Vorzeit (173),
     especially the fifth volume that presents his notion of
     theology. For a brief survey and bibliography, see Schoof
     (250), pp.30-44.

5   See Aubert (81).

6   To a great extent this phase received its reflective focus
     in questions centering on the meaning of the church and on
     the Christian approach to being-in-the-world; see Aubert
     (81), pp.33-39.

7   Kasper (166), p.197.

8   Despite this distinction I perhaps should stress that
     Lonergan is very much a "theologian", as will be
     explained in this Introduction.

9   See Bourke (96). A brief survey and additional biblio-
     graphy may be found in Tracy (30), pp.24-31.

10   See Lonergan (1). Much of the biographical information
     on Lonergan that I have included in this section is from
     his article, "Insight Revisited" (6r).

11   See Lonergan (4), p.107.

12   See Lonergan (2).

13   See Auer (83). On the relevance of this existentialist
     approach of Aquinas to contemporary theology, see Oeing-
     Hanhoff (210).

14   See Lonergan (2), p.ix.

15   So Lonergan, in his Epilogue to Verbum, explains his purpose
     in writing Verbum by reference to the challenge issued by
     Pope Leo to Catholic scholars, vetera novis augere et per-
     ficere. For Lonergan, the basic task is the determination
     and evaluation of the vetera, for only then is one in a
     position to transpose the vetera to the present day.

16 See Lonergan, *Verbum*; the entire book rests on this fact, but for an example see p.79: "...grasp the nature of your acts of understanding and you have the key to the whole of Thomist psychology. Indeed, you also have what Aquinas considered the key to Aristotelian psychology...".

17 For a brief account see Lonergan (6e).

18 It could be said that Lonergan was attempting to uncover the foundations of human historicity (Geschichtlichkeit) in the invariant structure of the conscious and operating human subject.

19 See Lonergan (3).

20 So Lonergan (6r), p.268.

21 Ibid., p.269.

22 See Lonergan (3), pp.xvii-xxx.

23 For Lonergan's brief description of this transcendental method, contrasting it with that of Otto Muck and comparing it with Scholastic and Kantian usage, see (4), pp.13-14, footnote 4.

24 Ibid., pp.24-25.

25 See Lonergan (6r) for this and the following data.

26 Ibid., pp.264-265.

27 Lonergan agrees with Coreth's assessment, that what has come from Maréchal is not a school but a movement, not a ready-made set of opinions repeated in unison by members of a uniform group, but a basic line of thought that has developed in several different manners. See Lonergan (5m), especially pages 203 and 220.

28 See Lonergan (6r), pp.276-277, as well as his Foreword in Tyrrell (17), pp.ix-x, for this contrast between faculty psychology and intentionality analysis.

29 See Lonergan (5n).

30 See Klibansky (174).

31 This introduction to Lonergan's doctoral work is on file at the Lonergan Center (Regis College) in Toronto.

32 See Tracy (30), pp.270-278, who lists these Latin writings.

33 This is simply Lonergan's approach to "historical consciousness", described in the important essay, "Theology in its New Context" in (6), especially pp.60-61. See also his two initial statements (5ð,5p).

34   I shall return to this distinction in Chapter Four. In
      the words of Kasper, one first distinguishes among the
      various traditions in the church, then works out an
      interpretative understanding of them: (170), esp. pp.
      213-215.

35   It is an effort to ease the tensions in theology between
      exegetes and historians on the one hand, and doctrinal
      and systematic theologians on the other; see Vorgrimler
      (269) and Kasper (161), pp.187-196.

36   See Tracy (30), pp.24-27, who notes the need for such work.

37   Directly or indirectly, the following discuss Lonergan's
      interpretation of medieval Scholasticism: Burrell (100),
      (99); Crowe (105), (106); Lamb (48); Langlois (24); Richard
      (238); Stewart (24); and Torrance (27).

38   See Sala (29) on Lonergan and Kant; also Lamb (28) on
      Lonergan and Dilthey. Other comparative studies remain
      unpublished.

39   For a bibliography to 1970, see Tracy (30). Later works are
      included in my own bibliography.

40   See Tracy (30).

41   See especially (25), (26), and (27).

FTN/I

I. THE PROBLEM OF PLURALISM IN THEOLOGY

FOOTNOTES

1   Lonergan (9), p.37.

2   See Barden (86), p.32. Also Berger and Luckmann (87),
     esp. pp.1-18. For the origins and development of the
     notion of common sense see Gadamer (126), pp.19-39.
     Lonergan's most complete analysis of common sense is
     found in Insight, esp. pp.173-244.

3   See Glazik (132) and also c.II from "The Church Today"
     of the Second Vatican Council.

4   See the Commission's report (152), pp.52-60; in the same
     volume see Nemeshegyi's application to Asia, pp.180-203.

5   See ibid., p.55; also Glazik (132), pp.117-126.

6   Specialization is not just the result of trying to meet
     the challenge of cultural pluralism; still, the awareness
     by theologians of cultural pluralism tends to call forth a
     greater attention to the fact of specialization and its
     need, as will be indicated in the next section.

7   See Mennekes (193), p.114, where he notes the views of
     Berger and Luckmann (88). See also Laszlo (182), pp.5-6,
     where he refers to Frankl's description of the existential
     vacuum. More recently, Ludwig (188). Also Lonergan (5p).

8   See Chapter Two of the present work.

9   See Hahn (141) and Stuhlmacher (264). Also Lehmann (183),
     pp.54-93.

10   See Kasper (163b), pp.45-65. Also Küng (177).

11   This is a dominant theme in the more recent writings of
     Karl Rahner; for example, see Rahner (230a), pp.18-25.

12   For an overview see Weinzierl (272).

13   See Ebeling (113). Also see vol. 46 of Concilium (1969)
     that is devoted entirely to articles on the current
     transitional phase of fundamental theology.

14   Pannenberg (214), p.137.

15   For what immediately follows see Pannenberg (219).

16   See Pannenberg (215a), pp.7-26, where he clearly indicates
     that his main concern is for the Wissenschaftlichkeit of
     theology.

500

17 See my bibliography (213) to (221) for the writings of Pannenberg that I have drawn upon.

18 See Pannenberg (214), pp.91-114.

19 Ibid., p.101. Also his "Stellungnahme..." (220), pp.347-349.

20 See Pannenberg (214), esp. pp.144-146.

21 See Pannenberg (213), pp.226ff; such is the "Vorgriff der Vollkommenheit", a basic notion in his thought. Also Pannenberg (215a), pp.286f., and 311f.

22 See esp. Pannenberg (220), pp.343-347; (218), p.169; (213), p.227; and (215), pp.299-348.

23 Pannenberg (220), pp.344-345.

24 See ibid., p.351.

25 For example see Rahner (233), pp.97ff: this is his essay on methodology in theology, that appears in Vol.XI of the English "Theological Investigations".

26 Ibid., pp.95-113 for what immediately follows here.

27 Ibid., p.98.

28 See esp. pp.28-34.

29 There would seem to be several different ways of answering the question regarding what is fundamental in Rahner's theology. A theoretical answer would identify the basis in the central category of Rahner's theology, and I agree with van der Heijden (267) that Rahner's main category is the Selbstmitteilung Gottes. A variation on this would further specify the category as christological, for in Christ the Selbstmitteilung Gottes to the human subject achieves its fullness: thus Eicher (116) and (117), pp.347ff. As well, one can shift from categories to the way (method) in which Rahner arrived at the categories, or the way (method) that any one of us can reach categorial expression. With this shift one speaks of the process from religious experience of divine mystery to the objectification of this experience by drawing on the expressions of the Christian tradition. Rahner himself suggests this approach (his "first level of reflection"), and I believe this dimension pervades the work of Fischer (124). While I do not disagree with the general theoretical findings of both van der Heijden and Eicher, I find the work of Fischer to be more in line with Rahner's notion of theology. See Waldenfels (271) and Lehmann (184).

30 Rahner (229), pp.117-118. Eicher (119) suggests that Rahner's notion of "Erfahrung" is ambiguous. I would hope that Lonergan's distinction between experience and self-knowledge will help clarify this ambiguity: see Chapter Three.

30a See Rahner (230a), pp.61-64, where he distinguishes transcendental and a posteriori knowledge of God; the former is the knowledge of immediate experience and is pre-reflexive, prior to questioning what is experienced; also Rahner (233), pp.30-31, 43-44, 78.

31 See Rahner (230a), pp.54-96; (229); and (231), pp.105-109.

32 Note the structure of Rahner's Grundkurs, that moves from the fact of religious experience towards the interpretation of that experience in Christian terms.

33 Rahner (233), pp.148-149; see ibid., pp.90-95.

34 To date there has been no extensive study of Rahner's ecclesiology. For some preliminary reflections see O'Donovan (209). I suspect that Rahner's understanding of "church" is co-extensive with the community of those who are responding to God's gift of love in experience of mystery, whether this experience has a Christian focus or a focus in some other religious tradition; see Rahner (234).

35 See Rahner's own bibliography in (233), p.48, footnote 13.

36 Rahner (233), p.48. Also ibid., pp.73-74, 91-92, 167-168; and (230a), p.14: Rahner's first-level is neither Christian Existenz nor theoretical reflection on that Existenz, but rather the insight into the difference between these two; see ibid., pp.27-28, where he speaks of the "Spannung zwischen ursprünglichem Wissen und seinem Begriff", with its double movement of linguistic expression and withdrawl towards communion with the reality being expressed.

37 Rahner (233), p.91.

38 Ibid., p.92.

39 Rahner, in Fischer (124), pp.404-405.

40 See ibid., p.409. This distinction between religious experience and theology is found also in Rahner (230a), p.28.

41 Rahner (233), pp.114-115 (emphasis mine).

42 See Metz (194a), p.25, and (196).

43 See Metz (194a), pp.25-26, 42.

44 See Metz, ibid., p.14; and (196).

45 See Metz (194a), pp.5-8, 14.

46 Ibid., pp.14-15.

47 See ibid., pp.13-28; Metz notes the achievement of the Tübingen School, however, as a genuine attempt to come to terms with the problems of Enlightenment (though for some reason Metz assigns this achievement to the end of the eighteenth century! - p.15).

48 See _ibid._, pp.20-25, and also Metz (198), (200), and (201), where he stresses the need for a truly academic theology.

49 Metz (194a), p.26.

50 See _ibid._, pp.44-74, for what immediately follows in my text: the foundations of theology are to be found in the praxis of the present. This interpretation of Metz is shared by Lamb (28), pp.38-39.

51 Metz (194a), p.54.

52 _Ibid._, p.55.

53 See ibid., p.49.

54 See _ibid._, p.3, 104-119, and 181-194.

55 See _ibid._, pp.152-157, 181-194.

56 See my footnote 48 in this chapter.

57 See Metz (194a) for the critique of historical reason, especially pp. 191ff.

58 This is clear from Metz' concern for the "Subjekt-werden" of all people, described by him in cc. II and III of (194a).

59 For example see Eicher (117), pp.460-464, and 433-439; further, see Eicher's article (118), pp.36-38. Also Schilson (247), pp.90-100; Lamb (28), 21-38 and (180), pp.165-171.

60 See Eicher (117), pp. 419-421 and (118), pp.34-36. Also Wenisch (273); and Schilson (247), pp.80-89.

61 See Kasper (168), pp.57-60; and Oeing-Hanhoff (210), pp.253ff.

62 See Schmithals (249). Juxtaposition and compromise seem often to be the initial stage in the process of reception; see Grillmeier (137).

63 See Seckler (257); and Eicher (117), pp.483-543.

64 Such derivation should not be confused with classicist deductivism; the former is simply an application of some central notion to various areas of theological reflection.

65 This spirit seems to have pervaded the liberal and so-called modernist theologies of recent times. It is to be distinguished from the legitimate concerns of much secularization theology.

66 See Copleston on Feuerbach (104), Vol.7, Part 2, pp.61-62, regarding Feuerbach's efforts to substitute anthropology for theology.

67 The word "sacralism" is my own invention.

68 Again, I am only pointing to a possible trend, and thus am
    suggesting something of a model. A dialectical examination
    would be needed to discern if any given theological system
    or viewpoint were guilty of such "sacralism", or, on the
    other hand, were re-emphasizing the legitimate sacral and
    religious dimensions of theology, perhaps against secularism.

69 Gnostic tendencies or "enthusiasm" are ever-recurrent in
    religious matters. They seem to mix religious experience
    with common nonsense, and highlight the need for a truly
    critical theology. Such gnostic tendencies seem to arise
    whenever there is a new differentiation of consciousness
    or specialized horizon operative in Christianity: the
    creation of a new group is often accompanied by rejection
    from those who do not understand the new ways, and these
    latter simply turn to simpler living.

70 See Lonergan (4), pp.97-99, on former varieties.

71 My aim in presenting this and other "solutions" is merely
    to offer a model that might be useful in developing a
    notion of theology that avoids exclusive attention to only
    one element.

II. BACKGROUND: FROM MEDIEVAL THEOLOGY
TO THE NEW STUDY OF RELIGION
FOOTNOTES

1   Lonergan (6h), p.109.

2   There are broad lines of similarity between Lonergan's scheme of historical process based on specialization, and Schulz' study of modern culture (253).

3   Lonergan (12).

4   Ibid., p.165; this passage is central to Lonergan.

5   Ibid., p.167. Also Lonergan (4), pp.235-237, on the meaning of "horizon"; and Ryan (244).

6   Lonergan (12), p.167; also (4), pp.27-30.

7   See Lonergan (9), pp.27-28; and (4), p.327.

8   See Lonergan (4), p.139; also Kasper (161), p.222.

9   See Lonergan (12), p.177.

10 Metz too suggests we analyze the stages in the history of theology according to theology's interaction with its cultural contexts: (199), columns 64-65.

11 See Lonergan (12), pp.177-179, and (4), p.138.

12 Lonergan (12), p.177.

13 Note that Lonergan's doctoral work examined this emergence of systematic meaning in Christianity, centering on the problem of reconciling grace and freedom.

14 Lonergan (4), p.138; also (1), (2), and (8) treat this development fully; in shorter form: (6b), (6q). Further, the work of Congar (103) and Harnack (143) is useful, as is that of Ebeling (112) and Beumer (90).

15 Common sense is richly differentiated, and Lonergan notes it can use a rich number of tools like myth, saga, legend, apocalypse, typology: (4), p.306.

16 Lonergan (3), p.177. The relevant distinction here is that between language and meaning: see Lonergan (8), p.vii; also Ricoeur/Jüngel (155).

17 Such is generally known as the "transformation" or "re-formulation" of canonical biblical texts to a new level of thought and speech, or to a new cultural context. See Stock (262). On narrative theology see Kasper (168),

esp. pp.57-60; <u>Concilium</u> (1976), No.5; Metz (194a);
Jüngel (154), pp.415ff. A recent study of Lonergan's
thought as related to narrative is J. Haught (144).

18   On reconstructing the common sense of another, see
     Lonergan (18), pp.87-89; Gadamer (126), pp.267-274.
     On the adaptation evident in scriptural writings, see
     Lonergan (4), 305-307; (10), p.23; Frör (125), pp.71-78;
     Lohfink (185), pp.18-26; (186).

19   See Lonergan (10), pp.23-24.

20   See <u>ibid.</u>, pp.24-25, and reference there given. Allegory
     seems to provide a transitional phase from commonsense to
     systematic thinking; see Gruber (139).

21   See Grillmeier (136) for a presentation and bibliography.

22   See my footnote 14 of this chapter.

23   See Kasper (162a), pp.208-213 (ET: 175-179).

24   <u>Ibid.</u>, pp.212-213.

25   See <u>ibid.</u>, pp.209-210.

26   Lonergan (8), pp.136-137. It would be fair to say that the
     course of the debate on hellenization attended, in a first
     phase, only to the trinitarian question; in a second phase
     to both the trinitarian and theological questions (Kasper
     and others); and, in Lonergan, to the hermeneutical
     question as grounding both other questions.

27   See Lonergan (6b), p.23.

28   See Lonergan (8), pp.1-17.

29   Lonergan (6b), p.22, where he refers to the claims of
     Leslie Dewart.

30   See Lonergan (6q) and (15). Durrant (110) reaches the same
     conclusion as Lonergan regarding Augustine's imprecise
     notion of person.

31   On the limitations of logic see Lonergan (3), pp.573-577;
     on Pelagianism see Pelikan (224), pp.278-292.

32   See Hilary's <u>De Synodis</u>, PL 10.

33   Clearly, orthodox doctrine may be found in non-systematic
     or symbolic expression, esp. in worship texts; see Pelikan
     (224), p.339, and Barden (26).

34   "Autonomous" here does not mean "independent" but rather
     "distinct"; see Lonergan (9), pp.50-51 and (4), 311-312.
     The main question prompting this move into metaphysics was
     the Byzantine discussion of <u>enhypostasia</u> and <u>anhypostasia</u>:
     see Lonergan (4), p.308, and the work of Evans there cited.

35 For example, see Lonergan (12); and Congar (103), cols. 347-410 on Christianity's reception of Aristotle and the corresponding shift from Platonic categories.

36 Lonergan (12), p.178. Also Seckler (256).

37 See Congar (103), column 354.

38 See for example Lonergan (4), pp.305-312.

39 See ibid.

40 Ibid., pp.278-279.Also Congar (103), cols.366-374, and Beumer (90), pp.71-72.

41 See Lonergan (10), pp.27-28, and (4), p.138.

42 See Lonergan (4), p.309.

43 See Congar (103), columns 251-252.

44 See Lonergan (1), pp.6-9, and (3), p.528. For Anselm's view of his relation to Augustine see the preface of his Mono- logion (p.28, ed. Schmitt); also Roques (242), pp.143-293.

45 See Lonergan (1), p.8. For a summary of Abaelard's position see Gilson (131), pp.3-30, and Congar (103), cols.366-367.

46 See Lonergan (1), pp.11-13. Also Copleston (104), Vol.2, Part 1, p.189.

47 See Lonergan (1), p.16.

48 See Lonergan (4), p.310.

49 Ibid., pp.309-310.

50 See Lonergan (5h); Aquinas' distinction between orders of knowledge is found in S.T. IIa-IIae, q.1, art.5. On the unity of faith and reason see Grabmann (134), pp.32ff.

51 See Lonergan (5h), pp.131-132.

52 See ibid., pp.132-135; also p.127 on the meaning of scientia subalternata.

53 See Congar (103), columns 347-349.

54 See ibid., column 350.

55 See ibid., columns 352-353.

56 See Lonergan (2), pp.vii-x.

57 See Lonergan (6d), pp.43-47. The use by Aquinas of Aristotle is presented clearly by Copleston (104), Vol.2, Part 2, pp. 144-145, who stresses that Aquinas did not simply take over the entire Aristotelian system, but rather adapted it care- fully to Christian truth.

58   Lonergan (12), pp.165-166.

59   Lonergan (3), p.527. Also Copleston (104), Vol.2, Part 2,
     pp.151-152, who comments that once philosophic thought
     had gained a certain autonomy, it was not to be expected
     that it would be content to sit at home, like the elder
     son in the parable of the prodigal; Aquinas' synthesis,
     then, contained a latent tension: see ibid., Vol.3,
     Part 1, pp.13-18.

60   See Lonergan (10), p.6.

61   See Lonergan (2), pp.vii-ix, and (9), p.20.

62   Lonergan (4), pp.314-315.

63   See Copleston (104), Vol.2, Part 2, p.151.

64   Ibid., pp.279-280.

65   Lonergan (2), p.211; see (4), p.280.

66   Lonergan (10), pp.30-31; see (3), pp.403-404.

67   See Lonergan (2), pp.210-211.

68   See Lonergan (3), pp.527-528. Copleston notes that it
     would be quite untrue to say that all modern philosophy
     is autonomous from theology (think of Pascal, Malebranche,
     Locke or Berkeley), yet adds that a progressive emancipation
     can be noted since the medieval period: (104), Vol.4, p.18.

69   See Lonergan (6f), pp.69-75, for what follows.

70   See Lonergan (12), p.170, and (10), p.6; also (2), p.vii.

71   Lonergan (6e), pp.55-56. For the historical background see
     Copleston (104), Vol.3, Part 1, pp.25-30; Schulz (253),
     pp.8,17; Kuhn (175), p.6.

72   The comment of Lonergan occurs in the transcript of an
     unpublished lecture in 1967, on file at the Lonergan
     Center, Toronto (file no. LB 195.1); see also Lonergan
     (3), p.112, and Matson (192), p.15.

73   See Schulz (253), p.12, and Kuhn (175), c.IX.

74   See Lonergan (12) for what follows. Lonergan studies the
     natural sciences only to get a preliminary notion of method.

75   This has changed the whole basis of modern science from a
     search for proof to a more modest quest for verification;
     see Lonergan (3), pp.304ff., and Ladrière (178). The
     mathematical principles are discussed by Polanyi (228).

76   See the discussion in Schulz (253), pp.130-144.

77 See Lonergan (4), pp.4-6, and (3), pp.3-170. The non-logical is basic also to Kuhn's paradigms.

78 See Schulz (253), p.92, on the importance of "meaning".

79 See Lonergan (6h), pp.105-106, and Schulz (253), pp.12, 17-19, on the confused relation of science and philosophy at the present time.

80 Copleston (104), Vol.3, Part 2, p.245. Also Lonergan (3), pp.423-430, and Lamb (28), p.vi.

81 See Lonergan (4), pp.85-96 for a schematic structure.

82 Ibid., pp.93-94.

83 See ibid., pp.94-95.

84 See ibid., p.94.

85 See ibid., pp.94-95; also my chapter three.

86 Ibid., p.96.

87 See Lonergan (6h), p.108.

88 Lonergan (6e), pp.56-57.

89 Lonergan (3), p.386.

90 Ibid., p.xvii.

91 For a comparison of Kant's and Lonergan's notion of "a priori", see Sala (29). Also Hirschberger (149), p.106.

92 Lonergan (3), p.408.

93 Ibid., p.411.

94 Ibid., p.412.

95 Ibid., p.413; also p.339 for the role of Galileo.

96 Ibid., pp.413-414. Also Copleston (104), Volume 6, and Patzig (223), esp. pp.54-66.

97 Lonergan (6f), p.78.

98 See Lonergan (3), p.415.

99 See ibid., p.416.

100 Ibid., p.417.

101 Ibid., p.373. Also Pöggeler (227), p.148.

102 Lonergan (3), pp.373-374.

103 Ibid., p.374.

104 Ibid., p.425. Also Schulz (253), pp.103-104, who stresses
     Kant's distance from actual scientific research; in a
     similar way, Toulmin wonders about the relevancy of much
     "philosophy of science" to actual scientific procedure.

105 Lonergan (3), p.393.

106 Ibid., pp.428-429.

107 Ibid., p.429.

108 The terminological issue, then, is far from settled. For
     Lonergan's usage see (18), p.87, for the distinction
     between systematizing and scholarly sciences; for his
     understanding of Geisteswissenschaften as hermeneutics
     and critical history see (6r), p.277. Also Schulz (253),
     pp.12-13, 17-18.

109 Lonergan (6p), p.234. Also Snell (260), pp.246-263.

110 See Snell (260), p.248.

111 Lonergan (4), p.97. Also Snell (260), p.257.

112 This is noted by Lonergan in an earlier draft of Method
     in Theology, on file at the Lonergan Center, Toronto
     (Batch VI, Folder 1, section a, p.25). See Schulz (253),
     p.543, and pp.473-475.

113 Lonergan (9), pp.7-8.

114 Lonergan (4), p.185. Also Hazard (145), pp.46-72, 213-231.

115 See Lonergan (4), pp.185-186, and (12), p.168. The impact
     of natural science on historical scholarship is well-
     known. Scientific inquiry often yielded results that
     contradicted traditional interpretations of classical and
     religious texts; here, one has only to recall the problems
     of Kepler and Galileo in reconciling their scientific
     views with the prevailing interpretation of scripture.
     See Schulz (253), p.481.

116 See Lonergan (19), p.346, and Schulz (253), pp.482-491.
     The same period is discussed by Copleston (104), Vol.6,
     Part i.

117 Lonergan (6n), pp.194-195; see also (9), p.70. Further:
     Hünermann (151) and Frör (125), pp.28ff.

118 See Snell (260), p.259.

119 See Lonergan (4), pp.209-212, and (19), pp.346-348.

120 See Lonergan (19), p.346.

121 See ibid. Also Lonergan (4), p.208, and Gadamer (126),
     pp.162-173, 208.

122 See Lonergan (19), pp.346-347; Schulz (253), pp.514-522;
    and Gadamer (126), pp.173-234.

123 Gadamer (126), p.192.

124 See Lonergan (19), p.347, and (4), pp.210-212. Also
    Crowe (24), pp.25-26, and Lamb (28), pp.110-193.

125 See Lonergan (4), pp.204-205.

126 See ibid., pp.175,197.

127 Lonergan (19), p.346.

128 See Lonergan (4), p.318, and references there given.

129 Lonergan (3), pp.373-374.

130 See Lonergan (4), p.316; and p.96. Also (6q), p.242;
    (19), pp.351-352; (6i), pp.122-123. Further: Schulz
    (253), pp.635-642, who acknowledges this concern for
    praxis in both traditional and modern philosophy, yet
    adds that such efforts have been largely unfruitful because
    of attempts to ground ethics on a metaphysical basis or,
    more recently, on a scientific or linguistic basis.
    Schulz himself urges a new grounding that would bring
    ethics to the center of current philosophy.

131 See Lonergan (6q), p.242.

132 See my previous section on the autonomy of scholarship.

133 Lonergan (19), pp.348-349; see also (10), pp.12-13;
    (6e), pp.60-61; and (6g), pp.92-93.

134 The foregoing is from Lonergan (5p), pp.262-263; see
    also (4), pp.72-73, 205.

135 See Lonergan (4), p.264, and Hirschberger (149), p.175.

136 Lonergan (19), p.351.

137 Lonergan (6q), pp.242-243.

138 Lonergan (6f), p.86.

139 See ibid.

140 See my introduction to the present work.

141 Note, in particular, the excellent work of Lamb (28).

142 Lonergan (12), p.169. See Lamb (28), pp.72, 147-148.

143 Lonergan (6e), p.55.

144 See ibid., pp.55-57.

145 Ibid., p.57.

146 See Lonergan (10), pp.30-31.

147 See *ibid.* It should be noted that the major barrier to the renewal of theology in the modern era did not stem from the fact that the medieval synthesis was metaphysical, but rather from the fact that 14th century theologians were concerned with necessary truths and logic. It is this clinging to logic in an exclusive manner that prevents a discipline from adapting to a new context; see Lonergan *ibid.*, pp.6,31,45-47. For an account of this period see Pannenberg (215a), pp.230-244; Beumer (90), pp.90-109. For a summary of Cano's thought see Duss-von Werdt (111), pp.75-79. Also Lang (181) and Grabmann (133).

148 See Lonergan (9), p.9.

149 See Lonergan (6e), pp.58-59.

150 Lonergan (5h), p.133. See also (4), pp.335-338.

151 See Lonergan (6e), pp.59-60. Also Congar (103), cols.432f.

152 Lonergan (6p), pp.231-232.

153 See *ibid.*, pp.232-234; also (4), pp.362-363.

154 See Lonergan (4), pp.xi,362-363.

155 Lonergan (6n), p.206.

156 Lonergan (6p), pp.237-238.

157 Lonergan (6h), p.109.

158 See especially Pannenberg (213), pp.252-295.

159 In (6j), pp.135-148.

160 *Ibid.*, pp.138-139.

161 See for example Lonergan (4), p.180.

162 See *ibid.*, pp.175-180.

III. FOUNDATIONAL UNITY: FROM RELIGIOUS EXPERIENCE

TO SPECIALIZED RELIGIOUS KNOWLEDGE

FOOTNOTES

1   Lonergan (4), p.327.

2   As Aubert mentions (81), pp.37-39, the question of a theological anthropology, formerly treated as the question of the relation between the natural and supernatural orders, began to be debated under new viewpoints during the first half of the present century. The new disciplines of science and scholarship, as well as the concern for Existenz and Geschichte in modern philosophy, greatly enriched our apprehension of what it means to be human, and this could not but have had an impact on theology. See also Kasper (164), pp.95-114.

3   See Lonergan (6j), esp. pp.147-148.

4   The reference is to Rahner (232), pp.43-65, who repeats this theme in his Grundkurs, pp.35-36.

5   See Kasper (161), pp.120-124; and Lonergan (6h).

6   See Lonergan (6h), pp.111-116 for what follows.

7   Lonergan (6L), p.186.

8   See Lonergan (6h), pp.113-114; (11).

9   Lonergan (6h), pp.115-116. Just as one can employ "humanism" in a pejorative sense, connoting a denial of religion, so Lonergan urges a positive meaning of the word that seems closer to the more neutral term "hominization".

10   Kasper (161), pp.123-124. This conviction pervades the work of Jüngel (154). As well, both Pannenberg and Rahner clearly philosophize within theology, while Metz tends towards this same procedure.

11   See Lonergan (10), pp.11-14. For a study of Lonergan's transition, see Tyrrell (31).

12   Lonergan (6e), p.63.

13   See Lonergan (13), p.229.

14   Lonergan (4), p.270.

15   See my chapter one, section 3. Also, Lonergan (6e), pp.63-64.

16   See Lonergan (4), p.270.

17   See ibid.

18   See _ibid._, pp.270-271.

19   Lonergan, "Variations in Fundamental Theology", the
      second in a series of four Larkin-Stuart Lectures under
      the general topic, Revolution in Roman Catholic Theology?,
      at Trinity College in the University of Toronto, Nov. 13,
      1973 (unpublished; a tape of the lecture is on file at the
      Lonergan Center, Toronto, from which the passage quoted was
      taken).

20   My main sources for what follows will be Lonergan (21);
      and (4), chapters one and four. An extensive study of the
      shift in meaning of the word "experience" is offered by
      Kambartel (157); see also Grom (138).

21   See Lonergan (21), pp.72-75.

22   See Lonergan (3), pp.381-383; and (5n).

23   Lonergan (6L), p.172.

24   Lonergan (21), p.73.

25   See _ibid._, pp.73-75, plus references there given

26   See _ibid._, pp.74-75. His book, Insight, is a series of
      exercises designed to help us experience, advert to,
      understand and know our conscious and intentional operations
      that normally are not adverted to, not understood, and not
      known. Such is the meaning of "self-appropriation" or
      "heightening of consciousness" or "generalized empirical
      method" in Lonergan's work.

27   Here, the two chapters from Lonergan's Method in Theology
      on "The Human Good" and "Meaning" are relevant. Our context,
      especially our linguistic context, is the means by which we
      develop (even religiously) and interpret our world and
      ourselves; see Lonergan (4), pp.112-115.

28   See Lonergan (21), pp.75-78; and (4), pp.108-109.

29   See Lonergan (21), p.76. See also Eliade (121).

30   See Lonergan (21), pp.75-76.

31   Ibid. See also Lonergan (6k), esp. pp.157-163; and (6f), p.86.

32   See Lonergan (6h), esp. pp.107-109; and (21), pp.76-78.
      Also Eliade (120), who stresses that regardless of increasing
      specialization and secularization, the sacred remains an
      integral dimension of human consciousness that can receive
      expression in a large variety of orientations.

33   Lonergan (4), p.80; see also Kasper (170), who also urges
      that the issue is not tradition vs. progress, but rather
      tradition and progress vs. truth; and truth is authenticity.

34 See Lonergan (19), p.349.

35 See Lonergan (21), pp.77-78.

36 See Lonergan (10), p.17; (21), pp.78ff.; and (20).

37 See Lonergan (6L), pp.168-169.

38 See Lonergan (21), pp.80-81; (6k); and (10), p.50, where Lonergan acknowledges that he makes this identity between unrestricted loving and religious experience on theological grounds. On the need for this reservation at the current stage of scholarship, see Mueller (56). On the identification of religious experience with love, see Jüngel (154), pp.430-453.

39 Lonergan (21), p.80.

40 See ibid., pp.80-81.

41 See ibid., pp.81-82.

42 See ibid., pp.82-83.

43 See Lonergan (3), pp.380-381.

44 See ibid.

45 Lonergan (6L), pp.169-170; see also (3), pp.458-483. Also Schulz (253), p.464.

46 See Lonergan (5ö), p.241.

47 See Lonergan (6L), pp.170ff.

48 See ibid.; also (5ö), p.243, and (5p), pp.252-253.

49 See Lonergan (20), p.50.

50 See Lonergan (6L), p.167. Such critical judgment marks the ancient transition from mythos to logos: see Kasper (170), pp.204-205, plus references there given.

51 See Lonergan (6L), pp.168-169; and (20), p.51.

52 See Lonergan (22), pp.313-314.

53 Lonergan (15), p.48.

54 See Lonergan (6L), pp.168-169, and (4), pp.111-112. Also Schulz (253), pp.272-334.

55 See Lonergan (6f), pp.85-86, on the alienation consequent upon attending only to the insecurity of human achievement.

56 See Lonergan (22), p.314.

57 See Lonergan (4), pp.122-123, and (10), p.38. Also Grom (138), pp.59-60.

58 Lonergan (4), p.115; see pp.115-118 for what follows. This is similar to Jüngel's statement (154), p.466: "Glaube ist also keine nur theoretische, sondern vielmehr eine in der Erfahrung göttlicher Liebe entstehende Gewissheit." But to what extent Jüngel's understanding of faith resembles that of Lonergan would require extensive study, not so much of the notion of faith, but of the notion of (religious) experience itself.

59 Lonergan (4), p.115; see pp.30-41 for his notion of "feeling" and "value".

60 See ibid., pp.116-117.

61 See ibid., pp.110-111.

62 Ibid., pp.117-118; see Lonergan (3), pp.225-242.

63 See Lonergan (4), p.79.

64 See Lonergan (21), pp.71-72.

65 Lonergan (4), p.118.

66 See ibid.

67 For background see Lonergan (3), pp.703-712; (6g); and (4), pp.41-47, 118-119.

68 See my footnote No.33 in this chapter. For Lonergan, religious experience, faith, and religious belief are constitutive of religious communities or, sociologically, ecclesial communities. (Theological) reflection arises precisely from within such community living, and thus Lonergan here is preparing the way for the ecclesial dimension of theology - its Kirchlichkeit.

69 Lonergan (4), pp.41-42.

70 See ibid., pp.43-44; also my footnote No.35 in this chapter.

71 Lonergan (4), p.45.

72 See Lonergan (6g), pp.90ff.

73 See Lonergan (4), p.243.

74 Lonergan (6g), pp.97-98.

75 Lonergan (8), p.7. His phrase, "As consciousness develops so too does religion..." contains perhaps the key to his entire project for method in theology.

76 See my Chapter Two; also Lonergan (10), pp.1-14.

77 See Lonergan (4), p.28, where he draws upon Piaget.

78 See ibid., pp.86-87, plus references there given.

79 See *ibid.*, pp.87–88, 108; and (10), p.2.

80 See *ibid.*, p.89.

81 *Ibid.*, p.90; see pp.76–81 on the functions of meaning.

82 Lonergan (10), p.4; see also Lonergan (4), p.82.

83 See Lonergan (4), pp.92–93.

84 See Lonergan (10), pp.4–5.

85 *Ibid.*, p.5.

86 See Lonergan (10), p.6, and (4), pp.93–96.

87 See Lonergan (4), p.95. It was to such a brand of systematic thinking that medieval theologians turned.

88 *Ibid.*, pp.82–83.

89 *Ibid.*, pp.94–95; see also p.316.

90 See *ibid.*, on this and the foregoing, esp. p.83.

91 Lonergan (10), p.8.

92 On contrast and continuity with Aristotle see Lonergan (12), pp.169,173.

93 See *ibid.*, for what follows in my text.

94 Lonergan here notes that this was evident in his own study, *Verbum* (2).

95 Method, then, for Lonergan refers to the actual conscious intentionality of human subjects – as intending truth, value, or as in love; it does not refer to his or anyone else's account of such conscious intentionality, nor is it a list of guidelines and rules for reaching truth and value.

96 See Lonergan (4), p.83.

97 Lonergan (3), p.xxviii.

98 The main source for what follows is Lonergan (22) and the first chapter of his Method in Theology. Regarding the phrase, "generalized empirical method" see Lonergan (3), pp.243–244, and also p.72 for the rationale behind this terminology. He also calls this method "transcendental method"; this term, however, has a meaning for Lonergan that stands in contrast to meanings usually assigned to that notion, so that I find the phrase "generalized empirical method" less likely to awaken in the reader a host of philosophic images and misconceptions. Lamb (28) employs the term "meta-method; see esp. pp.60–61.

99   Lonergan, in (22), p.322, says that method yields "ongoing and cumulative results". In (4), p.4, he spoke of "cumulative and progressive results". It seems possible that he was sensitive to criticisms of the word "progressive", and chose the less philosophic term "ongoing" to state what he meant. For one example of criticism see Lash (27), pp.128-133.

100   Lonergan (22), p.323; note his attached footnote, and see Lonergan (4), pp.13-14 (footnote 4), and p.212. Also Duss-von Werdt (111), p.37, and Winter (274), pp.135ff.

101   See Lonergan (4), p.286.

102   See Lonergan (4), pp.20-25.

103   On this isomorphism see ibid., pp.6-13, 21 (footnote 7); also Lonergan (5i), and references in index to "isomorphism" in Insight.

104   See Kasper (166), pp.196ff.

105   Lonergan (4), p.266.

106   See for example Lonergan (12), p.167, and (4), pp.85-89.

107   See Lonergan (18), p.89.

108   Lonergan (4), p.23.

109   See ibid., chapter one.

110   See Lonergan (6m).

111   See my Chapter Two for a fuller account.

112   See Lonergan (6e), p.61, and (9), pp.2-9.

113   Lonergan (19), p.347.

114   See my Chapter Two on the autonomy of scholarship.

115   See Lonergan (4), pp.224-233.

116   See Chapter Two and references there given, where Lonergan draws upon the work of Gadamer.

117   See Lonergan (19), p.347.

118   Lonergan (18), p.89.

119   See ibid., pp.95-99; and (4), pp.191ff.

120   See Lonergan (19), pp.348-351; and (4), pp.110-112, 235-266.

121   Lonergan (19), pp.348-349.

122 See _ibid._, p.349.

123 See Lonergan (4), p.52.

124 The main references to Lonergan's thought on conversion
     are (3), on intellectual and moral conversion; and (4),
     that includes as well an account of religious conversion,
     pp.235-244. For the relation of this to his doctoral
     work see Colleran (35). See also Curran (25), pp.41-59,
     and Lonergan's response, pp.225-230. A rather thorough
     analysis has been done by Conn (36).

125 Lonergan (4), p.238.

126 See Lonergan (22), pp.315, 327; also (4), pp.238-239.

127 See Lonergan (4), p.240.

128 See Lonergan (3), pp.187ff.

129 See Lonergan (4), pp.27-55; also Winter (274); Gadamer
     (127); and Schulz (253), pp.782-785.

130 Lonergan (6f), pp.82-83. See also Schulz (253), pp.782-
     783; Auer (82), (83), (84), and (85).

131 See Lonergan (4), p.50.

132 See Lonergan (6f), p.79, and (3), pp.607-619; also
     Auer (85), p.313.

133 See Lonergan (4), p.240, and (6L), pp.168-169. The
     different grounds from which self-determination can pro-
     ceed, as noted by Kant, Fichte, and especially Schelling,
     is a fact traced by Schulz (253), p.726.

134 See Lonergan's account of bias in (3), pp.191-242; also
     Schulz (253), pp.721-727, 765-780, 794-796, 810-821.

135 See Lonergan (4), pp.240-241.

136 See Lonergan (19), pp.345-351.

137 See _ibid._, pp.351-352.

138 _Ibid._, p.351.

139 See _ibid._, p.352.

140 See Lonergan (13), pp.230-231.

141 See Lonergan (4), p.85.

IV. THEOLOGICAL UNITY

METHOD AND METHODS IN THEOLOGY

FOOTNOTES

1   Lonergan (4), p.288.

2   See Chapter Two. On the link of theology to Christian living see Lonergan (4), p.144, and (19), pp.352-353. See also Schupp (254), pp.132-179, on this move from symbolic to literal meaning; Schupp notes that the move to literal meaning in no way ended symbolic thinking, that itself underwent a purification process.

3   See Lonergan (4), pp.125-126.

4   See ibid., p.125.

5   See ibid., pp.149-150.

6   Lonergan (12), p.166; see (4), p.126, where Lonergan notes that field specialization is simply a division into material parts. Commonly, it would be a division of labor based on the selection of different data.

7   In classicist terms this is a division according to material and formal objects; in more modern terms it is a division according to branches of knowledge.

8   See Lonergan (4), p.126. The fact of subject specialization sets the problem of interdisciplinary collaboration, viz., the relation of one conceptual classification to any other. For Lonergan the solution is to be found, not on the level of concepts, but of method.

9   See Chapter Two on the medieval distinction of theology from philosophy.

10   See Lonergan (10), p.33; and Chapter Two on the autonomy of science.

11   This is close to the view of Pannenberg, and perhaps also of Tracy (265), both of whom stress a theology in oratione obliqua. See my concluding remarks.

11a Gilkey (25), pp.76-101 asks if Lonergan wants a notion of theology based on an analogy with natural science; see Lonergan's response (25), pp.224-225.

12   See Lonergan (4), p.127; also de Vries (109).

13   See the article by Blum (95).

520

14   See Lonergan (4), p.153. Also Gadamer (126), pp.153-
      234, and Ebeling (114), for the historical background.
      For a useful overview of the function of exegesis
      within theology and church, as well as of the inter-
      dependence of exegesis and hermeneutics, see Blank
      (93); also Sauter (245), pp.52-53, on exegesis as
      reconstruction.

15   Lonergan (4), p.127; also pp.229-230, for the
      distinction between understanding and explaining,
      yet their convergence in both history and science.

16   See ibid., p.128.

17   See ibid. The universal viewpoint, for Lonergan, is
      provided in the functional specialty, dialectic. See
      Pannenberg (215),passim, on the reception of critical
      history into theology and on the special problem of
      church history. A concise, recent, and informed dis-
      cussion of the issues is by Ruhbach (243), who stresses
      that judgment is the central task of the historian, p.76.

18   Dialectic as method should not be confused with
      "dialectical theology" or with "comparative religions".

19   Lonergan (4), p.130.

20   See the various volumes of Concilium on fundamental
      theology. "Foundations", as presupposing Christian
      scholarship and dialectic, is for many a stumbling-
      block in understanding Lonergan: e.g. Gutheinz (45),
      esp. pp.451-454.

21   See Lonergan (4), p.132, (9), and the chapter on
      "Doctrines" in Method in Theology.

22   Lonergan (4), p.132, who insists that it is one thing
      for theologians to establish the truth that is to be
      mediated, and quite another to work out the apparent
      inconsistencies in various expressions of that truth;
      it is this distinction that grounds the two distinct
      specialties, doctrines and systematics.

23   Ott (25), p.141; see Kasper (163b), pp.5-8.

24   See Lawrence (26), pp.167-217, and Gadamer (126),
      pp.235-274.

25   See Lonergan (4), pp.133-136, for what follows.

26   Ibid., p.133: this is the religious tradition to which
      the theologian is correlative.

521

27 See Lonergan (6e), p.62; this locates theology within history: within the context of the Christian message and tradition, and within the broader context of human history.

28 Lonergan (4), p.133; see my Chapter Three.

29 *Ibid.*, pp.133-134.

30 *Ibid.*, p.134.

31 See Lonergan (19), p.346.

32 See my Chapter Three,4,(2); also Lonergan (4), p.24. It seems useful here to make a threefold distinction regarding the relation of generalized empirical method to theology: (1) as operative in theological work, but as non-objectified as method; (2) as operative in theological work and as objectified by religiously differentiated consciousness (e.g. Rahner); (3) as operative in theological work and as objectified by interiorly and religiously differentiated consciousness: this is Lonergan's proposal and it yields a method in theology both in oratione obliqua and, as in Rahner, in oratione recta.

33 Functional specialties are not specifically theological: see Lonergan (13), p.233.

34 See *ibid.*, p.229; also Lonergan (4), p.135.

35 See Lonergan (4), p.135.

36 See *ibid.*, pp.149-151; for an example, see Aland (78), p.xii.

37 See Lonergan (4), p.127; on interpretation, pp.153-173; (18), pp.89-99; and (3), pp.562-594.

38 Lonergan (4), p.155.

39 See footnote no.37 of this chapter for references.

40 For a similar account of the tasks of the interpreter see Ricoeur (239); also Frör (125), pp.48ff., who stresses the centrality of understanding in the task of interpretation.

41 See for example Pannenberg (27), pp.90-96. The distinction between understanding and judgment is a principal achievement of Lonergan's Insight.

42 Lonergan (4), p.133. Lonergan's discussion of history in his Method in Theology comprises two chapters: "History" centers on the main task of the historian, viz., historical judgment (knowledge); "History and

Historians" is the bridge to the following chapter on
dialectic, inasmuch as it pinpoints the conflicts
involved in historical work that admit a solution
only by moving to a higher perspective.

43 Ibid., p.78.

44 See ibid., p.181. Also Kasper (163b), pp.42-43, on
anamnesis.

45 See Lonergan (4), p.182.

46 See ibid., p.185.

47 See ibid., p.186; cf. pp.178-179.

48 See ibid., pp.189-194. On the operations of the
historian see Marrou (189), esp. pp.115-143, and
Fischer (123).

49 Lonergan (4), p.133.

50 See ibid., p.235; on dialectic see pp.235-266.

51 See ibid., pp.249-250.

52 Ibid., p.250; cf. p.247. Also Lonergan (8), p.viii,
and his discussion of the universal viewpoint (3),
pp.564-568. The work of Küng (176) commonly is
dialectical.

53 Lonergan (4), pp.134-135.

54 See ibid., p.135.

55 See ibid., p.267.

56 See Lonergan (6e), p.62.

57 See Lonergan (13), pp.230-231; and (4), p.333.

58 See Lonergan (4), p.267.

59 Lonergan (19), p.351; also (4), p.268.

60 See Lonergan (13), p.229; and (4), pp.269-270.

61 See Lonergan (13), pp.227ff.; and (4), pp.268-271.

62 See Lonergan (6ö), pp.217-218; and (4), pp.150-151.

63 Lonergan (4), p.271; and see also (13), pp.227-228.

64 See my Chapter Three,5,(3).

65 See Lonergan (4), p.136.

66 The full account is Lonergan (4), pp.267-368.

67 See ibid., p.133.

68   See *ibid.*; also Lonergan (10), pp.14,17, where he notes that religious conversion is basic inasmuch as it provides a new horizon in which questions about God are significant.

69   Lonergan (4), p.268.

70   See *ibid.*, p.270. The positions and counter-positions are revealed by dialectic: *ibid.*, pp.251-254.

71   *Ibid.*, p.285.

72   *Ibid.*, p.292.

73   See *ibid.*, pp.288-291.

74   See *ibid.*, pp.292-293.

75   *Ibid.*, p.133.

76   *Ibid.*, p.299.

77   See *ibid.*, pp.295-298.

78   This is simply to point to the fact that expressions of Christian truth proceed from a wide variety of sources, each differing in normativeness.

79   See Lonergan (4), pp.298-299. Also Schmaus (248); Kasper (168), p.56, and (163b), pp.24-32.

80   See Lonergan (4), pp.300-330, and (9).

81   Lonergan (4), p.133.

82   *Ibid.*, p.335.

83   *Ibid.*, p.336.

84   See *ibid.*, p.337; also Lonergan (10).

85   See Lonergan (4), p.337, and (6i).

86   See Lonergan (4), pp.337-340, and (6n), pp.203-204; also Kasper (169), pp.101-104.

87   Lonergan (4), p.345. This distinguishes Lonergan's notion of mystery from that of Pannenberg, whose systematic theology is grounded on the hypothesis of God as problem and not as mystery. Again, Rahner has made mystery the starting point of theology, and the theologian is understood to be the custodian of mystery; for Lonergan, on the other hand, mystery is the ground of religious experience and the term to which we are orientated in our quest for cognitional, moral and religious self-transcendence: hence the relevance of mystery (1) to the theologian as human subject, for mystery is the ground

and term of authentic development; (2) to the theologian as theologian, inasmuch as mystery evokes interpretation, interpretation occurs within historical contexts, and these contexts generate the problems with which theologians attempt to deal (cf. _ibid._, p.344).

88   See _ibid._, pp.345-350.

89   See _ibid._, pp.350-351.

90   See _ibid._, pp.132-133.

91   See _ibid._, p.133.

92   See _ibid._

93   _Ibid._, p.358.

94   See _ibid._, pp.361-367.

95   _Ibid._, pp.297-298.

96   See, e.g., Joest (153), p.10; Peukert (226), p.21; Sauter (245), p.12.

97   See Kasper (163b) for an example of this notion of method.

98   See my Chapters One and Two.

99   See Lonergan (4), p.125. The notion of "group" is borrowed from mathematics; see _ibid._, pp.27-30.

100   From the dust jacket of the Seabury edition of Lonergan's _Method in Theology_.

101   See Lonergan (3), pp.562-594, and (10), pp.45-60.

102   See Lonergan (3), pp.573-577; (18), pp.87-88, 97-98; (4), pp.81-83, 138; and (10), pp.4-6, 7, 45-50.

103   See Lonergan (3), pp.573-577 on the limitations of the treatise; this is fundamental to his thought.

104   _Ibid._, p.573.

105   _Ibid._, p.575.

106   See _ibid._, p.577; also Schulz (253), pp.92-93; and O'Farrell (212).

107   Lonergan (4), p.17.

108   See _ibid._, p.136. Thus, Lonergan describes method, not as a fixed blueprint, but as a framework for collaborative creativity (_ibid._, pp.xi-xii).

109 The unity, then, is to be foundational, performative, and contextual. The foundational unity was uncovered in Chapter Three, the performative unity is our present concern, and the contextual unity, dynamically integrating theological performance with concrete living in church and human society, will be noted in Chapter Five.

110 See Lonergan (4), pp.140-144, for what follows.

111 An example of this would be Zimmermann (275): see p.17.

112 Lonergan (4), p.141; see also p.12.

113 See ibid., pp.136-137.

114 See ibid., p.141; see also pp.12-13.

115 See ibid., p.141.

115a See Jüngel (156), esp. pp.34-35.

116 Lonergan (4), p.142. Distinguish, then value as context (foundations), truth as context (doctrines), intelligibility as context (systematics), communicability as context (communications), where each is but a more determinate context than the previous.

117 Functional specialization is a distinction of specialties and not specialists: see ibid., pp.136-137.

118 For the context of theology itself, see Chapter Five.

119 See Kasper (165).

120 See Lonergan (4), p.143; and Kasper (163b), pp.33-44 on the exploitation of historical method by apologetics.

121 On the autonomy of the theologian, see Lonergan (4), pp.330-333; and Blank (94), esp. pp.59-60.

122 See Lonergan (4), pp.143-144.

123 Lonergan (4), p.144.

124 See ibid., p.144.

125 See ibid., p.140, and my next chapter.

V. CONTEXTUAL UNITY:

FROM THEOLOGY TO THE CHURCH IN SOCIETY

FOOTNOTES

1   Lonergan (6e), pp.62-63.

2   See Lonergan (4), p.144.

3   For some background see Pannenberg (215a), pp.230-240, 426-442.

4   E.g., see Heinrichs (147), esp. pp.72-73.

5   So Schuster in his article "Praktische Theologie" in SM. This is similar to Rahner (235), esp. p.64.

6   This second variety is prevalent today, and has provided a much needed corrective to earlier simplistic views; its limitations will be noted in due course.

7   See Lonergan (4), pp.361-362.

8   For a good survey of the development of pastoral theology see Weinzierl (272).

9   Lonergan (4), p.139.

10   See ibid., pp.356-358 for what follows. It is the process from intersubjectivity to the constitution of community, and from there to the ongoing development of community in history.

11   Ibid., pp.356-357.

12   See ibid., pp.357-358, and the references to Insight there given; see Lamb (28), p.423.

13   See the authors cited in footnotes 4 & 5 of this chapter. Such theorizing about practice or about the meaning of the theory-practice mediation is constitutive meaning; but it seems constitutive only of the community of practical theologians, and not of the human or Christian community.

14   See Lamb (180), and Hennelly (148).

15   See Lonergan (4), p.362.

16   Ibid.

17   See e.g. Lonergan (6p), pp.232-233; Rahner (235).

18   Lonergan (4), p.362.

527

19 See *ibid.*, p.363.

20 See *ibid.*

21 See *ibid.*

22 Lonergan (4), p.364; see (3), pp.742-743.

23 See Lonergan (4), p.363, and cf. the chapter on the hunam good in *ibid.*

24 See Chapter Two.

25 See Lonergan (5), pp.121-141, esp. pp.139-140.

26 See esp. pp.743-747.

27 Lonergan (3), p.744.

28 *Ibid.*, pp.744-745.

29 *Ibid.*, p.745.

30 See the essays in Siemers (259).

31 See esp. pp.364-367.

32 Lonergan (4), p.24.

33 One does not speak of method without including both subject and object in correlation. And while the object is a unity, that unity is grasped in the unity of the intending subject's basic pattern of operations.

34 See also Lonergan (3), pp.103-139, and (4), pp.364-365.

35 See Winter (274), pp.137ff.

36 Performance precedes reflection on that performance, so that experimentation in collaboration is urged.

37 See Lonergan (4), p.365.

38 *Ibid.*

39 *Ibid.*

40 See *ibid.*, pp.365-366.

41 *Ibid.*, p.367; see also (11), esp. pp. 59ff.

42 See Lamb on Dilthey (28), p.537, and the quote from Dilthey there included.

CONCLUDING REMARKS

FOOTNOTES

1   Lonergan (4), pp.297-298.
2   Ibid., p.xii.
3   Ibid., p.119.
4   Ibid., p.149.
5   Ibid., pp.253-254.
6   Ibid., p.282.
7   Ibid., p.285.
8   Ibid., p.291.
9   Ibid., pp.323-324.
10 Ibid., pp.332-333.
11 Ibid., p.353.
12 Ibid., p.355.
13 Pannenberg (215a), p.349.
14 See ibid., esp. pp.374-383.
15 Ibid., p.350.
16 Ibid., p.439. Similarly for Tracy (265).
17 Lonergan (4), p.292.
18 See ibid., p.282.
19 See Rahner (25), pp.194-196.
20 See Lonergan , "Functional Specialties in Theology", in Gregorianum 50(1969), pp.485-504.
21 Lonergan (6ð), pp. 210-211.
22 See Lonergan (6k), p.156.
23 See Lonergan (10), p.67.
24 See Lonergan (4), pp.290-291.
25 See Rahner in Fischer (124), p.405.
26 1 Cor. 2,14f, quoted by Lonergan (13), p.228.
27 Lonergan (4), p.120.

28   See Lonergan (3), pp.426-427.

29   Lonergan (5n), p.223.

30   Lonergan (7), p.90.

31   See Pannenberg (27), esp. pp.97-99.

32   See Kasper (166), esp. pp.196-203 on the possibility of understanding theology in reference to symbol.

BIBLIOGRAPHY

WORKS BY LONERGAN

1. Grace and Freedom: Operative Grace in the Thought of St. Thomas Aquinas. Ed. by J. Patout Burns, Intro. by F.E. Crowe. London: Darton Longman & Todd, 1971; New York: Herder and Herder, 1971. Reprint of the articles on "St. Thomas' Thought on Gratia Operans", Theological Studies, 1941-1942.

2. Verbum: Word and Idea in Aquinas. Ed. by David B. Burrell. Indiana: University of Notre Dame Press, 1967. Reprint of the articles on "The Concept of Verbum in the Writings of St. Thomas", Theological Studies, 1945-1949, with addition of an Introduction by the author and a Foreword by the editor.

3. Insight: A Study of Human Understanding. London: Longmans Green, 1957; revised students edition, New York: Philosophical Library, 1958; 3rd edition, with publisher's Foreword by Thomas Kiernan, New York: Philosophical Library, 1970; 4th (paperback) edition, New York: Harper & Row, 1978.

4. Method in Theology. London: Darton Longman & Todd, 1972, 1973^2; New York: Herder and Herder, 1972; New York: Seabury paperback edition, 1979.

5 Collection: Papers by Bernard Lonergan, S.J.. Ed. by F.E. Crowe. London: Darton Longman & Todd, 1967; New York: Herder and Herder, 1967. Contents:
   a. The Form of Inference (1943), pp.1-15.
   b. Finality, Love, Marriage (1943), pp.16-53.
   c. On God and Secondary Causes (1946), pp.54-67.
   d. The Assumption and Theology (1948), pp.68-83.
   e. The Natural Desire to See God (1949), pp.84-95.
   f. A Note on Geometrical Possibility (1949-1950), pp.96-113.
   g. The Role of a Catholic University in the Modern World (1951), pp.114-120.
   h. Theology and Understanding (1954), pp.121-141.
   i. Isomorphism of Thomist and Scientific Thought (1955), pp.142-151.
   j. Insight: Preface to a Discussion (1958), pp.152-163.
   k. Christ as Subject: A Reply (1959), pp.164-197.
   l. Openness and Religious Experience (1961), pp.198-201.

531

m. Metaphysics as Horizon (1963), pp.202-220.
n. Cognitional Structure (1964), pp.221-239.
ס. Existenz and Aggiornamento (1965), pp.240-251.
p. Dimensions of Meaning (1965), pp.252-267.

6. A Second Collection: Papers by Bernard J.F. Lonergan,
S.J.. Ed. by W.F.J. Ryan and B.J. Tyrrell. London:
Darton Longman & Todd, 1974; Philadelphia: Westminster,
1975. Contents:
a. The Transition from a Classicist World-View to
Historical-Mindedness (1967), pp.1-9.
b. The Dehellenization of Dogma (1967), pp.11-32.
c. Theories of Inquiry: Responses to a Symposium
(1967), pp.33-42.
d. The Future of Thomism (1968), pp.43-53.
e. Theology in its New Context (1968), pp.55-67.
f. The Subject (1968), pp.69-86.
g. Belief: Today's Issue (1970), pp.87-99.
h. The Absence of God in Modern Culture (1969), pp.101-116.
i. Natural Knowledge of God (1969), pp.117-133.
j. Theology and Man's Future (1969), pp.135-148.
k. The Future of Christianity (1969), pp.149-163.
l. The Response of the Jesuit as Priest and Apostle in the
Modern World (1970), pp.165-187.
m. The Example of Gibson Winter (1970), pp.189-192.
n. Philosophy and Theology (1970), pp.193-208.
ס. An Interview with Fr. Bernard Lonergan, S.J., Ed. by
Philip McShane (1971), pp.209-230.
p. Revolution in Catholic Theology (1972), pp.231-238.
q. The Origins of Christian Realism (1972), pp.239-261.
r. Insight Revisited (1972), pp.263-278.

7. Theologie im Pluralismus heutiger Kulturen, Hrsg. v. G.
Sala. Freiburg: Herder, 1975. German translations of
various articles from Collection and A Second Collection.

8. The Way to Nicea. The Dialectical Development of
Trinitarian Theology. A translation by Conn O'Donovan
from the first part of De Deo Trino (1964). London:
Darton Longman & Todd, 1976.

9. Doctrinal Pluralism. Milwaukee: Marquette University
Press, 1971.

10. Philosophy of God, and Theology. The Relationship between
Philosophy of God and the Functional Specialty, Systematics.
With a Foreword by P.B. O'Leary. London: Darton Longman
& Todd, 1973.

11. *Bernard Lonergan: 3 Lectures.* Ed. and with an Intro. by R.E. O'Connor. Montreal: Thomas More Institute for Adult Education, 1975. Contents:
   a. The Redemption (1958), pp.1-28.
   b. Time and Meaning (1962), pp.29-54.
   c. Healing and Creating in History (1975), pp.55-68.

12. "Aquinas Today: Tradition and Innovation", in *The Journal of Religion* 55(1975), pp.165-180.

13. "Bernard Lonergan Responds", in *Foundations of Theology* (bibliography #25), pp.223-234.

14. "Bernard Lonergan Responds", in *Language Truth and Meaning* (bibliography #26), pp.306-312.

15. "Christology Today: Methodological Reflections", in *Le Christ hier, aujourd'hui, et demain.* Ed. by R. Laflamme and M. Gervais. Québec: Les Presses de l'Université Laval, 1976, pp.45-65.

16. "Dialectic of Authority", in *Authority.* Ed. by. F.J. Adelmann. Boston College Studies in Philosophy, Vol. III. Boston College and M. Nijhoff (The Hague), 1974, pp.24-30.

17. "Foreword", in B. Tyrrell (bibliography #31), pp.ix-x.

18. "Merging Horizons: System, Common Sense, Scholarship", in *Cultural Hermeneutics* 1(1973), pp.87-99.

19. "The ongoing genesis of methods", in *Studies in Religion/ Sciences Religieuses* 6(1976-1977), pp.341-355.

20. "Religious Commitment", in *The Pilgrim People: A Vision with Hope.* Ed. by J. Papin, Villanova: Villanova University Press, 1970, pp.44-69.

21. "Religious Experience", in *Trinification of the World.* Ed. by T.A. Dunne and J.-M. Laporte. Toronto: Regis College Press, 1978, pp.71-83.

22. "Religious Knowledge", in *Lonergan Workshop - Vol. I.* Ed. by F. Lawrence, Missoula: Scholars Press, 1978, pp.309-327.

23. "Prolegomena to the Study of the Emerging Religious Consciousness of our Time", in *Studies in Religion/ Sciences Religieuses* 9(1980), pp.3-15.

WORKS ABOUT LONERGAN

24. Spirit as Inquiry: Studies in Honor of Bernard Lonergan,
    S.J., a Lonergan Festschrift that appears as Continuum
    2(1964), Vol.3. Ed. by F.E. Crowe, who also offers an
    Introduction.

25. Foundations of Theology. Ed. by Philip McShane. Papers
    from the International Lonergan Congress 1970. Dublin:
    Gill and Macmillan, 1971. Editorial note by P. McShane,
    Foreword by J.D. Collins.

26. Language Truth and Meaning. Ed. by P. McShane. Papers
    from the International Lonergan Congress 1970. Dublin:
    Gill and Macmillan, 1972. Introduction by P. McShane.

27. Looking at Lonergan's Method. Ed. by P. Corcoran, SM.
    Dublin: The Talbot Press, 1975. Foreword by P. Corcoran.

28. Lamb, Matthew, History, Method and Theology. A Dialectical
    Comparison of Wilhelm Dilthey's Critique of Historical
    Reason and Bernard Lonergan's Meta-Methodology, Missoula:
    Scholars, 1978. (Note: the references in my text are from
    the original dissertation edition of Lamb's study.)

29. Sala, Giovanni, Das Apriori in der menschlichen Erkenntnis.
    Eine Studie über Kants "Kritik der reinen Vernunft" und
    Lonergans "Insight", Meisenheim am Glan: Hain, 1971.

30. Tracy, David, The Achievement of Bernard Lonergan, New
    York: Herder and Herder, 1970.

31. Tyrrell, Bernard, Bernard Lonergan's Philosophy of God,
    Dublin: Gill and Macmillan, 1974.

32. Braxton, Edward K., "Bernard Lonergan's Hermeneutic of
    the Symbol", in ITQ 43(1976), pp.186-197.

33. Butler, B.C., "Method in Theology", in Clergy Review
    57(1972), pp.579-596.

34. Carmody, Denise Lardner, "Lonergan's Religious Person",
    in Religion in Life 44(1975), pp.222-231.

35. Colleran, K., "Bernard Lonergan on Conversion", in
    Dunwoodie Review 11(1971), pp.3-23.

36. Conn, W., "Bernard Lonergan's Analysis of Conversion",
    in Angelicum 53(1976), pp.362-404.

37. Connell, D., "Father Lonergan and the Idea of Being",
    in ITQ 37(1970), pp.118-130.

38. Crowe, F.E., "The Origins and Scope of Bernard Lon-ergan's Insight", in ScEc 9(1957), pp.263-295.

39. Crowe, F.E., "Bernard Lonergan", in Modern Theologians, Christians and Jews, Indiana: University of Notre Dame, 1967, pp.126-151.

40. Crowe, F.E., "Early Jottings on Bernard Lonergan's Method in Theology", in ScEc 25(1973), pp.121-138.

41. D'Souza, Lisbert, "Lonergan's Metaphysics of Proportionate Being", in The Thomist 32(1968), pp.509-527.

42. Edwards, Mark, "Theological Expression", "Transcendental Method", "Knowing and Doing", "Transcendental Precepts", and "On Meaning", in The Priest 31(1975), No.1: pp.27-30; No.2: pp.25-28; No.3: pp.38-41; No.4: pp.37-40; No.5: pp.39-42.

43. Fox, Richard W., "Insight into Insight", in Modern Schoolman 46(1968/69), pp.268-270.

44. Frings, Manfred S., "Insight-Logos-Love: Lonergan-Heidegger-Scheler", in Philosophy Today 14(1970), pp.106-115.

45. Gutheinz, Luis, "Methode in Theologie – kritisch betrachtet", in ZKTh 95(1973), pp.443-458.

46. Johnson, Donald, "Lonergan and the Redoing of Ethics", in Continuum 5 (1967), pp.211-220.

47. Lapierre, Michael J., "God and the Desire of Under-standing", in The Thomist 33(1969), pp.667-674.

48. Lamb, Matthew, Review: Verbum: Word and Idea in Aquinas, in Continuum 5(1967), pp.425-431.

49. Lash, Nicholas, "Insight into Lonergan", in New Blackfriars 49(1968), pp.303-310.

50. Ledwith, Michael, "Method in Theology: Report of a Seminar", in ITQ 39(1972), pp.288-298.

51. Marsh, James L., "Lonergan's Mediation of Subjectivity and Objectivity", in Modern Schoolman 52(1975), pp.249-261.

52. McCool, Gerald A., "The Philosophical Theology of Rahner and Lonergan", in God Knowable and Unknowable. Ed. by R.J. Roth. New York:Fordham Univ., 1973, pp.123-157.

53. McKenzie, John L., "An Exegetical Answer to Lonergan's Method in Theology", in Listening 10(1975), No.1, pp.2-12.

54. Meynell, Hugo A., "Lonergan's Method: Its Nature and Uses", in Scottish Journal of Theology 27(1974), pp. 162-180.

55. Muck, Otto, Review: The Subject, in ZKTh 91(1969),p.93.

56. Mueller, Philip J., "Lonergan's Theory of Religious Experience", in Église et Théologie 7(1976), pp.235-251.

57. O'Donovan, Leo J., "Lonergan: Emergent Probability and Evolution", in Continuum 7(1969), pp.131-142.

58. O'Donovan, Conn, "Masters in Israel: Bernard Lonergan", in Clergy Review 54(1969), pp.666-679.

59. Ogiermann, H., Review: The Subject, in ThPh 44(1969), pp.139-140.

60. Reiser, William E., "A Note on Lonergan's Notion of Truth", in the Modern Schoolman 46(1968/69), pp.142-147.

61. Reiser, William E., "Lonergan's Notion of the Religious Apriori", in The Thomist 35(1971), pp.247-258.

62. Reiser, William E., "Lonergan's View on Theology: An Outline", in Scottish Journal of Theology 25(1972), pp.1-19.

63. Sala, G.B., "L'analisi della concienza umana in B. Lonergan: contributo priliminare al problema christo-logico", in La Scuola Cattolica 94(1966), pp.187-213.

64. Sala, G.B., "Oltre la Neoscolastica, verso una nuova filosofia. Quale?", in La Scuola Cattolica 96(1968), pp.291-333.

65. Sala, G.B., "Il Metodo in teologia di Bernard Lonergan", in La Civilta Cattolica 123(1972), pp.468-477; "Aspetti filosofici del Metodo in teologia di B. Lonergan", in ibid. 124(1973), pp.329-341; "Aspetti teologici del Metodo in teologia di B. Lonergan", in ibid. 124(1973), pp.553-567.

66. Schouborg,Gary, "A Note on Lonergan's Argument for the Existence of God", in Modern Schoolman 45(1967/68), pp.243-248.

67. Shannon, David T., "Methodology in the Thought of Bernard Lonergan", in Perspective 14(1973), pp.95-106.

68. Sharratt, Michael, "Lonergan on Method in Theology", in Clergy Review 56(1971), pp.958-963.

69. Shea, William M., "The Stance and Task of the Foundational Theologian: Critical or Dogmatic?", in The Heythrop Journal 17(1976), pp.273-292.

70. Surlis, Paul, "Rahner and Lonergan on Method in Theology", in ITQ 38(1971), pp.187-201; and 39(1972), pp.23-42.

71. Tracy, D., "Foundational Theology as Contemporary Possibility", in The Dunwoodie Review 12(1972), pp.3-20.

72. Tracy, D., "Method as Foundation for Theology: Bernard Lonergan's Opposition", in Journal of Religion 50(1970), pp.292-318.

73. Tyrrell, Bernard J., "The Dynamics of Conversion: A Review of Bernard Lonergan's Method in Theology", in Homiletic and Pastoral Review 72(1972), pp.56-65.

74. Tyrrell, Bernard J., "Phenomenon of Bernard Lonergan", in America 122(1970), pp.298-300.

75. Vaas, George/Mathews, William, "Lonergan's Method: Two Views", in Heythrop Journal 13(1972), pp.415-435.

76. Wilson, Patricia, "Human Knowledge of God's Existence in the Theology of Bernard Lonergan", in The Thomist 35(1971), pp.259-275.

OTHER WORKS MENTIONED

77. Abbott, W.M., The Documents of Vatican II, New York: America Press, 1966.

78. Aland, K., Synopsis Quattuor Evangeliorum, Stuttgart: Württembergische Bibelanstalt, 1967.

79. Apel, K.-O., "Sprache als Thema und Medium der transzendentalen Reflexion", in Man and World 3(1970), pp. 323-337.

80. Arnold, F.X., et al. (eds), Handbuch der Pastoraltheologie, 5Bde, in 6 Teilbänden (Bd.5: Lexicon), Freiburg: Herder, 1964-1972 (some in revised 2nd editions).

81. Aubert, R., "Die Theologie während der ersten Hälfte des 20. Jahrhunderts", in H. Vorgrimler/R. Vander Gucht (eds.), Bilanz der Theologie im 20. Jahrhundert, Bd.II, Freiburg: Herder, 1970^2, pp.7-70.

82. Auer, A., Autonome Moral und christliche Glaube, Düsseldorf: Patmos, 1971.

537

83. Auer, A., "Die Autonomie des Sittlichen nach Thomas von Aquin", in K. Demmer/B. Schüller (eds.), Christlich Glauben und Handeln, Düsseldorf: Patmos, 1977, pp.31-54.

84. Auer, A., "Ein Modell theologisch-ethischer Argumentation: 'Autonome Moral'", in A. Auer/A. Biesinger/H. Gutschera (eds.), Moralerziehung im Religionsunterricht, Freiburg: Herder, 1975, pp.27-57.

85. Auer, A., "Tendenzen heutiger theologischer Ethik", in G. Bitter/G. Miller (eds.), Konturen heutiger Theologie, München: Kösel, 1976, pp.308-325.

86. Barden, G., "The Symbolic Mentality", in Philosophical Studies 15(1966), pp.28-57.

87. Berger, P./Luckmann, T., The Social Construction of Reality, Garden City: Doubleday, 1966.

88. Berger, P./Luckmann, T., "Secularization and Pluralism", in Internationales Jahrbuch für Religionssoziologie 1(1966), pp.73-84.

89. Bertsch, L.(ed.), Beiträge zur praktischen Theologie. Theologie zwischen Theorie und Praxis, Frankfurt: Knecht, 1975.

90. Beumer, J./Visschers, L., Die theologische Methode, Freiburg: Herder, 1972 (Bd.I, Fasz.6, of Handbuch der Dogmengeschichte).

91. Biesinger, A. - see Auer, "Ein Modell...".

92. Bitter, G./Miller G. (eds.), Konturen heutiger Theologie, München: Kösel, 1976.

93. Blank, J., "Geht es mit der Bibel weiter?", in Zukunft der Theologie. Theologie der Zukunft, Freiburg: Herder, pp.155-177.

94. Blank, J., "Das politische Element in der historisch-kritischen Methode", in P. Neuenzeit (ed.), Die Funktion der Theologie in Kirche und Gesellschaft, pp.39-60.

95. Blum, O.J., "Methodology (History)", in New Catholic Encyclopedia, 15 Vols., New York: McGraw-Hill, 1967.

96. Bourke, V., Thomistic Bibliography: 1920-1940, Saint Louis: Modern Schoolman, 1945.

97. Brosseder, J. - See Seckler et al., Begegnung....

98. Bsteh, A. (ed.), Universales Christentum angesichts einer pluralen Welt, Mödling: St. Gabriel, 1976.

538

99. Burrell, D.B., _Exercises in Religious Understanding_, Notre Dame: Univ. of Notre Dame Press, 1974.

100. Burrell, D.B., "Aquinas on Naming God", in _TS_ 24(1963), pp.183-212.

101. Chenu, M.-D., _La théologie au douzième siècle_, Paris: Vrin, 1957.

102. Cobb, J.B. - see Robinson, J.M./Cobb, J.B., _Theologie....._

103. Congar, Y., "Théologie", in _Dictionnaire de théologie catholique_, 15 Vols., Paris: Letouzey et Ané, 1903-1950; Tables générales by B. Loth/A. Michel, 3 Vols., 1951-1972.

104. Copleston, F., _A History of Philosophy_, 8 Vols., Garden City: Doubleday, 1962-1967.

105. Crowe, F.E., "Complacency and Concern in the Thought of St. Thomas", in _TS_ 20(1959), pp.1-39, 198-230, 343-395.

106. Crowe, F.E., "St. Thomas and the Isomorphism of Human Knowing and Its Proper Object", in _ScEc_ 13(1961), pp.167-190.

107. Dawson, C., _The Age of the Gods_, New York: Fertig, 1970 (1928[1]).

108. Demmer, K./Schüller, B., _Christlich Glauben und Handeln_, Düsseldorf: Patmos, 1977.

109. de Vries, J., "Forschung", in _LThK[2]_.

110. Durrant, M., _Theology and Intelligibility_, London: Routledge, 1973.

111. Duss-von Werdt, J., _Theologie aus Glaubenserfahrung_, Zürich: Benziger, 1969.

112. Ebeling, G., _Word and Faith I_, London: SCM, 1963.

113. Ebeling, G., "Erwägung zu einer evangelischen Fundamental-theologie", in _ZThK_ 67(1970), pp.479-524.

114. Ebeling, G., "Hermeneutik", in _RGG[3]_.

115. Eckert, W.P. (ed.), _Thomas von Aquino_, Mainz: Matthias-Grünewald, 1974.

116. Eicher, P., _Die anthropologische Wende_, Freiburg: Herder, 1970.

117. Eicher, P., _Offenbarung. Prinzip neuzeitlicher Theologie_, München: Kösel, 1977.

118. Eicher, P., "Du sollst Dir kein Bildnis machen. Möglichkeiten und Grenzen theologischer Anthropologie heute", in G. Bitter/G. Miller, Konturen..., pp.21-44.

119. Eicher, P., "Erfahren und Denken", in ThQ 157(1977), pp.142-143.

120. Eliade, M., "The Sacred in the Secular World", in Cultural Hermeneutics 1(1973), pp.101-113.

121. Eliade, M./Kitagawa, J. (eds.), The History of Religions, Chicago: The University of Chicago Press, 1959.

122. Engelhardt, P. (ed.) - see Gadamer, H.-G., "Über die Möglichkeit...".

123. Fischer, F., "Aufgaben und Methoden der Geschichtswissenschaft", in J. Scheschkewitz (ed.), Geschichtsschreibung, pp.7-28.

124. Fischer, K., Der Mensch als Geheimnis. Die Anthropologie Karl Rahners, Freiburg: Herder, 1974².

125. Frör, K., Biblische Hermeneutik, München: Chr. Kaiser, 1967.

126. Gadamer, H.-G., Truth and Method (ET by G. Barden), New York: Seabury, 1975.

127. Gadamer, H.-G., "Über die Möglichkeit einer philosophischen Ethik", in P. Engelhardt (ed.), Sein und Ethos (Vol.I of the Walberger Studien), Mainz: Matthias-Grünewald, 1963, pp.11-24.

128. Geffré, R.P.C., (a) Un nouvel âge de la théologie, Paris: Cerf, 1972; (b) ET: The New Age in Theology, New York: Paulist, 1974.

129. Geiselmann, J.R., Die katholische Tübinger Schule, Freiburg: Herder, 1964.

130. Gervais, M. - see Laflamme, R./Gervais, M. (eds.), Le Christ....

131. Gilson, E., Unity of Philosophical Experience, New York: Chas. Scribner's Sons, 1937.

132. Glazik, J., "Ortskirche-Weltkirche", in A. Bsteh (ed.), Universales Christentum, pp.107-126.

133. Grabmann, M., Die Geschichte der katholischen Theologie seit dem Ausgang der Väterzeit, Freiburg: Herder, 1933.

540

134. Grabmann, M., Die Geschichte der scholastischen Methode I, Darmstadt: Wissens. Buchges., 1956.

135. Griesl, G. - see Weinzierl, E./Griesl, G. (eds.), Von der ....

136. Grillmeier, A., "Die altkirchliche Christologie und die moderne Hermeneutik. Zur Diskussion um die chalkedonische Christologie heute", in Theologische Berichte 1, Zürich: Benziger, 1972, pp.69-169.

137. Grillmeier, A., "Konzil und Rezeption", in ThPh 3(1970), pp.321-352.

138. Grom, B., "Erfahrung und Glaube", in G. Bitter/ G. Miller (eds.), Konturen..., pp.59-81.

139. Gruber, W., Die pneumatische Exegese bei den Alexandrinern, Graz: Akadem. Druck- u. Verlagsanstalt, 1957.

140. Gutschera, H. - see Auer, "Ein Modell...".

141. Hahn, F., "Probleme historischer Kritik", in Die Zeichen der Zeit, 10/77, pp.361-370.

142. Hampe, J. (ed.), Die Autorität der Freiheit, Bd.I, München: Kösel, 1967.

143. Harnack, A., Die Entstehung der christl. Theologie und des kirckl. Dogmas, Gotha: Klotz, 1927.

144. Haught, J., Religion and Self-Acceptance, Glen Rock,NJ: Paulist, 1977.

145. Hazard, P., The European Mind 1680-1715, Middlesex: Penguin, 1964.

146. Heinen, W./Schreiner, J. (eds.), Erwartung-Verheissung-Erfüllung, Würzburg: Echter, 1969.

147. Heinrichs, J., "Theorie welcher Praxis?", in Bertsch, L. (ed.), Beiträge..., pp.9-85.

148. Hennelly, A.T., "Theological Method: The Southern Exposure", in TS 38(1977), pp.709-735.

149. Hirschberger, J., Kleine Philosophiegeschichte, Freiburg: Herder, 1961.

150. Horney, K., The Neurotic Personality of our Time, New York: W.W. Norton, 1937.

151. Hünermann, P., Der Durchbruch geschichtlichen Denkens im 19. Jahrhundert, Freiburg: Herder, 1967.

541

152. Internationale Theologenkommission, <u>Die Einheit des Glaubens und der theologische Pluralismus</u>, Einsiedeln: Johannes, 1973.

153. Joest, W., <u>Fundamentaltheologie</u>, Stuttgart: Kohlhammer, 1974.

154. Jüngel, E., <u>Gott als Geheimnis der Welt</u>, Tübingen: J.C.B. Mohr (Paul Siebeck), 1977[2].

155. Jüngel, E.,/Ricoeur, P., <u>Metapher. Zur Hermeneutik religiöser Sprache</u>, München: Chr. Kaiser, 1974.

156. Jüngel, E., "Das Verhältnis der theologischen Disziplinen untereinander", in Jüngel/Rahner/Seitz, <u>Die praktische Theologie zwischen Wissenschaft und Praxis</u>, München: Chr. Kaiser, 1968, pp.11-45.

157. Kambartel, K., "Erfahrung", in J. Ritter (ed.), <u>Historisches Wörterbuch der Philosophie</u>, Bd.I, Darmstadt: Wissens. Buchges., 1971ff.

158. Käsemann, E., <u>Der Ruf der Freiheit</u>, Tübingen: J.C.B. Mohr (Paul Siebeck), 1968.

159. Käsemann, E., "Vom theologischen Recht historisch-kritischer Exegese", in <u>ZThK</u> 64(1967), pp.259-281.

160. Kasper, W., <u>Einführung in den Glauben</u>, Mainz: Matthias-Grünewald, 1972.

161. Kasper, W., <u>Glaube und Geschichte</u>, Mainz: Matthias-Grünewald, 1970.

162. Kasper, W., (a) <u>Jesus der Christus</u>, Mainz: Matthias-Grünewald, 1974; (b) ET <u>Jesus the Christ</u>, London: Burns & Oates, 1976; New York: Paulist, 1977).

163. Kasper, W., (a) <u>Die Methoden der Dogmatik. Einheit und Vielheit</u>, München: Kösel, 1967; (b) ET <u>The Methods of Dogmatic Theology</u>, Glen Rock, NJ: Paulist, 1969).

164. Kasper, W.(ed.), <u>Unser Wissen vom Menschen. Möglichkeiten und Grenzen anthropologischer Erkenntnisse</u>, Düsseldorf: Patmos, 1977.

165. Kasper, W., "Christsein ohne Tradition?", in <u>Diskussion über Hans Küngs 'Christ Sein'</u>, Mainz: Matthias-Grünewald, 1976, pp.19-34.

166. Kasper, W., "Dogmatik als Wissenschaft", in <u>ThQ</u> 157(1977), pp.189-203.

167. Kasper, W., "Karl Adam: Zu seinem 100. Geburtstag und 10. Todestag", in ThQ 156(1976), pp.251-258.

168. Kasper, W., "Systematisch-theologische Neuansätze", in ThQ 156(1976), pp.55-61.

169. Kasper, W., "Das theologische Wesen des Menschen", in W. Kasper (ed.), Unser Wissen..., pp.95-114.

170. Kasper, W., "Tradition als Erkenntnisprinzip. Systematische Überlegungen zur theologischen Relevanz der Geschichte", in ThQ 155(1975), pp.198-215.

171. Kasper, W./Schilson, A. - see Schilson, A./Kasper, W., Christologie....

172. Kitagawa, J. - see Eliade, M./Kitagawa, J., The History....

173. Kleutgen, J., Die Theologie der Vorzeit, 5 Vols., Münster: Theissing'sche Buchhandlung, 1874[2].

174. Klibansky, R./Paton, H.J. (eds.), Philosophy and History. Essays Presented to Ernst Cassirer, Oxford: Clarendon, 1936.

175. Kuhn, T., The Structure of Scientific Revolutions, Chicago: The University of Chicago Press, 1970[2].

176. Küng, H., Justification: The Doctrine of Karl Barth and a Catholic Reflection, New York: Thomas Nelson, 1964.

177. Küng, H., Theologe und Kirche, Einsiedeln: Benziger, 1965[2].

178. Ladrière, J., Les limitations internes des formalismes, Louvain: Nauwelaerts, 1957.

179. Laflamme, R./Gervais, M (eds)., Le Christ hier, aujourd'húi et demain. Colloque de christologie tenu à l'Université Laval, Québec: Pr. de l'Univ. Laval, 1976.

180. Lamb, M., "The Theory-Praxis Relationship in Contemporary Christian Theologies", in The CTSA Proceedings 31(1976), pp.149-178.

181. Lang, A., Die 'loci theologici' des Melchior Cano. München: (priv.), 1925.

182. Laszlo, E., Introduction to Systems Philosophy, New York: Harper & Row, 1972.

183. Lehmann, K., Gegenwart des Glaubens, Mainz: Matthias-Grünewald, 1974.

543

184. Lehmann, K., "Erfahrung", in Sacramentum Mundi I, Freiburg: Herder, 1967.

185. Lohfink, G., Die Bibel: Gottes Wort in Menschen Wort, Stuttgart: KBW, 1967.

186. Lohfink, G., "Erzählung als Theologie. Zur sprachlichen Grundstruktur der Evangelien", in StZ 192(1974), pp.521-532.

187. Luckmann, T. - see Berger/Luckmann.

188. Ludwig, H., Die Kirche im Prozess der gesellschaft- lichen Differenzierung. Perspektiven für eine neue sozialethische Diskussion, Mainz: Matthias-Grünewald, and München: Chr. Kaiser, 1976.

189. Marrou, H.-I., Über die historische Erkenntnis, Darmstadt: Wissens. Buchges., 1973.

190. Maslow, A., Religions, Values and Peak Experiences, New York: Viking Press, 1970.

191. Maslow, A., Towards a Psychology of Being, Princeton: Van Nostrand, 1962.

192. Matson, F.W., The Broken Image: Man, Science and Society, Garden City: Doubleday, 1966.

193. Mennekes, F., "Praktische Theologie - Theorie wirk- lichkeitsorientierter Praxis", in Bertsch, Beiträge..., pp.86-148.

194. Metz, J.B., (a) Glaube in Geschichte und Gesellschaft, Mainz: Matthias-Grünewald, 1977; (b) ET Faith in History and Society: Towards a Practical Fundamental Theology, New York: Seabury, 1979).

195. Metz, J.B., (a) Zur Theologie der Welt, Mainz: Matthias-Grünewald, 1973[2]; (b) ET Theology of the World, New York: Seabury, 1969[1]).

196. Metz, J.B., "Kirchliche Autorität im Anspruch der Freiheitsgeschichte", in Metz/Moltmann/Oelmüller, Kirche im Prozess der Aufklärung, Mainz: Matthias- Grünewald, 1970, pp.53-90.

197. Metz, J.B., (a) "Politische Theologie", in SM III; (b) ET "Political Theology", in SM V.

198. Metz, J.B., "Technik-Politik-Religion", in Heinen/ Schreiner, Erwartung..., pp.157-183.

544

199. Metz, J.B., "Theologie", in _LThK²_.

200. Metz, J.B., "Zu einer interdisziplinär orientierten Theologie auf bikonfessioneller Basis: Erste Orientierungen anhand eines konkreten Projekts", in Metz/Rendtorff (eds.), _Die Theologie in der interdisziplinären Forschung_, Düsseldorf: Bertelsmann, 1971, pp.10-27.

201. Metz, J.B., "Der zukünftige Mensch und der kommende Gott", in H.J. Schultz (ed.), _Wer ist das eigentlich Gott?_, München: Kösel, 1969, pp.260-275.

202. Miller, G. - see Bitter, G./Miller, G. (eds.), _Konturen...._

203. Moltmann, J. - see Metz, "Kirchliche...".

204. Muck, O., _The Transcendental Method_, New York: Herder and Herder, 1968.

205. Nemeshegyi, P., Commentary on the 9th thesis, in Internationale Theologenkommission, _Die Einheit_, pp.52-60.

206. Nemeshegyi, P., "Versuch über die Einkulturierung des Christentums in Asien. Neue Aspekte des theologischen Pluralismus", in Internationale Theologenkommission, _Die Einheit..._, pp.180-203.

207. Neuenzeit, P. - see Blank, J., "Das politische...".

208. Newman, J.H., _An Essay in Aid of a Grammar of Assent_, London: Longmans, Green & Co., 1947.

209. O'Donovan, L.J. (ed.), "A Changing Ecclesiology in a Changing Church: A Symposium on Development in the Ecclesiology of Karl Rahner", in _TS_ 38(1977), pp.736-762.

210. Oeing-Hanhoff, L., "Thomas von Aquin und die gegenwärtige katholische Theologie", in Eckert, _Thomas..._, pp.245-306.

211. Oelmüller, W. - see Metz, "Kirchliche...".

212. O'Farrell, F., "Aristotle's, Kant's and Hegel's Logic", in _Gregorianum_ 54(1973), pp.477-515, 655-677.

213. Pannenberg, W., _Grundfragen systematischer Theologie_, Göttingen: Vandenhoeck & Ruprecht, 1971².

214. Pannenberg, W., _Offenbarung als Geschichte_, Göttingen: Vandenhoeck & Ruprecht, 1970⁴.

215. Pannenberg, W., (a) _Wissenschaftstheorie und Theologie_, Frankfurt a.M.: Suhrkamp, 1973; (b) ET _Theology and the Philosophy of Science_, Philadelphia: Westminster, 1976.

545

216. Pannenberg, W., "Christologie und Theologie", in
     KuD 21(1975), pp.159-175.

217. Pannenberg, W., "Das christologische Fundament christ-
     licher Anthropologie", in Concilium (1973, No.9, pp.
     425-434).

218. Pannenberg, W., "Die Offenbarung Gottes in Jesus von
     Nazareth", in Robinson/Cobb (eds.), Theologie...,
     pp.135-169.

219. Pannenberg, W., "Reden von Gott angesichts atheistischer
     Kritik", in EK 2(1969), pp.442-446.

220. Pannenberg, W., "Stellungnahme zur Diskussion", in
     Robinson/Cobb (eds.), Theologie..., pp.285-351.

221. Pannenberg, W. - see Seckler/Pesch/et al., Begegnung....

222. Paton, H.J. - see Klibansky/Paton (eds.), Philosophy....

223. Patzig, G., "Immanuel Kant: Wie sind synthetische
     Urteile a priori möglich?", in Grundprobleme der
     grossen Philosophen. Philosophie der Neuzeit II,
     Göttingen: Vandenhoeck & Ruprecht, 1976, pp.9-70.

224. Pelikan, J., The Christian Tradition: A History of the
     Development of Doctrine. Volume i: The Emergence of the
     Catholic Tradition 100-600, Chicago: The University of
     Chicago Press, 1971.

225. Pesch, H.O. - see Seckler et al., Begegnung....

226. Peukert, H., Wissenschaftstheorie-Handlungstheorie-
     Fundamentale Theologie, Düsseldorf: Patmos, 1976.

227. Pöggeler, O., "G.W.F. Hegel: Philosophie als System",
     in Grundprobleme der grossen Philosophen. Philosophie
     der Neuzeit II, Göttingen: Vandenhoeck & Ruprecht,
     1976, pp.145-183.

228. Polanyi, M., Personal Knowledge, London: University
     of Chicago Press, 1958.

229. Rahner, K., Das Dynamische in der Kirche (QD 5),
     Freiburg: Herder, 1958.

230. Rahner, K., (a) Grundkurs des Glaubens, Freiburg:
     Herder, 1976; (b) ET Foundations of the Faith, New
     York: Seabury, 1978).

231. Rahner, K., Schriften zur Theologie - Bd.III, Zürich:
     Benziger, 1967[7].

232. Rahner, K., <u>Schriften zur Theologie - Bd VIII</u>, Zürich: Benziger, 1967.

233. Rahner, K., <u>Schriften zur Theologie - Bd.IX</u>, Zürich: Benziger, 1970.

234. Rahner, K., "The Individual in the Church", in <u>Nature and Grace</u>, New York: Sheed & Ward, 1963, pp.5-83.

235. Rahner, K., "Die Praktische Theologie im Ganzen der theologischen Disziplinen", in Jüngel/Rahner/Seitz, <u>Die Praktische...</u>, pp.46-64.

236. Reinhardt, R. (ed.), <u>Tübinger Theologen und ihre Theologie</u>, Tübingen: J.C.B. Mohr (Paul Siebeck), 1977.

237. Rendtorff, T. - see Metz, "Zu einer...".

238. Richard, R.L., <u>The Problem of an Apologetical Perspective in the Trinitarian Theology of St. Thomas Aquinas</u>, Rome: Gregorian, 1963 (Vol.131 of <u>Analec. Greg.</u>).

239. Ricoeur, P., "Philosophical hermeneutics and theological hermeneutics", in <u>Studies of Religion/Sciences Religieuses</u> 5(1975/1976), pp.14-33.

240. Ricoeur, P. - see Jüngel/Ricoeur, <u>Metapher...</u>.

241. Robinson, J.M./Cobb, J.B. (eds.), <u>Theologie als Geschichte</u>, Zürich:TVZ, 1967.

242. Roques, R., <u>Structure Théologique de la Gnose à Richard de Saint-Victor</u>, Paris: Pr. univ. de France, 1962.

243. Ruhbach, G., <u>Kirchen- und Dogmengeschichte</u>, Gütersloh: Gerd Mohn, 1974.

244. Ryan, W., <u>Intentionality in E. Husserl and B. Lonergan</u>, Louvain: (unpublished) doctoral dissertation, 1972.

245. Sauter, G./Stock, A., <u>Arbeitsweisen Systematischer Theologie</u>, München: Chr. Kaiser, and Mainz: Matthias-Grünewald, 1976.

246. Scheschkewitz, J. (ed.), <u>Geschichtsschreibung. Epochen, Methoden, Gestalten</u>, Düsseldorf: Droste, 1968.

247. Schilson, A./Kasper, W., <u>Christologie im Präsens</u>, Freiburg: Herder, 1974.

248. Schmaus, M., "Bemerkungen zu einer zukünftigen Theologie", in <u>Zukunft der Theologie...</u>, pp.69-81.

249. Schmithals, W., "Die Wahrheit der Heiligen Schrift und das Konzil", in Hampe, Die Autorität..., pp.197-208.

250. Schoof, T.M., A Survey of Catholic Theology: 1800-1970, Paramus,NJ: Paulist, 1970.

251. Schreiner, J. - see Metz, "Technik...".

252. Schultz, H.J. - see Metz, "Der zukünftige...".

253. Schulz, W., Philosophie in der veränderten Welt, Pfullingen: Neske, 1972.

254. Schupp, F., Glaube-Kultur-Symbol, Düsseldorf: Patmos, 1974.

255. Schuster, H., "Praktische Theologie", in SM III, Freiburg: Herder, 1969.

256. Seckler, M., "Thomas von Aquin und die Theologie", in ThQ 136(1976), pp.3-14.

257. Seckler, M., "Über den Kompromiss in Sachen der Lehre", in M. Seckler/H.O. Pesch/J. Brosseder/W. Pannenberg, Begegnung. Beiträge zu einer Hermeneutik des theologischen Gesprächs, Graz: Styria, 1972, pp.45-57.

258. Seitz, M. - see Jüngel et al., Die Praktische....

259. Siemers, H. (ed.), Theologie zwischen Anpassung und Isolation, Stuttgart: Kohlhammer, 1975.

260. Snell, B., The Discovery of the Mind. The Greek Origins of European Thought, New York: Harper & Row, 1960.

261. Stekel, W., Compulsion and Doubt, New York: Grosset & Dunlop, 1962.

262. Stock, A., Umgang mit theologischen Texten, Zürich: Benziger, 1974.

263. Stock, A. - see Sauter/Stock, Arbeitsweisen....

264. Stuhlmacher, P., "Thesen zur Methodologie gegenwärtiger Exegese", in Die Zeichen der Zeit, 10/77, pp.371-376.

265. **Tracy, D., Blessed Rage for Order. The New Pluralism in Theology**, New York: Seabury, 1975.

266. Vander Gucht, R. - see Aubert, "Die Theologie...".

267. van der Heijden, B., Karl Rahner. Darstellung und Kritik seiner Grundposition, Einsiedeln: Johannes, 1971.

268. Visschers, L. - see Beumer/Visschers, Die theologische....

548

269. Vorgrimler, H., <u>Dogmatic versus Biblical Theology</u>, Montreal: Palm, 1965.

270. Vorgrimler, H. - see Aubert, "Die Theologie...".

271. Waldenfels, H., "Anthropologia Negativa", in <u>ZM</u> 60(1976), pp.55-60.

272. Weinzierl, E./Griesl, G. (eds.), <u>Von der Pastoral-theologie zur Praktischen Theologie 1774-1974</u>, München: Pustet, 1976.

273. Wenisch, B., "Zur Theologie Karl Rahners", in <u>MThZ</u> 28(1977), pp.383-397.

274. Winter, G., <u>Elements for a Social Ethic</u>, New York: Macmillan, 1968.

275. Zimmermann, H., <u>Neutestamentliche Methodenlehre</u>, Stuttgart: KBW, 1974[4].

276. <u>Zukunft der Theologie - Theologie der Zukunft</u>, Freiburg: Herder, 1971.

*

553